# Medals to the Navy

## 1588 to 2013

### Including the Dieppe Raid of 1942

Roger Perkins

**Published privately
2015**

# MEDALS TO THE NAVY

Published privately
Torwood Cottage, Haytor, Newton Abbot, Devon TQ13 9XR
Email for the book: medalstothenavy@gmail.com
Email to the author: haytor.history@gmail.com
Telephone: 0044 (0)1364 661220
Copyright Roger Perkins 2014
ISBN 978-0-9506429-6-3

By the same author:

For Kenneth Mason, Havant, Hampshire
(1982, co-authored with Captain K J Douglas-Morris, RN, retd)
*Gunfire in Barbary - The Battle of Algiers, 1816*

For Picton Publishing, Chippenham, Wiltshire
(1983, co-authored with J W Wilson)
*Angels in Blue Jackets - The Messina Earthquake of 1908*

Also for Picton Publishing of Chippenham, as sole author:
*The Kashmir Gate - Lieutenant Home and the Delhi VCs* (1986)
*The Punjab Mail Murder -
The Story of an Indian Army Officer* (1979 and 1986)
*Operation Paraquat - The Battle for South Georgia 1982* (1986)
*The Amritsar Legacy -
Golden Temple to Caxton Hall, The Story of a Killing* (1989)

Published privately as sole author:
*Regiments of the Empire, A Bibliography* (1992)
*Pathfinder Pilot - The Search for Selwyn Alcock DFC* (1992)
*Regiments of the British Empire and Commonwealth, 1758-1993
A Critical Bibliography of their Published Histories* (1994)
*Military and Naval Silver -
Treasures of the Mess and Wardroom* (1999)
*The War Dead of Chudleigh, Devon* (2002)

Cover and book design by Susan Davie
Printed by CPI Antony Rowe, Chippenham, Wiltshire

# Contents

**Author's Introduction**     Page 1

**Part One - 1588 to 1792**     Page 3
The Spanish-Portuguese Armada and its causes, the battles off Lowestoft, Dungeness, Barfleur, La Hogue and Vigo Bay and the Siege of Gibraltar.

**Part Two - 1792 to 1840**     Page 23
The wars with Revolutionary and Napoleonic France, early frigate actions, The Glorious First of June, smugglers employed in the Royal Navy, the Spithead and Nore mutinies, the war with America, fleet actions in Navarino Bay and off Syria.

**Part Three - 1840 to 1860**     Page 45
The anti-slavery campaigns off West Africa and in the Indian Ocean, the war with Imperial Russia, the two campaigns in the Baltic Sea, actions on the coasts of Siberia and the Sea of Azoff.

**Part Four - 1860 to 1890**     Page 61
The invasion of Abyssinia, border defence in Canada, the war against the Zulu Nation, the invasion of Egypt.

**Part Five - 1890 to 1914**     Page 79
The Russo-Japanese War, the Second Anglo-Boer War, the Boxer Rebellion, the "Jackie" Fisher revolution, naval gunnery, the eve-of-war visits to Kronstadt and Kiel.

**Part Six - 1914 to 1939**     Page 97
Early failure in the Mediterranean, references to the Royal Yachts, the Dardanelles disaster, the Mesopotamia campaign, the birth of naval aviation, operations against the Bolsheviks in North Russia, South Russia, Siberia and the Caspian Sea.

**Part Seven - 1939 to 1945**     Page 125
The U-boat war, rapid expansion of the Fleet Air Arm and the carrier fleet, early disasters in the Far East, Royal Navy submarine operations off Malaya, the battle for Malta, operations of the British Pacific Fleet.

**Part Eight - 1945 to 1982**     Page 157
Operations off Palestine against Jewish immigration, the war in Korea, Britain's second invasion of Egypt (the Suez campaign), the Falklands war, the story of the Canal Zone, two retrospective awards.

*Continued over*

**Part Nine (A) The Awards That Never Were - 1820 to 1945      Page 175**
Actions in Latin America, the Battle of Shimonoseki (Japan), the war with Imperial Russia, the First Anglo-Boer War, wartime services of the Merchant Navy, the Sino-Japanese war, the Spanish Civil War.

**Part Nine (B) The Awards That Never Were - 1945 to 2013      Page 197**
The Beira Patrol, the three Cod Wars, the war against Libya, the Kuwait intervention, the demise of British aviation capability at sea, the Grenada affair, questions regarding the future of the Royal Navy.

**Farewell to the Crimson and White**                            Page 231

**For Valour**                                                   Page 233

**Addendum**                                                     Page 237

**Fabian Ware**                                                  Page 238

**Dieppe 1942 - Who Was to Blame? A Personal View**              Page 239

**Index of Battles and Campaigns**                               Page 285

**Index of Medals**                                              Page 286

**Index of British Warships**                                    Page 287

**Index of Personnel**                                           Page 291

**About the Author**                                             Page 295

## Voices from the past, they said it first

We should provide in peace what we need in war
*(Publilius Syrus, 42 BC)*

Seek peace but prepare for war
*(William Cecil, the Lord Burghley, c.1580)*

A man-of-war is the best ambassador
*(Oliver Cromwell, c.1650)*

It is upon the navy, under the good Providence of God, that the wealth, safety and strength of the kingdom do chiefly depend
*(King Charles II, 1672)*

A decisive naval superiority is to be considered as a fundamental principle, and the basis upon which every hope of success must ultimately depend
*(George Washington, 1780)*

No price is too great to preserve the health of the fleet
*(Admiral the Lord St Vincent, 1796)*

A good navy is not a provocation to war, it is the surest guarantee of peace
*(President Theodore Roosevelt, 1901)*

Speak softly and carry a big stick
*(also said by President Theodore Roosevelt, 1901)*

Nothing in the world, nothing you may think of or dream of, or anyone else may tell you, no arguments however seductive, must lead you to abandon that naval superiority upon which the life of our country depends
*(Winston Churchill, 1918)*

Superior firepower is an invaluable tool when entering negotiations
*(General George S Patton, 1945)*

Sea power is as ancient as the Minoan galleys of 5000 years ago, and its meaning has not changed essentially. Sea power is that force which utilises the oceans to defend the nation against invasion and to attack an enemy power at its own shore line. It may also deny an enemy use of the ocean
*(Fleet Admiral Chester Nimitz, 1946)*

Those who cannot remember the past are condemned to repeat it
*(George Santayana, 1905)*

## Author's Introduction

MEDALS are signposts along the highway of armed conflict. They point us back to the distant past, back to disputes which at the time inspired men to fight, kill and die. Of battles fought at sea barely a handful of names are embedded in the national conscience - the Spanish-Portuguese Armada, Trafalgar, Jutland, the 1982 Falklands campaign, as examples. For the rest, perhaps too little is known other than to the naval collector and historian.

This book is rooted in a series of articles published between 2010 and 2013 in the *The Review*, the Quarterly Journal of the Naval Historical Collectors & Research Association. Sadly, the Association disbanded in January 2015, but I am indebted to the Editor and Committee for having granted - through the medium of that excellent Journal - the opportunity to further develop my long-standing interest in Great Britain's naval heritage .

In the light of additional research, the ten original articles have since been corrected and greatly expanded but with the original style of presentation retained for ease of reference. Happily, I am blessed with a daughter who possesses the professional skills needed to develop the material in hard-back format. She is Susan Davie and, without her expertise and wise counsel, this book would never have been brought to fruition. Apart from pursuing her own high standards of picture research and enhancement, she has frequently brought forward suggestions intended to improve the narrative's general appeal to the non-specialist. It is our shared hope that the following pages will indeed touch a chord with readers who enjoy history simply for its own sake.

The articles as first published in *The Review* were aimed at naval actions which resulted either in the granting of a medal or, arguably, did merit such recognition but then never received it. The period covered was, in total, more than four hundred years. During those centuries our sailors (and latterly our naval aviators) were committed to a multitude of varied engagements in every region of the world. The intention, therefore, was to select from the vast storehouse of recorded maritime history just a few of those events. Chosen because they appealed to me personally, they may also stir the curiosity of the reader. If any of these articles stimulate an urge to research deeper - from other sources - they will have served a useful purpose.

Whenever possible, prominence is given to medals for which all ranks were eligible and which were impressed or engraved with the details of the recipient. There is no mention of medals awarded for long service or meritorious service. They are outside the scope of what was intended. I have, however, gone beyond the original remit of *"Medals to the Navy"* by discussing in pages 212 to 230 the current status of the Royal Navy and its possible future role in a fast-changing world. The evidence - both factual and hypothetical - is disturbing and worthy of debate.

One of the recurring themes is the relationship between surface and sub-surface sea-power on the one hand and maritime air power on the other. Over the past thirty years the policies pursued by successive British governments have created an unbalanced navy, highly capable at one level, woefully inadequate at others. Time and again over the past one hundred years, at the cost of much blood and treasure, experience has demonstrated the crucial influence of wings over the waves. It would be pleasing to think that future policy makers might take on board the evidence provided by the many episodes quoted in the second half of the following pages.

In a broader context, every man and woman currently serving with the Senior Service, or planning to join it, should gain from this book an even greater appreciation of its history and the exemplary dedication of their forebears.

It is said that "a book without an index is a treasure chest without a key". An unexpected bonus of this new publication was revealed when I came to compile the indexes. The combined narrative runs to little more than 110,000 words, a length which in publishing terms is relatively modest. I was mildly astounded therefore to discover that 357 Royal Navy ships have been mentioned, 282 British service personnel, 163 different campaigns or battles, 74 related medals. I then realised that a book such as this not only gives permanence to the articles published previously in *The Review*, it also provides an additional source of reference for future researchers. Without *"Medals to the Navy"*, many of us might forget those ships, the people who served in them and the campaigns in which they fought.

For the rest, it is my hope that all these stories will provide as much pleasure and interest to the reader as they have given to me in assembling them.

Roger Perkins.
Haytor, Devon.
2015

# Part One - 1588 to 1792

THE HISTORY OF ENGLAND is bathed in blood, mired in violence. The time of the Tudors was especially nasty. And yet, ironically, it generated a folk memory which endures to this day as an exemplar of British pluck and daring. A portent of England's future naval power, it was the destruction of "the Invincible Armada".

Why did King Philip II of Spain decide to mount that expedition? The first seeds had been sown eight decades earlier when, in 1509, Henry VIII ascended the English throne as the second Tudor monarch. His queen was Catherine of Aragon, widow of his brother Arthur and daughter of the joint rulers of Spain, King Ferdinand and Queen Isabella.

Catherine's successive pregnancies failed to produce the male heir Henry so desperately wanted. Having fallen in love with a lady of the Court, Anne Boleyn, he submitted a petition to the Pope for his marriage to Catherine to be annulled. When his request for a divorce was refused, Henry was infuriated. He broke all ties with Rome and declared himself in 1534 to be Supreme Head of the English Church.

His next step, beginning in 1536, was to dismantle the infrastructure of the Pope's power base in the British Isles - the 850 monasteries, abbeys, convents and friaries. Within five years they had all been reduced to ruin, their lands and valuables seized, their wealth transferred to the Royal Treasury or gifted to his favourites. The

*King Henry VIII depicted at the height of his powers. It was his father Henry VII who in 1495 ordered the construction of the first royal dockyard, Portsmouth. Two more were ordered by Henry VIII (Woolwich in 1512, Deptford in 1513, both located on the Thames). The other portrait is that of his second wife, Anne Boleyn. Before she was executed in 1536 on a fabricated charge of treason, she bore him a daughter, Elizabeth. After that infant girl grew to womanhood and ascended the throne, England went on to become an increasingly influential maritime power. For her and for her successors, the 1588 defeat of the Spanish-Portuguese Armada was the beginning of a new era.*

monks and nuns were driven out to survive as best they might in the countryside. Anyone who protested was condemned to a barbaric execution.

The great cathedrals were spared from destruction because the Bishops either did as they were told or were replaced. Even so, they were obliged to hand over their treasures and to dismantle every tangible symbol of "popery". All of this was viewed by the rulers of France and Spain as a legal dispute, not an abandonment of Catholic doctrine and ritual *per se*. They were right. Henry might have broken the controlling influence of the Papacy in his own kingdom but - and even though he had been ex-communicated - he remained throughout his life a devout Catholic and ensured that his people also continued in the ways of "the old religion".

He died in 1547, age 55, and was succeeded by his son, the nine year-old boy King Edward VI. He reigned for only six years before succumbing to ill-health but, in that time, a Protestant Reformation of the English Church swiftly gathered pace. Edward gave a free hand to his Regency Council to crack down hard on all forms of Catholicism. Why? Mainly because the Crown and a great number of the gentry and nobility had become immensely wealthy when the monasteries were dissolved and plundered. They had no intention of giving back what they had gained. Before he died, Henry had squandered his own share of the loot on unsuccessful campaigns against the Scots and the French. The Royal Treasury was massively in debt.

Edward's short reign continued his father's destruction of the old order. Beginning in 1547 it was the turn of the Parish churches to be raided. The Regency Council ordered every cleric in the land to adopt Archbishop Thomas Cranmer's innovative Book of Common Prayer and William Tyndale's first English-language version of the Bible. Their unwilling congregations were legally obliged to pay for these books, thereby generating more cash flow for the young King and his friends. Town and village churches were stripped of their valuable bronze bells, of their modest silverware, of all the many artefacts so important to parochial spiritual and social life. These and other radical changes caused deep resentment and popular uprisings in the West Country, Kent, East Anglia and the northern counties. The protests - known collectively as "the Prayer Book Rebellions" - were put down with astonishing cruelty by the King's troops and by Swiss and Italian mercenaries imported from France. Thousands of ardent Roman Catholics were massacred.

Not yet sixteen years of age, Edward died in 1553 and was succeeded by Henry VIII's elder daughter, Mary. A devout Roman Catholic, she soon set about the suppression of all forms of Protestantism. The Reformation shifted dramatically into reverse. Her four years on the throne brought continuing religious turmoil. Thousands more people - this time Protestant commoners, nobles and clerics - were imprisoned or put to death. Mary ordered 284 of them, including Archbishop Thomas Cranmer, to be ritually burned alive at the stake. Others were publicly semi-throttled, disemboweled, then chopped into pieces or, if they were lucky, simply hanged. Her four years reign of terror earned her the bitter *sobriquet* "Bloody Mary".

One year after gaining the throne, with the aim of restoring full Papal authority in England, she married her cousin, Prince Philip, son of Charles V, Emperor of the Holy Roman Empire. Before the wedding, to give him regal status to match that of

Mary, Charles made him King of Naples. Two years later, on the death of his father, he became additionally King of Spain. When he (age 27) and Mary (age 37) wed in Winchester Cathedral on 24 July 1554, he became *de facto* King of England and Ireland. The marriage, and Philip himself, were welcomed by those of the English nobility and gentry who were staunchly Catholic (or declared themselves so to be). Apart from a few Protestant strongholds, the Latin Mass was quickly restored in Parish churches.

There was some unease that during his first year in England he might try to import the Inquisition - the systematic persecution in Spain of all "heretics" - but Philip quickly adapted to English ways. For Mary, it was a genuine love match and her husband proved to be an able administrator. In the event, he did persuade her that they should go to war against France and, a year before she died, to send an army to reoccupy Calais. That port-city had been England's last remaining foothold on the Continent. It was a heavy blow to English pride and prestige when Philip's Anglo-Spanish relief force was defeated in battle and, after 210 years, Calais was lost for ever.

It was left to the new Queen to pick up the pieces. As Elizabeth I, the younger daughter of Henry VIII, she reigned for forty-four years. Beginning with her accession in 1558, those decades witnessed the next stage of the Reformation started by her father. A second Act of Supremacy made her Head of the English Church. She declared: "there should be outward conformity with the Established religion, but opinion should be left free". Even so, there was continuing tension throughout the land between Catholics and Protestants. It came to the boil when Elizabeth was declared by Pope Pius V to have no valid claim to the English throne. He opened the door for her cousin Mary, Queen of Scots, to pursue her own claim. She recruited a Catholic army to invade England. Defeated in battle near Glasgow, she became Elizabeth's prisoner. This triggered a major plot to secure her release, to dethrone Elizabeth and, with the aid of an invading Spanish army, to restore Roman Catholicism as the sole religion in the British Isles. The plot was stirred by Jesuit priests acting secretly on behalf of Philip. There was no longer any doubt in Elizabeth's mind that Spain was her greatest enemy. Showing her mettle as a strong Queen, she punished the conspirators without pity.

Neither of the two principal contestants was any longer at his or her best. At the time of the Armada, Philip was sixty-one years of age and had occupied the Spanish throne for thirty-two years. Elizabeth was fifty-five and had been Queen of England and Ireland for thirty years. By the standards of the time both were elderly, but this in no way diminished their determination to preserve the religious *status quo* in their respective domains. It had taken three decades but, finally, a climactic trial of strength between their two countries was about to erupt.

There were several considerations leading to Philip's decision to invade. He had maintained peaceful relations with England following Mary's death in 1558 and had even sent a proposal of marriage to her half-sister, Queen Elizabeth. They had come to know each other well during his two years at the English court. He enjoyed his time in England, but for legal reasons had never been formally crowned. There was therefore no point in remaining in a country where, although he was so popular, he possessed no hereditary rights. If he wanted to regain the English throne in his own right he must fight for it.

As King of Spain, he regarded himself as the principal guardian of the Church of Rome in Western Europe. With Protestantism spreading in France, Germany and Holland, he worried that it might infiltrate his own kingdom. The King of France shared the same anxiety. On his order, 20,000 Huguenots (Protestants) were slaughtered in Paris in a single day. The survivors fled to England. When the people of the Netherlands (at that time a Spanish province) rebelled against their oppressors, Elizabeth sent money and troops to help them (a move which angered Philip greatly). So, following the defeat of Mary, Queen of Scots, England emerged as an anti-Catholic stronghold, a focal point for those similar movements in other regions of northern Europe.

Adding to Philip's concerns were the activities of the English "sea dogs". He needed money, a lot of money, to finance his intended Armada, and for that he was dependent upon the silver mines of Peru. When Pizarro's "Conquistadores" had landed in 1532 they were astonished by the Inca's abundance of silver jewellery and ornaments. Great tonnages of the precious metal were soon being shipped back to Spain and converted into coinage.

Elizabeth also needed money. She had inherited twenty-seven "navy royal" ships from her father but she was unwilling to commit them under her own banner to open warfare with Spain. Instead, she granted "privateer" licences (letters of *marque)* to English pirates and others having knowledge of distant waters. Sir Francis Drake had already circumnavigated the world, a voyage which enabled him to plunder Spanish treasure ships and settlements on the Pacific coasts of the southern and central Americas. An exceptional commander, he had been raised as a Protestant and therefore detested the "papish" Spaniards. He and his cousin Sir John Hawkins had made slaver voyages to the New World from West Africa, there were others like them based in Plymouth and Dartmouth.

Elizabeth let them loose with orders to attack the Spanish convoys crossing the Atlantic and to raid their New World ports. Most of the treasure ships arrived safely in Spain, but any loss of revenue was to Philip a severe irritant. His anger was further stoked when, on 29 April 1587, Drake daringly entered the harbour at Cadiz and destroyed thirty of the ships ear-marked for the intended invasion of England. Drake went on to storm the port of Sagres, at the extreme south-west tip of the Portuguese coast. He occupied it for several days and used it as an operating base against Philip's supply ships.

Spectacular though they were, these raids were not enough to halt the momentum of the invasion preparations in Spain, Portugal and Flanders. All they did was to delay them until the following year. Philip had immense resources available to him, the Spanish Empire extended throughout most of the known world. He had annexed the kingdom of Portugal in 1581 and could additionally call upon naval and military assets in Italy, Sicily, and North Africa. On paper, his planned Armada would indeed be "invincible".

Well aware of what was intended, Elizabeth ordered Charles Howard, the Lord Effingham, to start assembling an *ad hoc* fleet for the defence of her shores. He had not previously commanded a fleet at sea, but he was an experienced naval administrator. His second-in-command was Sir Francis Drake and, between them, they spent the winter months making their own preparations. To augment the number of "royal" and privateer ships, Howard appealed to the Mayors of various West Country ports, asking them and their citizens to provide ships, men and money. The North Devon port of Barnstaple, as an example, contributed five ships headed by the SWAN. Normally their Masters and crews were engaged in regular trade with Newfoundland and the Caribbean but now, supplied with the additional cannon and powder needed for a sea battle, they headed south around Land's End and the Lizard to join Grenville, Frobisher, Hawkins and the others gathering under Charles Howard's command at Plymouth and at various more south coast ports.

After a long delay at Lisbon, the Armada finally set sail from Corunna on 23 July 1588. The expedition was in part a military operation, in part a religious crusade. This confusion of purpose was one of its principal weaknesses. In some ships there were more soldiers than seamen, more priests than trained gunners. However, there were other factors which contributed to its eventual failure. Storms in the Bay of Biscay forced five of the original 135 ships to take refuge in French ports, but only two were lost in action as the huge fleet advanced up the English Channel towards its appointment with the Duke of Parma and his invasion army waiting at Bruges and on the coast near Dunkirk.

The English snapped continuously at its heels and there were clashes off Plymouth, Portland and the Isle of Wight before, on 6 August, adverse winds and tides forced it to drop anchor three miles out from Calais. The Armada was just twenty-four miles short of its intended destination, Dunkirk. Two nights later it was

*The Spanish-Portuguese fleet passing a fortified headland in the crescent formation which the English, led by Lord Howard of Effingham, found so hard to penetrate. The ship in the foreground is the Portuguese galleon Sao Martinho (48 guns), flagship of the Armada's commander, the Duke of Medina Sidonia. The vessel in the lower left corner is one of his four Neapolitan galleasses, each carrying 50 guns and propelled by sail and 500 convict rowers. The English ships are to the right.*

dispersed by English fire-ships but, even so, the Spaniards then managed to re-form a large part of the "crescent" formation which had so frustrated Charles Howard's attacks in the Channel. It sailed further up the coast until brought to battle off the Flanders port of Gravelines (at that time still in the Spanish Netherlands). Both sides were by then seriously short of powder, shot and provisions.

On 8 August, in unsettled seas and squally showers, the two fleets fought all day at close range. Howard's West Country ships were joined by a force coming south from the Kentish coast and, together, they tore into the Armada like wolves after sheep. The Spanish admiral, the Duke of Medina Sidonia, fought back with skill and courage, but immense damage was inflicted by the smaller faster-moving English. Four of the Duke's "great ships" were sunk or driven ashore, 1000 of his men were killed, 800 wounded. Howard's ships suffered little more than superficial damage, all of it repairable.

Denied by a rising unseasonal southerly gale any hope either of embarking Parma's troops or of escaping down-Channel, Philip's ships were obliged to head

*Charles Howard's flagship in 1588 was the Ark Royal (800 tons, 44 guns). First of the five British warships to successively bear that name, she had been built a year earlier at Deptford as a privateer to the personal order of Sir Walter Ralegh (Raleigh). It being the custom, she was named after her owner as the "Ark Ralegh". Persuaded by his Queen to let the vessel join the other "royal ships" and then renamed, she headed the English fleet which, after Gravelines, harried the Armada all the way up the North Sea to the Firth of Forth before breaking off the action. In 2011 the last of "the Arks" - an aircraft carrier - was sold by the Cameron/Clegg government to a Turkish scrap metal dealer.*

north past the Thames estuary, past the coasts of East Anglia and Northumbria, then onward around the north of Scotland. Having reached the Atlantic, twenty-five of them were wrecked on the unforgiving rocky headlands of Ireland while others were sunk in storms. In total, and including thirty-six of his major vessels, one third of Philip's Armada ships were lost. Of the 29,453 souls who had departed Corunna on 23 July, at least 15,000 are said to have lost their lives before it was all over.

Earlier, while the risk still existed that the Spanish-Portuguese fleet might sail up the Thames and attack London, Elizabeth made her memorable speech at Tilbury to the 4000 militiamen charged with its defence. Best remembered is the line: "I know I have the body of a weak and feeble woman, but I have the heart and stomach of a king, and a King of England too". Less familiar is her concluding line: "I myself will be your rewarder of every one of your virtues in the field. I know already, for your forwardness, you have deserved rewards and crowns and, we do assure you, on the word of a prince, they shall be duly paid you".

Elizabeth lied in her teeth. None of her soldiers and sailors ever received their pay or their widows a pension. No more than one hundred of Howard's men had been lost in action but, when his ships returned to their home ports from the North Sea, great numbers were already dying of disease. They had survived the fighting but the ship-board contaminated water butts, rotting food and overcrowded insanitary conditions were in combination killing them off by the score. In the 550 ton ELIZABETH BONAVENTURE, for example, 200 of the 500 ship's company who had sailed from Plymouth in late July were dead a month later.

Even though that ship and others like her were "royal ships" - the property of the Queen herself - Howard's appeal to Elizabeth for money with which to pay wages and to support the sick and wounded brought this reply from her Secretary of State William Cecil, the Lord Burghley: "By death, by discharging of sick men, and such like, there may be something spared in the general pay". Strangely, at some stage during his forty years as one of Elizabeth's privy councillors, Lord Burghley advised her: "Seek peace but prepare for war". He should have taken his own advice. Several thousand seamen served in the 1588 English fleet. Ordered ashore as soon as the crisis had passed, great numbers died of their wounds or of sickness and starvation before the end of the year.

The physical condition of King Philip's men - those who managed to bring their battered ships back to Spain - was even worse than that of the English. They had been very much longer at sea. Philip and the Duke of Medina Sidonia responded by ensuring that they were given good medical care and received their arrears of pay prior to discharge. This disparity in the post-battle treatment of the two fleets explains much of what followed in later decades. As the horrified Charles Howard warned at the time: "It were pitiful to have men starve after such service .... if men should not be cared for better, we should hardly get men to serve". He made a good point. Long after 1588, patriotism alone was rarely enough to bring forward the number and quality of seamen needed whenever English maritime interests were under threat or overseas expeditions were being mounted.

Elizabeth may have been coldly callous in her attitude toward the sailors who

Photograph: Spinks *British Battles & Medals*, (6th Edition, 1988)

*The first medal generated by the defeat of the Armada was Queen Elizabeth's **Naval Reward**. She instructed her Court portraitist, Nicholas Hilliard, to produce the design and to supervise its casting. Hilliard was also responsible for **The Dangers Averted Medal**.*

Photograph: Spinks *British Battles & Medals*, (6th Edition, 1988)

*An example of **The Dangers Averted Medal** of which three (or possibly four) variants were produced. It is unlikely they were all made in the same year, hence some may be regarded more as commemorative pieces than rewards for services rendered. The bay tree standing on a small island is common to each reverse with the words, in Latin, "Not even dangers affect it".*

had saved her throne (and probably saved her neck), but she did reward her captains with a silver medal. It was intended for wear, and it was the first such naval award ever made by an English monarch. Over the following two centuries, through to 1792, fifty other types of medal would be authorised in recognition of a sea or land campaign. They were described and illustrated in exemplary detail by D Hastings Irwin in his monumental volume *War Medals and Decorations* (four editions, 1890 to 1910), but **The Naval Reward** of 1588 was their progenitor. Charles Howard had at various times 197 fighting ships under his command, so presumably that was the number presented to their captains. It is probable that others were struck for presentation to people who could claim some sort of share, direct or indirect, in the victory.

A year later an even more handsome piece was given to an unknown number of Elizabeth's sailors (there is no reliable record of its issue). It was **The Dangers Averted Medal,** cast or struck in gold, silver or copper, with an integral loop for suspension. Like **The Naval Reward** it had royal authority, but the popular belief

*Queen Elizabeth I was portrayed many times on canvas, but this image in particular demonstrates the immense importance attaching to the events of 1588. Engulfed in silks and jewels, she rests her right hand on a globe. The gesture is a statement. England is no longer a small island on the periphery of Europe, it is a claimant to world power. The small picture over her right shoulder shows her fleet pursuing the Armada towards Calais. In the other painting, Atlantic gales are hurling Spanish ships against Irish cliffs. The artist's intentions are unmistakable.*

that God had actively supported Elizabeth's cause prompted the marketing of unofficial commemorative medallions. "He blew with his winds, and they were scattered" was the wording on one of them. The chanciness of English Channel weather had indeed played a major role in settling the fate of King Philip's expedition. Coincidentally, it had decided in the much longer term the question of who would shape England's future religious, monarchical and legal institutions. It would be Canterbury, not Rome.

Exceptional page space has been devoted to this story. Why? Because the political and diplomatic consequences were far more important than the short-term triumph of the event itself. At home, Elizabeth reinforced her awesome reputation as a clever ruthless woman. The plots and rebellions continued throughout the remaining years of her long reign, but to challenge her proved exceedingly dangerous. Abroad, as other kings and queens came and went, the fate of the 1588 Spanish-Portuguese fleet made a lasting impression. English naval commanders and their men were perceived to be unbeatable. Even though she was named "Gloriana" by her people, the belief that "Britannia" ruled the waves had taken root.

In passing, and for the record, the ultra-patriotic song "Rule Britannia" was not written until 152 years after the Armada. It was first performed in 1740 as part of a private entertainment for Frederick, Prince of Wales. At that time, in what was known as "the war of Jenkin's ear", Great Britain was once again locked in conflict with Spain, the English Navy heavily engaged in attacking Spanish possessions in the Central Americas. When the general public first heard the rousing lyrics, they immediately identified with the references to "freedom" and "never never shall be slaves". The song has retained its popularity ever since, perpetuating the belief that the Royal Navy is the principal guardian of British liberty.

From the time of Christ onwards, the British Isles were colonised by a succession of foreign invaders - Romans, Angles, Saxons, Jutes, Vikings, finally the Normans. Following the departure of the Romans *circa* 410 AD, the land descended into a chaos resolved only partly by the creation in 519 of the Anglo-Saxon Kingdom of West Mercia. Eastern and northern areas had their own minor kings who became easy prey for Viking raiders. In 793 the Abbey on the island of Lindisfarne was the first to be laid waste. After that, year after year, land warfare between Vikings and Anglo-Saxons (interrupted by occasional peace treaties) characterised the history of England through to William of Normandy's invasion near Hastings in 1066.

The Vikings - with their savage style of warfare and frightening appearance - have at times earned "a bad Press", but they were brilliant ship builders and navigators. Their long-ships - the "dragon ships" - carried them far and wide to destroy, pillage and then settle wherever a major river gave them access to the hinterland. Their farmer warriors soon colonised chunks of Greenland, Normandy, Sicily, southern Russia, Ireland, the Scottish isles and, of course, England north of the river Humber (Northumbria). Viking command of the sea allowed them to strike all around Britain's coastline whenever they chose. The Angles and the Saxons had crossed the North Sea in the 6th century but had never maintained the sort of maritime force now needed to challenge the fearsome Viking fleets. On occasion, as many as 600 long-ships could gather for a single raid (as they did in 845 when they rowed up the River Elbe to sack Hamburg).

Things began slowly to change as English kings decided to fight back. In 851, King Athelstan of Kent fought a river estuary battle with Viking long-ships and captured nine of them. Best chronicled is a minor engagement in an unnamed Sussex river estuary in 896. That was in the reign of King Alfred, acclaimed by history as "the Great". To contest the repeated Viking raids along his shores, Alfred had ordered the construction of fighting vessels designed specifically to run alongside a Viking long-ship and seize it with a heavily-armed boarding party. Some of these fighting ships trapped a group of three Danish long-ships in shallow water on a falling tide. One escaped, the crews of the other two - 120 of them - fought and died to the last man. A thousand years later, Victorian writers drew upon that and similar episodes to romanticise Alfred as "the father of the Royal Navy". A nice idea, but a claim too far. Alfred's vessels were coastal troop carriers, not warships in any wider sense.

After Philip of Spain's defeat in 1588 there were other attempts at invasion, but most were half-hearted, seeming to lack any profound expectation of success. In 1805, the frustrated Napoleon Bonaparte began to disperse his 200,000-strong "Army of the Ocean Coast", sending it eastwards to perish, eventually, in the frozen steppes of Russia. At Boulogne he had inspected his troops, witnessed their attempts to operate landing barges and concluded that they could never survive a full-scale crossing without complete French naval control of the Channel. If his orders had been obeyed there would have been fifty-nine ships of the line assembled off Boulogne. They would have offered a serious if not insuperable challenge to any Royal Navy force attempting to attack the troop-carrying barges. Napoleon's plan collapsed when his senior naval commander, Admiral Pierre-Charles Villeneuve, lost his nerve and instead diverted thirty-three of the expected ships first to Cadiz and then to his disastrous encounter with Horatio Nelson off Cape Trafalgar on 21 October.

In 1940, his *Luftwaffe* defeated in the Battle of Britain, as ever fearful of the British Home Fleet, an equally frustrated Adolf Hitler abandoned his intended Operation *Sealion* invasion and repeated in Russia the same folly as Napoleon. As he confessed to his senior commanders: "On land I am a hero. At sea I am a coward". The enduring *mystique* of the Royal Navy had broken each man's earlier resolve.

In 1982, Admiral Jorge Isaac Anaya, head of the Argentine Navy, had argued strongly in favour of an invasion of the Falkland Islands but, when the Royal Navy began to arrive in the South Atlantic, he committed only one of his ships to challenge Vice Admiral "Sandy" Woodward's Operation *Corporate* task force. Following the destruction of the cruiser GENERAL BELGRANO by Commander Christopher Wreford-Brown's HMS CONQUEROR, Admiral Anaya ordered all his other surface ships back to port where they remained for the duration of the conflict.

The narrowness of our victory in 1588 demonstrated that we needed, urgently, to preserve our independence by establishing a strong permanent navy commanded by professional naval officers. That lesson was driven home less than one year later.

Elizabeth doubted that Philip had abandoned his ambition to invade. She knew that he was repairing and reinforcing his Armada ships in San Sebastian, Santander and Lisbon and might soon renew his campaign. Accordingly, she ordered Sir Francis Drake to attack those ports, destroy the warships harboured there and, of course, to seize any treasure ships he might encounter along the way.

When he departed Plymouth Sound in April 1859 he had under his command 150 ships - some "royal", the majority armed merchantmen. Knowing what had happened the previous autumn, Drake's seamen understandably wanted at least part of their wages to be paid in advance before they sailed. Elizabeth was obliged to cough up the ruinous sum of £50,000 to finance the expedition while City of London speculators were persuaded to invest a further £40,000. With excessive optimism, they thought Drake would occupy Lisbon. That would give them control of the lucrative trade with the Americas and West Africa.

Drake was approaching fifty and in poor health. For a variety of reasons he ignored his Queen's orders, tried to attack Corunna instead of Santander, then lost 4000 soldiers in a failed attempt to besiege Lisbon. The expedition ended in total failure, it was a fiasco. Elizabeth and the City investors lost all their money. Unpaid sailors and soldiers were rioting in the streets for months afterwards and Drake himself was in disgrace. Philip did not in the event make a second attempt at invasion but the navy of Spain continued to be the dominant force in distant waters for the next twenty years. Unsurprisingly, there were no "medals to the navy" for the ignominious 1589 episode.

Manning our ships was never easy. The best seamen preferred to go privateering (with the prospect of prize money) rather than serve in a ship of war (with the risk of death or of never being paid). The unhappy fate of Sir Walter Ralegh (Raleigh) taught their officers to avoid the perils of political intrigue at Court. The wars of religion did stimulate improved construction and armament of ships designed specifically for warfare, but selection of the officers was decided by their personal convictions, far less their knowledge of the sea. Roman Catholics were barred from holding a Commission even during periods of great peril and much of our military effort was expended on cruel suppression of the Catholic Irish and the Highland clansmen of Scotland.

Only in 1817, after Europe had already ceased tearing itself apart, did the House of Lords reluctantly approve The Military and Naval Officers Act. All ranks were then opened to both denominations, but that was still not the end of it. Ambitious Roman Catholic officers could not hope to develop a career in politics because they were banned from public office. The last barrier came down in 1829 when, under threat of imminent civil war, Prime Minister the Duke of Wellington persuaded the House of Lords to pass The Roman Catholic Relief Act. Freely elected Catholics were permitted at last to take their seats in the House of Commons. We may speculate in what ways the evolution of the Royal Navy and its administration might have been different if so many talented men had not been for so long excluded.

There was no formally established permanent English Royal Navy until the Restoration of the Monarchy under Charles II and his appointment in 1673 of

Samuel Pepys as the first Chief Secretary to the Admiralty. Henry VII and Henry VIII had set in train the construction of the royal naval dockyards and of specialist warships such as the MARY ROSE, but only in 1673 did we start to have a professional navy as we might understand that term today.

After Elizabeth was succeeded in 1603 by the Scottish Protestant King James I, England once again entered a period of great religious and political instability. Those years - the so-called Jacobean "Golden Age" - are best remembered in the story of Sir Guy Fawkes (the Gunpowder Plot of 1605) and the Protestant colonisation of Ulster (leaving scars unhealed to the present day). Largely forgotten is the story of one of the heroes of the Elizabethan decades, the great sea captain Sir Walter Ralegh. In 1584 he claimed for the English crown the territory which twenty years later became the Colony of Virginia, with Jamestown as its principal settlement. It was the first English-speaking foothold in the North Americas, the first source of imported tobacco and potatoes, and the seed-corn of the future United States.

Charged with the defence of England's south coast in the year of the Armada he was one of Elizabeth's favourites. He then fell foul of the machinations of the Jacobean court and was condemned to death for treason. Reprieved, he spent thirteen years jailed in the Tower of London until James, desperate for money, released him on the understanding that he would once again cross the Atlantic and bring home a cargo of gold. It was thought that a city of gold - "El Dorado" - was to be found somewhere up the Orinoco river in the jungles of the Amazon. Ralegh's "rules of engagement" bound him not to antagonise the local Spaniards. England was at that time, just for once, not at war with Spain.

Inevitably it all went wrong and a depressed Ralegh (his son Walter was killed in the fighting) came home with no gold and a lot of explaining to be done. The original death sentence was reinstated and in 1618 he was taken to Old Palace Yard where the axe-man removed his head. For England's naval explorers, service to the monarchy could be at times a question of "death or glory".

In 1624 we went back to fighting the Spanish and, three years later, the French. Then, in 1652, we went to war with our former friends, the Dutch. Charles I had been executed and England was, effectively, a Protestant republic. Initially it was known as the Commonwealth, then later the Protectorate (under Oliver Cromwell).

Holland also had become a Protestant republic, so Cromwell proposed that the two should merge. For a variety of reasons, the offer was not acted upon. In 1651, a resentful Cromwell retaliated with The Navigation Act. Despite its benign title, this Act was intended to wreck the Dutch economy while boosting our own mercantile trade. Inevitably, war followed. Over the next two years there were six running battles between the two navies, all with a single exception fought in the English Channel and the North Sea. The story of just one of them will serve to illuminate the nature of 17$^{th}$ century naval warfare. It was the Battle of Dungeness, fought on 10 December 1652 between a Dutch fleet of eighty ships commanded by Admiral Maarten van Tromp and an English fleet of forty-two ships commanded by General-at-Sea (Admiral) Robert Blake. Both were very experienced seamen.

Cromwell's advisors had assumed that the Dutch would not wish to fight in mid-winter, so half of our ships had been sent to the Mediterranean (where they were lost in the Battle of Leghorn). Blake, therefore, was outnumbered two-to-one and some of his ships were little more than armed merchantmen manned by temporarily impressed civilian officers and crews. Typically, these vessels displaced between 300 and 600 tons and were armed with thirty-five guns of mixed calibre. The largest, a Deptford-built "royal" ship, was the TRIUMPH (900 tons, 44 guns).

Abandoning its anchorage off the Kentish Downs, fighting a north-west half-gale, Blake's fleet hugged the coast westward towards the cape of Dungeness. The offshore wind prevented the Dutch from engaging them until the next day when the curve of the coastline forced the English out into the open sea. At three in the afternoon the two forces came together with a roar of cannon-fire and a crackle of musketry. It was all over in three hours, Blake pulling back to the Downs as darkness fell. He had lost three ships sunk, two captured and many damaged. Admiral van Tromp lost only one ship (it happened to catch fire). He returned to Holland, victorious, allegedly with a broom lashed to his masthead to show that "he had swept the sea clean of his enemies". Historians doubt the truth of this legend, but the story is too good to be ignored.

Blake, by contrast, was an angry man. Some of his civilian captains had maintained their traditional right to enter a battle or sail away from it whenever they chose. After reading his report, the Lords Commissioners ordered that, in future, impressed vessels must be commanded by naval officers whom they themselves appointed. They also published "Sailing and Fighting Instructions", rules intended to improve command and control in fleet actions.

The climax to this, the first of the Anglo-Dutch naval wars, came on 31 July 1653. The English blockade of Rotterdam and Amsterdam had brought starvation to their populations and the end was near. When van Tromp came out to break through at Scheveningen, the English fought him but then, obliged by battle damage to end the blockade, decided they had had enough anyway. Peace was signed (in England's favour) in April 1654. Sadly, the excellent Maarten van Tromp was killed in that final battle. Like Nelson many decades later, he was shot down on his own quarterdeck by a sniper.

Belatedly, in 1658, Parliament authorised production of **The Commonwealth Naval Medals**. There were three variant designs which, for obvious reasons, did not incorporate the bust of a monarch. The qualifying rules excluded Blake's 1652 defeat off Dungeness, but that affair has been described here anyway because of its important influence upon the management of future fleet actions. However, there was one other medal, unofficial, connected with those events. It deserves mention

*Four days of spasmodic fighting culminate in the Battle of Scheveningen (Texel) when, in shallow waters and violent weather, 247 warships batter each other until exhausted. The English emerge the winners. Thousands of spectators lined the shore to watch the spectacle, recorded in this oil by Willem van de Velde (the Elder).*

because so little is known about it. It is recorded as **The Triumph Medal**.

During the Dungeness battle, Blake's flagship caught fire. Fearful that her magazine would explode, the crew began to abandon her. There was then a move to go back aboard and save her. The fires were extinguished and TRIUMPH survived to fight another day. One source states that a medal was given to every man in her crew but, as it was made in gold and only one example has survived (now held by the British Museum), this seems unlikely. Perhaps Blake paid for a few as gifts for his ship's officers? **The Triumph Medal** remains a puzzling curiosity.

A decade later England was still at war with Holland. On 13 June 1665, forty miles east from Lowestoft, their fleets met in light winds to fight a confused battle which caused Charles II to authorise **The Dominion of the Sea Medal.** The statistics are impressive: 109 English ships armed with 4542 cannon and manned by 22,055 men facing 103 Dutch ships carrying 4869 cannon and 21,613 men. Admittedly the Dutch guns were of smaller calibre, but it was "the fog of war" which caused the Dutch tactical defeat.

Now we move forward to 1692. King James II had ascended the throne determined to reinstate Roman Catholicism as the sole Church in England. Failing to control events in England he fled to France, then raised a large Catholic army and naval fleet in Ireland. He was replaced in London by his son-in-law, the Dutch Protestant William III of the House of Orange. In France, King Louis XIV watched all of this with interest. He reasoned that if he supported James with an invasion and restored him to the English throne, Catholicism would once again dominate throughout the British Isles. With this in mind, in July 1690 he sent a reconnaissance force to test England's defences. His ships won a scrap off Beachy Head before cruising along the south coast to Devon (where, in the last foreign invasion of English soil, they plundered and set fire to the town of Teignmouth). Encouraged, the French Ministry of the Navy pushed forward with its plan for a major amphibious operation. William was busy persecuting the Catholics in

Ireland, but he was aware of the threat from France. His ships were scattered in penny packets around the English and Irish coasts, and it would take time to combine them with the Dutch fleet. The French hoped to strike before that could happen.

Their own ships were assembling in the ports of Rochefort, Toulon and Brest, and an army of 30,000 was awaiting embarkation at Cherbourg. Ten thousand of those foot soldiers were Catholic Irish who had been permitted by William to emigrate. At La Havre, dozens of barges were waiting to carry the artillery and cavalry across the Channel whenever the order came. The prospects for a great success were good. In overall command was the *Comte* de Tourville and, on paper, he had sufficient ships and troops for the task. But luck deserted him when the Toulon flotilla failed to break through the Straits of Gibraltar, the Rochefort flotilla was delayed, and lack of crews obliged him to leave twenty ships at their moorings at Brest. When his depleted force arrived off the northern coast of the Cotentin (Cherbourg) Peninsula, he had forty-four ships of the line to challenge the fifty-six English and twenty-six Dutch. They met on 29 May 1692 off Barfleur. A day and night of combat resulted in 5000 French sailors dead or wounded, 1700 English and Dutch. No ships were sunk, but most were severely damaged. Of the English ships engaged, several bore names which will appear later in this series of articles: EAGLE, BRITANNIA, DREADNOUGHT, VICTORY and LION

The French ships were scattered, literally to the four winds. Some escaped westwards to St Malo and Brest, three into Cherbourg (where they were burned by Dutch boarding parties), two even managed to return home by passing around

*The Commonwealth Parliament ordered a succession of Naval Rewards for actions fought between 1650 and 1653. This example commemorates a 1650 battle caused by the defection of six ships to the Royalist cause. The cypher "Meruisti" signifies "Thou hast merit".*

*Artists' interpretations of 17th century battles fought at sea tend to be very similar. This is the version, painted in oils, of the Battle of Barfleur (29 May 1692) as recorded by the marine artist Richard Paton (1717-1791). One of his most popular works was, curiously, the capture in 1779 of HMS Serapis off Flamborough Head (Yorkshire) by the American privateer Bonhomme Richard.*

Scotland into the Atlantic, but twelve others took refuge under the shore batteries at La Hogue (on the east coast of the Cotentin Peninsula). They included the AMBITIEUX (96 guns), L'FIER (80), and GRAND (84), powerful ships but with crews demoralised by the events of the past five days. All twelve were destroyed by English fire-ships and boat parties. The combined actions of 19-24 May 1692 led to Parliament authorising **The La Hogue Medal.** It was struck in gold and in silver with the conjoined busts of William and Mary, but published details of its issue are unclear.

King Louis abandoned his intended invasion, but Barfleur and La Hogue did not end his ambitions elsewhere. The damage to his fleet was quickly made good and, only one year later, de Tourville got his revenge when he ambushed a valuable Anglo-Dutch escorted merchant convoy off Lagos, southern Portugal. The financial loss for the owners and City underwriters exceeded that of the 1666 Great Fire of London.

Four years later the tables were turned yet again with the (first) War of the Spanish Succession. Admiral Sir George Rooke was leading an Anglo-Dutch fleet back to England when he learned that a convoy of merchantmen had arrived from the New World in the port of Vigo (on the Galician coast of Spain). Three were treasure galleons, laden with silver, the property of King Philip V. The rest were carrying mixed cargo owned by the traders of Amsterdam. Their powerful escort comprised fifteen French ships of the line. On 23 October 1702, they and the merchantmen were tucked deep within the bay, its entrance sealed with a log boom covered by shore batteries, but Rooke did not hesitate. He ordered the TORBAY (80 guns) to crash through the boom and she was followed by enough of his ships (half of them Dutch) to create mayhem in the anchorage. In the event, much of the silver had been unloaded before he arrived but, even so, he was able to send home seventeen captured galleons laden with valuable merchandise. All of the other enemy ships, French and Spanish, were burned at their moorings.

That action generated **The Vigo Bay Medal.** It bears the crowned bust of Queen Anne. She had gained the throne eight months earlier following the death in a riding accident of the widowed William III. Her twelve years as a Protestant monarch were marked by disputes at home between Whigs and Tories, and abroad by continuing warfare with France and Spain. There were many actions at sea during that time, but only one led to the issue of a specifically naval medal. It is the little-known **Callis Medal,** a silver award restricted to Captain Smith Callis and his officers who, in June 1742, attacked the French port of St Tropez and destroyed five Spanish galleys anchored there.

And so the carnage went on, seemingly without end. The following decades witnessed constant warfare throughout Europe, a major episode being our seizure in 1704 of Gibraltar (an event which later gave name to the only battle honour shown on the crest of the Corps of Royal Marines). The next seventy-five years were devoted to the Rock's fortification but, when a combined French-Spanish fleet began a blockade in 1779, the defences were under-manned and poorly provisioned. Almost four years of valiant resistance followed. They generated several commemorative medals and medallions of interest to the collector (notably **General Eliott's Medal** and **General Picton's Medal**). The strangest was **The Red Hot Shot Medal.**

On 13 September 1782, the French and Spanish launched a massive attack with 33,000 troops from landward and the artillery of seventy-eight assorted warships in the bay. To augment their close-range firepower, ten had been stripped out and converted at great expense into floating batteries. The dangerous technique of

*An aquatint version of the floating batteries assembling inshore at Gibraltar. None of the published sources are in agreement when describing these ships or their eventual fate. The most believable (and logical) state that they were manoeuvred into position by jib and stay sails only, but this artist (Clevely) gives them topsails and gallants.*

*The Red Hot Shot Medal*

loading cannon with an iron ball cooked to red heat had been invented long before by the Chinese. Aware that the garrison had the same capability, these ships were fitted with a sophisticated fire-fighting system. In the event, the first English shots set fire to the TALLA PIEDRA and PASTORA, both of which are said to have exploded. The fate of the remaining eight is uncertain. Some sources state that they were scuttled by their Spanish crews, but timber hulls do not sink readily and their semi-submerged wrecks would have been a navigational hazard for all the other ships in the area, so this version must be doubted. Another source claims that the crews destroyed their own ships by setting them on fire, but this account also is questionable. Eight blazing ships drifting through such a crowded anchorage would not have been at all desirable. Whatever the facts of the matter, the assault was a fiasco and the siege ended a year later. Production of **The Red Hot Shot Medal** seems to have been a commercial venture, a token offered for purchase mainly by the gunners involved. However, it was beautifully struck (in copper, one known in silver) with the names of the individual owners exquisitely engraved on the reverse. Such quality deserves deeper research.

At the time of the Gibraltar siege, England was standing alone against all the governments of Europe and was still deeply involved in the failed attempt to retain the American Colonies. A controversial but heroic figure from those decades was George Brydges Rodney. In 1759, flying his flag as Rear Admiral in HMS ACHILLES (60 guns), he led a flotilla of frigates and bomb-ketches across the Channel to attack the port of Le Havre. It was packed with stores and barges assembled there for an intended invasion of England. Immense damage was inflicted during fifty hours of continuous mortar fire to which the French offered little resistance, and that was the end of the latest attempt to occupy our island.

Twenty-one years later, in 1780, Rodney smashed a Spanish fleet off Cape St

Vincent. Then, in 1782, he routed a French fleet in the West Indies (the Battle of the Saintes). That victory "revived the expiring conviction in Europe that England was still Queen of the seas". The battle lasted eleven hours and was, according to Rodney, "one of the most severe ever fought at sea". Elevated to the peerage as Admiral Lord Rodney, he then retired after sixty years of almost continuous service at sea.

None of those actions resulted in the issuing of official medals so today they are forgotten. Such omissions support the author's introductory proposition that medals are indeed "signposts along the highway of history". Without them we could lose our way in pursuing the history of the Royal Navy. The preceding pages show that, at least until 1692, it was engaged almost exclusively in wars fired by religion or by disputed rights to kingship (often both in equal measure). The next article in the series (1792 to 1840) will describe a very different scenario.

*The book plate of Samuel Pepys, best remembered for his 1660-1669 diary record of the Plague, the Second Anglo-Dutch War and the Great Fire of London. The Latin motto signifies "Mind makes the man". Of humble origins, highly intelligent and self-driven, he started work at the Admiralty as a clerk. In time he rose to serve as its Chief Secretary in the successive reigns of Charles II and then James II. During those years, he imposed new standards which became the bed-rock of the navy's future administration.*

## Part Two - 1792 to 1840

PART ONE of this series dealt with wars of religion and inter-nation conflict fought at sea between 1588 and 1792. The scenario began to change in the wake of the American War of Independence (1775-1783) and the French Revolution (1789-1793). Theology was replaced by political philosophy, subservience by rebellion. Throughout Europe, age-old acceptances of authority were questioned by the oppressed classes. On the face of it, the aristocratic order in Europe needed either to become more liberal or risk being swept away by popular uprisings. Neither happened. Instead, Austria and Prussia invaded France with the aim of overthrowing the Revolution and restoring Louis XVI to his throne. Despite the turmoil within their own country, the French defeated the invaders and occupied the Austrian Netherlands. This brought conflict with Great Britain and the Dutch Republic and so, once again, we went to war with France and, soon after, with Spain (and then with the Dutch when they were forced into alliance with Revolutionary France).

That war was soon followed by yet another, this time with the France of Napoleon Bonaparte. Those two decades are commemorated by 228 different bars authorised for attachment to William Wyon's stunningly beautiful **Naval War Medal** authorised belatedly in 1848. Three more bars were issued for battles fought after the fall of Napoleon, but they will come later in the story. For the moment it is the Royal Navy of Nelson, of his "band of brothers", and of other officers of that tumultuous era, who command our interest.

Although first announced in *The London Gazette* as **The Naval War Medal,** authors such as D Hastings Irwin and other pioneers in the medal collecting field described it as **The Naval General Service Medal** (the **NGSM**). The present author chooses to follow their distinguished lead.

When it was introduced, the bars to be fixed to the **NGSM** recognised three different types of engagement at sea - fleet actions (involving ships of the line), frigate actions (when one, two or three were engaged, each having a bar named to the individual ship), and boat actions (usually beach landings or cutting-out expeditions from enemy harbours). Everyone who has read the accounts by William James and other early writers will know that the **NGSM** bars represent only a minority of all the actions fought, and that the 21,000 issued medals went to a lamentably small minority of the officers and men who had participated. Even so, they do give us the flavour of extraordinary times, years when Great Britain could so easily have succumbed without the skills and determination of the Royal Navy's senior commanders.

The earliest bar was **Nymphe 18 June 1793.** The NYMPHE was a frigate of 938 tons armed with thirty-six cannon of mixed calibre and manned mainly by an inexperienced crew of landsmen (Cornish tin miners) and impressed merchant sailors. Her commanding officer was Captain Edward Pellew, RN (he will appear later as Admiral Lord Exmouth). With the war against Revolutionary France only weeks old, with little time in which to "shake down", Pellew sailed from Falmouth in search of enemy frigates reported off South Devon.

Images: National Maritime Museum (NMM)

*The "young head" obverse created by William Wyon RA for the new **Naval War Medal** and other awards of that period. He also designed the reverse, bearing the motif "Britannia with seahorse".*

Soon he captured a privateer but then, at first light on 18 June, his lookouts reported another strange sail and he quickly closed her. She was the CLEOPATRE, a frigate of equal displacement and fire-power commanded by *Capitaine* Jean Mullon. Only five miles off the dangerous Start Point, the two Captains gallantly hailed each other, their crews gave a cheer, then the firing began. After fifty minutes of mutual battering, the CLEOPATRE had lost her mizzen-mast and, critically, her steering wheel. Out of control, she swung towards the NYMPHE and rammed her bowsprit across Pellew's main deck. When the two ships became locked together he led a boarding party into a savage fight in which *Capitaine* Mullon was killed and his ship seized.

Given a jury rig, the CLEOPATRE was sailed into Portsmouth harbour. She was purchased by the Admiralty Agent and taken into service as HMS OISEAU. It was the beginning of Pellew's prize money fortune, but the event had broader implications than that. Relatively minor in itself, the battle was seized upon by the English newspapers as proof that the Royal Navy did still rule the waves. For the fragile British government headed by William Pitt (the Younger), here was a golden opportunity to enhance its image and counter its critics. Only eleven days after his arrival in Portsmouth, Edward Pellew had been de-briefed, spruced up and rushed by carriage to London for an audience with King George III who dubbed him a Knight Commander of the Order of the Bath. For a junior captain, age thirty-six, this was heady stuff. Thanks to him and the Royal Navy, the London newspapers had "a good news day" and the government's critics were, for the time being, silenced.

By rare coincidence, the name of Pellew's ship came to attention again four years later following a brief battle off the coast of Wales. Under Captain John Cooke, RN, she and HMS SAN FIORENZO (Captain Sir Harry Neale, RN) tackled and captured two frigates of similar strength. The French LA RESISTANCE and LA CONSTANCE were sailing home after putting ashore near Fishguard a force of 1400 French soldiers and Irish mercenaries. It had been planned, optimistically, that they would raise the countryside and then march eastwards to attack Bristol. In the event, they were quickly rounded up by local farmers and men of the Pembrokeshire Militia. To commemorate the subsequent action at sea, the **NGSM** was fitted with the bars **San Fiorenzo 8 March 1797** (nine issued) and **Nymphe 8 March 1797** (five issued).

It had been a long time since our navy had fought a major fleet action, so it was not surprising that the battle known as "the Glorious First of June" was marked by confusion when it was fought on that day in 1794. It is important to examine the background. With Louis XVI under arrest and doomed to execution four months later, the Republic had been proclaimed in France in September 1792. The ensuing "Reign of Terror" sent at least 16,000 people to the guillotine, with perhaps 40,000 others randomly murdered. All France was "deluged in blood".

Amongst the victims were naval officers whose support for the Republic was, for one reason or another, questioned. Only a few were executed but hundreds were sacked or simply fled the country. Their replacements were in some cases junior officers of limited experience, but several of the best admirals were spared. Their ships were well built and well armed, their commanders only needed time in which to mould them into a formidable force.

They did not have that luxury because France was in the grip of famine. Bad harvests and the destruction of the land-owning classes had brought the countryside to its knees. The United States of America, grateful for the support given by France during their own revolution, agreed to ship a great quantity of grain across the Atlantic and to loan some of the vessels in which to carry it. Under command of a Dutchman, Rear Admiral Pierre-Jean Vanstabel, a convoy of 127 chartered French and American merchantmen sailed from Chesapeake Bay on 2 April 1794 and began its slow passage across the Atlantic.

Commanding our Channel Fleet was the veteran Admiral Lord Howe. Aware of its importance, he hoped to intercept the convoy as it approached the Bay of Biscay but that plan failed when he came up against Admiral Louis-Thomas Villaret-Joyeuse. The Frenchman had sortied from Brest with a force of twenty-six ships of the line, his orders being to protect the grain ships on the final leg of their long voyage. In a series of skirmishes beginning on 28 May, the French admiral very cleverly trailed his coat-tails, gradually decoying Howe's fleet away from the track of the out-of-sight convoy. Battle was joined in earnest on 1 June.

Howe and Villaret-Joyeuse at first followed the convention of deploying their ships in line ahead, in parallel, so that each matched the other's heaviest broadside batteries. Before he fled to France in 1688, King James II had held the post of Lord High Admiral. During his four troubled years on the throne his admirals were instructed that their battleships (those carrying the later equivalent of 74 guns or more) must always fight in a "line of battle" formation. Any captain disregarding that instruction - by following an independent course - took the risk of a speedy end

*The first ship to crash through the French line on 1 June 1794 is the 1600-ton HMS Defence (74) commanded by Captain James Gambier RN. Closely engaged with two French ships of the line, she loses all her masts but survives to fight another day (the Nile, Copenhagen and Trafalgar). In 1811 she will be caught in a storm off Jutland and driven ashore with immense loss of life.*

Image: National Maritime Museum (NMM)

*Admiral of the Fleet the Lord Howe KG, RN, (1726-1799), commander at the Glorious First of June. He quickly rose through the ranks of the Royal Navy and proved himself a brilliant leader. Nelson would later call him "our great master in tactics and bravery". Howe served as First Lord of the Admiralty (1783-88) during the Pitt administration. He is depicted here in 1794 shortly after the battle by naval portraitist J.S. Copley.*

to his professional career. Commodore Horatio Nelson ran that risk when, on 14 February 1797 off Cape St Vincent aboard HMS CAPTAIN, he ordered his flag captain, Ralph Miller, to break away from Admiral Sir John Jervis's battle formation and to then drive into the rear of the fearsomely strong Spanish fleet. It was an almost reckless move, but Nelson was Nelson. The CAPTAIN was severely damaged, *in extremis* until Nelson's great friend Captain Cuthbert Collingwood came to his rescue. Nelson got away with it - creating chaos among the much bigger Spanish ships - and was rewarded with a knighthood (KCB).

Unless an admiral ordered a "general chase", the same strictures applied long after the time of King James and they still applied when Lord Howe encountered Villaret-Joyeuse off Cape Ushant (western Brittany) on that "Glorious First of June". But, like Nelson three years later, Howe was prepared to ignore the rules if he thought that by so doing he could reap an advantage. A continuous "line of battle" was what Villaret-Joyeuse had expected, so he was astonished when he saw the English ships turning individually towards his own. Evidently Howe's intention was to rake the Frenchmen, fore and aft, as they crashed through in line abreast. This daring tactic was deserving of success, but it had not been rehearsed. Groping in light winds through dense banks of gun-smoke, bewildered English and French captains found themselves either out of range or close alongside. By the end of the day, Villaret-Joyeuse had lost seven warships (one sunk, six captured), 4000 dead or wounded, with 3000 taken prisoner, but the grain convoy reached Brest intact.

Despite its losses in the battle, the Revolutionary government had achieved a strategic victory by surviving the food crisis and thereby keeping France in the war. Even so, its navy became trapped in Brest and other ports by a blockade which the Royal Navy then maintained almost without pause through to 1814. Day and night, year after year, it was the hardest imaginable service but it was a campaign which earned few rewards for the officers and men committed to it. For Lord Howe's men, however, their reward came fifty-four years later when the bar **1 June 1794** was authorised. Remarkably, given that time-span, there were 540 successful claimants.

Lord Howe himself returned to England a hero - there was no question of censure for having ignored the Admiralty's "fighting instructions". To the contrary, King George III dubbed him a Knight of the Order of the Garter and, even though at seventy Howe was over-due to retire ashore, ordered that he should continue to draw pay as a C-in-C of the Channel Fleet.

King George also gave orders that a new award - **The Naval Gold Medal** - should be given to every senior officer who had distinguished himself in that battle. In later years it was awarded for other engagements, culminating in the war with America. There were two types, **The Large Naval Gold Medal** (for Admirals, twenty-two in total awarded) and **The Small Naval Gold Medal** (for Captains, 117 awarded). The last - one of the small variants - went to Captain Henry Hope, RN, of HMS ENDYMION (his story will follow later).

When William Pitt (the Younger) first became British Prime Minister in 1803, he inherited a near-bankrupt economy still recovering from the cost of fighting the American colonists. The continuing war with Revolutionary France was an immense drain on the Treasury. Despite all that, money was found to modernise the Royal Dockyards where the technologies of the new industrial age were put to work in improving the seaworthiness and armament of our warships.

After prolonged indecision, Their Lordships accepted the carronade, an innovative short-barrelled weapon first developed in the 1770s in the Scottish town of Carron. A commercial venture, it was purchased in its early years by the owners of merchant vessels as a self-defence weapon against privateers. It weighed one ton compared with the three tons of conventional naval 32-pounder cannon, had a faster rate of fire and could be handled by merchant sailors having only limited training in gunnery. It was a short-range "smasher", discharging either grapeshot, canister or ball.

In close quarter ship-to-ship duels such as Trafalgar it had immense impact upon timber, rigging and men's bodies. Horatio Nelson's HMS VICTORY carried two 68-pounders mounted on her forecastle. When she passed close astern of the enemy's 80-gun flagship BUCENTAURE, one of them discharged a canister of 500 musket balls into that hapless ship's stern gallery. They blasted a swathe through the windows and almost the full length of the French battleship's main gun deck with an effect needing little imagination. After a further two hours of battering the BUCENTAURE was a dis-masted hulk, half her crew dead or wounded. A junior officer of Royal Marines, Captain James Atcherley, was sent aboard with two of his men from HMS CONQUEROR to accept the surrender of the admiral commanding the Franco-Spanish fleet, Pierre-Charles Villeneuve. His flagship had been hit by eleven different British ships in succession, but the initial carronade blast had done much to knock the stuffing out of her.

In passing, and to give some impression of the great noise and violence of the sea battles of that period, just one 74-gun ship of the line possessed more firepower than that of all the artillery available to Wellington in his Peninsula land campaign

So the ships and their weapons were ready for war, but not the reserves of experienced personnel needed to man them. The long arm of the Impress Service rounded up all manner of men and youths to satisfy the numbers needed, but the unskilled majority were rated as no more than Landsmen. To meet the need and beginning in 1805, an Act of Parliament permitted the automatic impressment of men taken by Revenue officers from vessels engaged in smuggling. Even the suspicion of being a smuggler could condemn a man to the minimum of five years enforced service without benefit of a hearing by the Magistrates. Arrested men were taken directly into the nearest Royal Navy ship and confined in her pending transfer to "the next ship bound for any foreign station". The navy became, in effect, jailer for the civilian authorities. It did so gladly because most of the hundreds of smugglers detained each year by this Act were professional mariners. They were immediately advanced to the prime rate of Able Seamen and paid accordingly.

With France under continuing blockade, with silk and brandy in short supply but high demand, smuggling had become a major cross-Channel trade. To avoid Excise duty, it then continued long after the war's conclusion. When the Impress Service disbanded in 1816 a new Act of Parliament was needed to cover the particular circumstances of the smugglers. They remained liable to five years of continuous service at sea, and the Act was not rescinded until 1837. Having served their sentence, some of these men opted to make the navy their long-term career. The records reveal successful applications by former smugglers for the **NGSM** with the bars **Algiers** (1816) and **Navarino** (1827)**,** the **Army of India Medal** (1824-1826) with the bar **Ava,** and the **China War Medal** (1842).

Recruitment might have been easier if British society had been at ease with itself, but the English had spent two centuries impoverishing the Scots and the Irish with their religious persecutions and absentee landlord abuses. Few men from either of those two countries were inspired to serve under a British flag. In England, the revolutions in America and France had stirred the feelings of the common people. The House of Commons was a travesty of "democracy", half its Members being returned by "rotten boroughs" which either did not exist or which had, literally, a handful of residents eligible to vote. There was not a single Member to represent the fast-growing industrial cities such as Liverpool, Manchester, Birmingham, Sheffield and Leeds. For the mass of the people, including the families of the men serving in the King's ships, even basic survival was an exhausting struggle. Naval rates of pay had not changed since 1658. Combined with a brutal discipline inflicted too often by officers who knew how to punish but not how to lead and inspire, the calls for reform triggered two shipboard mutinies in home waters.

Lower deck unrest first came to a head on 16 April 1797 in the sixteen ships of the Channel Fleet. They were anchored at Spithead, off Portsmouth. By a prearranged signal from the ring-leaders in the ROYAL GEORGE, the sailors took to the yard-arms and rigging and stayed there. Ordered to come down, they responded with catcalls and "three hearty cheers for His Majesty the King". They had three basic demands - better pay, better food, and the removal ashore of 117 named officers regarded by them as cruel and unfit to lead.

Since long before Lenin and the 1917 Revolution, a red flag has often symbolised defiance against authority and one such now flew from every ship in the Fleet.

*(Left) Spithead anchorage, off Portsmouth, 16 April 1797. Thousands of men of the Channel Fleet defiantly refuse to set sail. (Right) 13 May, cheering sailors haul down their red flags and return to duty when shown by an officer the pardon signed by the King.*

Driven to desperation, the men had lost all fear of punishment. Commanding them was Vice Admiral Lord Bridport in HMS VILLE DE PARIS (although in fact he spent much of his time ashore). Named after a French ship of the line captured by Rodney at the Battle of the Saintes (*vide* Part One of this series), but then lost in a hurricane, the new VILLE DE PARIS was a Chatham-built battleship of 2359 tons armed with 110 cannon. Pitt and the Admiralty, headed by the Earl Spencer, agreed to meet the delegates' complaints, ordered Bridport to ignore the Articles of War, and persuaded the King to grant the men a pardon. The red flags were hauled down on 13 May and the Fleet proceeded peaceably to sea. There were no reprisals.

At the mouth of the Thames estuary was the naval port of Sheerness, its anchorage known as The Nore. In command was Vice Admiral Charles Buckner. On 12 May the red flag appeared on most of his twenty-nine ships at the time on station. This second mutiny was a much more serious affair because the men's demands were overtly political. The disaffected ships blocked the Thames estuary, cutting off London's mercantile trade until they quarrelled amongst themselves and dispersed. Believing the Spithead affair to have been handled too leniently, Pitt sponsored a Bill declaring The Nore leaders to be outlaws. Twenty-eight were hanged from the yardarm of HMS SANDWICH (the ship in which the mutiny had started) while many others were flogged, jailed or transported to the colonies. There were no more major mutinies in the Royal Navy until the Invergordon strike of 1931.

While all this was happening, our Mediterranean Fleet was maintaining a blockade of the Spanish naval port of Cadiz. In command was Vice Admiral Sir

*The Earl St Vincent's Medal*

John Jervis, flying his flag in HMS VICTORY. He had been leading the fleet since June 1795 with a reputation for harshness in applying the Articles of War and, at times, of inflicting bizarre punishments when his own Fleet Orders were transgressed. He was, however, capable of surprising acts of kindness and generosity, and this strand in his character may have prompted him to commission the medal known as **The Earl St Vincent's Medal.**

The following facts are relevant. Age 62, he was nearing the end of his fifty years at sea and his three years in the VICTORY when, on 14 February 1797, his fifteen ships of the line (with seven frigates) encountered, off Cape St Vincent (Portugal), a fleet of twenty-four Spanish ships of the line (also with seven frigates). It was a battle which, despite the odds, gave Jervis victory and earned him elevation to the peerage as the 1st Earl St Vincent. The war had been going badly - the Royal Navy having been forced to withdraw from the Mediterranean in September 1796 - so Jervis's victory was a much-needed boost to British morale.

Promoted Admiral of the White in February 1799, he remained at sea in the VICTORY until poor health forced him to give up his command off Cadiz and, in June of that year, to retreat to his family home in Essex. He returned to active command eleven months later, being appointed to replace Lord Bridport as C-in-C Channel Fleet in HMS VILLE DE PARIS. Six months at sea in this ship, blockading the French port of Brest, were enough to again put him ashore, this time to recuperate in the gentle climate of South Devon. He then resumed command in the VILLE DE PARIS until January 1801 when he came ashore for the last time upon his appointment as First Lord of the Admiralty. This biographical information has been set out here in detail because it demolishes the various published explanations for **The Earl St Vincent's Medal.**

One source states that it was a token of gratitude, "presented to the ship's company of the VILLE DE PARIS for not having joined in the mutiny at The Nore". This makes no sense whatever because he did not replace Lord Bridport in that ship until three years later. Furthermore, she was anchored at Spithead at the time of the mutinies, she was not at any time attached to Admiral Buckner's Nore

*His greatest years yet to come, Captain John Jervis RN was unemployed for nearly three years while in his thirties. During that time he was captured on canvas by the portraitist Francis Coates (1726-1770).*

Command. According to another source he gave the medal to "those officers, seamen and marines who had followed him from his flagship VICTORY to the VILLE DE PARIS and remained loyal to him during the mutiny at The Nore". Again, the chronology and the locations are totally wrong, and whatever might be intended by the word "followed" is unclear. Certainly, any officer of his seniority could request the Admiralty's permission to take with him a handful of trusted officers upon shifting his flag from one fleet to another - including perhaps a blood relative or the son of an old friend - but never a draft of ratings and marines. That was not the way the system worked.

Aware of the events at Spithead and The Nore, and of two particularly bloody mutinies in the Caribbean involving the murder of ships' officers, Admiral Jervis (as he was still) had removed his VICTORY detachment of Royal Marines from the seamen's mess decks and re-quartered them as a permanently armed *cordon sanitaire* to protect his own officers' accommodation. During his time off Cadiz there were the usual floggings for individual acts of disobedience, but nothing more.

Without access to all of St Vincent's private papers (if they still exist) it would be unwise to decide precisely why this medal was manufactured or who the recipients might have been. Some documents have survived - they show only that the contract for its manufacture was given to Matthew Boulton at his Soho Mint (Birmingham) and that the design was suggested by a Lady Spencer (presumably the wife of the then First Lord of the Admiralty). The meetings and correspondence associated with that procedure took place most probably during his first long period of sick leave in Essex (June 1799 to May 1800). Beyond that, there are more questions than answers. However, this author is of the opinion that neither St Vincent nor any other admiral of that period would ever have rewarded a ship's company for *not* having made a mutiny. The claim that the same "testimony of approbation" was given equally to the ship's officers is even more far-fetched. There must surely be another explanation.

The year 1812 witnessed a globalisation of the conflict. Although not recorded as such in the history books, this was truly the First World War. Napoleon's defeated frozen soldiers were departing Russia, his generals were struggling to hold the line against Wellington in Spain. For the British there was fighting in Italy, clashes with the warships of Turkey in the Mediterranean and of Spain around Latin America. For the Royal Navy, the war with France had spread to the Indian Ocean (Mauritius and Ceylon) and the East Indies (Java). Then, on 19 June, America joined the fray.

President James Madison and his government had three reasons for going to war with Great Britain - our support for the Indian tribes on their western frontiers, conflict on the borders with Canada, and disputed freedom of the high seas. American merchantmen were being stopped and searched by Royal Navy ships engaged in the long-running blockade of the French mainland and of the Caribbean ports. Cargoes were seized as "contraband", a term which covered almost anything conceivably useful to France's war economy.

Apart from interfering with America's legitimate export trade, we were often detaining their sailors and illegally impressing them into Royal Navy service. Together with men taken from free-lance American privateers, these men were forcibly enlisted into British warships where, as some recompense, they were at least paid according to their rates. Their circumstances changed dramatically for the worse on 18 June 1812 when war was declared. Two thousand two hundred of them stated that they were not prepared to fight their fellow-Americans. This made them "the enemy", hence they were "discharged with ignominy", sent ashore and confined as common criminals.

Beginning in 1813, the majority were sent to Dartmoor Prison. Construction of that infamous establishment had commenced in 1806 and the first of 10,000 French prisoners of war arrived in May 1809. Almost immediately an outbreak of measles killed 460 of them. The temporary conclusion of hostilities with France in April 1814 reduced the prison population for a few months but, for the American prisoners, there was little prospect of an early release. More were brought to Dartmoor from jails in other parts of the country and their number grew to 6000. The grossly overcrowded insanitary conditions led to a smallpox outbreak which killed 200 of them. Like the French dead, their bodies were buried at random in unmarked graves in the bleak surrounding moorland. Within the prison grounds there stands a monument (recently renovated) naming the 271 American prisoners whose remains are still out there, somewhere.

In late 1814, with Napoleon apparently safely tucked up on the island of Elba, there was no longer need for a blockade. Both sides recognised the futility of continuing the conflict so peace was signed by their delegates in Ghent (Belgium) on 24 December. The news crossed the Atlantic too late to stop the British from attempting to seize the city of New Orleans.

A fleet commanded by Vice Admiral Alexander Inglis Cochrane in his 80 gun flagship HMS TONNANT had been despatched from Bermuda to the Gulf of Mexico with 8000 troops embarked. The intention was to assist the army in regaining at least part of the territory sold by France to the United States in 1803 (the Louisiana Purchase). Blocking the seaward approaches were five gunboats. In what was the largest such operation of that war, Captain Nicholas Lockyer, RN, led forty-two ship's longboats into an action which destroyed the American vessels and cleared the way for the British landing. Lockyer's success was recognised by the last of the "boat service" bars to be fixed to the **NGSM**. It was stamped **14 Dec Boat Service 1814** (206 awarded).

In the event, once ashore, the British Army force was poorly handled by its commander, General Edward Pakenham. Heavily defeated in battle on 8 January 1815 by Major General Andrew Jackson, the survivors were driven back to Cochrane's ships and that was the end of it. The war with America was over.

The Americans held at Dartmoor were now free men. Marched down to Plymouth in parties of 250, they waited at Cattedown for ships to carry them home. The embarkation arrangements were a mess, they protested, the local escorting militia panicked, nine of the newly liberated men were shot dead. It was an unhappy conclusion to an unhappy episode.

Americans who avoided capture at sea had a much better time of it. The US Navy's frigates were well built, fast, heavily armed, and commanded by officers who owed their rank solely to ability. Their professional skills were grudgingly acknowledged by many of our own naval officers. Preble, Decatur, Bainbridge, Perry, Hull (of whom more later) won their spurs in the campaign against the Barbary pirates of North Africa.

In the First Barbary War (1805), temporary General William Eaton and 1st Lieutenant Presley O'Bannon, USMC, with ten marines and 450 assorted Greek and semi-mutinous Arab mercenaries, conducted one of the most amazing treks of the period. Or of any period! In fifty days they marched 500 miles across the desert from Alexandria to attack the fortified coastal town of Derna. That epic affair is perpetuated in the US Marine Corps hymn with its line: "From the halls of Montezuma to the shores of Tripolee". Montezuma was yet to happen - the 1840s war with Mexico - but the land battle on the shores of Tripolitania in 1805 was the first ever fought by US forces beyond their home shores. The Stars and Stripes have flown over many lands since then, but Derna started the ball rolling.

After the Barbary Wars the Americans faced the might of the Royal Navy, a contest from which they emerged three years later covered in glory. There are nine bars on the **NGSM** to record that period, four for "boat service" actions, the others for fights between frigates. One of these was **Shannon Wh Chesapeake.** It marks an action fought on 1

Image: Courtesy of the US Naval Historical Centre (USNHC)

*Stephen Decatur, at thirty-six, was and still is the youngest man ever to attain the rank of captain in the US Navy. Five American warships have been named after him, and the city of Decatur (Illinois) also is named in his honour. In 1820 he fought a duel with a fellow captain and died of wounds received.*

Right. Image: Courtesy of the US Naval Historical Centre (USNHC)

*Captain James Lawrence, USN. As he lay mortally wounded on the shattered deck of the Chesapeake, he commanded his men: "Don't give up the ship". That simple phrase became and remains legendary in American naval history.*

Below. Image: Reproduced courtesy of the US Navy Historical Centre (USNHC)

*With a fresh suit of sails replacing those damaged in the battle, the Chesapeake follows HMS Shannon into the Halifax anchorage. Purchased by the Admiralty Agent, she served as a Royal Navy ship under her original name until sold to the breakers in 1819.*

June 1813 a few miles out from the port of Boston, Massachusetts. There were at the time two frigates re-fitting in the naval yard, the USS CONSTITUTION and USS CHESAPEAKE. For the past fifty-six days, Captain Philip Vere Broke, RN, had been patrolling offshore in HMS SHANNON in the hope that one or both would come out and fight him. Running low on provisions, he despatched ashore a courteously-worded letter, challenging the Americans. The CONSTITUTION was not yet ready for sea, but Captain James Lawrence, USN, had already decided to take his CHESAPEAKE into action. It was a fatal decision for him personally and for forty-eight of his crew killed in a brief engagement which resulted in the boarding and capture of his ship. Captain Broke had a fully worked-up command, his opponent did not. Struck down and dying, James Lawrence called out to his men the words which passed into American naval legend: "Don't give up the ship!".

Philip Broke was severely wounded while leading the boarding party, but his officers brought the battered CHESAPEAKE safely to harbour at Halifax, Nova Scotia. In some ways a one-sided fight, the result bolstered the Royal Navy's damaged pride. The circumstances also reveal the exceptional good manners shown by both sides during that war. Six months previously, on 29 December 1812, Commodore William Bainbridge in the CONSTITUTION destroyed HMS JAVA (Captain Henry Lambert, RN). After a three hour ship-to-ship duel off the coast of Brazil, "his chivalry and personal kindness towards his defeated British opponents was a feature of the episode".

Earlier still, on 19 August 1812, when the CONSTITUTION (at that time commanded by Captain Isaac Hull, USN) engaged yet another British frigate, HMS GUERRIERE (Captain James Dacres, RN), the same courtesy prevailed. The two met 400 miles south east from Halifax, Nova Scotia. After a fierce close-quarter fight the American beat her opponent into submission. With the two ships locked together, Captain Dacres was able to walk across to the CONSTITUTION's quarter deck where he offered his sword as token of his surrender. Captain Hull declined the gesture "because he could not accept the sword of an officer who had fought so gallantly".

He then discovered that there were ten impressed American sailors serving in the GUERRIERE. Captain Dacres had sent them below before action commenced "because he did not wish to order them to fight their fellow countrymen". It was all very gentlemanly. Captain Hull's final act of consideration was to order a thorough search of GUERRIERE's 'tween decks to ensure that all her wounded were located and evacuated. Only after the search was completed did he put the wrecked British frigate to the torch (she exploded later when the flames reached her magazine).

That victory earned for the CONSTITUTION the name "Old Ironsides" and she is perpetuated in American naval history as such. Built in 1797, she is the oldest such warship still afloat. Beautifully restored and maintained, she is moored alongside in Boston Naval Shipyard. On 19 August 2012, the 200$^{th}$ anniversary of the battle, still a commissioned vessel of the United States Navy, she cruised under her own sail power around Boston Harbour.

The **NGSM** bar **Endymion Wh President** arouses the particular curiosity of this author. Of especial interest is the name of the British frigate involved. Endymion was a figure in Greek mythology, "a shepherd permitted by Zeus to keep his beauty forever in an eternal sleep". It was the title of an obscure and excessively long poem by John Keats (1795-1831). Why Their Lordships of the Admiralty should ever have thought it appropriate for a British ship of war is unknown, and yet it was given to five of them in succession between 1740 and 1891.

The ship commemorated on the **NGSM** was the third to be so named. A 50-gun two-deck frigate, she had exceptionally good sailing qualities. Having been logged at 14.4 knots (26.7 kph), she was said to have been the fastest such vessel in the Royal Navy. When the British West Indies Squadron encountered the USS PRESIDENT off New York, Captain Henry Hope's ENDYMION was alone in matching the American frigate's speed. A long chase concluded on 15 January 1815 with a fight in which the PRESIDENT lost most of her rigging. She was obliged to strike her colours when other British ships caught up with her.

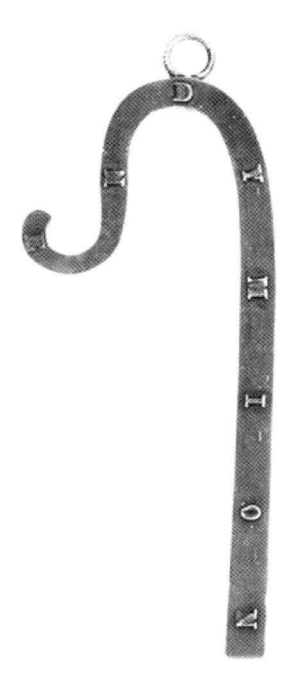

To mark their success, Captain Hope presented to each of his twenty-four officers a miniature silver shepherd's crook embossed with the ship's name. Known as **The Endymion Crook** (but recorded also, confusingly, as **The Midshipman's Badge**), it was intended for wear from an integral ring. One privately named example has survived (ex Payne Collection) but, for the rest, it is the most obscure of all (unofficial) naval awards. Captain Hope himself did not live long enough to claim the **NGSM** to which otherwise he would have been entitled, but he did receive a **Naval Small Gold Medal.** First introduced in 1794, Captain Hope's was the last to be awarded.

Two other **NGSM** bars resulting from the war of 1812-1815 are worth recording because the ships so named were fighting the Americans in the Pacific Ocean, not the Atlantic. Those bars, as stamped, were **Phoebe 28 March 1814** (thirty-one issued) and **Cherub 28 March 1814** (seven issued). The story behind them concerns Captain David Porter, USN, and his 850 ton frigate the USS ESSEX. Built in 1799 at Salem, Massachusetts, she was armed with the unbalanced combination of forty short-range 32 pounder carronades and six conventional long-range 12 pounder cannon. When he first assumed command, Captain Porter complained to the Navy Department that he would be in trouble if challenged by a British frigate of similar size. In the event, when ordered out into the Atlantic in the autumn of 1813, he succeeded in causing havoc in the shipping lanes where he captured ten British merchantmen and the 20 gun brig-sloop HMS ALERT (the first British warship to strike to an American).

That episode was yet another example of the chivalry which characterised the war. When David Porter first identified HMS ALERT coming over the horizon, he ordered most of his men to stay out of sight and kept his gun ports closed. Surprisingly, this deceived Captain T L P Laugharne, RN, into believing that the ESSEX was a merchantman. Accordingly, he approached almost alongside so that he could hail the stranger and call for her papers. Up went the gun ports, out rolled the guns and, after a single carronade broadside, the ALERT was on fire, a helpless wreck.

The two captains agreed how best to extinguish the flames, replace the masts and rigging and make the ALERT once again seaworthy. Captain Laugharne and his officers accepted the terms of Captain Porter's parole and set off unescorted first to Newfoundland and then New York. Honour bound, they rejected the temptation of heading for a British port. After landing in New York they remained at conditional liberty and their ship was taken into US Navy service. How many other wars have been fought in that way?

For Captain Porter, it was a case of "so far, so good". But he knew that the Royal Navy was searching for him and therefore, on his own initiative, he rounded Cape Horn and entered the Pacific with the intention of causing in that ocean even more disruption as a commerce raider. Over the following weeks he captured thirteen British whalers and a merchantman carrying $55,000 in gold. The money allowed him to purchase supplies at ports along the western shores of Latin America and so keep his ship fully operational.

It could not last, of course. He had been refitting and sheltering for six weeks in the Chilean port of Valparaiso when two of the Royal Navy ships then serving in the Pacific finally caught up with him. That was on 28 March 1814. They were the 36-gun frigate HMS PHOEBE (Captain James Hillyar, RN) and the 18-gun sloop HMS CHERUB (Commander Thomas Tudor Tucker, RN). As it happened, Hillyar and Porter had become acquainted when they were each serving in the Mediterranean at the time of the Barbary wars. There was a mutual regard and respect, but this did stop Hillyar from trying to kill his American opponent when they clashed off Valparaiso.

Fearing the arrival of more Royal Navy ships and despite ferociously bad weather, Captain Porter decided to make a break for the open sea. It was then that his luck deserted him. Even though he managed to hold off the British ships during two and half hours of spasmodic firing, he lost his main top mast in the gale-force wind and his carronades lacked the range needed to seriously damage the PHOEBE. Of his 315 men, fifty-eight were killed by gunfire and thirty-one drowned when they tried to swim ashore. The two British ships, in shocking contrast, lost only five dead and ten wounded. One of the seriously wounded was Commander Tucker, captain of the CHERUB, but he recovered and successfully claimed his **NGSM** when it was announced in 1848.

The American ship was repaired, taken back to England and accepted into service as HMS ESSEX. Also captured was her tender, the ESSEX JUNIOR. Captain Porter and the surviving members of his crew were soon released on parole. One of them was thirteen-year old Midshipman David Farragut, USN. Many years later he became the first officer to be promoted an Admiral in the United States Navy and a popular hero of his nation's Civil War. His old captain, David Porter, subsequently had a turbulent career and became Commander-in-Chief of the Mexican Navy. His captor, James Hillyar, also rose to high rank. One of the officers fortunate to be retained in full-time service after the massive post-war reduction in the size of the Royal Navy, Admiral Sir James Hillyar never received his **NGSM** because he died in 1843.

Hillyar's fellow-captain at Valparaiso, Thomas Tucker, was fated to join the many hundreds of other post-war redundant officers "on the beach". He was placed on half-pay in 1816 and never again served at sea. In 1840, when he reached the age of sixty-five, the Admiralty appointed him Rear Admiral (ensuring an adequate pension) and Queen Victoria made him a Companion of the Order of the Bath. It might not have been the career for which he had hoped as a young man but, unlike the ninety-four American and British sailors who died, he did at least live to tell his grandchildren the story of his long-ago fight with the Americans off the coast of Chile.

The defeat of Napoleon at Waterloo marked the onset of "the forty years peace". The great and the good met in Vienna to re-draw the lines on the map of Europe, but many major battles had been fought at sea before any of that could happen. Today, the best remembered are recorded with their own bars on the **NGS** medal: **St Vincent** (1797), **Camperdown** (1797), **Nile** (1798), **Copenhagen** (1801), **Trafalgar** (1805), and **Basque Roads** (1809). These and other great occasions like them can be studied in detail elsewhere. For the moment we may move forward to the last three **NGSM** bars: **Algiers** (1816), **Navarino** (1827), and **Syria** (1840).

The Battle of Algiers was fought on 27 August 1816 under the command of Admiral Lord Exmouth (formerly Captain Sir Edward Pellew, RN). This writer has already described that extraordinary affair in *Gunfire in Barbary,* a book co-authored with Captain Kenneth Douglas-Morris, RN, and published in 1982. Exmouth was, of course, an outstanding sailor and leader but, like all his contemporaries, he needed good men to lead. In his case, that man was his fellow-Cornishman, John Gaze. They served together almost continuously throughout the wars with France, Exmouth at first appointing him Quartermaster in the NYMPHE then, at Algiers,

Image: National Maritime Museum (NMM)

*Algiers, 27 August 1816. Under a skyline dominated by the Citadel and the high hills beyond, the Anglo-Dutch fleet concentrates its fire on the Mole batteries. This artist, George Chambers Sr, features (left to right) HNMS Melampus and HM Ships Minden, Albion, Queen Charlotte and Impregnable. The ship's longboat in the foreground is one of many fitted with small carronades or rocket launching apparatus and commanded that day by midshipmen.*

as his Fleet Sailing Master in the QUEEN CHARLOTTE. Both knew that, of the two, Gaze was the better ship-handler. His profound "feel" was crucial on that day, but sadly his name is now little known. He survived into old age to claim four **NGSM** bars: **Nymphe 18 June 1793, Indefatigable 20 April 1796, Indefatigable 13 January 1797** and **Algiers.** His old commander would have received the same combination, but Exmouth did not live long enough to submit a claim. Surrounded by the trophies and awards of a lifetime at sea, in 1833 he died peacefully at his fine Devonshire home, age 76.

The Congress of Vienna brought peace to Continental Europe but not to the Middle East. From the 15$^{th}$ to the 19$^{th}$ Centuries, the region had been dominated by the Ottoman Turks. Plagued by corruption and poor communications, their empire began to fall apart. In 1821, after 300 years of occupation, the people of Orthodox Christian Greece rebelled against their Muslim oppressors. In response, the Sultan of Turkey despatched two great armies to crush the revolt. One was driven off, the other perished miserably in the mountains.

Unable to subdue the Greeks, the Sultan then appealed to the Khedive of Egypt for military assistance. Modernised by French advisors, his army and navy quickly crushed the revolt in Crete and ravaged the southern Greek mainland. None of this was to the liking of the British, French and Russian governments. The British wanted to preserve their maritime dominance in the Mediterranean, the French to continue re-asserting themselves after their defeat in 1815, Russia to expand into Ottoman territories. In an early example of a United Nations "peace keeping" mission, they made a joint agreement to intervene.

The terms of that 1827 Treaty of London are interesting in the light of what has happened in later decades in many other countries when European forces have been committed to imposing their governments' policies in volatile situations. The Treaty "bound the three Powers to offer mediation with a view to establishing peace between Turkey and Greece, and in the event of either party refusing to accept the mediation, to put an end to the struggle by force". The implications were clear: "either calm down and sort yourselves out, or we shall bang your heads together".

There was no question of putting troops ashore, this would be a "gunboat diplomacy" operation. Each of the three nations contributed ships to a fleet which assembled in late 1827 off the Peloponnese coast under the overall command of Vice Admiral Edward Codrington. His orders were to make a show of force, to rattle his sabre - in effect to intimidate the Ottomans into giving the Greeks their freedom. But the plan did not work as intended. On 20 October, Codrington's twenty-two ships cruised into the confined waters of Navarino Bay where Ibrahim Pasha's combined Turkish-Egyptian fleet of seventy-eight lay quietly at anchor. A brief exchange of musical salutes and coldly polite signals quickly degenerated into an eruption of gunfire which, hours later, had killed or wounded 4200 Muslim sailors. Of the British sailors involved in this massacre, 1142 later received the **NGS** medal, bar **Navarino.**

The near total destruction of the Ottoman fleet left the empire even further enfeebled, so Russia was encouraged to attack again in 1828 (the ninth of the twelve Russo-Turkish wars). The Greeks did gain their independence in 1830, but

Codrington was censured by London and Paris for having hastened Turkey's decline. And it was that decline which led to the award of the last in the long series of **NGS** medals.

The Levant (Lebanon, Syria and Palestine) had been an Ottoman province since 1516. In 1833, shrugging off their nominal allegiance to the Ottoman Sultanate (an allegiance much weakened by the Navarino disaster), the Egyptians moved in and, with encouragement from France and Spain, claimed that territory for their own. There was little the Turks could do to remove them so, to prevent any further destabilisation of the region, a British-Austrian-Turkish fleet was assembled under command of Admiral Sir Robert Stopford and Commodore Charles Napier. And it was Napier who, with a very loose interpretation of Stopford's orders, hastened the collapse of the Egyptians by supporting a local rebellion. This he achieved by storming the historic ports of Beirut and Sidon before joining Stopford for a massive bombardment of the Crusader port of St Jean D'Acre. That assault (and the war) ended when an Egyptian powder magazine was hit by cannon fire, the enormous explosion killing 1100 men. Visitors to these ports will see Royal Navy cannon balls still embedded in the stonework of the ancient fortifications.

St Jean D'Acre was the first time Royal Navy ships propelled by steam-powered paddle wheels went into action. Two of them, CYCLOPS (2000 tons) and GORGON (1100 tons), were rated as frigates, the other four as sloops. Displacing 800 to 960 tons, they were HYDRA, PHOENIX, STROMBOLI and VESUVIUS. Being so responsive to the helm, these six innovative ships were ideal for a close-range ship-to-shore bombardment such as St Jean D'Acre (CYCLOPS in particular with her two fearsome 98-pounder guns).

*Flagship of Commodore Charles Napier, the 84-gun battleship HMS Powerful joins in the bombardment of the Crusader and Ottoman fortifications at St Jean D'Acre. In 1860, after half a century of sea service, she was decommissioned as a target ship.*

Images: National Maritime Museum (NMM)

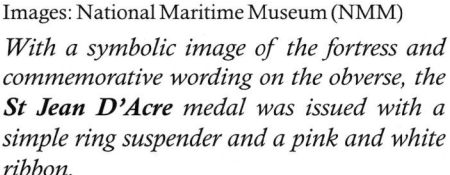

*With a symbolic image of the fortress and commemorative wording on the obverse, the* **St Jean D'Acre** *medal was issued with a simple ring suspender and a pink and white ribbon.*

*The original ribbon did not fit comfortably into the ring, so some recipients replaced it with a straight suspender to their own taste. The reverse bears the cypher of the Sultan within a laurel wreath.*

In 1842, the grateful Sultan Abdul Medjid Khan II ordered the despatch to London of a consignment of (unnamed) medals for presentation to (most of) the officers and men who had served under Stopford and Napier. The **St Jean D'Acre** medals in gold and silver were appreciated by the officers, but those struck in copper, allocated to ratings and marines, were greeted with derision (especially when it emerged that the Turkish sailors were receiving their medals struck in silver). More importantly, there was anger in Parliament and the London newspapers that a foreign potentate *did* recognise the services of our men but their own Queen did not. The anger rose to fury in 1843. While Stopford had been battering the Egyptians in the Levant, a British fleet on the other side of the world had been battering the Chinese (they were reluctant to buy our opium). That affair generated a silver "all ranks" **China War Medal.** But, thanks mainly to thirty years of obstruction by the Duke of Wellington, there were still no equivalent Sovereign's medals for all our other wars and battles of former decades. Under subtle pressure from Queen Victoria, Wellington's resistance crumbled and so the wheels began to turn in Horse Guards (the War Office), the Admiralty, and the Royal Mint. Announcements in *The London Gazette* of two new medals, a **Peninsular War Medal** and a **Naval War Medal,** made it plain that discrimination between the ranks was finally at an end. Looking back, we can see that the **St Jean D'Acre** and **China War** medals, when their stories are viewed in combination, mark a sea change in the evolution of British medallic awards.

When eventually it was issued, the **NGS** medal with bar **Syria** went to 6978 sailors, soldiers and Royal Marines, making it by far the most numerous encountered by the early generations of collector. Because the **NGSM** was always impressed with the recipient's name but not the name of his ship, and because his rank was not shown if he was a rating, some collectors replaced the **Syria** bar with a more desirable bar salvaged from a damaged medal. This was easily done if the man's name was the same as that of one known to have received, for example, the highly prized **Trafalgar** bar. The prudent collector considers this possibility before reaching for his cheque book.

Sources: *The East Suffolk Gazette* (19.11.1867), The Nelson Museum (Yarmouth)

*At Great Yarmouth, Norfolk, there stands a monument dedicated to the memory of that county's most famous son, Horatio Nelson. It was completed in 1819 and for nearly half a century its official keeper (seen here) was James Sharman. In 1799, age 14, working in Yarmouth at "The Wrestlers Inn", James had been press-ganged and sent to sea in the elderly 16 gun brig-sloop HMS Weazle (sic). After she was wrecked in March 1804 near Gibraltar, he was sent into HMS Victory with the rate of Ordinary Seaman. Eighteen months later, off Cape Trafalgar, he was one of those who carried the fatally wounded Admiral down from the quarterdeck to the cockpit where three hours later the great man died.*

Discharged from the navy in 1819, and on the recommendation of his former commander, Captain Thomas Masterman Hardy, James Sharman was appointed Custodian of Great Yarmouth's Britannia Monument and lived in a cottage provided by the Column's trustees. He lived there until his death in 1867, age 82. He received his **NGSM** bar **Trafalgar** in 1849.

On the night of 25 November 1827, James famously saved the sole survivor from the brig Hammond when she stranded in ferocious weather on the shore close to his cottage. Charles Dickens visited the town while he was composing his eighth novel, "David Copperfield" (set partly in Yarmouth) and heard the story of the rescue.

Image: Philip V Allingham

*First published as a book in 1850, Charles Dickens' novel "David Copperfield" ran to many editions. The popular "Household" edition, heavily illustrated by Fred Barnard, first appeared in 1870. For a Victorian readership, the story of the storm and the artist's depiction of the 1827 wreck of the Hammond had immense appeal.*

Intrigued, Dickens called on James and decided to take him as his model for the character Ham Peggotty.

In Yarmouth and his home county, the fame of James Sharman has never faded. His heroism, his association with Admiral Nelson, his years of dedication to the Monument, all are recorded on a recently installed memorial plaque. In 2008, his **NGS** medal was discovered in an attic. Offered for sale at auction in 2011, it attracted worldwide interest and sold for £27,000. He was also entitled to wear the Trafalgar commemorative medals commissioned by Matthew Boulton and by Alexander Davidson. His portrait photograph suggests that he received other similar tributes. Could James and his old lower deck shipmates ever have understood the 21st Century enthusiasm for the medals which once they wore?

Part Two of this series has been devoted mainly to a retrospective medal commemorating wind-driven battles fought at sea. Part Three (1840-1860) will examine an entirely new chapter in the story of the Royal Navy. There would be no more fleet-against-fleet actions until 1916. Meantime, the creation of our Empire committed the navy to supporting a succession of campaigns fought on land. The adaptability of "Jolly Jack" to changing styles of warfare would at times be stretched to the limit.

## Part Three - 1840 to 1860

SLAVERY is, paradoxically, as old as civilisation. For the black peoples of West Africa, it was the King of Portugal, Henry the Navigator, who in 1439 unintentionally sowed the seeds of future disaster. He sent expeditions to map the coastline leading south into the Gulf of Guinea. In 1441, one of his captains returned to Lisbon with, amongst other mementoes of his voyage, ten black men. Regarded initially as curiosities, they were the first of what soon became a flood of Africans transported to the sugar plantations springing up in Brazil and Cuba. Cane and its sugar derivative had been unknown outside India until the 16$^{th}$ century. Now its successful cultivation in the New World was creating an insatiable demand in Europe and, thereby, a huge requirement for labour to work the fields. It was met by establishing trading posts all down the western flank of Africa where manufactured goods were bartered for captives marched to the coast in shackles by their fellow Africans.

At first, Spain and Portugal were the prime movers. England did not enter the trade until 1562 when John Hawkins (soon joined by his cousin, Francis Drake) made his first slaver voyages. By 1627 there were 200 English ships operating across the 5000 miles of the notorious trans-Atlantic "middle passage". At its peak, the West African slave trade was exporting each year 100,000 men, women and children to a lifetime of servitude.

*The design incorporated into Josiah Wedgwood's Anti-Slavery Medallion. In just a few decades Britain went from being one of the most profitable slave trade nations to being at the vanguard of the abolitionist movement. With the high-minded morality of a new enlightened Victorian society the Royal Navy took on anti-slavery duties with almost puritanical zeal.*

Of the 1500 English-owned plantations in the Caribbean, many were the property of men powerful in Westminster politics. The British public gradually learned of the vile conditions within the slave ships, but the victims were regarded by Parliament as merchandise, not human beings. There was indifference to their suffering, entrenched opposition to any move for change. Liverpool and the City of London in particular were founded upon the new wealth created by what had become a major industry. Even so, campaigners for abolition of the slave trade did achieve a token success in 1788 when Parliament approved an Act limiting the number carried to "five males per three tons burthen". In other words, and depending upon the size of her hold, a typical slaver of 400 tons could continue to cram several hundred people into her dark stinking hold. The Royal Navy was not invited to enforce this Act, it was unenforceable.

The rules changed in 1808. The Abolitionists persuaded Parliament to prohibit trading in slaves and their shipment in British-flagged vessels. This was not the same as banning slavery. For that, a further Act was required and it came in 1833. Possession of a slave was then rendered a criminal offence. However, there were so many ways around the law that not until the 1890s was the West African trade brought to a halt. By then, the idealism of the Abolitionists had been overtaken by Britain's determination to colonise any territory which otherwise might be occupied by a competitor nation. This was "the race for Africa". Ironically, after nearly 500 years of cruel exploitation, it was European colonialism which lifted the yoke from the neck of the black African.

*The notorious Zong incident, November 1781. The Liverpool slave trade ship Zong is reaching the end of her trans-Atlantic passage. Disease has killed seven of Master Luke Collingwood's crew and sixty African captives. The owners are insured against loss resulting from the deliberate killing of slaves "to quell an insurrection" but not from death by natural causes. To protect the owners' investment, Collingwood orders his men to throw 133 ailing slaves overboard. The insurers mount a legal challenge, accusing Zong's owners of attempted fraud, but Collingwood cannot be tried for murder because slaves are "property" and not human beings.*

So, where did the Royal Navy fit into all of this? Beginning in 1808, a small West Africa Squadron was given the almost hopeless task of detaining any ship suspected of having slaves in her hold. With England in the middle of a fight to the death with Napoleonic France, there were few ships to spare for this new commitment. Those deployed were of shallow draft because the best way of catching a slaver was when she was loading her human cargo at a trading post sited within a river estuary. Major warships could not enter such places, so only small brig-sloops were employed. They were junior officer commands. Any Lieutenant with ambition knew there was no fame or glory to be gained here, it was "the white man's grave". Apart from battle casualties, he could lose fifteen or twenty percent of his men to disease in the course of a single commission.

Despite the navy's long-running devotion to it, the anti-slavery campaign did not generate a single medal. Going back to 1808 there had been many hard-fought actions in West African waters which arguably could have been recognised by the granting of a bar on the **Naval General Service Medal** (1793-1840) if the Warrant had been amended. Instead, it was an unrelated insurgency in one of our new colonies, the Gold Coast, which prompted the first of what later became a torrent of awards associated with that region. It was the **Ashantee Medal** (1873-1874), awarded to the ships' companies of eighteen Royal Navy ships which gave logistical support or whose men went inland to fight against that tribe with the Naval Brigade. In overall command was Colonel Sir Garnet Wolseley, a fast rising star whose name was already well established in London's corridors of power. We may wonder whether the Ashantee campaign, started and ended in just eight months, would have been recognised with a medal if it been commanded instead by an officer whose name did not carry the same clout.

Black enslavement began with Henry the Navigator and Sir John Hawkins, but it was not confined to West Africa. The Arabs had been trading and raiding down the length of East Africa since the 9th century. Propelled by the monsoon winds, their elegant *dhows* cruised south from Oman to Zanzibar and Kilwa, acquiring ivory, spices and slaves before returning north when the seasonal winds reversed. Following the 1808 Act, a newly-formed British East Africa Squadron was ordered to stop and search all *dhows* suspected of carrying slaves. The Squadron rarely had more than five ships on station. Responsible for 2000 miles of coastline, bound by restrictive "rules of engagement", they made little impact during the early decades. The Arabs continued to export 20,000 slaves each year from Zanzibar, only a few hundred ever being set free by the navy. It was diplomacy rather than firepower which ended the traffic.

In 1873 the Sultan of Zanzibar agreed (upon payment) to close the slave markets on his island. The deal was arranged by Sir Bartle Frere, a gentleman we shall encounter six years later. By then, all the European nations had followed the example set by the United States of America and Great Britain in banning slavery. When shipment by sea in the Indian Ocean became impractical, the Arab slavers simply moved inland, marching their captives along a network of routes extending 1800 miles north through Egypt and the Sudan. The name of one such route endured long after the trade had ceased. Followed by both the *Afrika Korps* and the

Image: Reproduced courtesy of the National Maritime Museum, Greenwich (NMM)

*A photograph which records a rare success for the British East Africa Squadron. Having been liberated from an Arab trading dhow by one of the Squadron's smaller vessels, these people have been brought aboard HMS London in Zanzibar harbour. Soon they will be set free on the mainland.*

8th Army in the 1942 battles in Egypt's Western Desert, it was the *Trigh el Abd* - "the track of the slaves". Like others, it led to the trading port of Suakin, on the Red Sea. Here there was always a cab rank of *dhows* and steamers ready to transport the Africans to similar commercial ports all around the Indian Ocean and Persian Gulf.

The second medal to recognise Royal Navy involvement in the region, even marginally, was the **East and West Africa Medal** (1887-1900). By then it was all over, most of the slavers driven out of business. Of its twenty bars, fourteen related to West Africa and were triggered by military punitive expeditions far inland. Of the six linked to the eastern half of the continent, only one involved a fight with Arabs. There were, of course, other "one off" awards authorised during that last decade of the 19th century which related directly or indirectly to the conquest of slave-catching tribes in the Gambia, Nyasaland, Uganda and West Africa. They were **The Central Africa Medal** (1891-1898), **The East & Central Africa Medal** (1897-1899) and **The Ashanti Medal** (1900).

By then, the issue of Africa-related medals had become a muddle. The confusion was swept away in 1902 by the introduction of **The Africa General Service Medal** which served its purpose right through to the Mau-Mau uprising of the 1950s. It was earned mainly by Colonial forces such as The West African Frontier Force, The King's African Rifles and locally raised police units. There were some individual naval recipients but, in general terms, it was not a "medal to the navy".

Going back to the early years, the Royal Navy's war against black enslavement had cost the lives of at least 2000 of its officers and men. Disease and wounds caused 20,000 others to be invalided out of the service. The most senior to die in action was Captain Charles Brownrigg, RN. In 1881 he was commanding the

British East Africa Squadron from the elderly two-decker HMS LONDON (4400 tons, 90 guns). Too big and too decrepit for chasing *dhows*, she was moored, as his depot ship, in Zanzibar harbour. A "hands on" officer of the old school, he set off on 27 November with ten men in LONDON's steam pinnace for a tour of inspection in local waters. Five days later he encountered a *dhow* flying (false) French colours. When he went alongside to inspect her papers, the pinnace was suddenly fired upon, then boarded by a screaming mob of sword-wielding Arabs who, in a hand-to-hand struggle, killed seven of his crew. Three other men jumped overboard and swam 700 yards to the nearest island.

Left standing alone at the vessel's stern, several of his fingers slashed off and half-blinded by blood from a scalp wound, Captain Brownrigg swung at his attackers with a rifle butt before going down to a bullet in the chest. When his body was recovered it bore the wounds of twenty sword cuts. The Royal Warrant did not at that time allow for a posthumous award of **The Victoria Cross** but, even if it had, it is unlikely that Charles Brownrigg would have been nominated. For the authorities at home, the distant low-key campaign to eradicate black slavery lacked the drama and popular appeal of much greater events which had been happening elsewhere. And this assessment takes us back in time to 1854, far from Africa, north to the shores of Imperial Russia.

The Crimean War (tenth of the twelve Russo-Turkish Wars) was in some ways a throw-back to the religious wars of an earlier age. In the late 1840s, a bitter dispute had erupted in the Ottoman province of Palestine where each of the three principal Christian churches had their representatives - Roman Catholic, Armenian and Russian Orthodox. The Catholics wanted to have their own key to the main door of the Church of the Nativity in Bethlehem and an exclusive right to repair the roof of the Church of the Holy Sepulchre in Jerusalem. The local Armenian and Orthodox leaders objected to both demands. When the monks started brawling, the Turkish authorities stepped in and appointed independent historians and theologians to seek a compromise. Their scholarly adjudication was rejected and the conflict then rapidly expanded far beyond arguments about spare keys and roofing contracts.

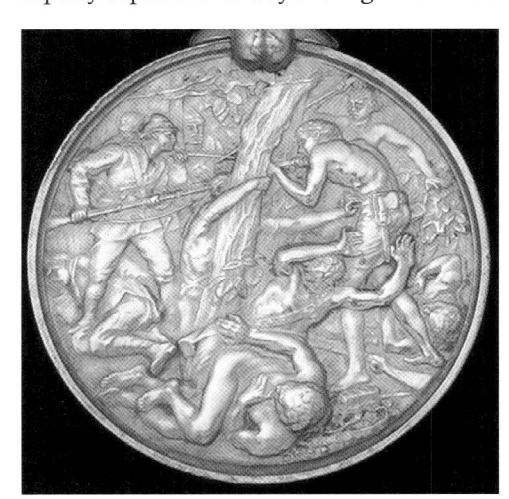

*Britain's early campaigns in West Africa resulted in a number of medals being produced.* **The Ashantee Medal** *(1873-1874),* **East & West Africa Medal** *(1887-1900) and the* **Central Africa Medal** *(1891-1898) all bear the same obverse and reverse designs. Depicted here is the reverse design showing British troops battling against Ashanti tribesmen between 1873 and 1874.*

Several governments felt the need to support whichever denomination was predominant in their own country and which also had a presence in the Holy Land. The arguments involved *inter alia* three of the most powerful nations in Europe - Russia, Great Britain and France. The former wanted, as ever, to absorb Ottoman-held territories into her own Empire, the latter two feared they might succeed. Apart from the religious considerations, there was concern at the fragility of the Turkish regime itself. Certainly there was no admiration for it in London and Paris. Indeed, there was in some quarters a general contempt for the Turks and for Islam in general. In 1851, Tsar Nicholas had branded Turkey "the sick man of Europe".

A major consideration was freedom of the high seas. By an international convention signed in 1841, the Ottomans could decide who might or might not send their ships through the Straits of Bosphorus and the Dardanelles. In practice, the convention blocked the Russian Navy from transiting those strategically important waters. As the British were to discover to their cost in 1915, they were impenetrable without the consent of the Turks. But in the event that the Russians might decide to force the issue by occupying Constantinople - either by amphibious assault or more likely by sending an army south through the Balkans - the Ottomans would collapse. The balance of maritime power in the Mediterranean (and very probably in more distant waters) would then change radically

By early 1853 it was becoming clear to the British and French governments that they might need to support the Ottomans in the event of a Russian attack. As a precautionary step they moved their Mediterranean fleets to the Dardanelles and the inland Sea of Marmora. Great Britain, France, Austria and Prussia jointly urged the Sultan to hand over to Russia, as a sop, his provinces bordering the Danube. Not surprisingly he refused, so Nicholas started a war which rapidly got out of hand. Full details of this miserable inconclusive conflict can be studied elsewhere. It is enough to say that the Royal Navy's role in the Black Sea was frustrated by the absence of a sea-going opponent. Apart from shore bombardments (Odessa, Kaleh and Kinburn) and a Naval Brigade which served some of the guns in the siege of Sebastapol, its main task was collaboration with the French fleet in coastal logistics and convoy escort work. Then, in June 1855, the dullness of this scenario was brightened by a great success at the Crimea's eastern extremity.

With their coastlines blockaded, the Russians had just two overland supply routes into the Crimea - south by land across the Perekop Isthmus or from the east by boat across the straits at Kertch. If they lost fortified Kertch there would be a 50% reduction in the flow of food and ammunition needed by the defenders of Sebastapol. Accordingly, the British launched an amphibious assault with fifty (mainly small) warships and 15,000 troops. They drove out the garrison and opened the gateway into the inland Sea of Azoff. The Royal Navy's rampage then shut down the water-borne traffic almost entirely. Four Russian warships were sunk and 246 merchant vessels either captured or destroyed. Having assisted in the Kertch assault, thirty-two of the Royal Navy's ships were engaged in that second phase of the operation. Their men received **The Crimea Medal** with the bar **Azoff.**

Although our one and only war with Russia is now commonly recorded in history books (and on the medal most associated with it) as "the Crimean war", it

Image: *Cassel's Illustrated History of England*

*The gun raft The Lady Nancy attacking Taganrog (Sea of Azoff), 11 August 1855, manned by volunteers from the flying squadron. The pulling boat in the foreground carries rocket-launching apparatus of the type developed by William Congreve. The standard missile used by the navy weighed 32lbs and had an effective range of 2750 yards. It was first used in action in 1806 when two hundred were launched into the port of Boulogne.*

drew the Royal Navy additionally into operations in the Baltic Sea, the Arctic Sea and the Pacific Ocean. Of these three, the best remembered is the campaign in the Baltic (mainly because it generated its own silver medal). When the war started and after Nicholas swiftly pulled his troops back from the Danube, the belief in London and Paris was that the Baltic offered the best means of defeating Russia. Great Britain was deemed to have the best navy while the French had the largest army. The former would damage Russia on her northern borders while the latter was containing any further aggressive moves by the Tsar in the Balkans. Between them, they would force Nicholas to make peace. Only later did a landing in the Crimea emerge as the central strand in the Allies' war plan.

When it was decided to mount a Baltic expedition, the Admiralty had difficulty in selecting an officer to take overall command. Most of the admirals in the Navy List were far too old. They chose, with some reluctance, 67 year-old Vice Admiral Sir Charles Napier, the officer who had played a key role in the 1840 Syria campaign (*vide* Part Two of these articles). Recently a revisionist historian has portrayed him as little more than a bad-tempered drunkard. While Napier may by then have been past his best, and certainly had a reputation for vigorously disputing all Admiralty decisions which he regarded as wrong-headed, there was no doubting his ability to command the Baltic expedition with a strong grip.

Napier had two immediate problems. The Admiralty could not provide him either with vessels of shallow draft (as he would need in the Baltic) or with sufficient experienced seamen to man the ships which did eventually sail. The Impress Service had disbanded in 1816, so desperate measures were used to make up the numbers required. In May 1854, Captain Byam Martin wrote from the recently recommissioned HMS NILE (92): "It is melancholy to see the poor old men ... dragged from their Coastguard stations to man the navy. They are too old to learn, too stiff to move, sending them aloft would be murder. So many infirm old creatures and so many raw uncouth youths from inland. It is a hopeless task". Byam was not alone with his manning problems. Of the 850 ship's company in the elderly HMS MONARCH (84), just eight were rated Able Seaman. There was a similar dearth of trained gunners.

Napier's fleet arrived in the Baltic in April 1854 (joined by the French on 12 June). With semi-trained ships and limited knowledge of his opponent's strength, he was bound to act with caution. English and Scottish merchants had been trading here for centuries, but Napier was ill-provided with charts. The Russians knew he was coming and, accordingly, they had doused the lighthouses, removed all navigational markers and withdrawn the pilots. They were thought to have 300,000 troops in the field, most of them positioned to defend their capital, St Petersburg, but with others ready to deal with a potential insurrection in Poland or already committed to the occupation of Finland. Their Baltic Fleet was even less prepared for war than the British. It was in such a poor state, in fact, that it was ordered to remain within its two fortified harbours - Sveaborg (on the south coast of Finland) and Kronstadt (near St Petersburg).

The Baltic Sea and its three adjoining gulfs are ice-bound from November to March. With little more than six months in which to act, Napier was under pressure from London and his own impatient captains to justify having been sent here in the first place. He despatched a "flying flotilla" far to the north, into the Gulf of Bothnia, to generally harass his enemy along the coast of Finland. It was commanded by Rear Admiral Sir James Plumridge, an officer whose previous combat experience had been as a 17-year old Midshipman in HMS DEFENCE (74) at the Battle of Trafalgar.

Image: Reproduced courtesy of Colonel Gerald W.A. Napier

*Admiral Sir Charles Napier (1786-1860), the colourful and controversial Commander-in-Chief of the Baltic Fleet in 1854. The perceived failure of his tenure as C-in-C allowed Their Lordships a period of reflection in which to reassess their objectives in the region as well as the composition of the Baltic fleet itself. In the immediate aftermath of the termination of his appointment Napier had to defend his actions to a hostile British public.*

*The Bombardment of the Russian Fort of Bomarsund by artist William Simpson. Those knowledgeable in the gunnery practices of the Royal Navy will recognise the impending danger faced by those huddled around the gun! This pleasingly dramatic painting proved popular with a British public who eagerly followed the events in new 'mass media' publications such as the Illustrated London News. War correspondents and illustrators, working alongside the combatants, brought the 1854-1855 campaigns vividly to life.*

His flagship was the small steam frigate HMS LEOPARD (18) sailing in company with two similar ships, VULTURE and ODIN. Ignoring his orders not to attack civilian targets, Plumridge burned numerous undefended villages and their fishing fleets. He came unstuck on 7 June at the small port of Gamlarkleby. When their pulling boats approached the shore they came under fire from Russian soldiers and Finnish Militia. Fifty-two men were lost.

There were comparable attacks along the coast of Latvia with towns burned and immense damage inflicted upon - amongst other properties - British-owned warehouses. Something positive was needed to quell the mounting criticism in London. A four-day reconnaissance of Kronstadt in June showed it to be too well fortified, so attention switched to the Aland Islands, midway between Finland and Sweden. Additional to the native Alanders, the capital Bomarsund had a garrison of 2000 Russian soldiers. To overcome them would require a military force, so 9000 French troops with artillery were shipped up from Calais. Accompanied by 600 British Marines they commenced an unopposed landing on 8 August and began a methodical advance inland. With them were the only representatives of the British Army to serve in the Baltic - six officers of the Royal Engineers and 103 other ranks of the Royal Sappers & Miners. Their initial task was the construction of access roads and batteries for the naval 32-pounders. Two forts in succession were forced into surrender before the final assault on Fort Bomarsund. It was carried after eight days by French troops under the suppressing fire of thirteen warships stationed offshore. The Sappers then moved in with their demolition charges. They laid the whole place flat, including the garrison church.

The French lost thirty-eight men in this affair. British casualties were thirteen seamen wounded and five Sappers who died of cholera. The sole Royal Engineer casualty was 21-year old Lieutenant the Honourable Cameron Wrottesley, killed on 15 August. It was a hollow victory because the King of Sweden was not interested in having the islands returned to him, and they had little value to the Allies. On 28 August the French army commander requested shipping to take his men back to France, and that effectively was the end of the 1854 campaign.

Having returned to England, Napier and all his senior officers were abruptly removed from their commands. He was replaced by the much younger (age 52) Rear Admiral Sir Richard Dundas, a well-connected officer currently employed as Second Naval Lord. Although he had served in the 1842 China War he had, like most of his contemporaries, been denied by the "forty years peace" any opportunity to shine as a fighting sailor. But now, with 105 ships and a French fleet in company, the Baltic should be his golden opportunity. In practice, he had much the same problems as his predecessor. The French Ministry of the Marine had quickly identified, in June 1854, the need for small shallow-draft steam-driven vessels equipped for close-range shore bombardments. Several hundred were built in French yards, many of them arriving in the Baltic in time for the 1855 campaign. The builders shared their ideas with British yards but, despite help from Isambard Kingdom Brunel, only twenty of these were available to Dundas when he entered the war zone in May.

At home, the public clamour was for a success, any sort of success, to off-set the catastrophic performance of the British Army in the Crimea. Accordingly, Dundas was ordered to attack the naval base at Sveaborg (something which Napier, lacking shallow-draft vessels, had prudently chosen not to do). The Russians had made

*Vice-Admiral the Hon. Sir Richard Saunders Dundas, KCB, RN (1802-1861). Having joined the Royal Navy as a volunteer in HMS Ganymede in 1817, Dundas saw service in the Mediterranean, North America, the East Indies and off Australia. He was made a Commander of the Order of the Bath for his actions during the First Opium War. At the outbreak of war with Russia, Dundas was serving as Second Naval Lord at the Admiralty. Following the end of hostilities, he went on to serve two terms as First Naval Lord until his untimely death in 1861.*

good use of the winter months preparing for an expected assault from the sea. It came on the morning of 9 August. Sandbanks, blockships and mines inhibited the deployment of the Allies' larger vessels, so most of the 6000 missiles hurled at the port and the nearby town of Helsinki were fired from the "bombs" (mortar ships). Great structural damage was inflicted but, after four days, the Allies had fired off all their ammunition. Peace with Russia was signed on 30 March 1856 and they never returned.

Even though he had achieved no more than his predecessor, Dundas and his men came home to a hero's welcome. Honours and promotions flowed freely and, in 1856, the Queen consented to a silver **Baltic Medal** being given to all ranks. Interestingly, despite the vicious criticism directed at Napier, L C Wyon's design for its reverse incorporated the fortresses of both Bomarsund (*vide* 1854) and Sveaborg (1855). In common with the majority of **Crimea Medals,** it was issued unnamed. However, all those given to Royal Engineer and Sapper personnel for their work at Bomarsund were impressed at the Royal Mint with the individual recipient's rank and name. Presumably, although there is no certainty, they were treated differently because their names were submitted by Horse Guards (the War Office), not the Admiralty. Sadly, given their rarity and therefore monetary value, it is not unknown to find fraudulently-named examples. Indeed, some years ago, two men were sent to prison after they commissioned the manufacture of a machine which exactly replicated the naming methods of the Royal Mint.

Of the 27,000 **Crimea Medals** awarded to the Royal Navy and Royal Marines, only 2000 were Mint-impressed with names and rank or rate (ships' names were excluded). Official permission was granted for some naval medals to be hand-engraved on contract by the firm Hunt & Roskill, others were named privately for the recipients. As revealed in Douglas-Morris's scholarly *Naval Medals, 1793-1856,* authenticity can be uncertain. Collectors unfamiliar with **The Baltic Medal** and **The Crimea Medal** may prefer to acquire examples of impeccable provenance or found in combination with one or more other named medals.

We turn now to the other side of the globe. The Russians had been established in the Pacific since the 17$^{th}$ century. They had settlements along the coast of Siberia and (through the Russian-American Company) they controlled Alaska. Their principal fortified bases were at Amur (on the Sea of Okhotskye) and Petropavlovsk (on the Kamchatka peninsula). An Anglo-French fleet of twenty-six vessels was ordered to disrupt their mercantile trade and to hunt down the four lonely warships of the Russian Pacific Squadron.

Apart from being hindered by the lack of coaling stations, our officers had few reliable charts for these unfamiliar waters. In command was Rear Admiral David Price, at sixty-four approaching the end of his naval career and evidently of unsound mind. The telegraph had not yet reached this part of the world so, lacking any dependable intelligence, his ships spent the summer months of 1854 searching thousands of miles of seaway without bringing their enemy to battle. A planned attack on Arub was aborted, its defences being thought too strong. The town of Ayub was stormed, but it was empty and undefended. The only residents were the Archbishop of Siberia and his *aide*.

In desperation, the Allied commanders agreed to attack the fortified port of Petropavlovsk. After an initial exchange of fire with the shore batteries on 29 August, a much heavier bombardment was commenced at dawn the next day. By mid-morning it was clearly having little effect so Admiral Price left the bridge of his flagship, HMS PRESIDENT, and took an early lunch. He then retired to his cabin and there shot himself. Command now passed to the French admiral, Febvrier-Despointes. He suspended the bombardment and ordered a landing for the next day. French and British marines and sailors forced their way into one battery before being counter-attacked and driven back to their ships.

On 4 September, Febvrier-Despointes - clearly made of sterner stuff than Price - ordered in a larger force but it was ambushed by Russian infantry and again forced into retreat. The withdrawal became a rout, and a lot of men died when they fell from the cliffs or drowned while attempting to swim to safety. Of the 700 who went ashore, 359 were killed, wounded or captured. This inglorious affair was to prove the sum total of two years' work by the Allied force in the Pacific.

The ships withdrew for the winter months to Vancouver (the British) and San Francisco (the French), then came back with more ships and new commanders in the Spring of 1855. They found Petropalovsk stripped of its artillery and stores and the garrison evacuated. The Russian admiral had removed his ships to the Siberian mainland coast so the Allies could do nothing more than set fire to the empty buildings. Commodore the Honourable H W Bruce, with the frigate SYBILLE (44 guns), the brig BITTERN and the steam corvette HORNET, was sent to look for the enemy vessels. He found them holed up in Castries Bay, but opted not to disturb them and they escaped. And that was the end of it.

The scene now changes again. British seafarers already had some familiarity with Arctic waters. Commencing in 1818, men such as Sir George Black and Sir John Franklin, with others, explored and charted the region and discovered its dangers. Their services were recognised by the award of **The Arctic Medal** (1818-1855). But then, in 1854, peaceful exploration was replaced by armed conflict when the navy was ordered to blockade the North Russian ports around the White Sea. A small Anglo-French flotilla operated there throughout the ice-free summer months of 1854 and 1855, seizing and burning merchant vessels and bombarding a few shore batteries. The blockade seriously affected the economy and maritime trade of Sweden. It stirred such anger that, at one stage, there was talk of Sweden abandoning her neutrality in favour of Russia.

The most successful action came in August 1854 when Captain Edmund Lyons, RN, navigated his 1100 tons steam corvette MIRANDA into the confined fast-flowing waters of the Kola Inlet (near modern-day Murmansk). His ship's gunfire and a follow-up landing party reduced the fortified town of Kola to ashes. Not a man was lost. When winter ice halted naval operations in the White Sea, he took his MIRANDA all the way around to the Black Sea in time to join the 1855 operations in the Sea of Azoff. The drive and skill of this officer were outstanding. He would have gone far in the service but in July he was killed while ashore under the walls of besieged Sebastapol.

Whether viewed separately or in combination, our naval operations in the

Baltic, Pacific and Arctic did nothing to alter the outcome of the war. However, they were successful in containing the Russian Navy within its home ports and in damaging Russian exports. Conversely, they tied up dozens of our warships at great cost and damaged our own exports. Traders on London's Baltic Exchange and commodity markets were probably harder hit than their Russian counterparts. Given Russia's immense landmass, the navy's efforts could be no more than flea-bites. And yet men had died while inflicting those puny blows, particularly at Petropalovsk. They and their shipmates are now forgotten because, even though they served in "the Great War with Russia", with one exception no medal was ever given to the men of the Pacific Fleet and the White Sea Squadron. The exception, of course, were those of HMS MIRANDA. They received **The Crimea Medal.**

Better remembered are the officers and ratings who fought, far inland, in the suppression of "the Great Sepoy Mutiny". In total, 290,000 British and Indian servicemen received the silver **Indian Mutiny Medal** (1857-1858) but, of these, just 786 were named to Royal Navy personnel. Its distinctive white and scarlet ribbon earned it the name, with some of the lads, "the Order of Blood and Bandages". Amusing perhaps, but entirely appropriate to the awful slaughter of that tragic war. The brilliant adventures of the Naval Brigade, particularly those of the redoubtable Captain Sir William Peel, VC, RN, have been described in print many times, so this author will not attempt a *precis* of those scholarly publications.

Similarly, the facts behind the **Ava** bar on the **The Army of India Medal** (1799-1826), **The China War Medal** (1842), the **Pegu** bar on **The India General Service**

Image: *A Pictorial History of the Russian War* by George Dodds

*The destruction by moonlight of Kola by HMS Miranda, 24 August 1854. Two men from the Miranda would later win the Victoria Cross for the Sea of Azoff action, Boatswain Henry Cooper and Lieutenant Cecil William Buckley RN.*

Images: *A History of the Royal Navy* by Sir William Laird Cowes

*Admiral the Lord Lyons, GCB (left) was one of the principal naval commanders during the latter stages of the war with Russia. He was showered with honours by a grateful government. His son, Captain Edmund Moubrey Lyons, RN (right) had struggled to emerge from his father's shadow and unwanted influence. This he finally achieved in both the White Sea and Black Sea as commander of the Miranda. Captain Lyons died of wounds received during the attacks on Sebastopol.*

Images: National Maritime Museum (NMM)

*Although the **Victoria Cross** was instituted by Royal Warrant on 29 January 1856, it was made retrospective to include the Baltic and Crimean campaigns. The first alphabetically listed in the London Gazette was Lieutenant C W Buckley of HMS Miranda. Also depicted is Boatswain Henry Cooper, late of the Miranda. Both were awarded the **Victoria Cross** for their actions at Taganrog. Henry Cooper's impressive array of medals includes the **VC, Baltic 1854-55, Crimea 1854-55** (bars **Sebastopol** and the rare **Azoff**), **Turkish Crimea** (Sardinian Issue) and the **French Legion of Honour**.*

**Medal** (1854-1895), **The South Africa Medal** (1834-1853), **The New Zealand Medals** (1845-1866) and **The (Second) China War Medal** (1856-1863), must be set aside for any reader who may wish to further his or her own researches into Royal Navy history.

Authorisation for each of these medals arrived in rapid succession. They must have placed great strain upon the staff at the Royal Mint and the clerks at the Admiralty still struggling with hundreds of late claims for the retrospective **Naval War Medal.** After the fall of Napoleon, and apart from the Algiers, Navarino and Syria campaigns (*vide* Part Two), the Royal Navy had had few commitments before the 1850s. Then, suddenly, that decade brought a dramatic increase in the administrative workload. It also exposed the limitations of traditional naval power in a fast changing world. Part Four will look at the navy's role in the creation of Victoria's British Empire.

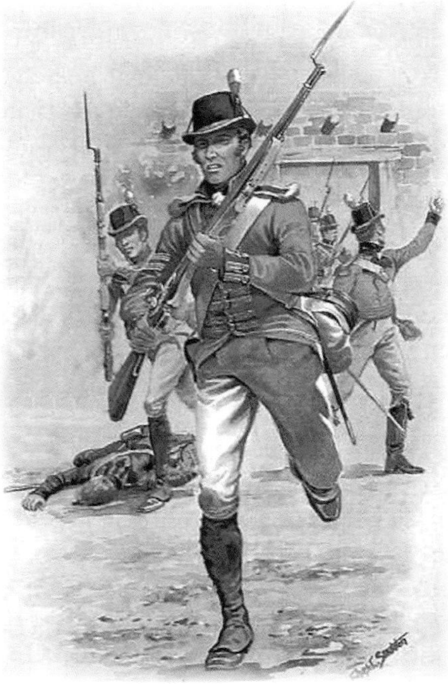

## Part Four - 1860 to 1890

ABYSSINIA was never regarded as a potential addition to the British Empire. When we invaded, we did so with the limited purpose of releasing a handful of Europeans held captive by the Emperor Theodore (Tewodros II). How and why they were imprisoned is a tangled story. It is enough to say that he went too far when he added an official British emissary to their number. At that point, national prestige demanded a military response and it was this which generated **The Abyssinia Medal** (1867-1868). Under the command of Lieutenant General Sir Robert Napier, a major expeditionary force was mounted in India and it began to come ashore in January 1868 on the Red Sea coast near Massawah. Its objective was Theodore's capital, Magdala, 400 miles to the south through some of the highest most precipitous unmapped mountains in all Africa.

Knowing that the logistical difficulties would be immense, Napier and his Staff were meticulous in their planning. They were all Indian Army men, Napier himself having entered the elite Bengal Corps of Engineers in 1828. Looking back, there is a startling difference between their outstanding professionalism when compared with the gross incompetence of the British Army commanders in the Crimea only fourteen years earlier.

Queen Victoria assented to a declaration of war on 19 November 1867. Barely five months later, on 13 April 1868, Magdala fell and it was all over. In the interim, 16,000 men (soldiers and sailors with experienced Indians to manage the great numbers of mules, horses and elephants) had been transported safely across the Indian Ocean. A port had been constructed where none existed previously, thirty miles of rail track laid, suspicious local chieftains mollified, two minor skirmishes fought. Total British losses in the campaign were two dead and twenty-seven injured.

It was the common British perception that the Abyssinians were savages who needed to be taught respect. And that was the tragedy of the whole affair. Theodore was demonstrably an unstable man, a schizophrenic, capable of ordering the torture and killing even of his own subjects whenever the mood so took him. At the same time, the record reveals a man of educated liberal views, unpredictably kind-hearted and considerate.

Image: Reproduced courtesy of the Victoria & Albert Museum (V&A)

*By contrast with the Punch caricature (next page), this image of the Emperor Theodore (based upon a portrait painted by an Abyssinian artist) shows the face of an intelligent and educated national leader.*

*Published in Punch magazine on 10 August 1867, this cartoon by John Tenniel barely requires a caption. British public outrage at the continuing imprisonment of Europeans in Magdala made inevitable the mounting of a military expedition. The figure of Britannia challenges the key-holding Emperor: "Now then, King Theodore. How about these prisoners?" It was a time when publishing costs were falling fast. Improved printing machinery and the fast-expanding railway distribution network enabled editors and politicians to sway popular opinion with an immediacy never before possible.*

He and his predecessors had been for years under pressure from neighbouring Islamic states. The Coptic Church, the oldest of all the world's Christian denominations, had been the established religion in Abyssinia since the appointment of the first Bishop in 330 AD. It is said that Mary Magdalene was born in the capital city (hence her name), but its history extends back long before that, back to the time of King Solomon and the Queen of Sheba. Although the Abyssinian Empire had at times extended into Egypt, Arabia and the Sudan, it began to shrink in the 18$^{th}$ century.

When Theodore ascended the throne in 1855, parts of his kingdom were falling into the hands of warlords some of whom wanted to replace the Christian faith with Islam. He appealed directly to each of the European leaders for help, but they all ignored him. He must have been frantic when told that a Christian-led army was coming to destroy him. Although he released his prisoners and despatched to Napier several offers of a peaceful settlement, it was too late. In despair, he shot himself in the mouth with a silver-mounted pistol sent to him fourteen years earlier and engraved with a message of goodwill from Queen Victoria.

Theodore's 7000 magnificently arrayed soldiers - banners flying, brave, disciplined, well led but armed only with spears and old muskets - had assembled outside the walls of the city. When they launched a mass charge they had no answer to Napier's naval rockets and his 3000 British and Indian riflemen. The city was quickly occupied, then burned to the ground.

An eyewitness to the final events of 10 April was the expedition's cartographer, Clement Markham: "As the king's (*sic*) forces charged down to meet our advancing troops, they were mown down in lines ... their most heroic struggle could do nothing in the face of such vast inequality of arms". After the discovery of Theodore's body, according to Markham: "The victorious troops gave three cheers over it, as if it had been a dead fox".

Attached to Napier's Staff was a civilian, Richard Holmes, Assistant Keeper of

Image: Cassell's *British Battles on Land & Sea* (1896)

*April 1868, Magdala is put to the torch. The city had already suffered a major assault when, in 1855, factional disputes resulted in its destruction. The new king (later emperor) Tewodros II then made it his capital and ordered the construction of a cathedral, an imperial palace and many fine residential buildings for the nobility. Even allowing for artistic licence, this engraving demonstrates the enormous logistical difficulties overcome by General Napier's expeditionary force.*

*General Sir Robert Napier, C-in-C of the Abyssinia expedition. A veteran of the First and Second Sikh Wars, the Indian Mutiny and the Second China War, he became briefly Governor General of India. He died aged eighty in 1890. By then Field Marshal the Lord Napier of Magdala, he was accorded the rare distinction of a State funeral. Despite their shared surname, he was not related to the Admiral Napier who commanded in the 1854 Baltic campaign (vide Part Three).*

Image: Leslie F. Thomson, *The Field*

*One of four Coptic Christian crosses purloined from Magdala in 1868. As a token of approval for their part in the expedition, it was presented by General Napier to the officers of "G" Battery, 14th Brigade, Royal Artillery.*

Manuscripts at the British Museum. It was known that Magdala and its cathedral housed a priceless library of books and other documents, a unique record of the flowering of Christianity from its earliest roots. Under Holmes' direction they were carefully crated, transported to the coast on the backs of 200 mules and fifteen elephants and then shipped to London. He was interested only in manuscripts so, before St Michael's cathedral and the lesser churches were put to the torch, Napier ordered them to be stripped of their other antiquities. Some were sold to his officers as keepsakes, the more valuable items he presented as tokens of appreciation to regiments which had performed particularly well.

Four of the most important were ornate altar or processional crosses fashioned variously in gold and silver. Two are still held by British regimental institutions each of which has requested this author not to reveal their names. The third went to the 1st Belooch Regiment, 27th Regiment of Bombay Infantry, and today it forms part of the Officers' Mess silver collection of their (Muslim) Pakistan Army descendant regiment. This one is additionally engraved with images of the Madonna and Child and the Twelve Apostles. The regiment's historian described it as "a trophy, displayed on special occasions".

The fourth cross was soon returned to Abyssinia. General Napier had given it to the 2$^{nd}$ Battalion, The Bombay Grenadiers (in the face of great difficulties, they constructed the section of railway to Kumavli from Zula on the coast). Returning to India, the officers presented this cross to St Thomas's Cathedral, Bombay. The battalion then began to lose its Indian-born officers, one after another, each dying in his prime and for no accountable reason. The number of deaths caused such concern that it was decided to return the cross to the rightful owners, the Coptic clerics in Magdala. This was done, and there were no more unusual deaths thereafter.

The British Government - influenced not by that story but by considerations of cool-headed diplomacy - also had second thoughts. The most spectacular of the objects stolen from Theodore's palace was the ancient crown of the Emperors of Abyssinia. For many years it was on display in London at the Victoria & Albert Museum. The crown was returned in 1930 when the Duke of Gloucester travelled to Addis Ababa as representative of his father, King Geoge V, to attend the coronation of Haile Selassie. For the rest, most of Abyssinia's treasures have been lost or dispersed to antiquity collections around the world.

The expedition not only punished Theodore, it punished his people by ripping the heart out of their culture. As his reward, Richard Holmes was appointed Royal Librarian and dubbed a Knight Commander of the Royal Victorian Order. General Napier's many rewards included elevation to the peerage as Lord Napier of Magdala. His men received **The Abyssinia Medal** of which 1981 went to Royal Navy personnel (they included a small Naval Brigade armed with 12-pounder rockets). The design reflected Victorian enthusiasm for the Neo-Gothic style, but it was the costly method of manufacture which made it unique. The recipient's details were embossed, not engraved or impressed, and this necessitated a separate die for each striking. It was a very expensive award commemorating a very costly smash-and-grab raid. Those named to Royal Navy men, especially if they served with the rocket contingent, are prized by collectors but perhaps not all are aware of what it represents.

While this was happening, far away in the North Americas, trouble had erupted which in 1899 generated the retrospective **Canada General Service Medal** (1866-1870). It commemorates, perhaps bizarrely, a series of events having their origins in the Protestant colonisation of Ulster in the 17$^{th}$ century. English persecution, and then later a cold indifference to Catholic Ireland's suffering when its staple food was wiped out by potato blight, caused great numbers to emigrate to America and Canada. Many took with them a profound hatred of the English. In America, they formed their own arm of the Republican Brotherhood - the Fenians - whose aim was to bring about a separation of Ireland from England and to establish an Irish Republic.

By 1866 the movement was causing havoc both in Ireland and on the mainland with raids and bomb explosions, and it was this which prompted their brothers in America also to take up arms. But these were not amateur terrorists, they had served as soldiers in the American Civil War and had access to the great quantities of weaponry left over from that conflict. With the intention of embarrassing the British, they planned a series of battalion-strength raids across the largely undefended border into Canada. The first came in April 1866 when a force of 700 men attempted to seize Campobello Island, New Brunswick. Forewarned, the authorities had ordered the steam corvette HMS PYLADES (1300 tons) to anchor nearby and despatched from Halifax a mixed force of 700 infantrymen drawn from the British Army garrison regiments. They arrived on 17 April aboard HMS DUNCAN (3720 tons) and joined forces with some hastily-raised local Militia. Seeing the scale of the opposition, most of the Fenians withdrew although a small contingent remained behind and occupied Indian Island before being driven off by a landing party from PYLADES.

The Fenians tried again two months later when a force estimated variously as 500 to 3000 men crossed the Niagara River and headed towards Fort Erie. This was a more serious affair. Despite shedding numerous deserters along the line of march, they successfully ambushed a force of volunteer Militia (Protestant Orangemen) at the hamlet of Ridgeway, east of Lake Erie. After a twenty-minute exchange of volleys, the ill-prepared Militia broke in confusion. Casualties were forty-seven

*Although it commemorated events which had occurred between 1866 and 1870, the* **Canada General Service Medal** *was not authorised until 1899. By then, Queen Victoria had been declared (in 1876) Empress of India, hence the "Regina et Imperatrix" on the obverse. Starting with William Wyon's beautiful 1847 "young head" design, Victoria's later widowhood and her advancing years led to British campaign medals being produced with a succession of seven different depictions of her before she died.*

Canadian dead or wounded, ten Fenian dead with "several" wounded.

The invaders defeated a second Militia force some days later before re-crossing the river and being arrested by American troops. And that, effectively, was the end of it. The American President Andrew Johnson invoked The Neutrality Act thereby denying the Fenians any future operating base. There were other ineffectual attempts at invasion, one of which was a raid by thirty-five men who managed to occupy a Hudson's Bay Company trading post near Winnipeg. They too were rounded up by the Americans.

Additional to the men of the DUNCAN and PYLADES, it is recorded (Spink's *British Battles and Medals*) that claims for the bar **Fenian Raid 1866** were submitted by personnel who declared that they had served in twenty-six other Royal Navy ships. Contemporary accounts of the raids published in Canada make no mention of any of them. Even so, if the Spink's entry was to be believed (twenty-six ships engaged), what was little more than a minor localised police action would have been a Canadian version of Trafalgar or Jutland.

In passing, the records do confirm that a vessel operated by the part-time Canadian Naval Company was involved. It had in its volunteer ranks a number of former Royal Navy people joined, for a short while, by a full-time serving officer. He was Toronto-born Midshipman E B van Koughnet, RN. His ship was HMS AURORA, currently moored at Quebec City. Before it froze over she was mother ship to smaller craft operating patrols along the St Lawrence River. Her captain gave the youngster leave to sail to the conflict area in the Toronto Naval Company's W T ROBB, a converted tugboat. This officer later served in Natal as Transport Officer during the 1899-1902 Anglo-Boer War.

Any reader having a taste for esoteric research is welcome to dig deeper into the question of entitlement. For the collector, however, a word of caution. Individual claims were being submitted and medals issued as late as 1928. Of these, some were engraved, some impressed, and there were at least five or six different styles of lettering. Then, in the late 1960s, the Royal Canadian Mint handed over to the Canadian War Museum an unknown number of surplus original unnamed medals which it began selling to the public. When attention was drawn to the risk of false naming and fraudulent attribution, the Museum made energetic efforts to recover the blank examples from collectors and dealers and stamped their remaining stock "CWM Specimen". It is likely that fewer than thirty escaped the net, but this background story should be kept in mind.

Why was authorisation for the medal (with its three different bars) delayed until 1899? The answer may be the continuing tension between English-speaking Upper Canada and French-speaking Lower Canada (such an award being politically sensitive). However, the Battle of Ridgeway was a seminal event in fostering a confederation of the Maritime Provinces and the eventual creation of modern Canada. With the last British Army garrison regiments departing in 1871, Canada's self-preservation demanded the creation of a strong Militia force and this was very successfully put into effect. The **Canada General Service Medal** is much less a campaign medal, much more a statement of an emerging national identity.

While the Canadian medal may be clouded with uncertainty, the story behind

Image: Reproduced courtesy of the National Portrait Gallery, London (NPG)

*Sir Henry Bartle Frere (1815-1884) had a long career in the Indian Civil Service. One recognition of his services was his appointment in 1867 as a Knight Grand Commander of the Order of the Star of India (hence the sash with its beautiful insignia resting upon his left hip). He was instrumental, in 1874, in negotiating the closure of the Zanzibar slave markets (vide Part Three). In 1877 he was appointed Governor of Cape Province with orders to form a "confederation" of British and Boer interests and to spread British control deeper into south east Africa. A civilian, essentially an administrator, he must have been unsettled by the arrival only a few months later of the brisk ambitious soldier, Frederic Thesiger (shortly to become Lord Chelmsford upon the death of his father). Thesiger had risen from Colonel to Lieutenant General in less than five years but had not previously commanded an army in the field.*

the **South Africa Medal** (1877-1879) is clear and well recorded both in print and on the cinema screen. Having started to evict the Dutch from the Cape in 1806, the British pressed ever deeper into Southern Africa with a succession of frontier campaigns against the Boer settlers and against any tribe standing in the way. Our strategy in that region was in total contrast with our long-standing policy in West Africa and East Africa. There, as described in Part Three of these articles, we devoted several decades to ending the enslavement of black Africans. The Royal Navy's tireless work in suppressing that vile trade should be remembered with pride. There is less satisfaction to be derived from its involuntary role in the final acts of conquest in Southern Africa. Gold and diamonds were not discovered until the 1880s, so the acquisition of territory was initially our sole objective.

The Royal Navy first became involved in 1877-1878. Sir Bartle Frere was the new Governor of Cape Colony and he was directing the Seventh Frontier (Kaffir) War in the Transkei. Short of troops, he obtained an all-ranks contingent of seamen and marines from the 3000-ton steam corvette HMS ACTIVE. Previously, in 1873, she had performed the same duty in support of Sir Garnet Wolseley's brief war against the Ashantee (*vide* Part Three). Armed with 12-pounder rockets, they came ashore at East London to take part in Frere's suppression of the Gcaleka and the Gaika. His new military commander, Lieutenant General the Honourable Frederic Thesiger (today remembered as Lord Chelmsford) persecuted the defeated tribes so mercilessly that the Cape Government felt compelled to rein him in. Having destroyed their *kraals* and grain stores and stolen their cattle, Chelmsford travelled north to Durban aboard HMS ACTIVE to prepare his invasion of Zululand.

Image: Cassell's *British Battles on Land & Sea* (1896)

*Early models of the Gatling gun discharged 200 x .30 calibre rounds per minute. Later marks had a theoretical rate of 1200 rounds, but 400 was the norm under field conditions. The six barrels were mounted on a hand-cranked revolving frame, the ammunition gravity-fed from a single hopper. All of these features are seen in this photograph of seamen from HMS Active, deployed ashore in Natal in 1879.*

It is not possible to write about Chelmsford and Frere and the men who succeeded them without a feeling of profound distaste. It is enough to say that what had once been the vigorous self-reliant Zulu nation - people who should have been our friends - were reduced to little more than a pool of cheap manual labour for the mines and for the European farmers. Inevitably, the word "enslavement" comes to mind, and that would have greatly surprised the 18$^{th}$ and early 19$^{th}$ century Abolitionists.

When, on 11 December 1878, Frere presented his impossible ultimatum to Chief Cetshwayo, he and Chelmsford had already agreed to destroy him. Without authority from London, Chelmsford invaded Zululand with three columns of British, Colonial and Native troops. He and his Staff accompanied the column commanded by Colonel Richard Glyn. Their intention was to cross the Buffalo river and head towards the plain and mountain known as Isandlwana with the ultimate aim of attacking Cetshwayo's *kraal* at Ulundi. A second column commanded by Colonel Charles Pearson crossed the 400 yards of the swift-flowing Tugela river and marched first towards the Norwegian missionary station at Eshowe. It was a mixed force which included officers and men from HMS ACTIVE. It was they who assembled and initially operated the prefabricated Tugela river "pont" ferry. While doing so, Able Seaman Dan Martin was swept away and drowned, so becoming the first casualty of the Zulu War.

Soon they were joined by a contingent of men from the steam corvette HMS TENEDOS. She reached Fort Pearson from the West Indies on 6 January. They in turn were reinforced by 398 officers and men from HMS SHAH, a big (6250-ton) armoured frigate which arrived at Durban from the Pacific on 7 March. The fourth major warship to enter harbour at Durban was the recently commissioned 3900-ton iron corvette BOADICEA. She should have arrived earlier, but had been held in quarantine following a shipboard outbreak of Smallpox. In total, 863 officers and men served ashore with the Naval Brigades in Zululand and thereby received **The South Africa Medal** with a bar. Those from ACTIVE who previously had taken part in the Seventh Frontier War had the bar **1877-8-9,** the rest carried the bar **1879.** Men of the ACTIVE, TENEDOS, SHAH and BOADICEA who did not go ashore were given the medal without a bar, as were those of four other vessels - EUPHRATES, HIMALAYA, ORONTES and TAMAR - each employed in coastal logistical duties.

The sole exception was the 455-ton steam gun boat FORESTER. Her Captain had surveyed the coast and recommended Port Durnford (the open beaches there) as a suitable location for landing supplies. While patrolling the mouth of the Tugela river she came under rifle fire from the shore which was silenced with a burst from her Gatling gun. None of her men went ashore but, on the strength of that encounter, they were deemed to have been in action and so were given the **1879** bar.

Chelmsford greatly under-estimated the strength and courage of his enemy. He soon ran into trouble. Full details of his grossly mismanaged war must be studied elsewhere. Just three episodes will be noted here to illustrate the types of situation in which individual members of the Naval Brigades found themselves. The first concerns Lieutenant Archibald Berkeley Milne, RN, a well-connected young officer chosen by Chelmsford to join his personal staff. On 22 January, having crossed the Buffalo river eleven days earlier and having left half his column comfortably encamped at Isandlwana, Chelmsford wandered off in search of the main Zulu army. It numbered at least 20,000 warriors, so he and his troops were in effect sheep hunting the wolves. Over breakfast he was told that something was amiss at Isandlwana. He ordered young Milne to climb to a high point and, with his naval telescope, to see whatever could be seen at that great distance. Milne, not surprisingly, reported that all appeared to be well. At that very moment, the Zulu were sweeping through the camp where, fighting desperately, 1700 of Chelmsford's men were being butchered or caught and killed as they tried to escape. One of them was Milne's servant, Signalman 1$^{st}$ Class W H Aynsley. He had been ordered to pack his officer's baggage and then rejoin him. When last seen he was trapped against a wagon, slashing at surrounding Zulu with, it is said, a naval cutlass. He went down after one of them crawled under the wagon and, pointing his *assegai* up through the spokes of a wheel, stabbed him in the back. He was the only Royal Navy man to die at Isandlwana. Milne, on the other hand, lived into old age. We shall meet him later (in Part Six) as Admiral Sir Berkeley Milne, serving in 1914 as C-in-C Mediterranean Fleet.

Image: Cassell's *British Battles on Land & Sea* (1896)

*The Battle of Isandlwana was fought on 22 January 1879. British forces subsequently made four visits to the site in order to bury the dead and salvage anything of value not already taken by the Zulu. This image records the fourth visit, on 21 May, when forty of Colonel Pearson's still serviceable wagons are being brought away. The definitive history of the campaign by Ian Knight and Ian Castle is required reading for everyone wishing to understand what happened on this great plain and along the route followed by the fugitives before they too were caught and killed.*

Less fortunate than Milne was Midshipman Lewis Cadwallader Coker, RN. During the action at the Inyezane river he distinguished himself while in charge of a Gatling gun. This fearsome machine gun had been patented by Dr Richard J Gatling in 1862 and it had caused hundreds of deaths in the American Civil War. Midshipman Coker was immensely proud of his command, this was the first time British forces had sent one of them to war on land. Despite being delayed by a broken limber pole, he moved his team rapidly to a key position at a critical moment and helped turn back the tide of attack. Four hundred and seventy Zulu were killed by his fire, by rifle fire and by the impact of the naval 24-pounder rockets.

Several navy men died of disease and hunger during the following three months while trapped at Eshowe, one of them the 19-year old Coker. He had insisted on sleeping in the rain beside his treasured Gatling gun. But, by contrast, tender years could sometimes be a life-saver. In the action at Gingindlovu, a Zulu *impi* charged forward through withering small arms and shell fire to start grappling with the British riflemen. With them was a young boy. An unnamed seaman reached over the stockade, grabbed the lad by the neck, hauled him inboard, boxed his ears and pushed him under cover. He was adopted as a mascot and later, it is said, inducted into the Royal Navy. That incident is one of the very few pleasing stories to emerge from the Zulu War. It ended in July with the destruction of the royal *kraal* at Ulundi and, soon after, the capture of Chief Cetshwayo.

Their job done, the men of the Naval Brigades returned to their ships, most of which went their separate ways. HMS BOADICEA, however, remained at Durban where she provided a contingent to fight in the First Anglo-Boer War of 1880-1881 (of which more later, *vide* Part Nine "A"). Those men were fated to be present at the Majuba Hill battle which left thirty-four of them dead. There was a world of difference between shooting a Zulu warrior armed with an *assegai* and leather shield or being shot at by a Dutch farmer armed with a modern rifle.

Leaping ahead seventeen years, the final chapter in the destruction of the Zulu nation did generate yet another medal. It was **The Natal Rebellion Medal** (1906). Zululand had been absorbed into the Crown Colony of Natal in 1879, but the Second Anglo-Boer War (1899-1902) had left the local economy in ruins. Desperate for revenue, Governor Sir Henry McCullum authorised a "hut tax" and then a "poll tax" on every Zulu tribesman age eighteen and over.

Supervising the collection of these taxes were men of the para-military Natal Police. In February 1906 two were murdered so, in reprisal, twelve Zulu men were tried by Court Martial and shot. Cetswayo's son and successor, Dinizulu, having seen what happened to his father, kept quiet but Chief Bambatha did not. He inspired a wave of protests and killings which prompted McCullum to declare Martial Law. He had a British Army garrison battalion in his capital, Pietermaritzburg, plus Royal Navy ships in local ports. Fortunately for them and for their reputations, he opted not to involve any of them in his punitive expedition into the Zulu heartland. South Africa was awash with adventurers, fortune seekers, remittance men, self-declared racists and enthusiastic Empire builders, all keen to "see a bit of action and have some fun". Titled "Militia Reserves", stiffened by the trained men of the Natal Artillery, Cape Mounted Rifles, Durban Light Infantry

*The **Natal Rebellion Medal** was authorised by the government of Natal Colony on 9 May 1907. The contract for its manufacture was given to the Goldsmith & Silversmiths Company of London. The quality of their striking is inferior to that of medals being produced by the Royal Mint during those same decades. The graceful figures of Britannia and Natalia give no hint of the violence of the genocidal campaign which led to its award.*

and Natal Carbineers, they conducted a series of "drives" through the Nkandla forest which killed, between April and June, at least 3000 Zulu (including their leader, Bambatha).

The climax came when the survivors were trapped under artillery fire in the wooded depths of the Mome Gorge. Casualties in that affair were three European dead, five hundred Zulu. The fate of the Zulu wounded cannot be imagined but, by the end of the campaign, 7000 had been captured (of whom 4000 were reportedly flogged).

In Spink's *British Battles and Medals* there are sixty-four unit titles listed as recipients of the silver **Natal Rebellion Medal** (of which 9979 were issued). Not included in that list is the Natal Naval Corp, a volunteer part-time coastal artillery unit raised in 1885 from the local British community for the defence of Durban (there was at the time a fear that Russian warships might attack the port). Some of its men had fought in the Second Anglo-Boer War at Ladysmith and now they were mobilised again, this time for active service in the Bambatha campaign. At least three medals named to individual Natal Naval Corps seamen are known in collections, but they are not comparable with the Naval Brigade awards already mentioned. The professional navy, happily, was not involved in the 1906 episode.

**The Egypt Medal** (1882-1889), with its bold blue and white ribbon and distinctive figure of the Sphinx on the reverse, points to a very different chapter in British Empire history. Beginning with **Alexandria 11$^{th}$ July,** thirteen successive bars were authorised. Officers and men of the Royal Navy earned twelve of them. There is no record of a navy entitlement to the bar **Toski 1899**, but that is the sole exception (a fact which underlines "Jack's" remarkable adaptability). The events leading to this medal's introduction are worth recording because they set the scene for three future British campaigns in Egypt - 1915, 1942 and 1956. At their heart, in each of those years, was command of the Suez Canal. The dynamics of international trade and maritime power changed radically when the Canal was opened in 1869.

Port Said stands at its northern entrance, but 150 miles to the east is the great port city of Alexandria. Over many centuries, back to the time of Cleopatra and beyond, it has always been a major commercial centre inhabited by people of many different racial descents and religious denominations. In the 1880s, Egypt was still nominally a province of the waning Ottoman Empire. At its head was the Khedive, a traditional title granted by the Sultans in Constantinople. The Egyptian masses gained little benefit from the Canal and their resentment grew when the Khedive sold his shares to the British. His country was bankrupt, sliding into chaos, its affairs largely controlled by European diplomats and businessmen. All of this produced a nationalist movement led by Colonel Ahmed Arabi and other officers of the Egyptian Army. There was nothing the new Khedive, Tewfik, could do to confront them when they declared their own government. Desperate for outside help, he appealed to the Western governments.

Political instability in Egypt was a particular threat to Anglo-French commercial interests so, in May 1882, both governments began to despatch warships to rescue Tewfik. Heading them was Admiral Sir Beauchamp Seymour with seven major warships, five smaller ships and six steam gunboats (plus a French squadron under Vice Admiral Charles Conrad). The intimidating sight of this foreign fleet fanned the fires of nationalism even further. Soon it was joined by vessels from other

Image: *Illustrated London News,* 1882

*The morning of 11 July 1882 aboard HMS Alexandra. One of her massive Armstrong 10-inch rifled muzzle-loaders is being fired into the city of Alexandria. The Mark I could hurl a 400lb shell up to 6,000 yards. Displacing 9,500 tons, this ship drew twenty-six feet under the keel, too deep for close range work, hence Admiral Seymour shifted his flag to the smaller Invincible.*

*Scenes all too familiar from too many wars. This was the once fine city of Alexandria after Admiral Seymour's fleet had completed its cannonade on 11 July 1882 and after fire had swept through the ruins. Almost identical photographs could have been taken in Ypres in 1918, in Smyrna in 1922, in Warsaw in 1939, or Berlin in 1945. There is a startling similarity also with photographs taken by officers of the Royal Navy who went ashore at Messina in 1908 after that city was struck by a violent earthquake.*

countries, sent to evacuate their nationals in the event of trouble. It came on 11 June. The mob turned on the city's large European, Jewish and Christian communities. There was serious rioting until Arabi's men restored order two days later. Admiral Seymour happened to be ashore on that first morning, lucky to escape unharmed back to his temporary flagship, HMS INVINCIBLE. Fifty Europeans were killed and many injured (one of them the British Consul). By 6 July all non-Egyptians who wanted to leave had done so. Seymour was then free to take action.

There were eleven forts guarding Alexandria harbour and its approaches. Over the past weeks, Arabi's men had been installing additional guns and throwing up fresh earthworks. To Seymour, they were a threat to his ships and an obstacle to any landing force. He issued Arabi with a warning that, if he did not desist, he would be attacked. In Paris, the government was still struggling with the fall-out from the 1870-1871 invasion by newly unified Germany. Wanting no part of yet another war, it ordered Admiral Conrad to withdraw all his ships. Admiral Seymour commenced a bombardment of the forts with his remaining Royal Navy ships on the morning of 11 July and maintained it for ten and a half hours. Despite its great violence and ear-shattering noise, the Egyptian gunners stuck to their task, inflicting damage and casualties on the British ships. Seymour ordered the "ceasefire" as darkness fell, but turmoil within the city continued throughout the night as the mob pillaged the affluent homes of the departed foreigners. Great damage had been caused also by the navy's "overs", and most of the city's fine buildings were burning and in ruin.

Undaunted, the Egyptians used the dark hours to repair some of the damage to their batteries. Next morning, observing that the Hospital battery was again ready for action, TEMERAIRE and INFLEXIBLE hit it with a few more shells before a white flag was seen. After a failed attempt at an armistice, preparations were made to resume a general bombardment but, by then, all of the forts were flying white flags. Uncertain of the situation on shore, Seymour sensibly waited forty-eight hours before sending in his landing parties. Then, with Tewfik in safe custody and the city under shaky control, the newly-landed British regiments with a small Naval Brigade set off in pursuit of the Egyptian Army retreating south towards Cairo. They caught up with it at Tel el-Kebir, so generating the second of the thirteen bars on **The Egypt Medal.** It is tempting to descend into a detailed account of each of them, but limitations of space do not permit that luxury and they are, in any case, covered admirably in Spink's *British Battles and Medals.* Instead, and turning away from medals, we shall conclude with a brief summary of the status of the Royal Navy as it was in the last two decades of the 19$^{th}$ century.

Since the 1820s and 1830s, the Admiralty had been advancing cautiously into a new world of technical innovation. Science and industry were presenting the naval architect and the gun maker with materials never previously used in the construction and armament of a warship. It was not that the designers refused to recognise their potential value, it was more a case of not knowing how best to employ them. Should they abandon sails for steam when boilers were still primitive and unreliable, when a worldwide chain of coaling stations did not yet exist? How to accommodate dozens of stokers in a ship already crammed with seamen and gunners? In any given situation, was the side paddlewheel more or less efficient than the screw propeller? What were the advantages of steel compared with wrought iron or cast iron? What was the effect of the high explosive shell on different types of armour? What was the ideal calibre? If traditional main batteries ranged along the sides of the hull were to be replaced by revolving heavy gun mountings fore and aft, what should be done with the masts and other obstructions limiting their arc of fire? How best (after 1895) to protect hulls from Whitehead's new self-propelled torpedo? And what was the navy *for?* Would it ever again fight at sea an enemy fleet of comparable strength? Or would it simply continue to be an adjunct to military campaigns fought on land? There were many questions, few certainties.

As the years rolled by, almost every ship emerging from the dockyards was a prototype. None of Admiral Seymour's ships at Alexandria in 1882 were identical. Each incorporated a new feature representing an improvement on what had gone before. But such rapid progress came at a high price, and not just in terms of soaring annual Naval Estimates. The hazards of pushing the pace too quickly were starkly exposed in September 1870 with the capsize of HMS CAPTAIN. Just eighteen men survived out of 500 or more.

Image: *Illustrated London News*, 1881

*In towering seas, caught in the grip of a powerful gale off Cape Finisterre, the experimental masted turret warship HMS Captain struggles against the maelstrom. The ship was under sail at the time and despite Captain Burgoyne's efforts to get the steam engine started, the Captain heeled over and capsized taking all but eighteen of her crew with her to the bottom. Captain H. T. Burgoyne VC, Captain Cowper Coles (her designer) and Midshipman Childers, the son of the First Lord of the Admiralty, were among the five hundred souls lost in the disaster. The subsequent inquiry, held aboard HMS Duke of Wellington, was the first to make extensive use of scientific experimentation and concluded that "the Captain was built in deference to public opinion expressed in Parliament. Never again should a warship be built privately against the wishes of the Naval Constructor".*

The first big advance came in 1860 with the launch of the innovative 9200 ton armoured frigate HMS WARRIOR. Built at Blackwall (London) by the Thames Ironworks & Shipbuilding Company to a design by the Admiralty's Chief Constructor Isaac Watts and Chief Engineer Thomas Lloyd, she was for a few years the most powerful warship in the world. Fully restored to her original condition she now has a permanent mooring at the Portsmouth Historic Dockyard. She is open to the public and a few exhilarating hours spent aboard will tell the visitor everything he or she might ever wish to know about the evolution of Victorian warship design.

*HMS Warrior 1860*          *HMS Dreadnought 1906*

The WARRIOR was followed between 1895 and 1904 by a succession of new "Class" ships - the ROYAL SOVEREIGNs, MAJESTICs, CANOPUSs, FORMIDABLEs, LONDONs, DUNCANs and QUEENs - but at a stroke all were rendered obsolete in 1906. When Admiral "Jackie" Fisher became First Sea Lord, one of his first moves was to appoint a committee of specialists having the remit to produce a battleship faster and stronger than anything that had gone before. With an eye to what was happening in Germany, Fisher ordered that the new HMS DREADNOUGHT must be launched within no more than twelve months from the day her keel was laid in Portsmouth Naval Dockyard. That target was missed by just twenty-four hours. She was followed by more "Class" ships, each resembling the DREADNOUGHT, each raising the bar for naval architects in every other maritime nation.

Although well-informed of the Imperial German Navy's massive building programme, our Admirals could feel every confidence in the tools the nation had placed in their hands. In Part Five we shall look at the ways in which they employed those tools between 1900 and 1914.

## Part Five - 1890 to 1914

THE ROYAL NAVY entered the final decade of Queen Victoria's reign with a massive inventory of ships of every kind. When they assembled in 1897 for the Spithead Review, the lines of anchored ships were thirty miles long. Manning those ships were men better educated and more technically competent than any previous generation of British sailors. They were commanded by high-born officers supremely certain of their place in society and confident in their individual professional abilities. The confidence was for a while dented after HMS CAMPERDOWN rammed HMS VICTORIA off the coast of Lebanon in June 1893. The sinking killed 358 officers and men. It also prompted vigorous debate regarding the extent to which an officer could or should disobey a wrong-headed order given to him by another of higher rank. The navy had become hidebound, the Nelsonian spirit of "turning the blind eye" largely forgotten. Even so, it was still the most respected maritime force in the world.

Confidence was boosted in May 1905 by the Battle of Tsushima. It was the time of the Russo-Japanese war which had erupted a year earlier. The Russian Baltic fleet of thirty-eight ships had steamed 18,000 miles to relieve Port Arthur on the coast of Siberia but then, after that place fell to the Japanese army, to reach safe haven at Vladivostok. When they attempted to pass north through the waters between Korea and the Japanese home islands, all but two were sunk, captured or interned in neutral ports. Nearly 4500 Russian sailors were lost (against 116 Japanese).

The ships which won this crushing victory were British-designed, built in British yards, fitted with British machinery and armed with British guns. The accurate shooting and hard hitting of the four battleships - MIKASA, SHIKISHIMA, ASAHI and FUJI - seemed to demonstrate that the Royal Navy's own ships, built in the same yards, would perform equally well in any future fleet-versus-fleet engagement. In the event, that belief would not be fully tested until 1916 in the North Sea (although, by then, warship design had advanced even further). Meanwhile, it was a "fleet in being", a magnificent icon of British national prestige frustrated only by a lack of opportunities to flex its muscles. Over the previous half century, our wars with the Russians, the Sepoy mutineers, the Abyssinians, the Boers, the Chinese and with various African tribes had committed it to little more than providing Brigades of sailors and marines to help the army on land. But, for the admirals and the captains of major warships, these were secondary roles, not primary. Personal reputations could not be built in that way. Fate then condemned them to yet another Cinderella commitment and, once again, it was in Southern Africa.

Beginning in 1806, the British had hounded the Dutch settlers always further north and further east out of the Cape. Following the Great Trek of 1834, the Boers (literally, in their language, "farmers") established two independent self-sustaining republics - the Orange Free State and the Transvaal. After initial conflicts with local tribes, they settled to doing what they did best, farming. Unfortunately for them, diamonds and gold were discovered in the 1880s and this attracted thousands of speculators and adventurers - the *uitlanders* - into their territories. Despite the harsh

*The shattered 12,650-ton armoured cruiser Peresviet lies abandoned in Port Arthur in the aftermath of the Russo-Japanese War. Having taken refuge there from the rampant Japanese fleet at sea, she had been reduced to ruin at her anchorage by long-range siege artillery. For the British, the 1870s and 1880s brought a succession of "Russian Scares" all of which proved unfounded. Then, in 1905, Admiral Togo's stunning destruction of Russia's Baltic and Pacific fleets marked his nation's emergence as a major naval power and the demise of any more Russian threats.*

lessons of the First Anglo-Boer war in which we gained a bloody nose but no medals (*vide* Part Nine "A"), people like Cecil Rhodes had no intention of leaving the Boers in control of such enormous new wealth. The Jamieson Raid in December 1895 was a portent of what was to come.

The President of the Transvaal, J P S Kruger, instructed his General Piet Joubert to prepare for a major conflict by modernising his one and only permanent full-time regular regiment, the *Staats Artillerie*, founded in 1874. Joubert wasted no time in obtaining Maxim "pom-pom" guns and heavy field pieces from Krupp (Germany) and Creusot (France). With them came Imperial German Army instructors. Of even greater influence in the impending battles was Joubert's purchase of the excellent German-designed Mauser magazine rifle, 30,000 of them. When war came, the Boers were as ready for it as ever they could be.

Leaving their farms and families, they mobilised themselves as fighting Commandos - boys and men of all ages, the officers appointed by common consent. Their knowledge of the terrain, their riding and shooting skills, their close bonds of family and community, and above all a devout love of their Church and homeland, made them an opponent to be respected. The British generals sent to fight them had no such respect and even less understanding of mobile warfare. The results were inevitable - disaster after disaster. The Boers were broken in 1901 only after our commanders changed tactics by burning their farms, stealing their cattle and forcing their women and children into concentration camps where 24,000 of them died of disease and starvation.

So, where did the Royal Navy fit into all of this? On 11 October 1899, driven to desperation by British demands, Kruger declared war and his Commandos quickly laid siege to Mafeking, Kimberley and Ladysmith. The British Army was incapable of relieving their garrisons without rapid reinforcement and so the fleet once again was required to provide a Naval Brigade for duty ashore. Twelve ships were already present in South African waters, nineteen more would join them over the following months. The first sailors to fight came from HMShips DORIS, MONARCH, and POWERFUL.

They were commanded by Captain Reginald Prothero, RN, an officer of violent temper known (behind his back) as "Prothero the bad". This was to distinguish him from a more agreeable contemporary of similar name. When he led his contingent

*Boer troops with a heavy gun of the type used to bombard Ladysmith. The Boers were at first content with long range shellfire but, on 6 January 1900, Commandant de Villiers made an attempt to force out the British lines at Waggon Hill and Caesar's Camp. The battle lasted throughout the day, with the defenders holding their ground until nightfall when the Boers withdrew having lost 52 men. They resumed bombardment of the town until it was finally relieved by Sir Redvers Buller on 28 February. Including deaths from disease, the garrison lost 89 officers and 805 men during the siege, nearly half of whom fell in the battle of 6 January.*

inland by rail from Durban to link up with the 8500 British Army force already in the field, he took with him from HMS DORIS an 18-year old Australian as his *aide de camp*. He was Midshipman Cymbeline Huddart, RN, the son of an influential Melbourne family which in 1895 had moved to London. Cymbeline was accepted for entry into the RNC BRITANNIA in that same year and was soon heading for a successful Royal Navy career. In late 1899, the name of this 18-year old youngster would come to prominence both in London and in his native Australia.

Captain Prothero's 350-strong Naval Brigade had the misfortune to be placed under the command of the newly-promoted Lieutenant General Lord Methuen. He had not long departed India where, during the Tirah Expedition of 1897-1898, he was employed as Press Censor. His orders were to raise the siege of Kimberley (the dusty township which had grown up around its fabulous diamond mine). Advancing up the line of the railway, his force arrived at Belmont Station on 23 November 1899. When Boers were seen near the station on a line of low rocky hills (*kopjes*), Methuen ordered a dawn attack to dislodge them.

Any night-time forward movement by a large body of troops requires detailed reconnaissance and, ideally, a rehearsal. Neither happened and so, not surprisingly, daylight came before the attacking infantry had begun to climb the higher ground. Even so, the three battalions of the Guards Brigade persisted under constant fire. They reached the summit to discover that the Boer marksmen had scuttled down the reverse slope, mounted their ponies tethered in readiness, then galloped off to a new position overlooking Graspan Station.

Methuen lost 200 Guardsmen at Belmont. Boer casualties (if there were any) were reported as "slight". The naval contingent took no part in this affair, and Captain Prothero let his views be known. He and his men wanted to show the soldiers what they could do, given the chance. Methuen was glad to give them the lead at Graspan. For two hours, their four 12-pounder naval guns banged away at the hidden Boer positions and then 245 of them rose up to advance with bayonets fixed. Marines on the left, seamen on the right, they walked forward in a rigid line with four paces between each man. The formation soon buckled in the rough terrain and they fell into the trap of "bunching", small groups clustered almost shoulder to shoulder. The Mauser rifle was sighted for ranges up to 1200 yards. The Boers held their fire until the Naval Brigade was 650 yards away, then began methodically "to pick them off like rabbits". Of the original 245, fifteen were killed, seventy-nine (including Captain Prothero) seriously wounded.

Like the Guards at Belmont, they stuck to their task with the greatest courage but it was all in vain. Reaching the high ground, they found nothing but heaps of spent cartridges. The Boers had again slipped away. Amongst the fallen that morning was Midshipman Cymbeline Huddart. In a display of magnificent youthful bravery, he continued to lead his party of sailors up the rising ground even though he had been hit already by two of the heavy Mauser bullets. Still pressing forward, he was then struck down by a third bullet and died later that night.

Inconsiderate and ill-mannered he may have been, but Captain Prothero ensured that the circumstances of the boy's death were reported back through command channels to the Admiralty. When the story reached Queen Victoria she

*Midshipman Cymberline Alonso Edric Huddart, RN. He is commemorated by a plaque in St Paul's Anglican Cathedral, Melbourne. The Naval Brigade went on to fight at the battles at Modder River (28 November 1899), Magersfontein (11 December 1899), the relief of Kimberley (February 1900), the battle of Paardeberg (17-27 February 1900) and the capture of Bloemfontein in March 1900.*

wrote a letter of sympathy to Cymbeline's parents and authorised a new award, **The Conspicuous Service Cross** (the **CSC**). Inaugurated on 15 June 1901, it was intended for "acts of gallantry in the face of the enemy" by naval Warrant Officers and junior commissioned officers whose conduct might have qualified them for admission into **The Distinguished Order** if they had been of higher rank**.** Only eight were ever awarded before it was replaced in October 1914 by **The Distinguished Service Cross.**

Of those eight recipients, four were rewarded for the action at Graspan. Additional to Cymbeline Huddart, they were Midshipman T C Armstrong, RN, Midshipman R B C Hutchinson, RN, and Warrant Gunner E E Lowe, RN, all of whom survived. Given its great rarity and the unusual circumstances under which it was won, the **CSC** is for the collector one of the most desirable of all "medals to the navy".

With hindsight, the Graspan affair was a shocking waste not only of life but of highly-skilled seamen, some of them specialist tradesmen. They did not deserve to fall victim to a commander like Methuen, and the navy should not have entrusted such a precious resource to the military. But it was to happen time and again during that conflict, good men thrown away in futile frontal attacks to no good purpose.

Interestingly, the war underlined yet again the tactical values of "fire and movement" and the use of natural cover. Having been put into practice with success by the British Army when it deployed "the green jackets" in North America and in the Peninsula, both were later forgotten (except by our soldiers campaigning on the North West Frontier of India). But they *were* emphasised in the new Infantry Training Manual produced by the War Office in 1908. Ironically, many of the senior officers who blundered in South Africa later commanded in the war of 1914-1918. Entrusted on the Western Front with the lives of the enthusiastic volunteers of the New Armies, they threw the 1908 Manual out of the window. The consequences are too well known. In terms of infantry tactics, the war against the Boers turned out to be a rehearsal in miniature for the industrialised carnage of the war with Germany.

After Graspan, Methuen pushed on to the Modder River which he successfully forced on 28 November. But, again, the tactics were faulty, the casualties excessive. He was then fought to a standstill with even heavier casualties thirteen days later at

Magersfontein. Everything that happened thereafter in the war is abundantly recorded in the many published accounts, so we may return now to the subject of medals. There were two - the **Queen's South Africa Medal** (the **QSA**) followed, after Victoria died, by the **King's South Africa Medal** (the **KSA**). Only thirty-one **KSA** went to sailors and marines because the Naval Brigades returned to their ships in 1901. Surviving examples are, of course, excessively rare and collectable.

By contrast, of the total 177,000 **QSA** medals issued to all services, 5700 went to Naval Brigade men and they qualified for one or more of the twenty-six authorised bars (the maximum to an individual naval recipient was eight). Their shipmates who did *not* go ashore were given the **QSA** without a bar. For the collector, one of the fascinations of this medal is the range of possible combinations of bars and of other medals which it offers. Much sought after, as an example, are medals to HMS TERRIBLE. Her men gained *inter alia* the desirable **Relief of Ladysmith** bar before being sent to China where they qualified for the **China War Medal** (1900) with the equally prized **Relief of Pekin** bar. But before we sail off to China, there is a tailpiece to the **QSA**.

Although the Naval Brigades were returning to their parent ships in 1901, the war was far from over and the Royal Navy's commitment to it far from ended. Despite the arrival in the war zone of tens of thousands of additional troops from all over the British Empire, the Boer Commandos were on the rampage, penetrating deep into Cape Colony and even at one point thought (wrongly) to be a threat to Cape Town itself. The navy's task was to patrol the 1500 miles of coastline between Walvis Bay (German South West Africa, now Namibia) all the way around to the mouth of the Limpopo River (Portuguese East Africa, now Mozambique). There were many places where contraband-runners could land, or where coastal settlements needed protection and reassurance. Five ships in particular put men ashore for the latter purpose - the 1$^{st}$ Class cruiser NIOBE (11,000 tons), the 2$^{nd}$ Class cruisers NAIAD, SYBILLE and TERPSICHORE (each of 3400 tons), and the steam gunboat WIDGEON (805 tons). Those of their men detached for service on land, perhaps for only a few days at each location, received the **QSA** with the bars **Cape Colony** and/or **South Africa 1901** (or in the case of the little WIDGEON, **Natal**). On the face of it, these medals are not nearly as desirable to collectors as those bearing scarce (for the navy) "battle" bars such as **Tugela Heights**, **Laing's Nek** or **Diamond Hill**, but they do represent an interesting series of adventures.

The most dramatic was that experienced by HMS SYBILLE. On the evening of 15 January 1901, she arrived off Lambert's Bay (180 miles north of Cape Town on the Atlantic coast) under command of Captain Hugh Williams, RN. There were reports that a Boer Commando was approaching from inland with the intention of attacking the small settlement and its storehouses. Captain Williams went ashore with fifty men to generally assess the situation, passing command of the ship to his First Lieutenant, Hubert Holland. In a fast rising gale, Holland prudently weighed anchor and put to sea for the night. Dawn brought calmer conditions, so he returned to what he thought was the original anchorage. Unfortunately he had not appreciated the strength of the current streaming along that coast and he was six miles too far to the south. For whatever reason, he and his Navigating Officer and the Officer of the Watch allowed their ship to drive onto rocks 300 yards from the shore where she became a total loss. One man died, Able Seaman William Jones. The three officers were tried subsequently by Court Martial, severely reprimanded and "dismissed the ship". It was an unhappy footnote to the navy's otherwise impeccable services in that war.

But there was another war in progress, one in which the Royal Navy was also taking a significant role. In the inventory of British campaign medals, there are three which relate to Eastern Asia - the **China War Medal** (1842), the **China War Medal** (1856-1863), and the **China War Medal** (1900). Imperial China reached the pinnacle of its magnificence and maritime power between the $14^{th}$ and $17^{th}$ Centuries. The Emperors of the Ming dynasty sent their "tributary" fleets to many parts of the world and their officers (notably Admiral Zheng He) made the earliest known maps of the Antipodes, India, Africa and the Americas. China's wealth was further boosted by the silver mines of Columbia.

Imperial Chinese diplomatic missions arrived in Florence in 1421 and 1434. They brought with them the scientific knowledge which ignited the European phenomenon known as the *Renaissance* (the *Rinascimento*). For a while, China's civilisation was by far the most advanced and cultured in the world. But then the long decline, hastened by internal disputes and natural disasters, enfeebled the country to the point at which European nations were tempted to take control. Inevitably there was resentment, aggravated by the influx of Christian missionaries.

The third and final crisis came in early 1900. At first, the government headed by the Dowager Empress Tzu Hsi was not inclined to confront the Europeans directly, but she did nothing to discourage the various nationalistic martial arts devotees such as "The Society of Righteous and Harmonious Fists", translated by the British as "the Boxers". Their aim was simple - to free their country of all Christian foreigners. One of their first moves was to isolate the European trading posts, the Christian mission stations and the foreign Legations in the Imperial capital, Pekin. Each Legation compound was routinely guarded by its own troops. In the case of the British, they were seventy-eight Royal Marines. Subsequently they (and others who joined them later) received their **China War** medals with the desirable bar **Defence of Legations.**

Clearly, they needed speedy reinforcement. There was much confusion within the various Chinese factions - some radical, others moderate - and the railway from the coast to the city was still intact. On 31 May, an international naval brigade of 435 men (including seventy-five Royal Navy) travelled the eighty miles with little difficulty and joined the small garrison. Their numbers were still inadequate, so Vice Admiral Sir Edward Seymour assumed the task of leading up from the coast, in person, an *ad hoc* force of 2000 seamen and marines (mainly British). It was a remarkable decision for a man of sixty-one, a veteran of the Crimea and the Second China War, and now Commander-in-Chief of the China Fleet.

Abandoning the comfort of his flagship (the 10,500 ton battleship HMS CENTURION), he set off in the rising summer heat for his big adventure. But Chinese resolve had hardened in recent days. With the rail track partially dismantled in front of it and behind it, Seymour's train was cut off and under heavy attack. Taking to the countryside, he marched on towards Pekin along the line of the Pei-Ho river but, on 18 June, he was brought to a halt by lack of food and the burden of 200 wounded. Then, by chance, his scouts discovered the Imperial arsenal at Hsi-Ku. It was packed with Krupp field guns, Mauser rifles, abundant ammunition and tons of rice. His immediate problems resolved but now surrounded, Seymour dug in to await rescue. It came a week later when 900 Russian infantry and 500 British seamen fought their way through the encircling Chinese and, after setting fire to whatever stores they could not carry, escorted Seymour's force away to safety.

Meanwhile, on the coast, the railhead town of Tianjin had fallen and also needed relief. That operation called for a much larger military commitment ashore plus a naval element to bombard and destroy the Taku forts which guarded the town's seaward approaches. It was not without its difficulties. The approaches were too shallow for any of Seymour's larger ships to come within effective range. He therefore ordered in a multi-national flotilla of shallow-draft vessels under command of the American Rear Admiral Louis Kempff to provide covering fire for the storming parties. Two of his ships were HMS ALGERINE and HMS WHITING. Both were hit by Chinese artillery but not seriously damaged. The forts were beaten into submission and the way was then open to escalate the campaign.

Seymour had initially underestimated the difficulties, but now they were appreciated in full. In total, the Allies brought in 55,000 troops (half of them Japanese and Russian) while Seymour's thirty-five ships - assembled off the mouth of the Pei-Ho - provided firepower whenever needed and more men for the fighting ashore. Overall command on land was given to Major General Sir Alfred Gaselee, an Indian Army officer with a fine record of campaigning in Afghanistan, Abyssinia and on the North West Frontier. After his Japanese contingent re-occupied Tianjin on 14 July he set off for Pekin with 20,000 Allied troops (others spreading out into the disaffected areas). Opposing him were 70,000 disorganised Imperial troops and between 50,000 and 100,000 poorly-armed Boxers. Two minor skirmishes delayed him only briefly, his main problem being the weather (oppressive humidity and temperatures exceeding 40 degrees C).

Pekin was occupied on 14 August and the Western world rejoiced. A peace agreement between the Imperial Court and the Eight-Nations Alliance (weighted heavily in favour of the victors) was signed a year later. Russia and Japan took possession of Manchuria, the other participants all gained "spheres of influence". The imposed level of reparations ensured that the Chinese Treasury would be impoverished for the next thirty-five years. The traders and speculators could tighten their grip on the economy, Customs levies made even more punitive, the Roman Catholic and Protestant missionaries free to continue their evangelising.

*A group of RMLI men pose (together with a solitary bluejacket) somewhere in the debris of a British Legation building, Pekin. In modern times, informal photographs taken by our lads serving overseas and sent home to their families are commonplace. This rare image, more than a century old, sets the tone.*

*Nine representative fighting men of the Eight Nations Alliance which defeated the Boxer uprising in 1900. The British Empire is represented twice in this photograph. To the left is a British Army corporal, fourth from the left is an Indian Army man, a Sikh. His sword suggests he holds the senior rank of those present. With the British Army heavily involved in fighting the Boers in South Africa, only the 2$^{nd}$ Bn, The Royal Welch Fusiliers, is available for the China expedition. All the other British Empire military units came from the Indian Army.*

The peasantry, debilitated by still greater imports of British opium, could be dispossessed without recourse to law and executed if they resisted. All in all, the outcome was a great success. Unless you were a Chinaman.

When the British withdrew, General Gaselee handed over to a German general, Alfred Graf von Waldersee. What happened over the following twelve months under his command is an enduring stain upon the reputations of France, Russia, Japan and his own country. At the time of the Second China War, in 1860, the sprawling 1000-year old Summer Palace had been stripped of its priceless treasures and its buildings burned to the ground. But much of China's immense artistic heritage had survived and that too was now pillaged. Every afternoon, in the British Legation compound, fortunes were made from the auctions of looted antiquities. They were "conducted in the most orderly manner".

All over northern China, the occupying armies were given *carte blanche* to indulge in an orgy of sadistic cruelty. Thousands of Chinese girls and women, having witnessed their fathers and husbands tortured, bayoneted or beheaded, killed themselves rather than be raped. Many thousands more failed to avoid that fate. The French general explained that the mass rapes were due to his soldiers' "Gallic gallantry". When some of the German troops were embarking for China, Kaiser Wilhelm II made a speech endorsing the atrocities and naming Attila the Hun as their inspiration. There is no evidence that British servicemen were guilty of such crimes, but the fact remains that Seymour and Gazelee had unwittingly kicked open the door for von Waldersee. Both were decent honourable men. Neither they nor the British sailors, marines and soldiers they commanded could have had any inkling of what was to come. However, with hindsight, the medal they were awarded does today arouse mixed feelings.

Now we leave the agony of northern China for the ordered calm of Whitehall. On 21 October 1904 - Trafalgar Day - the Admiralty building was struck by a hurricane. It came in the form of a short stocky man named John Arbuthnot Fisher. His pugnacious face gave fair warning: "I do not suffer fools gladly". This was the day he took up office as First Sea Lord and, after years of dissatisfaction with the state of the navy, he was at last in a position to do something about it.

He was not alone in believing that the fleet was "not ready to fight". Lord Tweedmouth and then Reginald McKenna, MP, held the political appointment of First Lord, both of them supporting Fisher's overdue reforms. They were followed in December 1911 by a third politician, Winston Churchill. Until recently he had voted against any increase in the defence budget, arguing that the money was better spent on social care projects at home. He changed his mind after studying reports of what was happening in German shipyards and after spending time at sea in ships of the Home Fleet. Appointed to the Admiralty by Prime Minister Herbert Asquith, he became Fisher's champion in squeezing out of the Treasury the money he needed for his modernisation programme.

Apart from possessing exceptional energy for a man of sixty-three, Fisher had the advantage of not belonging to the aristocratic officer class which dominated the higher levels of command. To the contrary, his origins could not have been more modest. Born in Ceylon, the son of an unsuccessful army officer turned even less successful coffee planter, one of a family of eleven children (seven survived childhood), he owed his promotions entirely to drive and ability.

To list all the reforms he drove through - often in the face of determined resistance - would fill a book. His best-remembered achievement was completion of HMS DREADNOUGHT, a ship which at her launch in 1906 instantly made obsolete every other battleship in the world. But the Fisher revolution went much further than that. He shone his light into every cob-webbed crevice of naval life, not caring whose sensitivities he might offend. A particular worry was the appallingly low standard of gunnery. Years of supporting colonial wars on land and conducting grand "spit and polish" prestige cruises had taken their toll. Fisher himself was a gunnery specialist. One problem was that most of his senior officers were still wedded to the age-old practice whereby each weapon was aimed and fired by its individual gun captain. The best of these were rewarded with the **Naval Good Shooting Medal** introduced (for ratings only) in 1902. It was not until 1912 that every capital ship was fitted with a central Director and fire control system. In this, Fisher had the informed technical support of Captain Percy Scott, RN, and Captain Frederic Dreyer, RN. After they and one or two others came forward with working designs, it was the Dreyer equipment and gunnery tables which prevailed. The loss of HMS HOOD in 1941 is attributed in part to the fact that, alone of all the navy's major units, hers were not updated during the inter-war refits.

While "Jackie" Fisher was fighting his Whitehall battles, Britain's diplomats were removing at least two of his potential causes for concern. The Anglo-Japanese Agreement of 1902 affirmed that the two governments had no conflicts of interest in the Far East. The Anglo-French *entente* of 1904 meant that, at long last, their two navies could stop glowering at each other. Imperial Russia had lost her Baltic Fleet

Images: The US Navy Historical Centre (USNHC)

*As professional heads of their respective navies, Fisher and von Tirpitz pioneered the construction of a radically new generation of warship. Each believed that a future conflict would involve heavily-gunned ships forming lines of battle, challenging each other in the style of Trafalgar. Their policies diverged only in respect of light cruisers (intended to protect British Empire trade routes) and Fisher's concept of the lightly armoured "hit and run" battlecruiser.*

*Authorised by the Admiralty in 1902, the **Naval Good Shooting Medal** was struck on its obverse with the bust of King Edward VII and on its reverse with the naked figure of King Neptune. By 1914 all major units had been fitted with centralised fire control systems and, with the wartime suspension of all shooting competitions, the medal then fell into abeyance.*

in 1905 in the Straits of Tsushima and her entire Pacific Fleet at the Japanese siege of Port Arthur in that same year. With the families of Tsar Nicholas II and King Edward VII so closely allied by blood, and with the Tsar having agreed a pact of non-belligerency in 1904, Russia's remaining ships offered no threat to Great Britain. It was the navy of Kaiser Wilhelm II which worried him. Under the direction of Grand Admiral Alfred von Tirpitz and with almost unlimited funding from Wilhelm's Treasury, German yards had been hard at work since 1898. The aim was to create, by 1917 or earlier, a modern fleet of forty-one battleships and twenty heavy cruisers. Fisher and von Tirpitz, without knowing it, were setting the scene for Jutland.

Meantime, there was other work to be done. There were still uncharted regions of the oceans to be investigated. The appointment of Admiralty Hydrographer dates from 1795 but his role was consolidated in 1905, under Fisher's direction, as the Hydrographic Office. Captain Robert Scott's first expedition to reach the South Pole led in 1904 to authorisation for **The Polar Medal** (to be fitted with appropriate date bars and struck in either silver or bronze). Then, and although the Zanzibar slave markets had been closed in 1873 (*vide* Part Three), illicit Arab *dhows* were still active in the Red Sea, Arabian Sea and Persian Gulf. Their business was slave-running, gun-running and piracy. It needed to be stopped, and that was a job for the navy. For the first time since 1840 (*vide* Part Two, Syria), this campaign was a purely naval affair, unrelated to land wars fought by the British or Indian Armies. There was a call, therefore, for a new dedicated **Naval General Service Medal** to be fitted with commemorative bars whenever appropriate. The first was **Persian Gulf 1909-1914.** Struck in silver, the medal was authorised on 6 August 1915, the Warrant restricting its issue "for service in minor naval war-like operations". It was never intended to recognise battles such as Coronel, Falklands, Heligoland Bight or Dogger Bank, each of them fought before its introduction. Even so, the medal did gain sixteen bars before, in 1962, it was superseded by the all-services **Campaign Service Medal.** We shall be visiting some of those bars in due course, but first we turn to the pivotal events of 1914.

"Jackie" Fisher retired in 1910 after six momentous years in office. His successor was sixty-eight year old Admiral of the Fleet Sir Arthur Wilson, VC. He had gained his **Victoria Cross** in a hand-to-hand fight with Arabs at the 1884 Battle of El Teb (the Egypt campaign). As a former Comptroller of the Navy (1897-1901), he had welcomed the Fisher reforms and was now brought back from retirement as guardian of that legacy. Of the twelve full Admirals on the Active List, half wanted to push forward with modernising the navy, half wanted to turn the clock back. Unfortunately, Wilson in his advancing years had become "abrasive, inarticulate and autocratic". He lasted little more than a year in the job before being replaced by Admiral Sir Francis Bridgeman. Although in poor health, this officer might have provided a steadying hand at the Admiralty helm if he and the newly appointed First Lord, Winston Churchill, could have worked together in harmony, but they could not. Bridgeman was forced out of office in just eleven months.

His successor was the affable but very competent Admiral the Prince Louis Alexander of Battenberg. In the Spring of 1914, with all Europe seemingly at peace

*When, at Kronstadt, Czar Nicholas presented Rear Admiral David Beatty and his officers with gifts to commemorate the visit, he was repeating a similar gesture of ten years earlier. In February 1904, off Inchon, Korea, the 5600 ton cruiser HMS Talbot (Captain Bagley RN) was caught up in the Russo-Japanese War. In the Battle of Chemulpo Bay, the Russian warships Varyag and Korietz were sunk by a Japanese fleet, the survivors being then rescued and repatriated by the Talbot. In appreciation, the Czar gave to the ship this magnificent inscribed punch bowl and ladle. Fashioned in the Pan-Slavic revival style, nearly two feet in length and weighing 263 ounces, it was crafted by the Court jeweller, Peter Karl Fabergé. Today owned by the RN Trophy Centre, it is occasionally displayed in the official residences of senior officers.*

following the termination of the two Balkan wars, Churchill and Battenberg obtained the agreement of the King and of the government that the time was ripe for gestures of friendship with Russia and with Germany. Accordingly, in June, the 1st Battlecruiser Squadron was despatched to the Baltic where it visited Riga and Revel under the command of Rear Admiral David Beatty. Flying his flag in HMS LION, he had with him the INDEFAGITABLE, NEW ZEALAND, PRINCESS ROYAL and QUEEN MARY escorted by the cruisers BLONDE and BOADICEA. They next came to anchor at the great naval port, Kronstadt. The Imperial Court and senior government ministers travelled the short distance north from the capital, St Petersburg, and over the following days there was much to-ing and fro-ing between ship and shore. The assembled warships were reviewed by Czar Nicholas II from the Imperial yacht, the opulent 5557 ton Danish-built STANDART. He was accompanied by the Czarina and their children (all murdered exactly four years later) and everyone had a splendid time.

Early on the morning of 23 June, 400 miles west from Kronstadt, the 2$^{nd}$ Battle Squadron entered the recently completed German naval base, Kiel. In command was the very experienced Vice Admiral Sir George Warrender in the 23,400 ton Dreadnought HMS KING GEORGE V. Additional to his flagship, the force consisted of the battleships AJAX, AUDACIOUS, CENTURION and NEPTUNE supported by three ships of the 2$^{nd}$ Light Cruiser Squadron, BIRMINGHAM, NOTTINGHAM and SOUTHAMPTON. As at Kronstadt, the Kiel visit featured a succession of official receptions, gala dinners, and the exchange of gifts. Ships' companies were encouraged over the following eleven days to mix, to compete in sporting events (the Germans won everything except the football) and generally come to know each other. There was intense interest amongst the sailors who had heard so much about each other's newest ships but who previously had not had an opportunity to make comparisons. Great Britain and Imperial Germany had never fought each other, either on land or at sea, hence there was no residual antipathy from former decades as there might have been with a visit to a French port. Indeed, *The Times* correspondent referred to the sailors "together making merry ashore".

Image: Reproduced courtesy of the Bundesarchive, Berlin

*A dramatic impression of the Kiel naval review, 25 June 1914. Progressing through the anchored lines of warships is the 6800-ton white-hulled Imperial yacht Hohenzollern (the second to bear the name). In the foreground, numbered U-1, is the kerosene-powered senior boat of the submarine training flotilla. Launched in 1906, it was already approaching obsolescence. Despite the overall welcoming warmth of the occasion, it is likely that von Tirpitz did not wish to expose to British eyes his latest diesel-powered designs.*

Emperor Wilhelm II arrived from Berlin on 24 June and next day processed along the lines of moored British and German ships in the Imperial yacht, the HOHENZOLLERN. Commanding his ships was "the father of the Imperial German Navy", Grand Admiral Alfred von Tirpitz in the FRIEDRICH DER GROSSE. Also present were the FRIEDRICH KARL, KAISER, KAISERIN, PRINZREGENT LUITPOLD and WITTELSBACH. The British Royal family was not represented either at Krondstadt or at Kiel. Even though the Czar and the Kaiser had the central roles at each, these were, according to *The Times*, "essentially naval occasions intended to display in a positive spirit the power and prestige of the respective fleets". As the paper's correspondent concluded on 5 July: "The visit to Kiel was a great success and gave proof of naval comradeship the world over and of German hospitality. The reception was warm and sincere ... it was not an empty convention ... but rather a symbol of brotherhood in arms. There were no politics at Kiel". Winston Churchill had been invited to attend, to meet Prince Henry of Prussia, Inspector General of the Navy, and his senior admirals. No doubt Winston wanted to be there, but Foreign Secretary Sir Edward Grey rightly feared the possible political ramifications.

On 4 July, his ships proceeding to sea for their voyage home, Warrender flashed to von Tirpitz a final signal: "friends in the past, friends forever". The general enthusiasm had been temporarily dampened when, on 28 June, news came through of the assassination in Sarajevo of the Archduke Franz Ferdinand of Austria-Hungary. While their ships carried them back across the North Sea, the more thoughtful amongst the Royal Navy's officers may have pondered the implications for themselves and for their service.

Seven weeks later the world as they knew it came to an end. Within little more than two years scores of them were dead. Of the ships mentioned above, the 23,000 ton AUDACIOUS (Captain C F Dampier, RN) was the first to be lost. On 27 October 1914, she struck a German mine off the coast of Northern Ireland. Twelve hours later she blew up but not a man was lost, the big White Star liner OLYMPIC and the light cruiser HMS LIVERPOOL having taken off the entire ship's company of 900 officers and men.

But then came the Battle of Jutland. At Kiel, the gunners had been kept busy firing 17-gun and 21-gun salutes to honour the arrival and departure of assorted dignitaries. At times, the harbour had been swathed in white smoke, hiding the ships from the onlookers ashore. All of that stopped after 4 August 1914, blank rounds replaced by live.

On 31 May 1916, the 28,000 ton QUEEN MARY (Captain C J Prowse, RN) was struck by plunging fire which penetrated deep into her hull and caused her to explode. Of the sixty officers and 1215 men on board, only three officers and six ratings survived. At almost the same time, the 18,750 ton INDEFATIGABLE (Captain C F Sowerby, RN) was likewise hit in a magazine and blew up. All but two of the 1012 ship's company were killed.

The 5400 ton cruiser NOTTINGHAM had had a narrow escape from being sunk on 28 August 1914 at the Battle of the Heligoland Bight, but her luck ran out on 19 August 1916. Part of a screening force for the Grand Fleet, she was struck by two

Image: Bundesarchive, Berlin

*Lead ship of her five-strong class, the 27,000 ton SMS Kaiser entered service in 1911. Her first major deployments were prestige cruises to Latin America and South Africa. They were intended to demonstrate Germany's global projection of sea power but at the same time to test the reliability of her British designed (Parsons) turbine engines. Conventional reciprocating engines provided the propulsion for the German navy's other ships. Just six months after the grand occasion at Kiel, she fired her first shots in anger. On 15/16 December 1914 she was part of the force which bombarded the east coast towns of Scarborough, Hartlepool and Whitby, escaping without damage. Next, heavily involved in the Battle of Jutland, she survived two hits by large calibre shells with only one man wounded out of her total complement of 1084 all ranks. Her end came on 21 June 1919 when the High Seas Fleet scuttled itself in the shallow waters of Scapa Flow. Salvaged in March 1929, the SMS Kaiser was taken to Rosyth and broken up for scrap.*

torpedoes fired from U-52 (*Kapitanleutnant* Hans Walther). Her sister-ship DUBLIN came to her aid but, thirty minutes later, a third torpedo from U-52 put Captain C B Miller's ship beyond salvation and she was abandoned. Thirty-eight men died in the explosions.

With one exception, the German ships which had given such a hospitable reception to Admiral Warrender's men at Kiel all survived the war years. The sole casualty was the 9000 ton armoured cruiser FRIEDRICH KARL. On 17 November 1914, operating with a large force in the Baltic Sea, she struck a Russian mine thirty miles west of Memel. Other ships managed to rescue her crew before she sank. After that, only the battleship WITTELSBACH was missing from the surrendered High Seas Fleet when, under the terms of the Armistice, it was escorted into the anchorage at Scapa Flow in November 1918. Outdated, she had been removed earlier from operational service and was broken up in Germany.

Together with seventy other warships, the FRIEDRICH DER GROSSE, KAISER, KAISERIN and PRINZREGENT LUITPOLD all went to the bottom when their crews opened the sea-cocks on 21 June 1919. Disfigured by years of weed and mud, they were raised and scrapped in the 1920s and 1930s. Did the Scapa Flow salvagemen understand what had once been? The bands and the bunting, the gleaming brasswork, the white-scrubbed decks, the immaculate guards of honour, the senior officers welcoming their guests aboard, all the pomp and glitter of June 1914 at Kiel? The memory lived on for those who had been part of that extraordinary episode but, for the rest, corrosion and decay removed all trace.

Although it was unimaginable at the time, Kronstadt and Kiel each marked the end of the old Europe. Only five years later, the aristocratic governance of Imperial Russia and of Imperial Germany vanished under a tide of social revolution. Nicholas was dead, Wilhelm exiled to Holland. The last of the Ottomans were gone, Franz Josef's Austria Hungary dismantled. Having come to the aid of the Allies in 1917, the United States of America withdrew into an isolation from international affairs which persisted until 7 December 1941.

The century of "Pax Britannica" may have ended in 1914, but in the 1920s and 1930s the British Empire alone provided continuity and stability in a re-shaped world. At its head was our Royal family, quietly adapting itself to the radical changes in society. Across the seven oceans, the latent power of that Empire was symbolised by the ships of the Royal Navy and of the Royal Australian, Canadian, New Zealand and Indian Navies. How the world then began to change once again will be examined in Part Six (1914-1939).

## Part Six - 1914 to 1939

PIP, SQUEAK AND WILFRED. Never before or since have three such emotive medals been labeled in this way. They were characters in a long-running cartoon strip first published in *The Daily Mail* in 1919. The ex-soldiers who gave those names to their awards, when they received them after "the Great War", had gone through all sorts of hell to earn them. Many had little reverence for such things. The medals were, of course, the familiar "trio" of **The 1914-15 Star**, **The British War Medal,** and the British version of **The Allied Victory Medal.**

Known unofficially as the **"Mons Star"**, there was a fourth medal in the series. Identical in design to the 1914-15 version, it incorporated at its centre the date symbols **Aug Nov 1914**. Of this pattern, 378,000 were issued. They went to men who had fought in August and September at Mons, Le Cateau, the Marne and the Aisne with the British Expeditionary Force but also to the largely forgotten soldiers of the Indian Corps. Ill-equipped for the cold and wet of the Western Front, they fought with enormous bravery in October and November in three crucial early battles - La Bassee, First Messines and Armentieres. In combination, those were seven of the major actions which halted the German Army's drive towards the Channel coast and thereby started four years of static trench warfare.

Soldiers who that autumn had served under fire rather than along the lines of communication were issued also with a slim brass bar sewn onto the watered-silk ribbon. It was impressed with the dates **5$^{th}$ Aug 22$^{nd}$ Nov 1914**. When Kaiser Wilhelm II sneeringly described the British Expeditionary Force as "this contemptible little army", our soldiers gleefully seized upon his remark and named themselves "the Old Contemptibles". The "Mons Star and bar" is still today identified mainly with those Regulars and Territorials of the first five Divisions to land in France, thousands of whom did not survive to celebrate "the Christmas truce" of 1914.

However, there are rare and even more collectable exceptions to those predominantly British Army awards. A limited number of the **1914 Star** was awarded to certain officers and men of the Royal Naval Air Service (RNAS) and the Royal Marines Light Infantry (RMLI). On 27 August, at the order of the First Lord of the Admiralty Winston Churchill, an ill-prepared RMLI brigade was despatched to assist the Belgian Army in its ultimately failed attempt to keep the Germans out of Antwerp. On the same day, a small number of RNAS personnel commenced operations along the Flanders coast under the buccaneering Commander C R Samson, RN.

On 27 August he led the RNAS Eastchurch Wing across the Channel to act as airborne Intelligence gathering eyes for the army. Soon after, with the aid of a few friends who owned Rolls Royce motor cars, he formed an impromptu RNAS

Armoured Car Section which conducted reconnaissance patrols on the ground for the same purpose. He and his men qualified - together with the marines - for the so-called **"Mons Star"**.

With those exceptions, **"Pip, Squeak and Wilfred"** were given to every sailor and marine who had been on the strength of an operational unit during the first phase of the war. Men who joined later, after 31 December 1915, received **The British War Medal** and **The Allied Victory Medal** without the bronze Star. This pairing was nick-named **"Mutt and Jeff"**, two characters featured in a popular American cartoon series dating from 1907 and syndicated to several British newspapers. Distribution of the medals did not commence until the early 1920s, hence great numbers of the men named on the reverse or rim never knew they had been rewarded in this way. Or in *any* way, even. Long dead, their medals were delivered in small cardboard boxes to their next-of-kin by the local postman.

Approximately 2,366,000 **1914-15 Stars** were issued. Of these, 283,500 went to personnel who had served with an operational unit of the Royal Navy, Royal Naval Reserve, Royal Naval Volunteer Reserve, Royal Marines Light Infantry or Royal Marines Artillery before 31 December 1915. It was awarded also to seamen who served under special terms of engagement in merchant ships operating under Admiralty control (the Fleet "oilers", for example). They qualified additionally for the bronze **Mercantile Marine Medal** (of which more later, *vide* Part Nine "A").

When, shortly after the outbreak of war, General Kitchener appealed to the nation for volunteers, it was the needs of the army which he had in mind, not the navy. Under the direction of "Jackie" Fisher, the Royal Navy had expanded to the point at which it already had in its inventory most of the larger ships (and therefore the sailors to man them) needed for this new conflict. To build a ship and train its officers and ratings could take months or years. An infantryman could be trained in weeks, a new battalion formed at the stroke of a pen. By 1918 the British Army consisted almost entirely of valiant "civilians in uniform". The navy, by contrast, continued in the main to be a full-time professional force throughout. But, whether they wore khaki or navy blue, all had shared the perils of the "war to end all wars" and thereby rightly qualified equally for a "trio" or a "pair" as described above.

This article will look at some of the less familiar activities of the Royal Navy during those tumultuous years. All of the major engagements - Coronel, (first) Falklands, Heligoland Bight, Dogger Bank, Jutland - have been described many times in the past. This author chooses to open with Gallipoli. For the people of Australia and New Zealand, it is a name which still today evokes great pride in their forebears who fought on that barren peninsula in 1915. Just as Canada later "came of age" on Vimy Ridge, so did their countries emerge from Gallipoli with a distinct sense of national identity. But first we must set the scene for the late summer and autumn of 1914.

On the eastern front, Imperial Russia is losing the fight with the armies of Imperial Germany. To prevent a collapse, France and Britain must help the Russians with war materials. The only warm water access to their ports is through the Mediterranean and the Black Sea. This means free passage through the Dardanelles channel to the inland Sea of Marmora and then up through the Straits of

Bosphorus. The Germans have serious ambitions in the Middle East. For years they have been influential in Turkey's internal affairs. Beginning in 1888, they have extended their railway system so that it can carry freight (and troops) almost without interruption from Berlin to Baghdad. A German military mission headed by General Liman von Sanders is training the Turkish Army in the use of the artillery and machine-guns provided by Berlin.

The ordinary people of Turkey might fear Russia, but certainly not the British or the French. After all, we propped them up in the Crimean War. However, in July 1914, the British suddenly become very unpopular indeed. Their government has asked them to contribute to a fund for the purchase, from Great Britain, of two new battleships. As a matter of national patriotic pride they have responded by donating their personal savings. Both of these 27,000 ton ships are nearing completion in Vickers yards at Barrow in Furness where British-trained Turkish Navy officers and key ratings are "standing by". The First Lord of the Admiralty is Winston Churchill. As the war clouds gather over Europe, he instructs Vickers to break the contract. The ships are instead transferred to the Royal Navy as HMS ERIN and HMS AGINCOURT. It is a huge slap in the face for the Turks.

Adding to their anger is the inconsistency of Churchill's decision. To them, it is a betrayal. Following in the wake of the 1908 "young Turks" revolution, the British have maintained in Constantinople a permanent Naval Mission headed successively by Vice Admirals Sir Douglas Gamble, Hugh Pigot Williams and Arthur Limpus. Their job is helping the Turks to modernise their much neglected navy. It is through their negotiating skills that Vickers have won the battleship contract and an additional contract to build a new naval dockyard for the Turkish Navy at Ismid. To do so, these three officers have beaten off fierce competition from Krupps and other German industrial concerns. They have already, in previous years, persuaded the Turks to purchase forty-odd lesser warships from British yards

Even more importantly, in the diplomatic context, they are accredited as "naval advisors" to the Turkish government which, in 1912, appoints Arthur Limpus as Commander-in-Chief of the Turkish Navy. As a gesture of trust and confidence, it

*HMS Erin about to launch a kite balloon. She was intended to be named Reşadiye. The design was based on that of HMS King George V, but with some features of the Iron Duke.*

could not be bettered. He holds this post until 2 September 1914 when his accreditation is withdrawn and, together with his staff, he leaves Constantinople for Malta.

Despite his two years of intimate experience of Turkish affairs at the highest level, Vice Admiral Limpus is immediately appointed Superintendent of the Malta Naval Dockyard. This is surely a very strange move by Battenberg and Churchill. It would have made much better sense to bring Limpus back to London and keep him there for a few months. He is uniquely qualified to tell Whitehall about the individual personalities within the disunited Turkish leadership and to advise the Foreign Office how those men might possibly react to any particular set of circumstances. At this critical time, he should be updating the Admiralty's knowledge of the Turkish Navy and its capabilities. Instead, he is sent to manage the dockyard in Valetta. There he replaces an officer we shall meet again later, Rear Admiral Sackville Carden.

At this point another British Vice Admiral appears on the scene. He is Sir Archibald Berkeley Milne, commanding the twenty-seven ships of our Mediterranean Fleet. On 4 August, war with Germany now declared, the Admiralty orders him to hunt down the only two German warships then present in the Mediterranean. They are the battle-cruiser GOEBEN and the light cruiser BRESLAU. Neither Milne nor anyone else can know it, but how he responds to this order will shape dramatically the course of this new war and, in the longer term, the political landscape of the entire Middle East. It is necessary, therefore, to consider his fitness for the task.

Archibald Milne first appeared in these articles as the youthful naval *aide* to Lord Chelmsford in the 1879 Zulu War (*vide* Part Four). In time he came to be the type of "social officer" Fisher had tried but failed to unhorse during his 1904-1910 tenure as First Sea Lord (*vide* Part Five). Milne owed his Baronetage to his father's services in 1816 at the Battle of Algiers. Flying his flag in HMS IMPREGNABLE, Vice Admiral Sir Alexander Milne served there as second-in-command to Lord Exmouth. For his heraldic motto he chose *Tam Marte Quam Arte* which signifies, oddly but perhaps prophetically: "As much by war as by skill". By the time he died (in 1897), he was an Admiral of the Fleet and a retired First Naval Lord. Much was expected, therefore, of his son.

In the event, Archibald proved to be a reliable and competent officer and he rose steadily through the commissioned ranks to Captain. Then, in 1891, he made what today we might describe as "a smart career move". He accepted command of the Royal Yacht OSBORNE (the second to bear that name). His contemporaries tended to avoid such sinecure appointments, fearing they might lose contact with "the real navy". The appointment usually went to Commanders, not Captains. However, with Europe at peace and the navy engaged in little more than "spit and polish" prestige cruises, the surest way of achieving flag rank was by patronage. Her Majesty's Yacht OSBORNE offered that opportunity.

He was tailor-made for it - tall, handsome, charming, attractive to women, at thirty-six still a bachelor. He had seen the face of war in Zululand (where he was wounded at the Battle of Ulundi) and then in the 1882 Egypt conflict. He had

*"Arky-barky", Rear Admiral Sir Archibald Milne, photographed aboard HMY Victoria & Albert III by the admiring Queen Alexandra. Following the Goeben and Breslau fiasco, he received no further sea-going employment. His second-in-command, Rear Admiral Sir Ernest Troubridge, was tried but exonerated by Court Martial. Milne himself, with indirect support from the king, was likewise officially cleared of all blame but without the privilege of a Court Martial. He died in 1938, age eighty-four.*

medals on his chest and a fund of tales to tell over the dinner-table. Fairly or otherwise, his hobbies were reported as "collecting rare orchids and entertaining royal ladies". The Royal family was entranced by him, the future Queen Alexandra calling him "Arky-barky". Astonishingly, Queen Victoria retained him in OSBORNE for nine years. Two years was the normal tour of duty for a "yottie" officer. Reluctant to let him go after Victoria died, King Edward VII made him an honorary *Aide de Camp* and dubbed him a Knight Commander of the Order of the Bath.

By 1900 the Admiralty was probably asking Buckingham Palace "please can we have our officer back?". Queen Victoria consented to his release and he was given his first significant command with the "real navy". She was not just any old ship, she was one of the newest to join the Mediterranean Fleet. Two years earlier, Fairfields of Govan had completed the ninth (and last) of the 5600 tons ECLIPSE Class armoured cruisers. She was HMS VENUS. The current C-in-C Mediterranean was Admiral Sir "Jackie" Fisher, future professional head of the navy. During the two years he had Milne under his command, Fisher had ample opportunity to form an opinion of his capabilities. As we shall see later, it was not favourable.

It is reasonable to conclude that in 1900 there was royal influence again at play. Milne could have been given command of a less modern ship on a distant Station - China, the West Indies, or in some other region where - out of sight, out of mind - a career might too easily fade away. Instead he gained an almost brand-new ship in Britain's most important Fleet. A "tick in the box" in his *curriculum vitae*, it was soon completed. In 1903, he was recalled to service with the Royal family as Commodore and soon after as "Flag Officer Commanding His Majesty's Yachts". This was a new title having no precedent. The job was hardly demanding. Apart from OSBORNE, there were only four other royal yachts in service at various times during those years. The smallest were ELFIN (97 tons) and ALBERTA (390 tons). The largest were VICTORIA & ALBERT II (2470 tons), and the palatial VICTORIA & ALBERT III (4700 tons).

In 1906 he was again parted from the elegant life of the Court when appointed Second-in-Command Atlantic Fleet and then commander of the $2^{nd}$ Division, Home Fleet. With hindsight, it would surely have been helpful to him if at around this time he had been ordered to attend one of the war studies courses at the Royal Naval College, Greenwich. Commenced in 1901, they taught all aspects of naval strategy and related subjects to officers (including flag officers) being groomed for greater things. The opportunity was missed, overtaken by events.

The Royal family did not lose contact with their favourite naval officer. In 1912, with an exceptional gesture of friendship, the recently crowned "sailor king" George V granted him the highest honour within his personal gift, Knight Grand Cross of the Royal Victorian Order. In that same year, Milne was promoted full Admiral and this brings us to a turning point in history. A new C-in-C of that rank was needed for the Mediterranean Fleet. An unusually demanding post, it required an understanding of the history, cultures and politics of the thirteen diverse countries sharing the coastlines of that land-locked sea. Diplomacy and an understanding of strategy were as important as experience in seamanship and leadership. Before the introduction of the under-sea communication cable network in the 1860s and Marconi's system of wireless telegraphy in the early 1900s, our Admirals were often required to exercise their own judgment and then hope Their Lordships and the Foreign Office would approve what they had done.

The navy at various times operated numerous Fleets and Squadrons around the world - amongst them the Pacific, China, East Indies, Channel, Home, Atlantic, North Americas and West Indies - but the Mediterranean was always the "plum" job, the height of ambition for every senior Admiral before he finally settled ashore. Going back to 1757, Admiral Sir Charles Saunders was the first in a succession of fifty-one officers appointed C-in-C Mediterranean. All, without exception, had previously commanded a Fleet or a Squadron, had served as a Sea Lord, or had held a senior independent appointment. Typically, Admiral Sir Edmund Poe commanded the East Indies Station and then the Cape of Good Hope Station before being rewarded with the Mediterranean in 1910.

Before him, between 1908 and 1910, the Fleet was commanded by Admiral the Honourable Sir Assheton Curzon-Howe, a high-born officer enjoying close ties with the Royal family. He was the paternal great-grandson of Admiral Lord Howe, hero of the 1794 battle recorded as "the Glorious First of June" (*vide* Part Two). Queen Victoria and King Edward VII each in turn appointed him as their Naval *Aide de Camp*, and he had easy access to the highest in the land. This did not mean that Curzon-Howe was anything other than a very professional officer. Before moving to the Mediterranean he commanded the North America Station and then the West Indies Station.

Just four weeks after arriving on Malta in late 1908 he was faced with immediate decisions regarding his new command. Reports were coming through of a major earthquake under the Straits of Messina and an immense loss of life along the adjoining coastlines. He immediately did all the right things, made the right decisions, ensuring not only that many lives were saved but also that the Royal Navy would emerge from the disaster with its prestige even more enhanced. That story is told in detail in the book *Angels in Blue Jackets, The Navy at Messina, 1908*, by Roger Perkins and J W Wilson (Picton Publishing, Chippenham, 1985).

Admiral Poe retired from active service, age 63, in June 1912. This coincided with the arrival on stage of the other principal character in the Gallipoli drama. After an astonishingly swift rise from freshman MP to Home Secretary in only ten years, 38 year-old Winston Churchill was moved from the Home Office to the Admiralty as First Lord. It was he who decided that Sir Berkeley Milne was the right man to succeed Poe in the Mediterranean. According to published sources: "the views of the King were taken into account". Given all that had gone before, we may be certain that Milne's appointment was, in fact, the direct result of noises emanating from Buckingham Palace.

Although he had retired two years earlier, "Jackie" Fisher had not lost his taste for a fight. When told the news he protested to Churchill that to give Milne command in the Mediterranean was "a gross betrayal of the navy". Presumably he had three considerations in mind - Milne's lack of senior independent command experience, his unchallenging twelve years (total) of courtly duties in the Royal Yachts, and the rapidly escalating crisis in Greece, Turkey and the Balkans. His protest was ignored. Any further objection would have come from the current professional head of the navy, Admiral Sir Francis Bridgeman. However, this was precisely the time when Bridgeman's various disputes with Churchill were reaching their climax. His opinions counted for nothing. On 9 December 1912, after less than a year in office, he was replaced by Admiral the Prince Louis of Battenberg.

So friendship with the King and his family, combined with Churchill's ingrained deference to royal wishes, steered Milne into a role for which, through absolutely no fault of his own, he was totally unprepared. He was given his new job at a time when, on the face of it, the Mediterranean region was, like the rest of the world, at peace. The impression was illusory. All the ingredients for a global conflict were already in place before his arrival on Malta in June 1912. Storm warnings began to fly four months later when, in October, Serbia, Greece, Montenegro and Bulgaria - united as The Balkan League - went to war with Turkey. This was by any standard a very big war. Tens of thousands of soldiers were killed in battles on land, inconclusive actions were fought at sea. The Turks were beaten, all their continental European territories occupied and shared out amongst the victors. Although sympathetic to the Turks, the British government steered well clear of that First Balkan War, just as it did when Bulgaria and Greece fought each other in the Second Balkan War eighteen months later.

It might be supposed that Sir Berkeley Milne's Mediterranean Fleet could have been involved in those conflicts, if only peripherally. There were naval clashes in the Aegean and around a peninsula whose name - Gallipoli - would soon become painfully familiar in England, Australia and New Zealand. The Turks encroached

*The dissolution of the old order in Europe began in 1912, not 1914. Three seminal decisions were made in that year. Winston Churchill was given unrestricted political control of the Royal Navy, King George V persuaded Churchill to gift the Mediterranean Fleet to his friend Sir Berkeley Milne, Foreign Secretary Sir Edward Grey failed to adequately warn Churchill and Milne of the pressures building in the Balkans and their potential threat to British interests. The editor of the weekly Punch magazine was more perceptive. Published on 2 October 1912, just four months after Milne replaced Admiral Poe, this sketch gives prominence to the leaders of Russia, Germany and Austria-Hungary. Great Britain and France are still at this stage discreetly in the background, but their costly Gallipoli and Salonika campaigns are not far away.*

even further into the Royal Navy's back yard by sending the Armstrong Whitworth-built 4000 ton cruiser HAMIDIYE (Captain Rauf Bey) to conduct a commercial blockade down the Levant and Sinai coastlines as far south as Port Said, then through the Suez Canal and into the Red Sea. Admiral Milne would have been bound to react if she had interfered with British-registered merchantmen, but prudently she did not.

The Balkan wars and their aftermath boiled over at Sarajevo on 28 June 1914. The assassination of the Archduke Franz Ferdinand by a Bosnian Serb nationalist,

Gavrilo Princip, soon fired a salvo of declarations of war by all the major European powers. Great Britain's war with Germany was declared on 4 August, then with Turkey on 5 November. Without access to official archives it is not known how much advice or information was being fed through to Admiral Milne from Whitehall during those final darkening weeks but, whatever it was, the evidence indicates that he did not understand its relevance to him or to his Fleet. By then he had gained two years of experience as C-in-C, time enough to think about what was happening in the Balkans, in Greece and in Turkey, time enough to weigh his options. He could not know what was about to happen, but a more thoughtful officer would have ordered his staff to draw up a set of "what if" contingency plans

The Mediterranean Sea has just three points of entry and exit - the Straits of Gibraltar, the Suez Canal and the Dardanelles. Trapped within that sea was Rear Admiral Wilhelm Souchon with his two lonely warships, GOEBEN and BRESLAU. An officer with a strong sense of initiative, Souchon had anticipated the outbreak of war by placing his small force off the coast of French Algeria. He immediately bombarded the French Army's embarkation docks at Bone and Philipeville. It was a good start but, sooner or later, with so few coaling stations open to him, he might be forced either to attempt a breakout into the Atlantic or seek refuge in a neutral port. The Straits of Gibraltar were probably too tightly guarded, he could not use the Canal and, if he found sanctuary in a port in the upper Adriatic, Milne had more than enough ships to seal its southern end. Souchon's only option, therefore, was to head for neutral Turkey where his nation had for so long been embedded.

That same possibility did not occur to Admiral Milne. On an earlier occasion, when asked by one of his officers what he thought about a particular point, he had replied: "They pay me to be an Admiral, they don't pay me to think". He now proved his point by sending his ships on a wild goose chase which, although there were brief encounters off Tunisia, Sicily and Greece, allowed Souchon to steam 1600 miles eastwards to drop anchor at Constantinople on the afternoon of 10 August. Milne's thinking may not have been particularly clear at the best of times, but it was not helped by a succession of contradictory reports and orders being signalled to him by Winston Churchill.

Wilhelm Souchon's unexpected arrival caused total consternation in the Turkish Cabinet. The new democratic government formed in 1908 was still trying to recover from the enormous financial and human cost of the First Balkan War. It had no wish to get involved in yet another war. With anybody. The exception was the War Minister, Enver Pasha. He was furious with Churchill's cancellation of the Vickers contract and his anger was stoked by the German Ambassador, Baron Hans von Langenheim.

Events might have taken a different turn if the British government had been more strongly represented at the diplomatic level. During the simmering years between 1908 and 1913, our Ambassador to the Ottoman Empire was Sir Gerard Lowther. According to his biographer: "He is known for distributing anti-Semitic texts during his time in Constantinople, playing a crucial role in the spread of Arab anti-Semitism". Ensuring that the naive Admiral Milne was fully briefed would

Images courtesy of the Bundesarchiv

*The light cruiser SMS Breslau (renamed Midilli), one of the two German ships that brought Turkey into the war and which later saw much action in the Black Sea. She also contributed in 1915 this contingent of seamen to fight ashore on Gallipoli. In January 1918, she and the Goeben (renamed Yavuz) broke out of the Dardanelles to interrupt the convoys supplying British forces in Palestine and Salonika. Their surprise attack on the Aegean island of Imbros was rewarded with the sinking of the 4500-ton monitor HMS Raglan and the 540-ton M28. The German admiral came to grief when his ships ran into a minefield off Mudros. The ex-Breslau sank with heavy loss of life after striking five mines, the ex-Goeben was badly damaged and beached.*

have been a more helpful use of his time.

Lowther completed his five years tour of duty in 1913. There was then a hiatus while Sir George Barclay, our Ambassador to Romania, represented the United Kingdom at long range from Bucharest. The new British Ambassador in Constantinople, the last to take office before Britain's declaration of war on 5 November 1914, was Sir Louis du Pan Mallet. His appointment caused surprise at the time because he had no previous personal experience of Balkan and Turkish affairs.

Summing up, the Admiralty was in the grip of a thrusting young politician having no naval background, the Mediterranean Fleet was under command of an officer promoted far beyond his capabilities, the British Embassy was occupied by a diplomat still settling into his new job. The subsequent complex fast-moving events are best described in diary form.

Under international law, Turkey cannot allow the German ships to remain in her territorial waters under their own flag so they are transferred to Turkish government ownership. Rear Admiral Souchon replaces the British Vice Admiral Arthur Limpus as C-in-C of the Turkish Navy. His ships fly the Turkish flag and his sailors are issued with the *fez* (a gesture which challenges the view that Germans do not possess a sense of humour). Gilbert and Sullivan could not have imagined a more farcical story-line.

On 20 October, without the sanction of the full Turkish Cabinet, Souchon takes a flotilla of Turkish warships north into the Black Sea. They are led by GOEBEN and BRESLAU. They bombard five Russian ports including the naval bases of Odessa and Sebastapol. The Turkish government is deeply dismayed. It immediately apologises and there is talk of reparations.

In London there is disarray in the higher ranks. Battenberg had succeeded Bridgeman as First Sea Lord in December 1912, proving himself an able administrator but now his health is deteriorating under the impact of Churchill's impulsive fire-eating ways and the disgraceful hate campaign in the British popular Press. Despite his adoption of British nationality when he was fourteen, despite his forty-six years of dedicated service to the Royal Navy, the editors are stirring up public hysteria based upon his Germanic family name and lingering German accent. In October, only three months into the war, he feels obliged to resign. He is replaced by 74 year-old "Jackie" Fisher, recalled from retirement to sort out the mess.

Meantime, Milne is returned to England. The Admiralty issues a series of public statements - presumably at the prompting of the King - to the effect that he is not to blame for the escape of the GOEBEN and the BRESLAU, but he receives no further employment in the navy before retiring in 1919. The post of C-in-C Mediterranean Fleet will remain vacant until August 1917 (it is the first time since 1757 that no officer has been appointed to it). Placed in charge of the Dardanelles operation is 57 year-old Rear Admiral Sackville Carden. So far, this officer has followed an unremarkable career - service in the 1882 Egypt campaign and the 1897 Benin expedition, successive commands between 1902 and 1909 of four different pre-Dreadnought battleships, two years on half-pay leave when he married his second

*A photograph taken in late 1914, recording a key juncture in the relationship between the youthful Churchill and fatherly Fisher. The former has held office as First Lord since 1911, the latter is returning to the Admiralty as First Sea Lord after four years in retirement. In tandem, they will co-operate to good effect until May 1915 when, in the wake of the Gallipoli disaster, they go their separate ways.*

wife, then a brief spell at the Admiralty. For the past two years he has been employed as Rear Admiral Superintendent of the Malta Dockyard. That, broadly, is the sum total of his experience. For reasons unknown, Churchill decides that he is the very chap to take charge and promotes him to Vice Admiral. Just as he did too often in his long political career, Churchill puts his money on a willing but unfit horse.

On 3 November, Carden obeys Churchill's order to bombard the forts guarding the entrance to the Dardanelles Straits. Dozens of Turkish and German gunners are killed. Our excuse is the need to pursue the two German warships. It is an event of the first magnitude. It will make, irreversibly, a determined enemy of a country which for decades has been our friend. Turkey has declared for the Central Powers on 29 October, but the British Cabinet does not declare war on Turkey until 5 November. That is two days *after* Carden's attack on the forts. To what extent has Churchill consulted his Cabinet colleagues before despatching his fateful signal to Vice Admiral Carden? Was there still time for the sort of diplomatic jockeying which might have avoided all-out conflict? As events unfold, it will condemn the Allies to fighting the ensuing four major Middle East campaigns - Gallipoli, Mesopotamia, Palestine and Salonika. The likely explanation is that all eyes in London are focused on Belgium and France where the British Expeditionary Force has been fighting for its life, first at Mons and Le Cateau, then on the Marne and the

Aisne. Churchill, it would seem, is given a free hand in the Mediterranean. If Turkey had been left in amicable peace as a neutral or, better still, had been encouraged to become an active ally, the history of the 20$^{th}$ century would be very different.

Carden is ordered by Churchill to renew the assault. The French and their navy have their own ambitions in the Middle East. They refuse to be left out of the adventure. Carden, who had never previously commanded at sea anything more than elderly battleships now finds himself commanding a combined Anglo-French fleet of forty-one warships, six submarines and twenty-one trawlers fitted as minesweepers. The French commander is 59 year-old Rear Admiral Emile-Paul-Aimable Guepratte flying his flag in the 12,700 ton battleship SUFFREN. This officer has a well-rounded background of service in European waters and the Far East.

Carden intends to attack on 19 February and informs Churchill that he "will be in Constantinople within a fortnight". However, the first British attack, three months earlier, has alerted the Turks to weaknesses in their defences. The fortified shore artillery is reinforced with twenty-odd new mobile batteries. The Germans hurriedly supply them with twenty-six sea mines which they lay within the Dardanelles narrows (more than 300 will eventually be laid).

In the Far East, in 1904, offensive mine-laying by both the Russians and the Japanese at besieged Port Arthur has already demonstrated this weapon's unique destructive power. In combination, the Turkish mines and guns form a hangman's noose into which Carden, at the insistence of Churchill, obligingly places his head. For nearly a week the Allied ships push and shove, but it gets them nowhere. The shellfire is bad enough, but it is the mines which will cause the most destruction (especially after our civilian-manned trawlers unsurprisingly head back to the open sea).

Several ships are damaged before the attack is abandoned. On 15 March 1915, under the immense pressure of his unique circumstances, Carden has a breakdown and his ordered home. He will see no more active service. Granted a knighthood (KCMG) a year later, he will be permitted to retire in 1917 with the rank of full Admiral.

Carden's replacement is his Second-in-Command, Vice Admiral John de Robeck. Three days after taking over, on 18 March, de Robeck makes another attempt but he too is repulsed. He has ordered Rear Admiral Guepratte to take the lead. The French battleship BOUVET (12,000 tons) hits a mine and sinks in three minutes. Six men survive from the 670 on board. Also sunk are two other French battleships, IRRESISTABLE and OCEAN. At the same time, GAULOIS and Guepratte's flagship SUFFREN are badly damaged. They are followed into the same minefield by the Royal Navy's battleships IRRESISTIBLE and OCEAN (by odd coincidence they share the same names as their French counterparts). They too are lost and HMS INFLEXIBLE is badly damaged. John de Robeck expresses his admiration for the gallantry of Guepratte's officers, but the French squadron has effectively been wiped out. By the end of that disastrous day, the two Allies have for the time-being lost the main part of their shore bombardment capability.

*It is 18 March 1915, and the 15,000-ton HMS Irresistible has just struck a mine in the Dardanelles narrows. Smoke rises from her shattered rear section where 150 men have died in the explosion. Six hundred and thirty others are rescued before their ship, devoid of power, drifts inshore to be shattered and sunk by Turkish shore batteries*

Finally it had become obvious (as it should have done at the outset) that the Anglo-French fleet could never force a passage as long as both shores of the Dardanelles were in Turkish hands. The agreed solution was to mount a French amphibious assault on the mainland (Asiatic) shore and a British landing on the southern tip of the Gallipoli peninsula. And, by now, we had the troops to do the job. The all-volunteer Australian and New Zealand Army Corps (the ANZAC) was under training in Egypt in preparation for the Western Front. They were joined by regiments of the Indian Army and the British 29th Division. All were assigned to the expedition forming under the command of General Sir Ian Hamilton. What happened when his soldiers struggled ashore in the teeth of the Turkish machine-guns is a story too well known. A pilot flying low over Cape Helles reported: "The sea is red with blood thirty yards out from the beach".

That disaster, and all the others which followed it until we were forced to evacuate nine miserable months later (having lost 44,000 French and British Empire dead) is another story. It is enough to say that the navy did the very best it could to help the army. When Hamilton ran short of troops, it even gave him the unique 63rd (Royal Naval) Division - 11,000 seamen and marines hurriedly trained to fight as conventional infantry. From offshore, de Robeck's ships provided constant heavy gunfire support, the fall of shot reported by his Royal Naval Air Service pilots. When Turkish field artillery on the headland at Gaba Tepe was inflicting casualties on the beachhead, the captain of HMS BACCHANTE took the risk of placing his

12,000 ton ship just 600 yards from the cliffs and blasting the defenders with his 9.2 inch guns. If, by failing to catch GOEBEN and BRESLAU the navy had brought Turkey into the war as our unwilling enemy, it was certainly not failing now. And the Turks and the Germans were determined to do something about it.

One of the ships stationed off Morto Bay (Cape Helles) was the 13,000 ton pre-Dreadnought HMS GOLIATH. In the early hours of 13 May, in thick fog, *Kapitanleutnant* Rudolf Firle in the Turkish-German manned destroyer MUAVENET-I-MILLIYE slipped skillfully into the anchorage and launched three torpedoes into Captain Thomas Shelford's ship. Weeks later, Firle was presented with the Iron Class 1$^{st}$ Class. Years later, the postman delivered to their next-of-kin the cardboard boxes containing the **"Pip, Squeak and Wilfreds"** impressed with the names of the 570 GOLIATH men (including Shelford) who went down with her. That was not the end of it.

*Kapitanleutnant* Otto Hersing was still at the beginning of his extraordinary career when, early in 1915, he brought his U-21 into the Mediterranean. On 4 September 1914 he had made the first successful torpedo attack of the war by sinking the light cruiser HMS PATHFINDER off the Firth of Forth. His job now was to seek out the big British ships operating around the tip of Gallipoli. They were not hard to find. On 25 May he spotted the 12,000 ton HMS TRIUMPH anchored off Gaba Tepe, her anti-torpedo net booms spread and the destroyer CHELMER watching over her. Shortly after noon, both ships saw the wake of Hersing's periscope and opened fire, but a single torpedo somehow evaded the nets and struck TRIUMPH squarely amidships in a coal bunker. Even though her watertight doors were all clipped shut, she flooded and ten minutes later rolled over. It is to the credit of her officers and senior rates that only seventy-three lives were lost, 500 survivors being picked up by CHELMER.

With a U-boat lurking in the area, the navy began a massive hunt for it but, at this stage in the war, our ships had no effective means of detecting underwater targets. Aware of that deficiency, Otto Hersing boldly returned forty-eight hours later to sink TRIUMPH's sister-ship, HMS MAJESTIC. She too was anchored offshore, her anti-torpedo net booms spread, bulkhead doors shut tight, tucked in amongst a crowd of transport ships. Her task was that of gunfire support for the troops at "W" Beach. Having recharged his batteries overnight, Hersing brought U-21 at first light through the tangle of anchored merchantmen until he was only 400 yards from the massive bulk of his target. As before, his periscope was seen by alert lookouts and MAJESTIC opened fire, but it was too late. Two torpedoes struck home and, seven minutes later, 12,000 tons of British metal plunged to the seabed. Captain H F G Talbot, RN, survived along with, surprisingly, all but forty of his ship's company. As reward for his exceptional skill and determination, Otto Hersing received his country's highest award, the *Pour le Merite*. He survived the war having completed twenty-one patrols and sinking 145 Allied ships.

If the news of Firle's and Hersing's successes prompted celebration in Berlin and Constantinople, it caused profound dismay in London. "Jackie" Fisher had never been happy with the Gallipoli adventure. Having quarrelled with Winston Churchill, he resigned on 15 May. Two days later, Prime Minister Henry Asquith's

*Severe losses forced Admiral de Robeck to withdraw all his heavy units in May 1915 but his submarines continued to penetrate into the Sea of Marmara. The approach passage through the Dardanelles was made doubly hazardous by mines and by the great press of water passing through from the Black Sea to the Mediterranean. It was this powerful current which, on 17 April, drove E15 on to rocks under the guns of a Turkish battery. Her captain, Lieutenant Commander Theodore Brodie RN, was one of those killed. Here the stranded boat is inspected by German and Turkish officers. Desperate efforts by the Royal Navy to destroy the wreck finally succeeded and she sank in shallow water.*

Liberal government was replaced by a Coalition and Churchill was sacked from the Admiralty (and therefore from the War Cabinet). He rejoined the army and gained command of an infantry battalion on the Western Front. In the Mediterranean, Admiral de Robeck made the inevitable decision to withdraw all his heavy units to safer waters. Naval gunfire support for the Allied beachheads was reduced correspondingly, the initial landings made no further progress. All these sinkings had been witnessed by the troops serving ashore. The navy was their lifeline to the outside world. Horrified by what they had seen, their morale and confidence in the higher command never fully recovered.

Far away from Gallipoli, the navy was committed at three levels to the Allied theatre of war known as the Western Front. On land, it contributed the post-Gallipoli survivors from the 63rd (Royal Naval) Division. At sea it conducted coastal bombardments and, of course, the three well-known raids at Zeebrugge and Ostend. But it was in the air that the navy made its greatest day-after-day contribution right through to 1 April 1918. That was the day when the army's Royal Flying Corps (RFC) amalgamated with the Admiralty's Royal Naval Air Service (RNAS) to form an independent Royal Air Force. It would be controlled by a new government department, the Air Ministry.

Before it disappeared, the RNAS had an establishment of 67,000 officers and ratings (male and female), 2949 fixed wing aircraft and 103 airships. There were no more "flying sailors" until May 1939. In that month, when finally they were returned to full Admiralty control (dangerously late as Europe rushed towards war), the Fleet Air Arm was allocated just 232 aircraft (none of them of modern design).

By war's end, hundreds of RFC pilots had shot down five or more enemy aircraft and so qualified (unofficially) as "aces". Many became household names. Amongst the most famous were Albert Ball, James McCudden and Mick Mannock. However, less celebrated at the time (because inter-service rivalries in Whitehall meant they were permitted less publicity) were the "aces" of the RNAS. Four of the most remarkable were the Australian Major Stanley Dallas, DSC and bar (thirty-two victories before being killed in action), the Canadian Flight Commander Joseph Fall, DSC and two bars (he survived the war after thirty-six victories), the Australian Captain Robert Little, DSO and bar, DSC and bar (forty-seven victories until, wounded while attacking a Gotha bomber, he bled to death in his cockpit after crash-landing), and the Canadian Lieutenant Colonel Raymond Collishaw, DSO and bar, DSC, DFC (at least sixty "kills").

Of the English-born naval "aces", one of the highest scorers was Major Charles Booker, DSC (twenty-nine victories). Age twenty-one, he joined No 8 Naval

Image: Canadian Public Archives

*The steady gaze of a hunter, a pilot credited with sixty victories in the air. Raymond Collishaw began his adult life in 1908 as a cabin boy, age fifteen, in the Canadian Fisheries Protection Service. By 1943, at retirement, he was an RAF Air Vice Marshal, CB, OBE, DSO\*, DSC, DFC. Early in 1919 he led No 47 Squadron RAF to join the South Russia Relief Expedition. There his final victim was a pilot serving with the Bolshevik Red Air Force.*

Squadron just as the air war entered its most intense phase, the Spring of 1918. His guns sent down sixteen German pilots in less than two months. Promoted then to command No 1 Naval Squadron, he took off on the morning of 13 August in company with a recently-joined pilot with the intention of showing him the front-line boundaries. Like all such novices, that boy's life expectancy was seventeen days. They were found by fifty or more Fokker biplanes, ten of which immediately attacked. Charles Booker despatched three of them, drove off most of the others and allowed the novice pilot to escape before himself being shot down and killed. The very lucky Second Lieutenant G H Fowles beat the odds, he survived the war.

The "flying sailors" came from every corner of the Empire. They wanted to fight, not spend their war in a cruiser or battleship swinging at her mooring in Scapa Flow. Their spirit was admirable, but for every one who became an "ace" at least thirty others never reached that level of success in combat or died in training accidents even before arriving in France. Further, it must be remembered that the work of RNAS aircrew was not confined to the Western Front. In the autumn of 1914, in the first ever demonstrations of "strategic bombing", they mounted long-range raids against Zeppelin sheds and depots inside Germany itself.

The RFC aeronauts who served in tethered observation balloons - "the balloonatics" - were provided with parachutes. When attacked, or as attack became imminent, they could leap to safety and so live to ascend another day. There was no such hope for the pilots and their observers in British fixed-wing aircraft. The first practical folding parachute had been demonstrated in 1797 by a French inventor, Jean-Pierre Blanchard (he was involved with hot air balloons). In 1911, the American designer Grant Martin made the first jump from a fixed wing aircraft. By 1915, workable pack-type parachutes designed by the British engineer Everard Calthrop had become commercially available. The Whitehall mid-war committees managing the affairs of the RFC and the RNAS stubbornly refused to purchase them, and the same policy was then pursued by the new Air Ministry. The men who made that decision may have been well qualified in other ways, but only three held (pre-war) pilot's certificates and they themselves certainly never flew operationally over the Western Front. Their explanation was that, if an airman had a parachute, "he might be tempted to prematurely abandon a valuable item of Government property", or words to that effect.

Whenever an aircraft was hard hit in action, damage to the controls rendered it no longer flyable or the petrol tank caught fire. According to circumstance, the pilot then had four choices. First, he could remain in the cockpit and be roasted alive by the blowtorch flames. Secondly, rather than suffer that agony, he could shoot himself with his Service revolver. Thirdly, he could stay on board and be killed when his mount crashed into the ground. Last, he could jump out and fall 10,000 feet into the void. At least seven thousand of our airmen died one or other of those horrific deaths. It was not only a shameful waste of young lives, it was a stupid waste of their combat skill and experience.

The senior commanders of the *Luftstreitkrafte* - the German Air Service - followed the same policy until the final months of the war. They then decided that pilots were more important than machines. At least sixty are known to have saved themselves when they began to receive reliable parachutes. One who benefited was twenty-two year old Ernst Udet. He was the highest-scoring German "ace" to survive that war and a key figure in preparing the *Luftwaffe* - the new German Air Force - for the next. Another "ace" beneficiary was Hermann Goering. Like Ernst Udet, he also was a holder of the *Pour le Merite* ("the Blue Max"). Together with Adolf Hitler, he and others went on to create the National Socialist German Workers' (Nazi) Party and in 1935 he was appointed head of the nascent *Luftwaffe*. So, would history have been any different if those two men had not been given parachutes? Of the British dead, still in their early twenties, how many possessed the potential to achieve great things in their later years?

Three successive members of the wartime Whitehall committees were representatives of the Royal Navy. The first, Commodore Murray Sueter, was a multi-talented officer with a keen technical mind. Even before the war, he was involved in the development of submarines, airships, torpedoes, anti-aircraft artillery and armoured cars. In 1912, when the War Office announced that it was forming a Royal Flying Corps, the Admiralty responded by giving Murray Sueter the job of creating the RFC Naval Wing (renamed Royal Naval Air Service in July 1914).

By 1918, one quarter of all the British aircrew operating over the Western Front were successors to the "flying sailors" he had helped to raise in the early years. He did not survive Whitehall politics long enough to see them achieve final victory. In September 1915, after quarrelling with Their Lordships, he was removed from his post and despatched to Southern Italy to look after RNAS interests in that theatre. In effect, professionally, he was buried. After the Armistice, still only forty-six years of age, he was prematurely retired, promoted (for pension purposes) to Rear Admiral, given a couple of foreign awards but none from his own government. An examination of Committee Minutes might explain the reason for his downfall, but he had not helped his cause when he broke the conventions by writing directly to the King (presumably complaining of his treatment). Following that sorry end to his naval career, Murray Sueter changed course, went on to be elected a Conservative MP and then became a prominent advocate of the innovative Imperial Air Mail Service. For this he was knighted in 1934 by King George V. Long forgotten by most naval historians, the brilliant Murray Sueter should be acknowledged as the founding father of British naval aviation.

His successor as Director of the RNAS was an entirely different type of officer. He was Rear Admiral Charles Vaughan-Lee and his conventional career was based upon command of surface vessels and of the boys training ship HMS GANGES. He seems to have had no previous involvement with aviation, so presumably he was chosen as a safe pair of hands in committee proceedings. He departed in 1917 to become Superintendent, Portsmouth Dockyard.

By contrast with Vaughan-Lee, the third and final Director was an officer who, although a torpedo specialist, had become interested in aviation as early as 1911. He was Commodore (later Rear Admiral) Godfrey Paine. His enthusiasm for the subject was recognised a year later when he was appointed Commandant of the new bi-service Central Flying School (at Upavon, Wiltshire). His first step, age forty,

*The 20,000-ton modified cruiser HMS Furious was the Admiralty's initial experiment with a new concept, the aircraft carrier. Commissioned in June 1917, she is seen here in dazzle paintwork. She was able to launch a naval dirigible on her after-deck and a Sopwith 1½ Strutter on her tiny fore-deck. The immense superstructure (later removed) created great turbulence, a serious hazard for RNAS pilots.*

*Squadron Commander Edwin Dunning, DSC, made the first ever landing on any moving flight deck on 2 August 1917. Five days later, on final approach, his Sopwith Camel was caught in a sudden gust and tipped overboard. The 25 year-old pilot drowned in his cockpit.*

was to obtain a Pilot's Licence (No 217). By April 1916, the RNAS was expanding so rapidly that it needed its own depot and training establishment. Paine was given the task of creating that one also, at Cranwell, Lincolnshire, an appointment which ended on 1 April 1918 when it became RAF Cranwell.

The careers of Sueter and Paine demonstrate that there were men in Whitehall who, pilots themselves, were qualified to raise the issue of parachutes. As Admiralty representatives, they and Vaughan-Lee must have seen the reports reaching Whitehall from the RNAS commanders in France, but no pressure was ever exerted to reverse the "no parachutes" policy. Or, if there was such pressure, it was ineffectual. We may wonder what the Admiralty's reaction might have been if anyone had proposed that all lifejackets should be removed from warships on the grounds that, when their ship was sinking, the sailors "might be tempted to prematurely abandon a valuable item of Government property".

"Trios" and "pairs" awarded to Great War aviators have long been prized by collectors. By the time those medals were authorised, successively in 1917, 1918 and 1919, the wartime rank structures were changing radically. For example, until 1 April 1918, the lowest RNAS commissioned rank (equating to that of a Second Lieutenant in the army) was Flight Sub Lieutenant, RN. Following the amalgamation of the two forces, the same level of ranking changed to Pilot Officer, RAF. However, to muddy the waters, there was a transitional period when naval aviators absorbed into the RAF were being recorded with army ranks as used by the RFC. This explains the stated ranks of the five RNAS officers named in this article (Dallas, Fall, Little, Collishaw and Booker).

To muddy the waters even further, when their medals were issued in the first half of the 1920s, the naming impressed upon them was a mixture of the old and the new. Their **1914** or **1914-1915 Stars** showed their original naval rank while their **British War** and **Allied Victory** medals showed their transitional army rank. A search through the past auction catalogues of Dix Noonan Webb indicates that the lettering usually terminated with "R.N.A.S." on all three. However, if the recipient qualified only for a "pair", his service was normally (but not always) shown as "R.A.F.". How and why the responsible authorities got themselves into such a muddle will, at this distance in time, never be known.

Now we must go back to the next Middle East campaign - Mesopotamia (today's Iraq). What prompted us to invade? In a word, it was oil. Beginning in 1901, British companies had been searching for oil in Persia (today's Iran). The Anglo-Persian Oil Company finally found it at Kermanshah, up in the north-west near the borders with Russia and Turkey. They constructed 150 miles of pipeline to bring the oil down to their refinery at Abadan. The Royal Navy was converting from Welsh coal to oil imported from Texas and Burma. Persian oil was cheaper because the Anglo-Persian company had deceived the Teheran government with an unfair contract. Our Government became the majority share-holder, thus ensuring exclusive supplies for the Royal Navy. When war broke out, it was immediately obvious that Abadan was a vital strategic asset to be protected. As it happened, the Turks had never regarded Mesopotamia as being important to their own interests. They had one weak Division around Baghdad, another up north at Mosul, but almost nothing around the Shatt al Arab where the Tigris and Euphrates empty into the Persian Gulf and where Abadan is located.

On 6 November 1914, as a first move, the Royal Navy bombarded the ancient Turkish fort on the Al-Faw peninsula. The fort was garrisoned with just 350 soldiers. Intimidated by the shellfire, they could do nothing to prevent the landing of an Indian Army Division and its advance towards Basra. His troops having entered Basra unopposed fourteen days later, General Sir John Nixon, the Commander-in-Chief, was encouraged to bring in more Divisions from India and to advance northwards up the Tigris. In a classic example of "mission creep", he set his sights on Baghdad, 275 miles distant. It was pointless, the city had no strategic value either to him or to the Turks and its occupation would have no bearing upon his primary duty of protecting Abadan and the Kermanshah pipeline. Nevertheless, he committed his growing army of British, Indian and Gurkha soldiers to arguably the nastiest campaign of the war.

Starting in January 1915 under the immediate command of Major General Charles Townsend, the army struggled northward until brought to battle on 22 November at Ctesiphon, just 25 miles short of Baghdad. Behind it stretched a long trail of graves. The medical services arranged by GHQ Delhi were so grossly deficient that thousands of soldiers had died needlessly, and were still dying, of cholera, typhus, dysentery, malaria and exposure to the climate's extremes of heat and cold. The advance having run out of steam, Nixon ordered Townsend to retreat back down the line of the Tigris to the village of Kut al Amara. It lay within a big loop in the river so, with water on three sides, it should have been easy to defend. In the event, the British trapped themselves in a place from which they could not escape and which soon became impossible to supply.

The siege began on 7 December. The Turks were commanded by General Colmar von Goltz, an officer who had worked with them for many years. At seventy-six he was still full of energy. He not only sealed off the Kut perimeter, he placed artillery along the banks of the river to block any supply vessels coming north. From the outset, the Royal Navy had operated numerous locally-requisitioned commercial vessels on the Tigris in support of the army. Operating from the port of Basra, they kept pace as far as they were able with Townsend's 1915 advance towards Baghdad. Given the complete absence of roads and railways, he depended upon them to meet at least part of his logistical needs and to evacuate his great numbers of sick and wounded, but they were not enough.

Anticipating his problem, orders were placed in February 1915 for twelve shallow-draft 98 ton rivercraft to be shipped out to Abadan in sections and assembled there by local labour. Armed with a variety of weaponry, drawing little more than two feet under the keel, each manned by twenty-two officers and men, they were known as the "Fly" Class. Amongst the first to ascend the Tigris, in late 1915, were DRAGONFLY, FIREFLY and GREENFLY. Space does not permit a detailed account of all the work of their crews, it is enough to acknowledge their great courage and determination in attempting to reach Kut in the face of the Turkish gunfire. It was an impossible task and, on 29 April 1916, Townsend was forced to surrender. His garrison had rotted away from starvation and disease.

*Typical of the sixteen "Insect" Class eventually commissioned, this is HMS Aphis. Launched in 1915 she first served on the River Danube before joining the Yangtse Flotilla. Transferred to the Mediterranean in 1939, rarely out of action, she was scrapped in 1947.*

Nearly 10,000 British, Indian and Gurkha soldiers passed into a brutal captivity which at least 4000 did not survive. News of the British capitulation came only four months after the humiliating withdrawal from Gallipoli.

From one river we turn to another. The main branch of the Dvina flows 1000 miles north out of central Russia to reach the White Sea at Archangel. It was to this desolate place that Lieutenant Roger Fitzherbert-Brockholes, RN, was ordered in February 1919 with the appointment "Chief Mining Officer, North Russia Relief Expedition". At the mouth of the river was the elderly five-funnel 6500 ton Imperial Russian cruiser ASKOLD. Taken over by the Royal Navy and temporarily renamed HMS GLORY IV, she was "mother ship" for her flotilla of small warships operating deep inland. Their task was gunfire support for the British battalions fighting alongside the "white army" Czarists against the "red army" Bolsheviks. Amongst them were the 645 ton "Insect" Class ships which had served on the Tigris in 1916 and 1917 - GLOWWORM, CICALA, COCKCHAFER, CRICKET, MOTH and MANTIS.

The Dvina channels are deeper than those of the Tigris so, after the Spring thaw, these well-armed ships were able to penetrate 200 miles or more into the contested territory. The land fighting was severe, two Australian soldiers earning **The Victoria Cross.** Robert's job was detection and destruction of Bolshevik moored mines and the semi-submerged mines released upstream to drift with the current. It was one of the latter which killed him on 2 July 1919. In due course his parents received his "trio", and that raises an interesting question.

When it was instituted in August 1915, the Warrant for the new **Naval General Service Medal (NGSM)** stated that it would recognise "service in minor naval warlike operations". Including 994 medals to the Royal Indian Marine, approximately 6900 had been issued with the first bar **Persian Gulf 1909-1914**. Those sailors were not fighting the King's enemies, but certainly they were protecting Imperial interests by interrupting the flow of weaponry into territories where we had a vested interest such as Baluchistan and the Gulf emirates.

The next bar was wrongly dated **Iraq 1919-1920.** It commemorated, in fact, the peace-keeping services on the Tigris between 1 July and 17 November 1920 of the 1000-ton HMS ESPIEGLE and her tenders, TRIAD and CLIO. Having ejected the Turks, Great Britain was trying to establish order amongst the quarreling tribal leaders and steer them towards forming an independent kingdom. So that bar is perhaps understandable.

The third bar was **NW Persia 1920**, and it is a puzzle. According to published sources, there were only four recipients - Commodore D T Norris, CB, CMG, RN, Paymaster Lieutenant H G Pertwee, DSO, RN, Chief Petty Officer H Dickason and Able Seaman C B Haig (servant to the two officers). Each had qualified already for a "trio", but this bar was in no way connected with a "minor naval war-like operation". It recorded a diplomatic mission to Teheran to advise the government of Persia how best it might create its own independent navy for service in the Caspian Sea.

Commodore Norris was uniquely qualified to lead the mission. Following the collapse of the old Imperial order in Russia in 1917, huge tracts of the region had descended into chaos. Great Britain's strategic interests were jeopardised and so, despite almost losing our hold on the Western Front in March 1918 and despite still being in pursuit of the German-Turkish army in Palestine, we found the men to maintain a presence in Persia (Iran). In late 1917, Major General Lionel Dunsterville was ordered to raise an initial force of one thousand British Empire soldiers (mainly Indian Army, Canadians and New Zealanders) for operations in north-west Persia. He made his base at Hamadan, up near the Russian border. The title was Dunsterforce, and its task was countering the work of a German diplomat, Wilhelm Wassmuss. This man was known as "the Lawrence of Persia", an acknowledgement of his deep love of wild places but also his skill in working with tribal leaders.

The Byzantine complexities of the region's politics and power-plays defy summary. It is enough to say that the Allied military effort expanded enormously in 1919 with the formation of the South Russia Relief Expedition. More and more British and Indian units (with squadrons of the recently unified Royal Air Force) arrived to support Dunsterforce and to fight the Bolshevik forces in the Caucasus. By then, the influence of Wilhelm Wassmuss with the tribes was in steep decline, mainly because the gold promised by Berlin had not arrived

In 1919, Commodore Norris found himself required to relieve a Dunsterforce garrison stranded at the oil refinery port of Baku (on the western Russian shore of the Caspian Sea) and to generally sweep that sea clear of hostile shipping. Needless to say, the Royal Navy did not itself have a presence in the land-locked Caspian. Norris therefore, by a combination of guile, diplomacy, leadership and money, created an *ad hoc* Caspian Flotilla of eighteen locally-chartered merchantmen. He retained most of their polyglot crews and armed them with 4" and 6" guns. Flying the White Ensign, three were temporarily renamed HMS WINDSOR CASTLE, HMS DUBLIN CASTLE and HMS EDINBURGH CASTLE. The SS KRUGER became HMS KRUGER, and that would have amused the older hands who had served in South Africa.

Having rescued the Baku force in July-August 1919, the Caspian Flotilla was stood down on 2 September. Norris and his men departed for long awaited leave and postings to more conventional ships, but then he was recalled for the mission to Teheran. No doubt the journey was difficult, even dangerous, but its purpose was essentially political and diplomatic. So why was it commemorated with a campaign medal?

In 1918, by contrast, 4000 miles away on the other side of the Asian landmass, a multi-national army had landed at Vladivostok. Like the Allied expeditions sent to North Russia and South Russia, its purpose was to aid the Czarists in their failing fight with the Bolsheviks. It was titled the Siberia Relief Expedition and its ranks included 4160 Canadians. They comprised *inter alia* two units of infantry - the 259th and 260th Overseas Battalions, plus a squadron of the Royal North West Mounted Police (RNWMP). Few if any of these men had seen previous overseas active service and, in the event, they were to see little action in Siberia. Even so, it was an operational theatre of war and, in the absence of any alternative award, they were given the **British War** and **Allied Victory Medals** (the rules of entitlement having been amended). The impressed details concluded with "C.S.E.F" (Canadian Siberia Expeditionary Force). All but fifty of the British and Canadian servicemen came safely home a year later.

When King George V instituted the silver **British War Medal** in 1919, it was intended to mark the end of "the Great War" with the Central Powers and Turkey

*In addition to the three British post-war expeditions to mainland Russia, the Royal Navy sent a squadron to the Baltic. Leading it was Rear Admiral Sir Walter Cowan, a fire-eating Welshman whose aggressive style of command led to several minor mutinies but a number of important victories. One of these was the sinking of the Red Navy cruiser Pamiat Azova (seen here) in Kronstadt harbour on 18 August 1919. This daring raid by motor torpedo boats was led by Lieutenant Augustus Agar, RN, later awarded the Victoria Cross. Cowan himself retired in 1931, then rejoined in 1941 as a Commander RNR and served with Indian Army cavalry in the Western Desert. Always at the "sharp end", he was still in the front line in 1944, fighting the Germans in Italy at the age of seventy-three.*

and, accordingly, the reverse bears the dates "1914" and "1918". The **Allied Victory Medal** likewise commemorated the battles which preceded the Armistice of 11 November 1918. Given their prior service in that war, they appear in the "trios" and "pairs" issued to naval men who then went on to serve in the Caspian Sea in 1919 and on the Dvina in 1919-1920. But those two *post-war* campaigns had no connection whatever with the defeat of Imperial Germany, so surely they deserved an award of the **NGSM**? The costly campaign on the Dvina - in which Royal Navy ships were sunk and Robert Fitzherbert-Brockholes was killed along with 600 other British servicemen - was a "minor naval warlike operation", so it would have been logical to authorise bars **North Russia** and **South Russia.** Presumably for reasons of cost, "administrative convenience" or "political sensitivity", that never happened.

In the case of the Siberia campaign, the evidence suggests that the Royal Navy's involvement was minimal, so the question of a **NGSM** commemorative bar could never have arisen. That said, it may be noted that at least three ships of the China Fleet called at Vladivostok during the operational period, 1918-1920. They were the heavy cruiser HMS SUFFOLK (9800 tons) and the light cruisers HMS CARLISLE and HMS KENT (4190 tons each). Nine of their people became ill or were injured and, having been taken ashore, subsequently died. Buried locally, they included the SUFFOLK's Chaplain, the Reverend William Lewis Ford, and the only Royal Marine to find his final resting place in Siberia, Private William Reed, RMLI, also of the SUFFOLK.

With hindsight, it is extraordinary that the Siberia episode has been so largely forgotten. In total, 350,000 Allied troops were committed to it. They included 70,000 Japanese, 12,000 Americans, 12,000 Poles, 4000 Serbs, 4000 Romanians, 5000 Chinese and 18,500 French. For reasons which at this distance in time are even more difficult to understand, troops from the nascent Czechoslovakia were committed to the campaign. The suffered fifty percent casualties.

It was all in vain. Many years later, in 1949, with the temperature of the Cold War falling ever lower, Winston Churchill lamented "our failure to strangle Bolshevism at it's birth, to bring Russia, then prostrate, by one means or another into the general democratic system, lies heavily upon us today".

Siberia was a land campaign. The Royal Navy was not required to contribute sailors or marines to fight ashore. Its role was concentrated on coastal logistics and blockades and assisting in the evacuation to Japan - and then onwards to Canada - of hordes of distressed White Russians and their families. Commanding the China Station during those forlorn years were, successively, Rear Admiral Sir Frederick Tudor (1917-1919) shown here, followed by Vice Admiral Sir Alexander Duff.

Both were highly experienced and competent officers but barren Siberia, on the periphery of Russia's cataclysmic civil war, never held any prospect of fame and glory for them or for the men they commanded. If there were medals to be won, this was not the place to win them.

There is one more "no medal action" to be mentioned. During the years of the Spanish Civil War (1936-1939), dozens of merchant ships of several nations were engaged in supplying the warring factions with contraband. Enforcing the blockade were, amongst others, ships of the British, German and Italian navies. In such a time of European political tension there was the constant risk of confrontation at sea, but there was no medal to recognise the work done by the Royal Navy even though some of its men were killed by hostile action. That story will be told in "The Awards that Never Were, Part Nine (A)".

In those same years, we had ships patrolling the coast of Palestine, also in search of gun-runners. Conflict had broken out between the Palestinian Arabs and the Zionist settlers. Great Britain held the League of Nations mandate to govern Palestine and was therefore duty-bound to intervene. Over the next three and a half years, the Royal Navy deployed a succession of seventy-nine ships along that coast. Every man-jack of those ships' companies - 13,600 of them - received the **Naval General Service Medal** with the bar **Palestine 1936-39.**

Some ships called at local ports for fuel and stores while patrolling the coast, others were birds of passage, but there were no potentially hostile ships to challenge them. A twenty-four hour stop-over, "a quick run ashore", it was enough to qualify for the medal. Regardless of whether they remained in their ship or went ashore, they all received it and that was a radical departure from previous practice. Readers familiar with the medals generated by services in the Crimea, the Indian Mutiny, South Africa, all the Colonial campaigns, the 1908 Messina earthquake, and so forth, will know that a firm line was always drawn between "men who went shore" and those who did not. Ignoring Messina, the former received their Sovereign's medal with one or more bars, the latter received it without a bar. Palestine was different, everyone got both. It set a precedent and, given the nature of the world war about to erupt, it was both necessary and desirable.

# ROYAL NAVAL DIVISION
## HANDYMEN TO FIGHT ON LAND & SEA

**1ST BRIGADE**

BATTALIONS:
"BENBOW"
"COLLINGWOOD"
"HAWKE"
"DRAKE"

**RECRUITS WANTED**

**2ND BRIGADE**

BATTALIONS:
"HOWE"
"HOOD"
"ANSON"
"NELSON"

**RECRUITS WANTED**

VACANCIES FOR RECRUITS BETWEEN THE AGES OF 18 AND 38
CHEST MEASUREMENT, 34 in.   HEIGHT, 5 ft. 3½ in.
PAYMENT FROM 1/3 PER DAY.   FAMILY ALLOWANCES.

Besides serving in the above Battalions and for the Transport and Engineer Sections attached,

**MEN WANTED**

who are suitable for training as Wireless Operators, Signalmen, and other Service with the Fleet.
Apply to the Recruiting Office, 112, STRAND, LONDON, W.C.

## Part Seven - 1939 to 1945

ELEVEN FIFTEEN, the morning of Sunday, 3 September 1939. In every home, the family gathered around "the wireless" to hear the thin tired voice of the Prime Minister. Most could guess what Neville Chamberlain would tell them, few were inspired by the words: "You can imagine what a bitter blow it is to me that all my long struggle to win peace has failed". Indeed, too much of his speech was a feeble attempt to explain why he had believed that Hitler was a man to be trusted. But if Chamberlain failed to inspire, King George VI did not.

Speeches by the King were always a white-knuckle experience for his listeners as they willed him to master his stutter. A few hours after Chamberlain, he addressed the nation from Buckingham Palace. With barely a falter, he set out clearly and simply the issues at stake in this new war. Their King gave his people the rallying call his Prime Minister had so dismally failed to voice. For the Royal Navy in particular, his words gained added power when, next morning, the newspapers published the photograph of him sat before the BBC microphone in his uniform as an Admiral of the Fleet.

Even better, and after too many years in the wilderness, Winston Churchill was returned to the Admiralty as First Lord. Every ship in the Fleet received the signal: "Winston's back!" He most certainly was, and he unleashed a storm of demands at Sir Dudley Pound, the recently appointed but already ailing First Sea Lord (effectively, the navy's chief executive officer). The hundreds of major and minor events which resulted from that relationship and which then unfolded following Churchill's appointment as Prime Minister in 1940 and Pound's death in 1943 do not lend themselves to easy summary. Instead, this author will select just one or two episodes associated with each of the seven campaign Stars announced at the war's conclusion.

For the navy, **The Air Crew Europe Star** commemorates *inter alia* the contribution of the Fleet Air Arm (the FAA) to the Battle of Britain. Aircrew who flew with two of its squadrons qualified for this medal. They were Nos 804 and 808 NAS (Naval Air Squadrons) which operated from HMS SPARROWHAWK, the desolate naval air station at Hatston, near Kirkwall, Orkney. Equipped with the Gloster Sea Gladiator biplane, their task was defence of the Scapa Flow fleet anchorage from *Luftwaffe* bombers and high level photo-reconnaissance flights.

Additionally, in June 1940, fifty-three FAA pilots were loaned to Hugh Dowding's RAF Fighter Command. He had sufficient aircraft but not nearly enough trained pilots. After speedy conversion to the Spitfire and Hurricane, they joined "the Few" to fight their historic battle over south east England. In total, 2927 aircrew of a dozen different nationalities completed at least one operational flight between 10 July and 31 October 1940 and thereby qualified for **The Aircrew Europe Star** preceded by the highly-prized **Battle of Britain** clasp affixed to the ribbon of their **1939-1945 Star.**

Although their historic mission has since been largely forgotten, two other Fleet Air Arm squadrons operating from Hatston earned **The Aircrew Europe Star.** They were 800 NAS and 803 NAS. In April 1940 they were involved in contesting

*"Winston's back!"*
*Churchill and his First Sea Lord, Admiral Sir Dudley Pound, worked extremely well together and very closely in battling the German threat in 1939-40. Pound was a widely experienced officer. He had commanded the Colossus at Jutland and held the appointment of C-in-C Mediterranean Fleet (1936-39). He was appointed First Sea Lord and Chief of the Naval Staff shortly before Britain declared war on Germany on 3 September 1939. Crucially, he knew how to deal with the idiosyncratic Churchill and stood his ground when the latter made improbable or impossible naval strategy suggestions.*

the German invasion of Norway. Flying the first of the FAA's all metal low-winged monoplanes - the Blackburn Skua - sixteen of their two-man crews were sent to dive-bomb the 7700 ton light cruiser KONIGSBERG. Already damaged by Norwegian shore batteries, she was berthed alongside in Bergen. Their 500 pound bombs should in theory have been too light to penetrate her deck armour, but the Skuas gained at least six hits and they were enough to send her to the bottom. It was the first ever sinking by small bombers of a major operational warship and none were lost in the raid (one crashed on the return flight).

Of the FAA pilots who survived those early actions, several later lost their lives over Malta, the Western Desert and in the Far East. One who became a Battle of Britain "ace" was Sub Lieutenant (A) Richard John Cork, RN. He was credited with shooting down five enemy aircraft in the first half of September while flying a Hawker Hurricane Mk 1 with the RAF's No 242 Squadron (part of the Duxford Wing commanded by the legendary Douglas Bader). Over London, on the morning and afternoon of the climactic 15 September, the Wing twice engaged and dispersed large formations of Dornier 17 bombers. Two fell to the guns of Richard Cork. His reward, a **Distinguished Flying Cross,** was later replaced at Admiralty insistence with a **Distinguished Service Cross.**

By 1942 he was serving with No 880 NAS in the fleet carrier HMS INDOMITABLE in the Mediterranean. When the Malta-bound Operation *Pedestal* force departed Gibraltar, it came under heavy attack from the air. On 10 August, flying a Sea Hurricane, Richard shot down a Ju88 bomber. Then, the next day, between dawn and dusk, his ship under constant aerial attack, he launched four times from the carrier's flight deck to destroy five more enemy aircraft. An extraordinary performance, it was recognised by immediate admission to the **Distinguished Service Order.** Promoted Lieutenant Commander (A), he was next posted to Ceylon to join HMS ILLUSTRIOUS as a Corsair fighter-bomber Wing Leader. He died on 14 April 1944 in a taxying collision at the China Bay airfield, Trincomalee.

When Allied troops stormed the beaches of Normandy on 6 June 1944, it was the Royal Navy's job (working with our Allies) to put them ashore and then protect their cross-Channel supply routes. **The France and Germany Star** was given, in the main, to soldiers and aircrew who served in the subsequent North West Europe campaign. Most of the sailors, on the other hand, had already qualified for **The Atlantic Star** and so were given the additional "theatre clasp" on that ribbon. However, for younger men only recently qualified for sea duty, **The France and Germany Star** was possibly the one such campaign Star for which they were eligible before Hitler shot himself. Meantime, those posted to landing craft experienced the Walcheren landings and those to minesweepers the clearance of the Scheldt.

**The Atlantic Star**, by contrast, commemorates the longest battle of the Second World War. It began on its first day, 3 September, when U-30 (*Oberleutnant* Fritz-Julius Lemp) torpedoed and sank the 13,500 ton passenger liner ATHENIA (Captain James Cook) off the coast of Ireland. It ended in May 1945 when the last of Admiral Doenitz's submariners raised, as instructed, a black flag of surrender. During the intervening forty-four months, countless actions were fought to keep Great Britain and the Soviet Union supplied with the food and weapons needed first for survival and then for Nazi Germany's destruction.

One of Churchill's first actions was to endorse Admiral Pound's decision to re-instate the convoy system. It had been delayed far too long in the previous war. On 2 September, twenty-four hours before Chamberlain told the nation "we are now at war with Germany", a group of eight merchant ships departed Gibraltar under Admiralty instruction for Cape Town. It was the fore-runner of 2889 convoys to be escorted across the North and Mid Atlantic before war's end. But how best to escort them? The navy had an adequate inventory of battleships and cruisers which from time to time were available to shield an important convoy from attack by German surface raiders, but there was a grave shortage of the smaller ships needed for the day-to-day routine of shepherding trans-Atlantic convoys threatened by increasing numbers of U-boats.

The "greyhounds of the sea", the big fast Fleet destroyers, were too valuable for such mundane work. They were in any case needed to protect heavier units whenever they put to sea. The descriptions "frigate", "corvette" and "sloop" had been adopted by the Royal Navy from the French and the Dutch in the 18$^{th}$ century. In the 1940s they applied to relatively small vessels designed and armed for patrol and escort work, economical to build quickly in yards perhaps having little previous experience of navy contracts. Great numbers were built in British and Canadian yards. Compared with their 1914-1918 predecessors, they were made immensely more effective by the installation in those ships of ASDIC (Sonar) and RADAR - underwater and surface detection equipment developed by Professor Frederick Lindemann's scientists at Cambridge University. Weighing against those advantages until 1943 was the inadequacy of their numbers. In the Western Atlantic, convoys were escorted to and from mid-ocean by Royal Canadian Navy ships and, even before Pearl Harbour, by ships of the US Navy and US Coast Guard. Despite early problems with training and equipment, Canada's contribution was crucial. In 1939 the RCN had eleven ships, by 1945 that number had grown to four hundred.

In the Eastern Atlantic, escorts flying the White Ensign were manned predominantly by "HO" (hostilities only) ratings and by officers of the Royal Naval Volunteer Reserve and Royal Naval Reserve. Others flew the flags of the Free navies - the Polish, French and Norwegian. The merchantmen could expect protection as they approached British waters, but in the mid-Atlantic they were often on their own. It was decided, therefore, to requisition a number of liners having sufficient fuel capacity for the entire 3000 mile transit and to equip them for Admiralty service. One such was HMS JERVIS BAY, a 14,250 ton passenger-cargo ship fitted with seven elderly 6" guns. The exceptional gallantry of Captain Fogarty Fegan, RN, when he challenged the pocket battleship ADMIRAL SCHEER on 6 November 1940, 750 miles south of Iceland, is a tragic but familiar story. His sacrifice saved most of the thirty-seven ships in the convoy when it was ordered to scatter but, even if not attacked by a surface raider, big unarmoured ships such as his were excessively vulnerable to torpedo strike. Something more was needed to confront the U-boats and that could best be done with aircraft.

In 1917 and 1918, the Western Approaches had been patrolled by seaplanes and destroyers, British and American, based at Queenstown (Cobh). When the Irish Free State was created in 1922, the terms of the Anglo-Irish Agreement permitted the continuing use by British forces of Cobh and of two other Treaty Ports. In 1938,

*The passenger FW200 Condor first flew in 1937. A year later, a modified version flew non-stop from Berlin to New York. Military variants were developed for war service and, to quote Winston Churchill, they became in 1940 and 1941 "the scourge of the Atlantic". Fitted with radar, bomb racks and machine-guns, they roamed the Eastern Atlantic in search of convoys which they reported to the U-boats. They also bombed and sank 340,000 tons of shipping before being driven out of business in 1943 by the new escort carriers.*

to the dismay of the Admiralty and of the outcast Winston Churchill, MP, and to the great surprise of the Irish themselves the Conservative government of Prime Minister Neville Chamberlain formally renounced those Treaty privileges. It was part of a trade deal.

Apart from sacrificing Cobh's other naval assets which would have been so valuable in the fast looming Battle of the Atlantic - refuelling, repairs, hospitals - the decision reduced the effective range of our maritime patrol aircraft by two hundred precious miles. We shall never know how many ships and how many lives might have been saved if Chamberlain had not so stupidly betrayed them as he did, and if the Irish government had not thereafter persisted with its policy of neutrality. To that nation, the cataclysmic world-wide war of 1939-1945 was known as "the emergency", nothing more.

Other than the Short Sunderland flying-boat, the RAF's Coastal Command did not at first have any long-range long-endurance aircraft, and anyway there were too few of those. In 1940, short-range aircraft such as the twin-engined Avro Anson patrolled the North Sea, but their weapons were useless. On 3 December 1939, HM Submarine SNAPPER (Lieutenant W D A "Bill" King, RN) was returning from a North Sea patrol when the crew of a Coastal Command aircraft skillfully but mistakenly planted a 100-pound "anti-ship bomb" at the base of its conning tower. It failed to detonate, but the impact did break four light bulbs in the submarine's control room.

Clearly, there was a lot more work to be done even in home waters. In the Bay of Biscay, Coastal Command began slowly to gain ground with a succession of aircraft equipped and armed specifically to hunt and kill U-boats - the twin-engined Hudson, Whitley and Wellington, then the four-engined Flying Fortress, Halifax and Lancaster. But they were a temporary solution. Only after the first deliveries in late 1942 of the superb long-range American-built PBY Catalina and B24 Liberator could Coastal Command begin to operate effectively over the mid-Atlantic.

However, the problem with all these land-based types was the time lost on outbound and inbound flights. For every aircraft on station - circling a convoy or reacting to a U-boat sighting - another would be flying out from an Icelandic, Newfoundland or United Kingdom airfield to replace it, a third returning to base, with possibly a fourth on the ground for repair and maintenance. What were needed were ship-borne aircraft which stayed with a convoy throughout its perilous crossing of the 1000-mile mid-ocean "air gap" and which could be re-fuelled and re-armed in their parent ship. And that meant developing entirely new types of ship because our few conventional aircraft carriers were more urgently needed for major operations with the fleet.

Early provisional measures were the MAC-ships (merchant aircraft carriers with two or four Fairey Swordfish biplanes embarked) and the CAM-ships (catapult-armed merchantmen). The CAM-ships carried a solitary one-flight-only Hawker Hurricane. The task of its pilot was to drive away any circling *Luftwaffe* FW200 Condor maritime surveillance aircraft before returning to parachute into the ocean with the hope of being rescued. In total, ten Condors were claimed by CAM pilots. However, of these two makeshift types of carrier, the most operationally flexible

*The FAA flew four thousand sorties from the eighteen MAC-ships. Modified grain carriers had primitive hangars for their four Swordfish, modified tankers had no such luxury. Life for their handlers was hard but, able to loiter at 60 mph, Swordfish were very effective in forcing U-boats away from convoys in the mid-Atlantic "air gap". This one, operated by 860 (Dutch) NAS, is returning to the challengingly small flight deck of the 8000 ton Dutch-crewed MV Gadila. Owned by Royal Dutch Shell, she survived the war. The MAC-ships served through to 1945, but became less important after the introduction in early 1943 of the new escort carriers and the VLR (Very Long Range) Liberators and PBY Catalinas of the RAF's Coastal Command.*

were the civilian-crewed MAC-ships - oil tankers and grain carriers fitted with a short flight deck, still carrying 80% of their commercial cargo and retaining, like the early MV ACAVUS, their mercantile "motor vessel" designation. Despite the scale of the crisis, the first of the eighteen ships eventually modified and returned to the convoy routes did not become operational until early 1943. By then the tide was already beginning to turn.

It turned even faster when the new mass-produced escort carriers joined the battle. Even before it entered the war, the US Navy had anticipated a requirement for ships smaller and easier to operate than large complicated fleet carriers. The first was the USS LONG ISLAND, commissioned in June 1941. The Admiralty had been following the same line of thinking, the earliest comparable British vessel - HMS AUDACITY (11,000 tons) - being commissioned in that same month. In total, by 1945, the Royal Navy was operating (worldwide) forty-four escort carriers of various classes. Built almost exclusively in American yards under the Lend-Lease agreement, they were by then operating the excellent American Wildcat (Martlet), Hellcat, Avenger and Corsair. But they were yet to come, it was the maritime version of the stately Swordfish which held the line in the meanwhile. It was armed either with four 250 pound depth charges or six under-wing 60 pound rocket missiles.

For a Swordfish to fly at low level over a well-armed surfaced U-boat at 90 mph (or less) was not a good idea, so the stand-off rocket was the weapon of choice. The first success came in May 1943 when an 819 NAS aircraft operating from HMS

ARCHER rocketed and sank U-752. Sub-Lieutenant (A) Harry Horrocks' missiles were the innovative "rocket spear" fitted with a 25 lbs non-explosive cast iron head. Kinetic energy alone took it straight through the U-boat's pressure hull.

*Kapitantleutnant* Karl-Ernst Schroeter and twenty-nine of his men drowned, seventeen were rescued. Harry received his **Distinguished Service Cross** before being sent to HMS JACKDAW, the gale-swept Royal Naval Air Station at Crail, Fifeshire, for advanced torpedo-attack instruction with 785 NAS. It was an operational training unit. There, piloting a Fairey Barracuda, he crashed and died on 25 March 1944. The aircraft dived into the ground two miles from the airfield and caught fire.

Between 1918 and 1939, the Royal Navy possessed no strike aircraft of its own. Those operating from the inter-war carriers were flown by the Royal Air Force. As young Royal Flying Corps pilots, the senior officers of the 1930s RAF had fought their war in biplanes with open cockpits and fixed undercarriages and that was where their thinking stagnated for nearly two decades. But even if the Air Ministry *had* gone in to bat against the Treasury, the money available for research and development was minimal. Only after 1936, when the Ministry decided to order Supermarine's Spitfire and Hawker's Hurricane (both at first privately financed) could the RAF begin to re-equip its land-based fighter squadrons with modern designs. Barely in time, as it happened, to fight the Battle of Britain. The carrier-based squadrons on the other hand were the poor relations. Discounting the late-1930s under-powered Blackburn Skua and Blackburn Roc they were obliged for too long to fly slow antiquated biplanes. Throughout the war, the British failed to produce a single high-performance monoplane fighter designed and constructed specifically for the rough-and-tumble of carrier operations. For that, we depended upon the Americans.

The 1930s were a decade when the British general public was intensely "air minded", but this enthusiasm did not penetrate the Admiralty. Lack of interest in high places resulted in the navy entering the conflict with little understanding of air operations at sea. The middle-aged reservists recalled to HMS COURAGEOUS in August 1939 paid dearly for that neglect, but the civilian crews of the Allied merchant fleets paid a far higher price before it was all over. By 1945, more tankers and freighters had been sunk by torpedo than by surface gunfire, more U-boats sunk by aircraft than by surface ships. Escort and hunter-killer groups such as those led so brilliantly by Commander Donald Macintyre, DSO**, DSC, RN (in HMS WALKER and HMS HESPERUS), by Captain "Johnnie" Walker, CB, DSO**, RN (HMS STORK and HMS STARLING), by Commander Peter Gretton, OBE, DSO**, DSC, RN (HMS DUNCAN) and by Captain Daniel Gallery, DSM, USN (in the USS GUADALCANAL) helped to bring the U-boat offensive to its knees, but it was the humble aeroplane that made the difference. If at least a few of the Royal Navy's new escort carriers had been available in 1940 or 1941, the story behind **The Atlantic Star** would have been very different.

**The Burma Star** is, understandably, most commonly associated with the three-year jungle campaign to eject the Imperial Japanese Army from that country. Less obvious is its association with the war at sea. The Warrant gave entitlement to personnel who served in British ships which had operated in the Bay of Bengal, in the Andaman Sea, and eastwards as far as the Sunda Strait separating Sumatra from Java. The Royal Navy's war in the Far East could not have started more badly. As conflict with Japan became ever more likely, and with the intention of deterring its military leadership, Prime Minister Churchill ordered the creation of a new command, the British Eastern Fleet, to be based in Singapore. At its core would be three capital ships, the elderly battle cruiser REPULSE (Captain W G Tennant, RN), the modern battleship PRINCE OF WALES (Captain J C Leach, RN) and the fleet carrier INDOMITABLE (which in the event never arrived).

Flying his flag in PRINCE OF WALES was the newly-promoted and recently-knighted Vice Admiral Sir "Tom" Phillips. The Japanese were not so easily deterred. On 7/8 December 1941, they struck simultaneously at Pearl Harbour and throughout much of the Far East. The Malay peninsula was on their target list. When their landings were reported at Kota Bharu and on the east coast of Siam at Singora, Admiral Phillips departed Singapore with the intention of destroying the invasion convoys. As escorts he had four destroyers - ELECTRA, EXPRESS, TENEDOS, and the Australian VAMPIRE - but TENEDOS had fuel concerns and later was ordered back to port. On a calm sea, the flotilla (designated Force "Z"), headed ever northwards at 25 knots with no sign of the enemy.

In the event, the over-night Kota Bharu beach landings were fiercely contested by the 8th Indian Infantry Brigade and, next morning, by ten locally-based RAAF

*Singapore's strategic importance was in large part due to its extensive ship repair and refit facilities. One of these was a massive German-built floating dock, large enough to accommodate the RMS Queen Mary. Seen here, in one of the smaller drydocks, is the 10,000 ton cruiser HMS Dorsetshire. The Union flag painted on her "B" turret suggests that the photograph was taken sometime in 1941. She did not have long to live, being sunk in the Indian Ocean by Japanese carrier-borne aircraft in April 1942.*

Hudson bombers (half were lost while attacking the enemy transports). Japanese casualties in men and assault craft were severe, but the defenders were outnumbered and forced to retreat after hours of hand-to-hand fighting.

Five Dutch submarines had been ordered into the Gulf of Siam to monitor the reported invasion fleet. At dawn on 10 December, two of them found the Kota Bharu force anchored off the beaches and immediately attacked. The most successful was O.16, commanded by Lieutenant Commander A J Bussemaker, Royal Netherlands Navy. With exceptional skill and in only forty-eight hours (10-12 December), he sank five troop ships, a freighter and several landing craft. Returning to Singapore with empty tubes, his boat struck a mine and broke in half. Bussemaker and all but one of his men were lost.

Admiral Phillips knew nothing of this but, when his lookouts spotted three Japanese seaplanes observing his flotilla's speed and track, it was obvious that surprise was lost. The transports, their job done, would be returning with empty holds to their ports of embarkation. Deciding to abandon the pursuit, Phillips was next told that Japanese troops were coming ashore 200 miles further down the coast at Kuantan. That was not far off his intended return track for Singapore, so he ordered a change of course to investigate.

The information was in fact wrong. Lieutenant (A) C R Bateman, RN, was sent ahead in PRINCE OF WALES's Walrus at dawn on 10 December but, having overflown the town and its adjacent beaches, he signalled that there was nothing unusual to be seen. Next, and most strangely, Lieutenant Commander F J Cartwight's EXPRESS was ordered inshore to double-check Bateman's report. Sixty precious minutes were wasted before Cartwright returned to report that Kuantan was indeed "quiet as a wet Sunday afternoon". Even then, Admiral Phillips still hoped that something might happen to justify his foray into these waters. A day earlier, an unidentified tug had been sighted towing three barges. Were they part of an invasion fleet? Clutching at straws, Phillips set off with a 35,000 ton battleship, a 26,500 ton battle cruiser and his remaining three destroyers to relocate these four small vessels (they were innocent).

Adding to the sense of unreality were the previous day's exchanges between the Admiral and his captains, Tennant and Leach. They must have been puzzled by his suggestion that they might practice "forming line of battle". This was not Jutland, he had only two major units under his command, there was no time for such fancy evolutions. Or even, as it happened, time to agree a clear plan of action. Captain Tennant, inviting his Admiral (rather plaintively) to clarify his intentions in the event of contact with the enemy, offered several suggestions of his own. They included: "Propose to have one aircraft (Walrus) fuelled and at short notice to fly for spotting if anything worth our metal appears". Intelligence sources had identified the composition of the invasion fleets' covering force, hence Phillips' lengthy reply included the lines: "We may have the luck to try our metal against the old Japanese battle cruiser KONGO or against some Japanese cruisers and destroyers which are reported in the Gulf of Siam. We are sure to get some useful practice with the H.A. (high angle) armament".

That second line recognised the risk of attack by high-flying bombers but for the rest, and in the light of what shortly was to happen, the Admiral's choice of sporting metaphors was tragically incongruous. These were not pre-match briefings for a cricket team, they were orders which would determine the fate of five Royal Navy ships and of the 3000 officers and men serving in them. As it happened, his "metal" - all 61,000 tons of it - would soon be on the seabed.

Admiral Phillips had spent most of his career in Whitehall and as "naval advisor to King George V". His contemporaries regarded him as "a desk admiral", but he had caught the eye of Winston Churchill and it was he who pushed for Phillips' promotion and command of this new Eastern Fleet. It was an appointment strongly contested by the very experienced First Lord, Mr A V Alexander, MP, and by the First Sea Lord, Admiral Sir Dudley Pound. There is an uncanny echo here of the 1912 quarrel between Churchill and "Jackie" Fisher and the then First Sea Lord, Admiral Sir Francis Bridgeman, regarding the appointment of Admiral Sir Archibald Berkeley Milne as C-in-C Mediterranean Fleet (*vide* Part Six). Phillips had the analytical mind of a good staff officer, but that was not the only quality required of a fighting admiral. Like Milne before him, Phillips was thrust into a role for which, through no fault of his own, he was singularly ill-prepared. Not for the first time and not for the last, Churchill put his money on the wrong horse.

All that morning, Admiral Phillips kept his ships in a text-book controlled formation cruising off the coast at fifteen knots when instead he should have been steaming hell-for-leather south to the sanctuary of Singapore naval base. Why did he linger? He was a thoroughly professional officer in the traditional mould. But, like every admiral of his generation, he knew (or should have known) the story of the American Colonel "Billy" Mitchell. In 1921 and 1923, Mitchell had conducted trials which demonstrated, beyond any rational dispute, that a very small aeroplane could sink a very big warship.

Mitchell's experiments were conducted in peacetime under controlled conditions, but two young Greek officers had already shown the way forward ten years earlier during the Balkan wars. On 5 February 1913, flying in a primitive Farman MF7, Lieutenant Moutisis and Ensign Moriatinis attacked a Turkish fleet trapped at anchor in the Dardanelle narrows. Their four small bombs were too light to have done much damage and, in the event, they all missed. However, the potential of aerial assault against surface ships was further demonstrated by Lieutenant Edward Osmond, RN. In 1915, during the Gallipoli campaign, he scored a hit on the Turkish battleship BARBAROS HYREDDIN, his 100-pound bomb inflicting considerable damage.

Admiral Phillips was certainly aware that thirteen months earlier, on 11 November 1940, Admiral Andrew Cunningham had despatched twenty Swordfish aircraft from HMS ILLUSTRIOUS to attack at night the Italian fleet anchorage at Taranto (southern Italy). In the space of thirty minutes, for the loss of just two of those aircraft, their torpedoes and bombs sank or crippled three battleships, three cruisers and a destroyer. That was half the Italian Navy's main battle fleet. The only casualties were Sub-Lieutenant (A) G W L A Bayley, RN, and Lieutenant (A) Lieutenant H J Slaughter, RN. They died when their aircraft suffered a direct hit and exploded low over the outer harbour. The other lost crew, Lieutenant Commander

(A) Kenneth Williamson, RN, and Lieutenant (A) Norman Scarlett, RN, became prisoners of war.

Cunningham's small force of near-obsolete aircraft caused more damage to the Italians than the Royal Navy's entire Grand Fleet had inflicted - at a cost of 6094 lives and fourteen ships - when it fought the Imperial German High Seas Fleet at Jutland in 1916.

Japanese admirals studied the Fleet Air Arm's Taranto tactics and refined them for their own much bigger attack at Pearl Harbour on 7 December 1941. By contrast, the US Navy totally ignored the glaringly obvious lessons to be drawn from Admiral Cunningham's strike at Taranto. Commanding the US Pacific Fleet was Admiral Husband Kimmel, another of that generation of "big ship, big gun" officers having no previous involvement with naval aviation. The Taranto operation had been widely reported in American newspapers. Perhaps Kimmel never read them?

The Italian Fleet anchorage was strongly defended with balloon barrages and anti-aircraft artillery. The Swordfish crews described the rising tracer and shell-bursts as "looking like an erupting volcano". Even so, they scored a stunning success. Pearl Harbour, on the other hand, had no such proactive defence plan, so 2402 American sailors died. At minimal cost to the Japanese, the US Pacific Fleet lost four battleships sunk, four others put out of action.

Until a few weeks before being despatched to take command of the Eastern Fleet, Admiral Phillips had been working in London as Vice-Chief of the Naval Staff. The post-action reports of the sinking of the 41,000 ton BISMARCK must have crossed his desk. That powerful modern German battleship, comparable in many ways to the PRINCE OF WALES, had been destroyed as the direct consequence of being struck by a single air-launched torpedo. On the late stormy evening of 26 May 1941, having broken through the Denmark Strait and having obliterated HMS HOOD along the way, BISMARCK was heading for the west coast of France when she was found by a flight of Swordfish from HMS ARK ROYAL.

In the teeth of the German's fierce defensive fire, Lieutenant Commander (A) John Moffat, RN, secured a chance hit under the warship's stern where her twin rudder-posts and three propeller shafts protruded from the hull. The impact of that explosion was catastrophic. With her rudders jammed, able only to steer in circles, BISMARCK was a wounded stag waiting for the pursuing hounds to catch up. They arrived on the following morning when heavy units of the Home Fleet tore her to pieces. Without John Moffat's torpedo she would have reached safe haven at Brest or St Nazaire.

In the 1920s, American politicians and senior officers had become deeply irritated by "Billy" Mitchell and his persistent lobbying for greater maritime airpower. When he continued to press his case, he was Court-martialled, disgraced and driven out of the service. The same rejection of the vulnerability of their shiny expensive battleships - their "castles of steel" - prevailed amongst the admirals of the Royal Navy, and "Tom" Phillips was one of them. They were not alone. Winston Churchill "did not believe that well-built modern warships properly defended with armour and A-A guns were likely to fall prey to hostile aircraft".

*An anachronism even before it left the drawing-board, Fairey Aviation's open-cockpit fixed under-carriage Swordfish first flew with the Fleet Air Arm in 1936. Funded initially by its makers to a 1934 order from the Greek naval air service, it was taken on by the Air Ministry as a Fleet "spotter". Under the pressure of war, it became a multi-role maid-of-all-work. It is claimed that aircrew named it "the string bag" because, like a housewife's string shopping bag, it could be shaped and expanded to accommodate all manner of payloads - bombs, mines, torpedoes, rockets, ASV radar and additional fuel tanks. An alternative explanation is the biplane array of struts and wires, but that applied equally to the navy's two other "museum quality" designs, the Gloster Sea Gladiator and the Fairey Albacore. Whatever the answer, the Swordfish proved to be amazingly durable. In a dive, it could exceed 100 mph (just) but 60 mph was the normal cruising speed. Several British companies tried to design a replacement - they included Fairey's own exceptionally ugly dangerous-to-fly Barracuda - but amazingly the Swordfish out-lived most of them and was still in operational service on the last day of the war.*

As the man responsible for the Gallipoli campaign, Churchill should have recalled the episode when Flight Commander Charles Edmonds, RN, demonstrated for the first time the potential of the air-launched torpedo. Flying a frail Short Type 184 from HMS BEN-MY-CHREE (an Isle of Man ferry adapted as a wartime seaplane carrier), he found and attacked a Turkish supply steamer in the Sea of Marmara. His single 14" torpedo was enough to sink her. That was on 12 August 1915. He repeated the performance one week later, sinking another Turkish steamer in the same way. Those two vessels were unarmed, but Charles Edmonds had opened an entirely new chapter in naval warfare. The lesson was there to be learned by every serving admiral of every nation who chose to think about it.

Twenty-six years later, cruising sedately along the Kuantan coast, Admiral Phillips simply could not grasp the near certainty that the Japanese would attack him from the air with torpedoes. Even when respectfully reminded by his officers that Japanese naval aircraft were poised on airfields barely 400 miles away in French Indo-China, he insisted that they posed no threat.

When the Japanese invaded Malaya, the RAF and RAAF had just 110 aircraft (fighters and light bombers) available to oppose them. Sixty were destroyed on the first day, mainly by ground attack. Amongst the early survivors was the recently formed No 453 Squadron (an all-Australian unit). With its eleven (serviceable) single-seat Brewster Buffalo fighters, it was on stand-by at Sembawang airfield (Singapore Island), ready to provide air cover whenever Admiral Phillips called for it. He never did, not even after the initial formations of Japanese aircraft were seen approaching.

So far he had maintained radio silence but when, beginning soon after midday, the first bombs and torpedoes struck home, his appeals to Singapore were for tugs and more destroyers, not aircraft. Even though the location of his ships was self-evidently no longer a secret, the signals were methodically encoded before transmission. More time was then wasted while they were decoded in the cypher office in Singapore.

In temporary command of No 453 Squadron was a Battle of Britain "ace", Flight Lieutenant Tim Vigors, DFC, RAF. When eventually he received local clearance to take off from Sembawang and lead the squadron north to Kuantan, the British ships were already under attack. The flying time was sixty minutes. Vigors and his pilots arrived over the site of the disaster just as the last Japanese aircraft was departing. Apart from the three destroyers there was nothing to be seen but oil,

*Nick-named "The Cigar" by its crews, code-named "Betty" by the Allies, the Mitsubishi G4M had various design defects but in 1941 it was still greatly in advance of anything in British naval service. It was a formation such as this which, descending to wave-top level, launched the fatal torpedo assault on Force "Z". Ironically, a British officer, the "ace" Wing Commander Roy Chappell, MC, RAF, had been posted to Japan in the 1930s to advise Imperial Navy pilots on the best ways of attacking maritime targets.*

Image: Reproduced courtesy of COFEPOW (Children & Families of the Far East Prisoners of War

*Lieutenant Iki Haruki at the controls of the "Betty" in which he attacked HMS Repulse. When his squadron arrived, the ship had already suffered its first torpedo hit. Later he recalled: "she was firing intensively and turning to starboard. After finishing our attack we watched her still firing but losing speed. Then she started to sink towards the port side".*

Image: Reproduced courtesy of the Trustees of the University of Glasgow

*Taken in January 1916, shortly before her launch at John Brown's Clydeside yard, this rare photograph shows the arrangement of Repulse's propellers and drive shafts. Under attack off Kuantan, they proved to be excessively vulnerable. Despite the relatively small size of her rudder, Captain Tennant was at first able to manoeuvre his ship "like a yacht".*

wreckage and men struggling in the water.

It is unlikely that the Australians could have prevented the attack entirely, but the lumbering seven-man Mitsubishi "Nell" and "Betty" torpedo carriers were unescorted (Japanese fighters then based in Indo-China lacking the necessary range). Under aggressive assault from the Buffaloes, their well-rehearsed pre-launch procedures would have been disrupted with far fewer strikes achieved. The portly Buffalo was not the finest aircraft to emerge from the American aviation industry in the 1930s, but its intervention on that clear sunny morning off Malaya on 10 December 1941 would have been decisive. Two major British warships would have been damaged, even seriously damaged, but surely not despatched irretrievably to the bottom of the sea.

The BISMARCK had been condemned by a single torpedo strike under her stern. Eerily, it was an identical blow which contributed to the fate of the PRINCE OF WALES. Severe flooding through the port outer propeller shaft was bad enough, but the force of the detonation wrecked the electrical motors in the tiller flat. With jammed steering (plus damage from three other torpedoes), she was helpless. Whether or not those two great ships, one German, one British, sank or survived was decided by a fluke, by just 220 kg of warhead striking in precisely the wrong place. Every other vulnerable part of their hulls was protected by thick armoured plate, but their rudders were always bound to be their Achilles heel.

The REPULSE also was crippled with a jammed rudder. Captain Tennant had handled his ship with outstanding skill, at times pushing the old lady to twenty-seven knots, but in the end he could not evade all of the fifteen or more torpedoes that came her way. Four in rapid succession found their mark, and she was doomed.

The almost clinical destruction in ninety minutes of the iconic REPULSE and the mighty PRINCE OF WALES by a few dozen twin-engined aircraft (only three out of sixty-six were shot down) caused shock and disbelief at home and throughout the Empire. The shock was compounded on 15 February 1942 by the news that Lieutenant General Arthur Percival had surrendered "the Gibraltar of the east", Singapore. Dozens of small vessels were lost as they tried to flee the island.

Defeat at Singapore resulted in 80,000 British, Commonwealth and Empire servicemen passing into a captivity of unprecedented barbarity which, over the following three years and eight months, too many would not survive. From the border with Siam all the way down the 650 miles length of the peninsula, the bodies of 7500 of their comrades killed in action lay lost and unrecorded in the rubber plantations and jungle forests of Malaya. Even as General Percival sat down with General Yamashita to be told the terms of the cease-fire, Japanese soldiers were rampaging through the city, bayoneting and raping just as they had in Nanjing in 1938 (*vide* Part Nine "A"). Untold numbers of Chinese and British women - including military nurses who refused to abandon their patients - were being gang-raped, mutilated and left for dead. Even if he had known, there was nothing the humiliated Percival could have done to protect them or indeed any of the other people in the city of Singapore for whom he was responsible.

The abject surrender resulted in the capture of eight Australian and British generals, thirty-four Brigadiers plus great numbers of battalion commanders and

*General Tomayuki Yamashita and Lieutenant General Arthur Percival represented two different empires, two contrasting modes of warfare and, above all, two utterly different cultures. The British simply could not comprehend the alien nature of their opponent. A Staff College study in 1936 had concluded that the Malay Peninsula was indefensible, but Japanese air power in early 1942 made defeat even more certain. Percival survived captivity and left the army in 1946. In that same year, Yamashita was hanged by the Americans for crimes committed by his forces in the Philippines.*

specialist Staff officers. In the longer term, their loss became a serious hindrance to the subsequent enormous expansion of the Indian Army. When two and a half million Indians volunteered for wartime service, there was a dearth of experienced leaders to take them into the protracted campaign in Burma. Instead, they were rotting in prison camps throughout the Far East.

Even before that disaster, Japanese forces were pouring into every part of the East Indies and establishing themselves ashore. In what became a pitiful attempt to stem the tide, the Dutch Admiral Karel Doorman was given command of a scratch force of fourteen American, British, Dutch and Australian warships (titled ABDA Force). His flagship was the 6500 ton light cruiser DE RUYTER. His principal units were the 6" gun cruiser HMAS PERTH and the 8" gun heavy cruisers USS HOUSTON and HMS EXETER (heroine of the 1939 GRAF SPEE battle). Admiral Doorman's orders were to attack the strongly escorted Japanese invasion convoys off Java and Sumatra but, before he could even begin to engage them, Admiral Takeo Takagi was attacking his ships from the air. Unlike Karel Doorman, the Japanese admiral had the support of carrier-borne aircraft. One of their first attacks destroyed the HOUSTON's main aft turret. It was not a good start.

Surface action commenced on the late afternoon of 27 February and continued with little pause for four days and nights with a series of engagements in the Java Sea, the Sunda Strait and the Bali Strait. Every one of the British and Australian ships was sunk - HMS EXETER, HMS ELECTRA, HMS ENCOUNTER, HMS JUPITER and HMAS PERTH  The only survivors were four American destroyers which skillfully evaded their way through the Bali Strait to reach Fremantle, Australia, on 4 March. All the other Allied ships were lost along with 2300 of their men (including the Dutch admiral). One Japanese destroyer was damaged, one transport sunk.

As a defeat it could not have been more comprehensive, but the agony was not yet ended. In early April, off the coast of Ceylon, the valuable heavy cruisers CORNWALL and DORSETSHIRE were both sunk by Japanese carrier-launched aircraft. At the same time and in the same area, the light carrier HMS HERMES with her escorting destroyer, the Australian VAMPIRE, also were found by Japanese naval pilots who sank them in just ten minutes. The old destroyer HMS TENEDOS - another survivor from Admiral Phillips' doomed Force "Z" - was bombed and sunk in Colombo harbour.

"Billy" Mitchell had died in 1936 a broken man, but in late 1941 and early 1942 his prophecies were being fully and brutally vindicated. Ironically, the Japanese Navy invested heavily in constructing battleships of its own. Two were the largest (74,000 tons) with the biggest guns (18.1") the world has ever seen - the YAMATO and MUSASHI. Both were sunk in the closing months of the war by American carrier-borne aircraft. The phrase "the biter bit" comes to mind.

*After Singapore, the Northern Australian port of Darwin suddenly gained great strategic importance. Japanese aircraft made repeated bombing raids, the last coming in November 1943. This image records the first and heaviest, the devastating attack on 19 February 1942. Eight ships were sunk at their moorings, ten more damaged. One of those destroyed was the MV Neptuna (6000 tons), laden with munitions. Her end is marked by the immense plume erupting above the black smoke from Darwin's burning oil tanks. In the foreground, preparing to engage in rescue work, is the 1000 ton corvette HMAS Deloraine.*

*Highly decorated for his leadership of America's aviation effort on the Western Front, Colonel "Billy" Mitchell later mounted a personal crusade against the US Navy's refusal to recognise the significance of air power. In 1924, on a visit to Pearl Harbour, he predicted, with stunning foresight, that one day it would be attacked by Japanese carrier-borne aircraft. The Royal Navy finally accepted his teachings in WWII, but much too late to avoid its bitter early losses in the Far East. The Mitchell creed is as valid today as it was ninety years ago.*

Before 1941, the White Ensign was to be seen all over the world. After Singapore, for the next four years, it disappeared almost entirely from the high seas except in the Atlantic, the Arctic and the Mediterranean. With no more than fifty years of naval tradition, Japan had mastered the secrets of modern ocean and amphibious warfare - the application of overwhelming force at a chosen point, surprise, up-to-date ship and aircraft designs, and the close integration of surface ships with carrier operations. The Royal Navy was, for the time-being, left far behind. Not until the industrial might of America came into full flow in 1943 could it begin to catch up.

Following all those early Royal Navy catastrophes, Japanese naval and air forces dominated the seas around the East Indies until 1945. The one weapon able to strike back was the submarine. When the Japanese Navy stormed into the Bay of Bengal and Indian Ocean in April 1942, we had not a single boat on station to oppose it. The Dutch had fifteen in East Indies waters, but only three survived the early onslaughts. Commanding what little was left of our Eastern Fleet was Vice Admiral Sir Geoffrey Layton, based in Ceylon. Responding to his urgent appeal, the Admiralty began to transfer from home waters and the Mediterranean units of the 1550 ton much-modified "T" Class. We did not possess ocean-going boats comparable with those of the Japanese and American navies. With ours dependent upon bases in Ceylon (and later Fremantle, Australia), range and endurance were critical factors and the "T" boats were the best available.

The first to arrive were TRUSTY and TRUANT. They were followed by eleven more of the same class, all having the primary task of interrupting the flow of stores and reinforcements in transit from Japan to Singapore, then onward through the Malacca Straits to Burma. As they were not designed for extended patrols in warm shallow seas, their crews (joined in 1944 by the crew of the Dutch "T" Class ZWAARDVISCH) suffered constantly from septic prickly heat sores and other debilitating skin conditions. Even so, for nearly three years, they kept up the pressure. In the process, they sank five submarines (two Japanese, three German) plus dozens of transports and small coastal vessels.

Additionally, off Penang on 11 January 1944, TALLY-HO (Lieutenant Commander Leslie Bennington, DSC, RN) sank the 5100 ton light cruiser KUMA. Eighteen months later, on 6 June 1945, the 13,300 ton heavy cruiser ASHIGARA was sent to the bottom by TRENCHANT. Lieutenant Commander A R "Baldy" Hezlet's attack was exceptionally skilled. Although his target was steering to avoid his torpedoes, he and his plotting team obtained five hits from his full salvo of eight at a range of 4700 yards. The ASHIGARA was *en route* from Batavia to Singapore with 1600 troops embarked. Of these, 1200 did not survive. Arthur Hezlet, however, did survive the war. He died in 2007, age 93, a highly-decorated Vice Admiral. None of the "T" boats were lost to enemy action although in May 1945 TERRAPIN had a lucky escape. She was heavily depth-charged and damaged beyond subsequent repair.

In 1944, the over-stretched "T" boats were reinforced by six small "S" Class (fitted with additional fuel tanks). Displacing 900 tons submerged - 300 tons less than their bigger sisters - they could operate closer to shore in search of small coasters and barges. The STATESMAN (Lieutenant Robert G P Bulkley, RN) was particularly adept at this work. Between August 1944 and August 1945, he sank forty-seven of them with his 4" deck gun (discharging in total 1200 rounds, a record for any Royal Navy submarine). But success came at a price. The STRATAGEM (Lieutenant D C Duncan, RN) was depth-charged and sunk off Malacca in November 1943, and STONEHENGE (Lieutenant D M Verschoyle-Campbell, DSO, DSC*, RN) failed to return in March 1944. Then, following a savagely fought surface action on 3 January 1945 off the Andaman Islands, SHAKESPEARE (Lieutenant David Swanston, DSC, RN) returned to port so badly damaged it was condemned as a constructive loss.

Between 1939 and 1945, worldwide, the submarine branch lost seventy-seven boats with 3100 of their men. That was a personnel casualty rate of 38.0% compared with 8.0% for the surface navy. The last boat to be sunk in Malayan waters was the elderly 1500 ton minelayer PORPOISE (Lieutenant Commander H B Turner, DSC, RN), destroyed by Japanese bombers and patrol vessels off Penang on 19 January 1945.

In the Pacific, the big US Navy GATO Class boats went on to annihilate Japan's merchant fleet, but the work of the "T" and "S" boats in the closely-guarded waters around Malaya should not be forgotten. Their crews received **The Burma Star** (as did those unfortunate enough to be caught up in the Kuantan, Java Sea and Sunda Strait actions).

In April of 1944, Churchill's War Cabinet overrode their Prime Minister's initial reservations by deciding that Great Britain must somehow become involved in America's Pacific Ocean war with Japan. We possessed no amphibious or submarine capability in the Pacific, but there was a determination that the Royal Navy's surface ships should contribute to the final battles of the war. Apart from our moral obligations as an ally, there was a powerful political consideration. If the

British were to recover their colonial possessions in the Far East they must be seen as willing to fight for them. The shame of Singapore must be erased, our prestige regained. Consequently, Churchill ordered the creation of a new command to be titled the British Pacific Fleet (the BPF).

Churchill's intention was more easily announced than put into effect. Apart from our commitments in the Mediterranean, the delay in allocating the required ships was due to the continuing threat of the 58,000 ton battleship TIRPITZ. She was lurking in a Norwegian fiord and thought by the Admiralty to be fully operational. If she broke out into the Atlantic she could either attack the North Russia convoys or attempt to sink the big Cunard liners QUEEN MARY and QUEEN ELIZABETH. In the build-up for the June 1944 Normandy landings and their subsequent exploitation, each was carrying 15,000 troops at a time on her round trips from North America to the United Kingdom. If TIRPITZ sank one or the other - with the associated enormous loss of life - it would have catastrophic impact upon American political opinion and popular support for an Allied invasion of Europe.

To counter that threat, the Admiralty needed to retain many of our most powerful ships in the Home Fleet. It was only when RAF Bomber Command

*The destruction of the battleship Tirpitz in a Norwegian fiord was a turning point in the war at sea. Described by Churchill as "The Beast", Hitler's last remaining modern battleship had, for too long and by her very existence, prevented the Royal Navy from joining the Americans in the Pacific. When the thirty-one Avro Lancaster bombers of the Royal Air Force's No 9 and No 617 Squadrons flew from Lossiemouth to Tromso Fiord on 12 November 1944, they were led by Wing Commander J B "Willy" Tait (seen here, fifth from the left, with his crew). Carrying the 5 ton "earthquake" bomb, the "Lancs" achieved two direct hits and four near misses. No ship ever built could withstand such a succession of impacts. The ship rolled over and settled in shallow water. Of her 1700-strong crew, barely 700 survived.*

destroyed TIRPITZ on 12 November 1944 that we could begin to release them for service in the Far East. Their Commander-in-Chief designate was Sir Bruce Fraser, the fighting Admiral who had destroyed the 38,000 ton battle-cruiser SCHARNHORST in the epic Arctic Ocean engagement off the northern extremity of Norway in December 1943. Assigned to the nascent BPF were four new battleships (HOWE, ANSON, KING GEORGE V and DUKE OF YORK), four fast armoured Fleet carriers (FORMIDABLE, INDEFATIGABLE, INDOMITABLE and VICTORIOUS), fourteen escort carriers, ten cruisers, forty destroyers, sixty-six smaller warships, and a hundred or more support vessels.

The BPF came into existence, on paper, on 24 November 1944, but there was much to be done before it could be assembled and made ready for action. Boosted by the inclusion of warships of the Royal Australian and Royal New Zealand navies and seamen from the South African Navy, the BPF would in time become numerically the largest strike force we had been able to bring together since Jutland. However, even at its strongest, by comparison with each of the US Navy's eleven independent Task Forces, it was modest. Bruce Fraser himself said later it was "insignificant". That statement alone shows just how colossal was the American campaign in the Pacific.

Ships ear-marked for the BPF passed initially to the Eastern Fleet based at Trincomalee, Ceylon. In the Spring of 1944 its commander was Vice Admiral Sir James Somerville. Between April and June of that year, he launched a series of destructive strikes against Japanese facilities on the Andaman and Nicobar islands (their bases in the Bay of Bengal) and Surabaya (Java). Then, on 25 July, he directed another aerial attack, this time against Sabang (Sumatra). Apart from damaging the Japanese, such operations provided experience which would prove invaluable when our ships began to operate in the Pacific.

It took time to transfer ships from UK home waters to the Indian Ocean. The weeks spent with the Eastern Fleet introduced their crews to the technical problems posed by service in a tropical climate. In August, Somerville handed over the Eastern Fleet to Bruce Fraser. His task was to prepare the bulk of the arriving ships for eventual transfer to the Pacific. On 22 November this duty passed to the new C-in-C East Indies, Admiral Sir Arthur Power, while Fraser went on ahead to establish his BPF command base in Sydney (Australia). From there he travelled widely to confer with his new American colleagues.

On 16 January 1945 the first sizeable component of the nascent BPF - the battleship HMS KING GEORGE V with the four Fleet carriers, three cruisers and ten destroyers - departed Ceylon for Australia. This group was commanded by Rear Admiral Sir Philip Vian, hero of the daring 1940 incident when, in HMS COSSACK, he rescued 299 British merchant seamen held captive in a Norwegian fiord in the ALTMARK.

Vian was now the designated commander of the BPF's carrier strike force and, on 24 and 29 January, *en route* to Australia, he launched a series of devastating air raids on the Royal Dutch Shell oil refineries at Palembang (eastern Sumatra). The bombing destroyed or seriously delayed a third of Japan's aviation fuel requirements. Flushed with this success, Vian's force arrived at Fremantle on 14

February 1945. The Java and Sumatra raids marked the beginning of a much happier time for the Royal Navy in the Far East and it resulted in the award of **The Pacific Star.**

Operationally, at sea, Bruce Fraser's battleships and cruisers were commanded by Vice Admiral Sir Bruce Rawlings, the carriers by Sir Philip Vian. For both tactical and strategic reasons, the BPF could never operate in a fully independent role. Instead, it was assigned to the US $5^{th}$ Fleet as one of the Task Forces commanded by the highly experienced Admiral Raymond A Spruance. A forward operating base was created in the Admiralty Islands. The anchorage at Manus became "Scapa Flow with palm trees", but it was in no way idyllic. The lack of air conditioning in our ships caused chronic debilitating skin conditions. To the sailors, it was "a hell-hole".

The British were now even further from home than the Americans. The supply chain from Britain was impossibly long and the Americans had logistical problems of their own. The Australians were crucially helpful in keeping the show on the road. The situation might have been easier but for the malign influence of the bitterly anglo-phobic Admiral Ernest King, C-in-C, US Navy. He was determined to exclude the British from the headlines or any post-war glory. That said, most of his subordinates did their best by generously supporting the BPF with whatever supplies they could spare and without Admiral King's knowledge.

Events were gathering pace with the prospect of striking directly at Japan's home islands and so ending the war. Before that could happen, the Allies' overall American theatre commander, General Douglas MacArthur, needed to continue ejecting the Japanese from some of the many small South West Pacific island groups which constituted Japan's outer defence perimeter. But first he had his eye on what was to him personally an even larger prize. When he had been driven out of the Philippines in March 1942 he told the world: "I shall return". Two years later he was able to keep his word. That campaign commenced with a violent surface and air battle at the centre of the Philippine group of islands in the Leyte Gulf. After Leyte was captured and transformed into an operational base, MacArthur could proceed with his planned reoccupation of the large northern island of Luzon. A preliminary naval and air bombardment commenced at Lingayan Gulf on 3 January 1945.

Admiral Fraser had arrived at Leyte from Pearl Harbour a few days earlier. He did not yet at that stage have his fleet fully assembled and ready for action, but he did need to continue familiarising himself with this Pacific war which was so different to the Royal Navy's operations in northern waters and the Mediterranean.

He studied American reports of the Leyte Gulf battle and the desperate suicidal *kamikaze* attacks on US Navy ships. The first of those aircraft had appeared on 25 October 1944. They were followed twenty-four hours later by swarms more of them swooping down on the American task force, hitting seven carriers and forty other ships (sinking five). Fraser felt that he could not send his BPF ships into such unprecedented dangers without first experiencing them for himself and learning how the Americans were dealing with them. Accordingly he embarked in the USS NEW MEXICO, one of the battleships assigned to support the Lingayen Gulf amphibious landings. With him was General Sir Herbert Lumsden, Churchill's personal representative in the Pacific theatre.

*On 4 May 1945, HMS Formidable was struck by a kamikaze Zero carrying a 250 kg bomb. Despite fifty-nine casualties and extensive damage, she resumed flying operations five hours later. She was hit again on 9 May, this time on her after-deck where aircraft were ranged ready for launching. One man was killed and nine wounded, eighteen Corsairs and Avengers were destroyed. Despite the chaos, she was out of action for just twenty-five minutes.*

On the morning of 6 January, observing the bombardment, they were standing together on the NEW MEXICO's bridge when it was struck by a *kamikaze* aircraft armed with a large bomb. Fraser had moved away to the other wing of the bridge to retrieve his binoculars. The explosion killed Lumsden, the ship's captain and many others (including Fraser's secretary, 36 year-old South African Sub-Lieutenant Bryan Morton, RNVR). Fraser himself survived the blood-bath with nothing more than severe temporary shock. It was a near-miraculous escape from death for one of the Royal Navy's highest ranking officers.

We now move forward in time and much further north from the Philippines. Having taken Iwo Jima, the Americans needed to occupy Okinawa, a densely populated mountainous island three times the size of the Isle of Wight. US Marine Corps landings commenced in April 1945 and the battle raged for eighty-two days. The loss of life, military and civilian, was enormous. It escalated even further when waves of *kamikaze* entered the battle. They had tried earlier to defend the Philippines and Iwo Jima, but now every day over Okinawa there were many dozens more. The result was even greater carnage. Almost five thousand US Navy sailors were killed, thirty-five of their ships sunk, two hundred seriously damaged. All four British carriers were attacked but, unlike the American carriers, they had armoured flight-decks and so were soon repaired. An American liaison officer commented: "When one of our carriers is hit, it's six months back at Pearl Harbour for repairs. When a Limey carrier is hit, it's 'Sweepers, man your brooms'". An exaggeration, but a reflection of the design and construction qualities of our ships.

Setting for one of the most historic events of the 20<sup>th</sup> century, the Iowa-class USS Missouri *(45,000 tons) rests at anchor in Tokyo Bay. The date is 2 September 1945. About to go aboard are Japanese emissaries ordered by their Emperor to sign the instrument of surrender drafted by General Douglas MacArthur, US Army. One of the Allied signatories, representing the British Crown and government, is Admiral Sir Bruce Fraser, Commander-in-Chief, British Pacific Fleet. The ships and men lost so tragically in the Royal Navy's defeats three years earlier are finally avenged.*

The Okinawa campaign ended on 2 July. The time had come to close in for the kill. The BPF moved north to attack shore targets on the big home island of Honshu. Our battleships had, at last, the chance to join in with their heavy batteries while Fleet Air Arm pilots roamed inland and along the coast. One of these was Lieutenant Robert Gray, Royal Canadian Naval Volunteer Reserve. He had already won, two years earlier, a **Distinguished Service Cross** while attacking the TIRPITZ in Norwegian waters. By mid-1945 he was flying Corsair fighter-bombers from HMS FORMIDABLE. On 9 August 1945, Robert was leading a section of aircraft against a flotilla of small warships passing close inshore. Armed with two 500 pound bombs, approaching at low level, he was hit by fire from the ships and from the shore. Over the radio he told his wingman that he had been wounded and, if necessary, to take over the lead. His aircraft caught fire but he completed his approach and scored a hit with one of his bombs. Moments later the blazing Corsair crashed into the sea. His target, the 870 ton escort vessel AMAKUSA, capsized and sank. In the event, the Japanese government agreed to surrender five days later, hence Robert Gray's **Victoria Cross** was the last of World War Two.

When the Labour Party won its landslide victory at the Polls in 1945 it did not have the needs of future medal collectors in mind. The country was almost bankrupt and so, for reasons of economy, it was decided to manufacture the new family of campaign Stars without stamping them with any details of the individual recipient. As the preceding pages show, our sailors and marines who served in the Far East qualified for either **The Burma Star** or **The Pacific Star** or both. If both, and depending upon time served, they were given a "theatre clasp" to be sewn on the ribbon of the Star they had earned first. For the naval collector-researcher, unless a group of medals includes a named award such as the **Naval Long Service & Good Conduct Medal** or is accompanied by original documents or personal photographs, there is no possibility of researching the man's career or identifying the ship in which he might have served. In the absence of such clues, we cannot even be certain whether he was a sailor, marine, airman or soldier. This is a pity because, if the 14th Army in Burma was "the forgotten army", the men who served under Admirals Phillips, Doorman, Somerville, Rawlings, Vian and Fraser have been overlooked even more. The exceptions were those recipients who took advantage of the service offered by Messrs Boots (Chemists) Limited. For a modest charge, they would stamp the man's details on the reverse, but few took advantage of it. Like their fathers before them in the 1920s, the majority wanted only to forget the war and get on with the rest of their lives.

Perhaps more readily remembered are the sailors who qualified for **The Africa Star** or **The Italy Star.** Here the same rules applied, a "theatre clasp" being affixed to the ribbon of the first gained. Unless he was killed in action, a man needed to serve a minimum of six months (accumulatively) in a specified theatre of war before he qualified for any of these Stars or clasps. Given the wide-ranging nature of naval warfare and the length of the war itself, it is not unusual to find "groups" consisting of two or three or even four Stars (the maximum was five not including **The 1939-45 Star).** Gunners who served on Defensively Equipped Merchant Ships (DEMS) seem to have gained more Stars and theatre clasps than the average Royal Navy man, and that is not surprising. A warship might spend most of its time in the Atlantic or the Mediterranean while a DEMS gunner would be constantly switching between convoys bound for every port between New York, Halifax, Liverpool, Murmansk, Gibraltar, Alexandria, Cape Town, and Colombo.

The Atlantic U-boat war did not reach its climax until May 1943, but the Mediterranean had already witnessed several turning points in the conflict at sea. The Italian surface navy was not large, but its ships were modern, fast and well armed. Their crucial deficiency was that of not being fitted with radar. Mussolini's fleet lost much of its strength when the Fleet Air Arm made its brilliant attack at Taranto in November 1940 and Admiral Andrew Cunningham fought his equally brilliant Battle of Cape Matapan in March 1941. To aid his struggling Italian partner, Hitler ordered Erwin Rommel to North Africa with the *Afrika Korps,* sent Goering's *Luftwaffe* to establish itself on Sicily and Sardinia, and Doentiz's U-boats to cause havoc from Gibraltar to the Lebanon.

The "Insect" Class now reappears in the narrative. It will be recalled (*vide* Part Six) that these extraordinary 645 ton riverboats were conceived originally in 1914 for service on the Danube. They were the sort of ship a child would draw - a big gun at each end with a funnel in the middle. Some were transferred in 1939 from the Far East to the Mediterranean where they saw more action than their 1914 designers could ever have imagined. Their small size and shallow draft allowed them to conduct close-range bombardments along the Libyan coast and carry supplies into the wreck-filled harbour at besieged Tobruk. Their maximum speed of fourteen knots made it hard to evade attack, and three were lost in rapid succession. The GNAT was torpedoed by an Italian submarine but survived to serve as an anti-aircraft gun platform protecting Alexandria harbour, LADYBIRD had the same role at Tobruk after being semi-submerged by bomb damage, CRICKET was wrecked by Italian bombs off Mersa Matruh. Remarkably, SCARAB and APHIS went on to take part in the Allied invasions of Sicily and mainland Italy in 1943 and of the French Riviera in 1944, operations which qualified for **The Italy Star.** Ton for ton, man for man, the antique "Insects" with their 6" guns were still punching well above their weight right through to the end.

Still looking at **The Africa Star** and the men who earned it, the story of Operation *Pedestal* has passed into legend. The Royal Navy paid a high price in August 1942 to fight that convoy through to Malta when the island's survival was in the balance. If Malta fell we would no longer be able to disrupt the Italian convoys supplying Rommel in the Western Desert, and his army would then have the strength to cover the last remaining miles to Alexandria and the Suez Canal. The implications were frightening. The navy had already conducted two major operations to shepherd supply convoys through to the besieged island, both had been very costly in both warships and merchantmen. This time the outcome was more important than ever. Malta was running out of food for its people, running out of aviation fuel for its few remaining aircraft, running out of ammunition for the anti-aircraft batteries.

While Vice-Admiral Edward Syfret was planning *Pedestal*, he was acutely aware of the dangers his ships would be facing. German Ju87 and Ju88 dive-bomber pilots had demonstrated already their skills in the battle for Crete and in other areas of the Mediterranean. The three-engined Savoia-Marchetti SM79s of the Italian Air Force each carried two 17" torpedoes, and their four-man crews were known to be well-trained and resolute. Submarines were a menace, but it was all these aircraft which caused the most anxiety. In passing, two of the dangerous SM79s were amongst the five "kills" scored on 11 August by Lieutenant (A) Richard Cork, RN (mentioned previously).

To escort and protect just fourteen merchant ships, Admiral Syfret was given forty-five warships (including four aircraft carriers and two battleships). Rarely can the Merchant Navy have enjoyed such mothering, and that reflects the enormous importance of the operation. The last 350 miles of the voyage were a raging battle. Some ships fell victim to German and Italian submarines and motor torpedo boats, but it was assault from the air which caused the greatest disruption. Only four of the original ten merchantmen - including famously the tanker OHIO - eventually crept into Grand Harbour, Valetta. The island was saved, but only just.

By early 1944 the Allies had occupied all of North Africa and Sicily and were steadily grinding their way northward up the mountainous spine of Italy. They needed enormous tonnages of *materiel* to maintain the momentum, and that meant large numbers of supply ships heading for Italian ports *via* the Suez Canal and the Gibraltar narrows. They were a juicy target for any U-boat commander, but he and his fellow captains were very aware that, for them, the Mediterranean Sea was a potential death trap. One such was twenty-four year old *Oberleutnant* Wolfgang Rahn. On the night of 5 January he successfully evaded the Gibraltar patrols but, two nights later, his U-343 was detected by the Free Polish Navy's SLAZAK (a "Hunt" Class destroyer, formerly HMS BEDALE). She raised the alarm and within minutes the order was given to launch a "swamp operation". This tactic involved sending every available aircraft and surface vessel into a reported area and forcing the U-boat to remain submerged until its batteries were exhausted. Once surfaced, it could be attacked and destroyed. That, at least, was the intention. In the case of U-343 it did not happen that way.

Vickers Wellingtons of No 36 Squadron were despatched from Blida (Algeria) and, in bright moonlight, three in quick succession found the surfaced submarine charging its batteries. In 1943, Admiral Doenitz had ordered all his boats to be heavily armed with multi-barrelled anti-aircraft weapons. His captains were instructed to remain on the surface and to fight back when attacked by aircraft. As the first Wellington made its long flat approach at fifty feet, it was met by a blizzard of automatic fire and crashed in flames. A second Wellington was badly damaged, driven off, and forced to make an emergency landing at Bone. A third Wellington of No 36 Squadron then attacked, caught fire and, like the first, fell into the sea. Only the pilot survived. The flames and tracer of those encounters guided to the scene a PBY Catalina of No 202 Squadron. As it flew towards its target, the wings of the big amphibian were so shredded that Flight Lieutenant J Finch abandoned the attack and staggered back to Gibraltar. When two No 179 Squadron Wellingtons arrived from Gibraltar, they also were greeted by the U-boat's fearsome "flak". Of the six aircraft which attempted to sink the U-boat, two were shot down while the others were all crippled to a greater or lesser degree. Seven aircrew were killed, four seriously wounded. The survivors were recovered from their dinghies by SLAZAK and HMS ACTIVE.

Wolfgang Rahn's boat was shaken by near-miss depth charges and one of his gunners was injured, but he succeeded in escaping the "swamp" and found safety in the French port of Toulon. After repairs and re-storing he headed south for the North African convoy routes. On 10 March he was found by HMS MULL. Although officially designated "armed trawlers", she and her sisters were designed to catch U-boats, not fish. One of the 197 wartime-built ships of the "Isles" Class, she was well armed with surface and anti-aircraft guns and carried thirty depth charges. It was the latter which killed Wolfgang Rahn and his fifty-man crew when U-343 sank 3000 feet into the abyss. If nothing else, the story of U-343 tells us that airborne radar and other new sophisticated aviation equipment did not themselves mark the end of Doenitz's U-boat war.

The HMS MULL episode is of additional interest because it demonstrates that, even in 1944 when highly organised Allied escort and hunter-killer groups were achieving such success, a small warship acting independently could still strike a deadly blow. Commanded by Temporary Lieutenant Bernard Gordon, RNVR, she had departed Algiers with orders to patrol off southern Sardinia. Her ASDIC operator was Leading Seaman John Rawlinson, RNPS. It was he who detected an underwater target and then, with remarkable mental concentration, tracked it without relief for the next five-and-a-half hours. This man had already been Mentioned in Depatches for his personal bravery during a German air raid at Algiers.

*With their small complement of forty all ranks, HMS Mull and her Isles Class sister ships carried relatively more firepower, man for man, than ships of much greater size. Seen here is HMS Ailsa Craig. Most were engaged in harbour defence and convoy escort work, twelve being lost to enemy action. Lieutenant Gordon had the unusual distinction of operating independently and far from his base when he encountered U-343.*

With only thirty depth charges available, Lieutenant Gordon needed total confidence in the accuracy of Rawlinson's reports before releasing any of them. Their patience was rewarded when, following the MULL's attacks, the ASDIC "pings" slowly faded into deeper water. The target was assessed initially as "probably" sunk, but Gordon received an immediate award of the **Distinguished Service Cross** and Rawlinson an immediate **Distinguished Service Medal.** Only later was it confirmed that their victim was the unfortunate Wolfgang Rahn and his U-343.

Authority for production of the seven familiar Stars was published in 1946. These are campaign medals, they recognise active service within an identified war zone over a specified period of time. However, there was an eighth theatre of war which, just like the others, witnessed heavy fighting and long casualty lists but which, for reasons unknown, was not acknowledged as such by the post-war Honours & Awards Committee. It is the region described broadly as "the Arctic".

Sixty-eight years after the end of the Second World War, the British government at last caved in to the unrelenting pressure applied by veterans' associations whose elderly members had served in merchant ships in the North Russia convoys. It was always argued that those operations were so hazardous as to merit a distinctive award. In the event, when in 2012 the Queen was invited to give her approval for **The Arctic Star**, the criteria were broadened well beyond the original concept of a medal for former merchant mariners.

Eligibility was extended to every British and Dominion serviceman and non-serviceman whose ship or aircraft or military unit had, at any time between 1939 and 1945, served north of the Arctic Circle. Interestingly, this means that a Royal Navy man who served in North Russia convoy escort duties but not for the full (accumulative) six months needed to qualify for **The Atlantic Star** before being sent off to the Mediterranean has at last received an acknowledgement of his time in those storm-bound northern waters. But, if he does already hold **The Atlantic Star**, he is not disbarred from applying for the new Star. The two can be worn together.

Much more interestingly, the new award applies to a range of very dissimilar actions fought north of the Arctic Circle but entirely unrelated to convoy escort work. Most are today forgotten. The first was the Namsos campaign of April and early May, 1940. German forces were invading the extreme north of Norway. Six and a half thousand British, French and Norwegian troops were sent to eject them. For a variety of reasons, they were unsuccessful. British Army casualties were less than 150 men, but six Royal Navy ships were lost to aerial attack. The carrier GLORIOUS and her brave escorts, ARDENT and ACASTA, were sunk on their way home.

During those same weeks the two violent point-blank Battles of Narvik were fought. Royal Navy losses were two destroyers sunk (HARDY and HUNTER) with two more seriously damaged (HOTSPUR and ESKIMO). The *Kreigsmarine* lost half of its total available destroyer strength. This was sea warfare at its most savage.

In May, it was discovered that the German navy had established a weather reporting station on the Norwegian-owned Bear Island. Standing lonely in the western Barentz Sea, it was a long way from the main scenes of action off Namsos and Narvik but, even so, the Admiralty needed to eliminate it. The heavy cruisers NIGERIA and AURORA, escorted by the destroyers PUNJABI and TARTAR, destroyed it with long-range shellfire.

Next came Operation *Claymore*, an amphibious landing on the Norwegian island of Lofoten. Five hundred Army Commandos and Royal Engineers went ashore on 4 March 1941 with the objective of destroying the factories producing fish oil and glycerine (used by German explosives manufacturers). The landing was uncontested. The Commandos demolished the factory and set fire to 3600 tons of fish oil. The expedition was supported by five ships of the 6$^{th}$ Destroyer Flotilla. They sank 16,000 tons of German shipping and, very importantly, recovered an Enigma machine from the German armed trawler KREBS.

Two months later, in May, the powerful battleship BISMARCK attempted to break out into the Atlantic by passing north around Iceland through the Denmark Strait. She was pursued by the tenacious heavy cruisers HMS SUFFOLK and HMS NORFOLK before being hunted to destruction in the Atlantic.

The second Arctic Circle amphibious raid was Operation *Gauntlet*, a brief occupation of the big isolated Norwegian coal producing island of Spitzbergen. On 25 August 1941, the RMS EMPRESS OF CANADA put ashore a force of Canadian infantry - detachments from The Loyal Edmonton Regiment and The Saskatoon Light Infantry - together with Royal Canadian Engineer demolition teams. The troopship was escorted by the cruisers HMS AURORA and HMS NIGERIA and five destroyers: ANTELOPE, ANTHONY, ECLIPSE, ICARUS and TARTAR. The soldiers were able to spend eight undisturbed days on

*Although the Lofoten Raid was given prominence on the cinema screens at a time when the British public was in serious need of good news, Operation Claymore was soon pushed into the background by stronger news stories coming from other theatres of war. Even so, immense damage was inflicted upon the German war economy. This photograph was taken from the destroyer HMS Legion. She was sunk alongside in Valetta harbour (Malta) in a bombing raid exactly one year later.*

Spitzbergen, evacuating the civilian population, destroying with explosives the mining equipment, and setting fire to 450,000 tons of coal which otherwise would have gone to Germany.

That episode was followed on 27 December 1941 by a hard-fought raid on the twin Norwegian islands of Vaagso and Malloy (Operation *Archery*). At the same time, a diversionary raid (Operation *Anklet*) was made against, once again, the Lofotens. The covering force included fifteen Royal Navy ships led by the light cruiser HMS ARETHUSA. In time, the accumulative value of these raids was to convince Hitler that Norway would be the place where the Allies would open their "second front". Tens of thousands of troops who otherwise should have been available to fight in his campaigns in North Africa and Russia were sent instead to man the northern arm of his "Fortress Europe".

Two years later, on 26 December 1943, came the action known as the Battle of North Cape. The 38,000 ton battle-cruiser SCHARNHORST had broken out of Alta Fiord (Norway) with the intention of attacking the Allied convoys then in transit to and from North Russia. It was essential that she be intercepted and sunk. In heavy snow-storms and the twenty-four hours blackness of the Arctic night, she was hunted down and brought to battle by Vice Admiral Bruce Fraser, C-in-C Home Fleet, in his flagship HMS DUKE OF YORK. After a complex series of exchanges, the German ship was overwhelmed by gunfire and torpedo strikes.

An unknown number of her 1968 officers and men went into the water when she capsized but only thirty-eight were rescued by the destroyers HMS SCORPION and HMS MATCHLESS. It was the heart-stopping cold of the Arctic Ocean which killed so many men of all nations whose ships were sunk from under them during those five years, and it was that which made operations in the Arctic so exceptionally perilous.

The other major German naval vessel to lose her life in northern waters was the superb battleship TIRPITZ. Completed in 1941, her continuing presence, lurking in Norwegian fiords, obliged the Royal Navy to launch repeated attempts at her destruction. In the event, it was the Lancasters of No 9 and No 617 Squadrons RAF Bomber Command, which, in November 1944, finally finished her off. It was their third attempt. The first had been mounted from the Soviet airfield at Yagognik, near Murmansk. It is unlikely that many, if any, of the aircrew and ground crew involved in that operation are still alive, even less likely that their families know enough about Grandad's wartime adventures to submit a claim for **The Arctic Star.** For men of Bomber Command it is unique, and it can be worn alongside their **Air Crew Europe Star** or **France & Germany Star.**

Looking back to the Spitzbergen raid of August 1941, how many families in Edmonton or Saskatoon are aware that one of their men represented their nation far north of the Arctic Circle before being killed in Sicily or Italy two years later? Politicians of a later and unaware generation dragged their feet for far too long before acknowledging that the Arctic was a distinctive theatre of war in its own right.

Between August 1941 and May 1945, fourteen hundred merchant ships carrying the weapons of war needed to keep Stalin's Soviet Union in the fight against

*The crew of a Luftwaffe Ju88 A-17 about to take off for yet another strike against a North Russia convoy. Their weapons are two F5b 21" torpedoes each carrying a 280kg warhead. The ferocious battles fought intermittently in the Arctic between 1941 and 1945 were in effect part of "the second front" Joseph Stalin had been so belligerently demanding. In May 2012 the Russians requested permission to grant their Medal of Ushakov to British convoy survivors. Seven months later, the British felt obliged to follow that lead with the long delayed Arctic Star.*

Germany were escorted through to Murmansk or Archangel. Eighty-five of them, from several different nations, were lost. Sixteen Royal Navy escorts were sunk. For the men who served in them, the violence of their shared experience was described by a young officer who served in the destroyer HMS TARTAR, Sub Lieutenant Ludovic Kennedy, RNVR. He wrote: "Seas the size of houses would come from every side, so that on duty one could barely rest, always bracing the body, bending body and knees to meet the motion of the ship like some frozen skier. The bows dug deep into the dark sides of the travelling water-hills, flung the spray upwards where the Polar winds caught it, flung it over the ship, on deck and superstructure and on the faces of crouching men, froze it on steel and skin. One saw nothing but an agony of water grey-green or blue-black, spume-tossed marble-streaked, heard nothing but the thunder of the seas against the sides, the yell of the wind above". Only wartime necessity could force men to hazard their lives and their ships in such a hideous ocean nightmare.

Superficially, the eight cheaply-made anonymous campaign Stars named in this article lack the emotional appeal (and certainly the artistic merit) of those commemorating earlier conflicts. Their bland exteriors conceal, however, a succession of events in Royal Navy and Royal Marines history matched only by the bravery and devotion recorded on the 231 bars fitted to the retrospective **Naval War Medal** of 1848.

## Part Eight - 1945 to 1982

THE UNCONDITIONAL SURRENDER of Imperial Japan on 14 August 1945 marked the end of the bloodiest disaster the human race has ever inflicted upon itself. Fifty million people were dead, six million of them Jews. The pitiful survivors of the Holocaust had only one ambition - to find sanctuary in "the Promised Land". The deeply unpleasant job of stopping them was given to the Royal Navy.

In 1920, Great Britain accepted a League of Nations mandate to govern Palestine until such time as the Arabs and the Zionists might agree to govern themselves. The mandate ended at midnight on 14 May 1948. It was the moment when the State of Israel was born and the First Arab-Israeli War exploded. Prior to that seminal event, fifty-three Royal Navy ships were at various times engaged in patrolling the coast in search of unauthorised migrant vessels. It was a replay - on a much more poignant scale - of the navy's work on this same coast a few years earlier. That first deployment had earned **The Naval General Service Medal** with bar **Palestine 1936-39** (the fourth in the series). The post-war operation was recognised with the bar **Palestine 1945-48.** Of the 7900 sailors who received it, few could have taken much satisfaction in turning back, sometimes with violence, those thousands of desperate men, women and children. Stateless, the only visible proof of identity for many of them was the concentration camp number tattooed on their left forearm. "Jack" is famed for his sense of humour. He needed every ounce of it then.

*Of the millions of Jews rounded up in the Holocaust, just 100,000 succeeded in embarking in ships heading for Palestine between 1945 and 1948. One hundred and twenty such vessels were engaged, most of them being intercepted by the Royal Navy. The immigration ship Exodus (seen here) was stopped on 18 July 1947 by the cruiser HMS Ajax, heroine of the 1939 Graf Spee action and the battles for Crete and Malta. To international outrage, the 4515 distressed passengers were sent back to camps in Germany. In other incidents dozens of people were bludgeoned or shot and 1600 drowned at sea. Palestine was not the navy's finest hour but, as ever, the politicians were calling the tune.*

What nobody could know was that there was more trouble ahead. As **The Korea Medal** today reminds us, it came in 1950 on the other side of the world. Following the removal from Korea in 1945 of the surrendered Japanese occupation forces, Moscow and Washington had agreed, as a stop-gap measure, to divide the peninsula into two areas of responsibility separated by the 38$^{th}$ Parallel. In the north, the Russians installed a Communist regime led by President Kim il Sung with his capital at Pyongyang. In the south, in Seoul, the Americans installed President Singman Rhee as head of a new Republic of Korea (the ROK). The Americans provided him with 500 instructors to train a ROK self-defence force before withdrawing most of their own troops to Japan and thence back to their homeland.

While the United Nations in New York were debating how best to create in Korea a democratically elected government of national unity, Kim il Sung and his generals were preparing an armed occupation of the south. Their planning was brilliant. They succeeded in assembling 200,000 soldiers in the hills along the 38$^{th}$ Parallel without alerting anyone in the south. The 58,000 American and ROK troops were almost swamped when these North Korean divisions erupted across the border at dawn on 25 June 1950 and drove them back 250 miles to the peninsula's south-eastern tip. There the exhausted US/ROK units formed a perimeter around the coastal city of Pusan. By holding its docks and airfield, they ensured a rapid build-up of reinforcements from Japan. The arriving American soldiers were told "here you stand, win or die".

Neither before nor since has the full membership of the United Nations (excepting the USSR) agreed to fight a full-scale war. And "full-scale" is what it rapidly became. Every member was asked to help in a "police action". Uniformed personnel of twenty-two nations would eventually serve under the blue and white flag. The British government responded immediately by sending two battalions of infantry from our garrison in Hong Kong. Later, serving alongside units from Canada, Australia, New Zealand and recently independent India, they and other British regiments won a fine reputation as the Commonwealth Division. Meanwhile, the North Koreans failed to break into bitterly-defended Pusan because their lines of supply were over-stretched. And this is where the ships of the Royal Navy first enter the story. In total, with the invaluable support of nine "Wave" Class oil and stores replenishment ships of the Royal Fleet Auxiliary, thirty-five of our warships operated in Korean waters at various times between 1950 and 1953. None were lost to enemy action although, unhappily, the US Navy had four of its own ships sunk by mines.

One of the early arrivals was the veteran 6" gun cruiser HMS BELFAST. The topography of Korea is such that most of the roads and railways are confined to coastal routes. They were vulnerable, therefore, to the long-range gunfire of ships such as BELFAST. In June and July of 1950 in particular, her guns inflicted serious damage on the supply columns moving south towards Pusan. Return fire from the shore caused casualties, but she continued to operate in company with the US Navy to great effect. Five more big Royal Navy cruisers operated at various times along this coast where they towered over the 1300 ton sloops such as BLACK SWAN and AMETHYST (names familiar from the 1949 "Yangtse incident").

Overall UN commander in the Far East was still the US Army's General Douglas MacArthur. To break the stalemate at Pusan, he ordered a spectacular amphibious operation on the west coast at Inchon. The landings began on 15 September 1950 and were timed to coincide with a breakout at Pusan. Operation *Chromite* had three objectives - to cut the enemy's north-south supply routes, reoccupy Seoul, then drive on north across the 38$^{th}$ Parallel. Tactically it was an outstanding success, strategically it developed into a profound embarrassment.

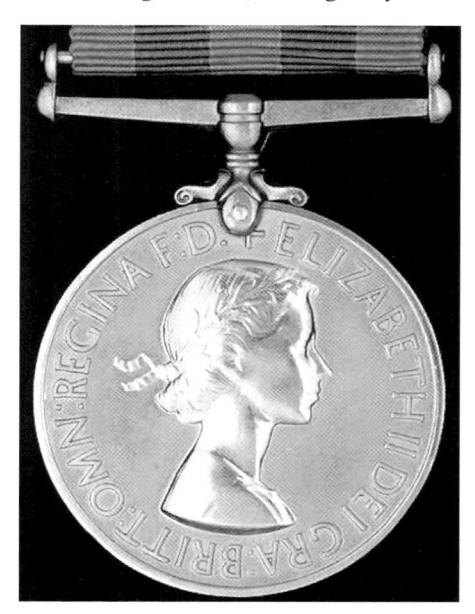

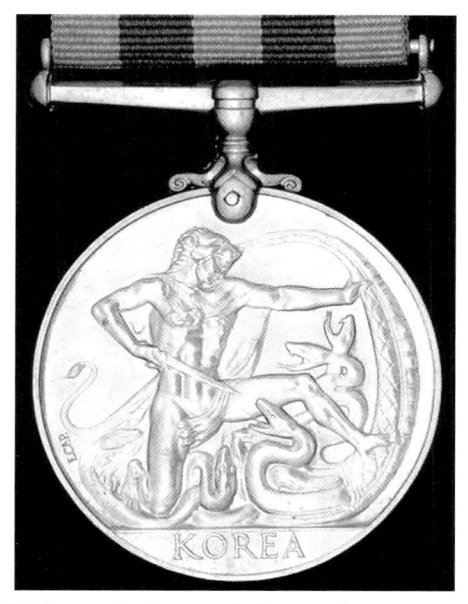

*The obverse of **The Korea Medal** (1950-1953) bears the image of the new but not yet coronated Queen Elizabeth II. The reverse is an oddity. Traditionally, in simplified terms, British campaign medals have been struck with a wide range of benign motifs each denoting victory. However, with the arguable exception of **The Punjab Medal** (1848-1849), the symbols have never been disrespectful of a defeated foe. They have followed the principal that "yesterday's enemy might be tomorrow's friend". Korea was the fourth in our successive wars with China. The earliest generated **The China War Medal** (1840-1842) having on its reverse a conventional "piled trophies of war" motif. It replaced an initially suggested design portraying a triumphant British lion trampling an Imperial Chinese dragon. With an eye to future trading and diplomatic relations, that version was never issued. Strangely, **The Korea Medal** harks back to Greek mythology and the Twelve Labours of Hercules. His second such task was to destroy the poisonous evil many-headed Lernaen Hydra. There is no doubting the medal designer's intent. Since then, China has become a major trading partner with the West.*

With a multi-national foreign army advancing rapidly up to her Yalu River frontier, China was bound to react. Mao Tse-tung's army of five million men became the key factor in the ground war. The full story of the next two years, leading up to the cease-fire on 27 July 1953, must be set aside while we return to the war at sea.

Having assembled such an enormous Pacific fleet in 1944 and 1945 to defeat Japan, the US Navy still had substantial numbers of ships in commission. It was this supremacy at sea that gave MacArthur the freedom to mount the Inchon landings (and later two more on the other side of the peninsula).

The ships of the British Pacific Fleet (the BPF) had gone home in 1945. Certainly there was work to be done - blockading, bombarding, escorting - but the big US Navy presence and the lack of a surface opponent rendered unnecessary a rebirth of Admiral Bruce Fraser's BPF. What *were* needed were aircraft. Five light carriers were despatched to Korea - GLORY, OCEAN, TRIUMPH, THESEUS and UNICORN. Displacing little more than 13,000 tons, they were not best suited to the often extreme weather of those waters. The dear old Swordfish biplane had by then taken her hard-earned pension. Her replacements were the Fairey Firefly and the Hawker Sea Fury. The Firefly dated from 1941 and had given good service over Norway (attacks on the TIRPITZ) and then with the BPF in 1945, but it was not in the same league as the Sea Fury.

Treasured examples of this beautiful and extremely powerful machine are still flown in "Classic aircraft" speed competitions. Over Korea it needed to be very fast indeed. When the war started, neither North Korea (devastated by half a century of

*Designed by the legendary Sidney Camm, the Hawker Sea Fury was the only high-performance piston-engined fighter ever produced specifically for the Royal Navy. Powered by the Bristol Centaurus 12-cylinder engine, its cruising speed was 390 mph (maximum 460 mph at 18,000 feet). Entering service in October 1945 (too late for World War II) it was replaced in 1955 by the first jets. Although at least one Mig 15 was shot down by a Sea Fury, ground attack was its primary role in Korea. Armed with four 20 mm cannon and twelve 3" rockets, this one departs HMS Glory on an unusually calm day. To avoid "friendly fire" encounters, it retains the black and white livery first adopted for the 1944 Normandy invasion.*

*Paired with **The Queens Korea Medal**, the English-language version of **The United Nations Korea Service Medal** was awarded to all United Kingdom and Commonwealth personnel who served at least one day in that theatre. Reflecting the international scale of the conflict, variants were produced with eleven other languages embossed on the reverse.*

*Marines from 41 Independent Commando RM lay demolition charges astride a key North Korean railway line. The "Independent" in the unit designation meant that the commanding officer, Lieutenant Colonel Douglas Drysdale, DSO, OBE, RM, had sole responsibility and was not always expected to consult higher authority when planning his covert operations.*

*Korea was essentially a land war supported by air power. Rear Admiral Sir William "Bill" Andrewes was already in theatre when the conflict started, taking command of the British Commonwealth naval forces during the early stages. Promoted Vice Admiral in 1950, he briefly led the UN Blockading and Escort Force. Having commanded the seaplane carrier Albatross in WWII and then the fast fleet carrier Indomitable, he had an exceptional grasp of air operations at sea. Furthermore, having served in 1945 under overall American control with Bruce Fraser's British Pacific Fleet, he was familiar with the ethos of the US Navy and its air-strike operational procedures. Officers appointed to command our new Queen Elizabeth class carriers may well envy him that wealth of experience.*

Japanese occupation) nor China (weakened by years of civil war) had any experience with warplanes. Like it or not, Soviet Russia was obliged to help them. Russian "advisors" organised "the Unified Air Force" and equipped it with the Mig15, a small nimble swept-wing jet fighter. Its technical superiority came as a shock to the American and South African pilots in their early straight-wing jets and 1944 Mustangs. Even the Sea Fury struggled to keep up.

The time needed to train the novice North Korean and Chinese pilots meant that the Mig15 would be flown mainly by Russians already familiar with it. Results came quickly. On 8 November 1950, a Russian pilot in a Mig15 shot down an American F80 Shooting Star. It was the first-ever jet-versus-jet engagement. In total, 3048 UN aircraft (mostly American) were brought down either in combat or by ground fire. Of these, 1106 were shot down by Russian pilots, a fact concealed at the time by both governments for fear of triggering a third world war. For a "police action", these are impressive statistics. Ironically, just as happened on the Western Front in 1918, the two sides finished up more or less where they had started. Two million civilians were dead.

**The Korea Medal** bears the laureated bust of Queen Elizabeth II and is sometimes known as **The Queen's Korea Medal** to distinguish it from **The United Nations Korea Service Medal** (the first in the long succession of UN peace-keeping awards). Her father had already given approval for a specifically British Commonwealth award as early as 1951 (shortly before his premature death on 6 February 1952). It is, therefore, the first "one off" war medal to be awarded in the reign of our present Monarch.

There have been plenty of other awards since then, the next in line being a fourteenth issue of **The Naval General Service Medal** (for sailors) and a thirteenth issue of **The General Service Medal** (for soldiers and airmen). Each was fitted with the bar **Near East** and it was geographically wrong. The regions where Great Britain's armed forces have ever served (especially in WWII) are always grouped under three broad headings - the Near East (Gibraltar, Algeria and Tunisia), the Middle East (Malta, Cyprus, Libya, Egypt, Palestine, thence through to Iran), and the Far East (India and beyond). The Honours & Awards Committee chose, for reasons never explained, to ignore the historical precedent. For the record, our servicemen did exactly what the British Prime Minister ordered them to do, not in the Near East but in the Middle East.

What precisely did Anthony Eden want? Privately, he wanted the death of the Egyptian President Gamal Abdel Nasser. He is on record as having said so. But that was perhaps a passing thought. There were much broader issues at stake. The most important was "how do we continue to control the Suez Canal in the face of rising Egyptian nationalism?". In years gone by, the Canal was "the lifeline to India", now it was "the jugular of Europe". Every year, 17,000 merchant ships passed through it. Two thirds were tankers carrying oil from the terminals around the Arabian Gulf.

This is not the place to examine all of the events which preceded Eden's decision to invade, but his was the central character in the drama about to unfold and so the following facts must be recorded. Educated at Eton College, served on the Western Front, won the Military Cross, went up to Oxford, gained a 1st Class Honours degree in Oriental Languages, studied the history of Islam, became fluent in Arabic, elected to Parliament, appointed Foreign Secretary, resigned in 1938 in protest over Munich, served in Churchill's wartime Cabinet with special responsibility for the Middle East. In other words, there was no other British politician nearly so well qualified to understand what was now happening in Egypt. It was not good.

The British had maintained a large military establishment in an area titled the Canal Zone since 1936. A year earlier, in October 1935, the armed forces of Benito Mussolini (Italy's self-styled "Duce") had commenced a large-scale invasion of Abyssinia (Ethiopia). Emperor Haile Selassie's people possessed no oilfields or other natural resources, hence few members of the League of Nations were interested in the destruction of his kingdom. Even though Mussolini's air force was using high-explosive and poison gas bombs against tribesmen armed with spears, Britain and France allowed him to get on with it. By closing the Canal to Italian transports they could have stopped the invasion in its tracks, but the policy of both governments was "peace at any price".

Despite the supine behaviour of the diplomats in Geneva and of the British Tory Prime Minister Stanley Baldwin, the Admiralty assumed (to its great credit) that the Royal Navy would surely be committed to action. What was the point of having a large and expensive Mediterranean Fleet if it was not allowed to protect from such cynical aggression a helpless independent nation like Abyssinia?

The C-in-C Mediterranean was the "fearsome" Admiral Sir William Fisher. One of his preparatory steps was to order the planning of a Fleet Air Arm attack on the Italian fleet anchorage at Taranto. This never happened because the First Lord at the Admiralty, Sir Samuel Hoare, received a direct order from Baldwin to ensure that there must be no confrontation of any kind with the Italian Navy nor, crucially, with the oil tankers upon which the Italian economy was entirely dependent. Admiral Fisher and his boss, Admiral of the Fleet the Lord Chatfield, had no choice other than to obey. And that was fortunate because a direct attack on Taranto, if it had gone ahead, would have kick-started a full scale war. Simply closing the Canal to all Italian vessels would have been a far less dangerous gambit.

Worried by the international community's refusal to prevent the rape of nearby Abyssinia, the ailing 68 year-old King of Egypt, Fuad I, became fearful that his own country could be next on Mussolini's hit list. Italy had begun to colonise neighbouring Libya in 1911 and had a significant military presence there. The British Army had maintained a small garrison force at Tel el Kebir in the 1920s and early 1930s but Mussolini's troops could walk across the Libya/Egypt desert frontier at any time if so ordered.

Nineteen thirty-six was a "crunch" year in shaping Europe's future. The "Pact of Steel" between the two dictators, Hitler and Mussolini, would not be signed until May 1939, but meantime they were each given a free hand by the rest of the world. In March 1936, while the League of Nations was still dithering over Abyssinia, Adolf Hitler took a huge gamble by ordering 32,000 troops into the Rhineland. It was an open defiance of the League, but France and Great Britain backed off and he got away with it. Even though the possibility seemed far-fetched, Italy's "Duce" might likewise take the gamble of facing down the British in Egypt. If that happened, he would gain control of the Canal.

Adding to London's concerns was the death in April 1936 of King Fuad and the succession to the throne of his 16 year-old son, Farouk. Italian aggression combined with inexperienced leadership in Cairo represented a worrying mix. To counter the risks, Anthony Eden (our then Foreign Secretary) travelled to Egypt and signed the Treaty which created a British military enclave, the Canal Zone. The initial strength was 10,000 troops, later it rose to 80,000. It became the largest garrison, of any nation, anywhere in the world. If Mussolini had held any serious thoughts of seizing the Canal they now evaporated.

King Farouk was deposed in 1952 by army officers committed to "Egypt for the Egyptians". Colonel Nasser was one of those officers. To them, British dominance in their country was intolerable. There is an echo here of the *coup de main* headed by Colonel Ahmed Arabi in 1882 (*vide* Part Four). Even before Farouk's departure to exile in France, *fedayeen* splinter groups connected with the Egyptian police and army had begun a campaign of kidnapping, sniping and road ambushes in and around the Canal Zone. Our local army commanders reacted with vigour and a lot of people, military and civilian, died.

Beginning in 1951, upwards of 500 British servicemen were murdered or seriously injured. Not until 2003, after much Whitehall debate, was the Queen invited to authorise retrospective awards of the long-defunct **General Service Medal** and **Naval General Service Medal,** each fitted with the bar **Canal Zone.** Neither was issued automatically. Former servicemen who believed they qualified for one of these medals needed to submit a personal application, hence many who met the criteria had already died of old age. However, their next-of-kin are still permitted to apply. In response to my recent enquiry regarding the number issued, the MoD civil servant spokesperson replied, bafflingly but perhaps typically, "this information is classified". Even so, and regardless of the Official Secrets Act, we may safely assume that ex-navy recipients are in the minority.

Now we must return to the events of 1955. Anthony Eden (once again Foreign Secretary) flew to Cairo for personal meetings with President Colonel Nasser. Their discussions were cordial, even friendly. It was agreed that the 1936 Treaty was a dead letter, the British would progressively vacate the Canal Zone and the last of our troops would be gone by June of the following year (1956). As a gesture of good faith, Eden undertook to supply Egypt with fifty-eight Vampire jet fighters and a squadron of twin-engined Meteor night fighters. He returned to London believing that he and Nasser had become good chums and that all would be well. There is an uncanny parallel here with the euphoria of Neville Chamberlain who in 1938 returned from Munich convinced that Herr Hitler was a nice chap really. Six months after his visit to Cairo, 56 year-old (but sickly) Anthony Eden replaced 80 year-old Winston Churchill as Prime Minister.

It was the time of the Cold War. Soviet Russia and the United States each had their own plans for the Middle East, both seeking to make Egypt a "client State". To the great alarm of Israel, Moscow radically augmented the strength of the Egyptian Air Force with 300 world-class Mig15 and Mig17 fighters and ninety Ilyushin bombers. Nasser's army gained 200 of the well-proven T34 tank. It was the massive influx of Soviet equipment and "technical advisors" (following hard on the heels of the British departure) which caused Washington and London to cancel their offer to finance the construction of a hydro-electric and irrigation scheme on the Upper Nile. The Aswan High Dam was (still is) central to Egypt's economy. On 19 July 1956, Nasser announced to a huge cheering crowd in Cairo that the Suez Canal Company now belonged to them. The revenue it generated would be used to pay for the Aswan project and compensation paid to the Company's share-holders.

Nationalisation is not in itself illegal. Our own post-war Labour government nationalised all the major British industries. In 1951 the Teheran government nationalised the Anglo-Iranian Petroleum Company (mainly British-owned, *vide* Part Six) and ejected the British workforce. It was Great Britain's largest overseas capital asset and a major earner of hard currency at a time when the nation was struggling to pay off its immense wartime debts. Our angry Prime Minister Clement Attlee responded by ordering a naval blockade which brought Abadan to a halt. The Foreign Office persuaded all the other oil producing countries to shun the Iranian regime. Attlee also ordered a Divisional-strength invasion force to be mounted from our garrison in the Canal Zone, but the Americans persuaded him otherwise. They had their own agenda for Iran. In 1954 the CIA master-minded a change of government which resulted in American oil companies gaining 40% ownership of the former Anglo-Iranian company. So, for the Iranians, the nationalisation *coup* of 1951 did not work out as intended, but that episode must have been on Nasser's mind in 1956.

When Colonel Nasser effectively removed the Suez Canal from British control, Anthony Eden was enraged. Within a week he ordered preparations for an invasion. Of the three Chiefs of Staff, Admiral of the Fleet Lord Louis Mountbatten was alone in expressing concern for the long-term implications. Early in November, with the Allied fleet approaching Port Said, he broke the conventions of service life by writing directly to the Prime Minister. In a powerfully reasoned case, he urged that the operation be cancelled because - a foretaste of the American-led invasion of Iraq forty-seven years later - the political consequences had not been thought through or even considered. Receiving no reply, he tried to speak with Eden on the telephone. The Prime Minister hung up on him. There were others who shared Mountbatten's anxiety. The government's own lawyers advised that an invasion in these circumstances was a violation of international law. In protest, three of Eden's key Cabinet colleagues resigned - the Lord Privy Seal and, most tellingly, the Foreign Secretary and the Secretary of State for Defence.

August 1956. Events are moving at startling speed. An Anglo-French planning staff is established on Cyprus under the overall command of General Sir Charles Keightley. The naval commander is Vice Admiral Robin Durnford-Slater flying his flag in the converted depot ship HMS TYNE. His fleet of 120 warships and support vessels - one third French - begins to assemble off Malta while great numbers of bombers crowd the airfields on Malta and Cyprus. The initial plan, Operation *Muskateer*, visualises an occupation not only of the Canal but also of Cairo and of Alexandria. In effect, all of Egypt. Deciding that this might perhaps be over-ambitious, the planners settle for Port Said and the Canal. The watered-down

Image: Reproduced Courtesy of Canadian State Archives

*Ignoring the objections of his own Cabinet and of world figures such as the Australian Prime Minister Robert Menzies and the UN Secretary General Dag Hammarskjold, Anthony Eden single-handedly ordered Great Britain's armed forces into a war which could not be won. It was an extraordinary act for a man whose entire adult life had, until 1956, been committed to measured diplomacy at the highest international levels. Here, as Winston Churchill's Foreign Secretary, he is greeted by US President Roosevelt at the seminal 1943 Quebec Conference.*

scheme is code-named *Muskateer Revise*. If successful, it might bring Nasser to the negotiating table or, as Eden hopes, topple him from power. The term "regime change" has not yet been invented.

D-Day will be 6 November. This worries Keightley's Deputy, the French Admiral Pierre Barjot. The Mediterranean's notorious autumn gales usually arrive in late October, and this operation will be entirely weather-dependent. His country has joined the expedition partly because its financial institutions are co-owners of the Canal and partly because French settlers and soldiers in Algeria are being killed with weapons supplied by Egypt. What he does not know, what nobody knows, is that the Israelis will be involved. Almost at the last hour, on 14 October, Eden agrees to a top-level French proposal that Israel should be a third partner. The deal is done in absolute secrecy. The British and French Cabinets are not told, our Chiefs of Staff are not told. This will be Eden's war, nobody else's. There is much coming and going at the United Nations, Nasser suggests a compromise solution, the US Navy's Sixth Fleet moves aggressively into the waters between Malta and Egypt, American U-2 spy planes monitor the build-up in Toulon, Malta and Cyprus. Washington is fearful that this "colonial adventure" might trigger a world war. The "special relationship" has never been so invisible.

Adding to Eden's worries is the unexpected discovery in the Eastern Mediterranean of Soviet submarines. Intelligence sources have indicated that there might be one in transit from the Black Sea southwards through the Dardanelles. The RAF hurriedly sends to Malta a detachment of No 210 Squadron's Lockheed Neptune (MR1) maritime reconnaissance aircraft to find it and to monitor its movements. Disturbingly, the Neptunes then find "several" Soviet submarines lurking along the intended track of Durnford-Slater's invasion fleet. With the US Sixth Fleet assembling in those same waters, the potential for serious international conflict increases by the hour.

The pressure on Anthony Eden, as a man, is becoming almost unbearable. It now escalates even further. Since 1951, the US Government's Information Agency has been operating a radio station transmitting the "Voice of America" foreign language programmes from a 5500 ton former US Coast Guard ship. Named the COURIER, she is anchored off the Aegean island of Rhodes. Amongst other themes, the broadcasts are encouraging insurrection in the countries of Soviet-occupied Eastern Europe. John Foster Dulles, the US Secretary of State, has announced: "To all those suffering under Communist slavery, you can count on us". On 23 October, the people of Hungary rise up in rebellion and, seven days later, the Soviet Premier Nikita Kruschev sends in a thousand of his Red Army tanks. Much of Budapest is flattened, 30,000 civilians die. The empty promise of John Foster Dulles proves to be just that, empty.

There is outrage throughout the free world, but how can the British government join in the condemnation when it is about to invade sovereign independent Egypt? Eden has placed himself between the proverbial "rock and a hard place". The pressure increases hugely when Kruschev threatens to destroy London and Paris with nuclear missiles if the invasion goes ahead.

The first sign of wobble is the order to Durnford-Slater to scale down his pre-landing bombardment at Port Said. Nervous that it will cause civilian casualties, Eden imposes a limit of one hour and nothing greater than 4.7" calibre. This will eliminate the magnificent French battleship JEAN BART and heavy cruiser GEORGES LEYGUE, also the Royal Navy's 6" gun cruisers CEYLON and JAMAICA. The war has in fact already started. On 29 October, troops of the Israeli Defence Force (the IDF) parachute into the Sinai. They occupy the Mitla Pass and open the way for their tanks. The plan is that Britain and France will claim they are intervening as "peace keepers". Such a claim ignores the fact that RAF Valiant and Canberra bombers based in Cyprus are already pounding Egyptian military airfields. The lie is further exposed when the GEORGES LEYGUE approaches the coast of Gaza and bombards Rafah in support of the Israeli army.

In the Red Sea, on the night of 31 October, the 8800 ton cruiser HMS NEWFOUNDLAND is patrolling the Gulf of Suez where she encounters the 1600 ton Egyptian frigate DOMIAT. Built in 1942, she is the former HMS NITH, a veteran of the Normandy landings. Challenged to heave-to, the DOMIAT turns bravely towards the British ship. She is struck by NEWFOUNDLAND's 6" gun main turrets at point-blank range. Badly damaged, DOMIAT responds with her 4" armament, scores hits, causes casualties, then rolls over and sinks (there are sixty-nine survivors, fifty-six others die). Any thoughts that the Egyptians will lack the guts to fight when we land at Port Said have been thoroughly disabused.

Three days later, further down the Red Sea, the 1350 ton sloop HMS CRANE is patrolling gently around the entrance to the Gulf of Aqaba. She is looking for an Egyptian frigate reported to be in the area, but the only warlike activity to be seen is the tank battle raging around Sharm el Sheikh. Believing the CRANE to be the Egyptian ship, five IDF Mystere fighter-bombers break the calm by attacking with rockets and cannon-fire. Manning one of her 40mm Bofors guns is young Able Seaman Roy Loader. Several men go down, including his number two. The gun is damaged but Roy keeps it in action. He hits two of the Mysteres, one of which crashes into the sea. His **Distinguished Service Medal** is the only one ever presented by the Queen for having shot down a "friendly" aircraft.

Durnford-Slater is bringing the invasion fleet along at a sedate 6.5 knots. There are close encounters with US Navy ships, but the main worry at this stage is the threat of attack from the air. He and Keightley, understandably, will not bring the fleet inshore as long as the Egyptian Air Force remains intact. In the event, knowing that his pilots lack experience with the precious Soviet aircraft received in June and August, Nasser disperses many of them to airfields in Syria where we cannot pursue them. The Ilyushin bombers are flown far south beyond Luxor (a French squadron finds them and they are destroyed on the ground). As the range shortens, our carrier-borne aircraft are able to reach the Egyptian military airfields. They conduct ground-strafing sorties to eliminate whatever aircraft have not already fled. Operating in conjunction with the French carriers ARROMANCHES and LAFAYETTE are the Royal Navy's EAGLE, ALBION and BULWARK. This is the first time the Fleet Air Arm has sent jet-propelled aircraft into action - the Sea Venom and the Sea Hawk. Both acquit themselves well.

Israel's main motive in joining the war is fear of Egypt's Soviet-supplied fighters and bombers. The Israeli Air Force is feeble compared with what it will become in future years, but the French and British pilots do the job of destruction for them anyway. Israel also gains control, for the first time since 1948, of Sinai and its adjacent waters. The price paid by the IDF in the fierce Sinai land battles is very high - 231 dead and 890 wounded. The Egyptian Army loses 900 dead, 4900 wounded, 6000 taken prisoner and most of its T-34 tanks.

Israel's war is won, there is nothing more to be gained. On 4 November, two days before the Port Said landings, Prime Minister Ben Gurion announces that his generals have pulled their tanks ten miles back from the Canal and he is ready to talk peace. Anthony Eden is enraged. Again.

The air threat removed, the next worry is the weather. It is still favourable for landings by parachute, but it cannot last. Under French pressure, the time-table is shortened by twenty-four hours. This means the lightly-armed Paras will be on their own until the next day when the main amphibious assault commences. It will be a gamble, the outcome depending upon how hard the Egyptians fight. At first light on 5 November, 500 French Paras seize the Al Raswa bridges linking Port Said to the mainland. They are followed by 520 French Foreign Legion men who drop on Port Fuad. Their job is to seal off the landing beaches. The initial British objective is El-

*Allied air strikes culminated on 5 November with attacks on and around Port Said. The plume of black smoke from burning oil tanks persisted long after the land invasion itself had been brought to its unplanned halt. Here, returning with flak-damaged undercarriage from yet another strike, a Fleet Air Arm Sea Venom of 895 NAS crash-lands on the flight deck of HMS Eagle.*

*A Centurion tank disembarks from HMS Puncher at Port Said before moving into the town's wrecked interior.*

Gamil airfield, near Port Said.

For speed and surprise, the first wave of 3rd Battalion, The Parachute Regiment, drops on El-Gamil from only 500 feet. They are all down in just ten minutes. The twenty-six Hasting and Valetta troop-carriers get away safely, but the Paras are plunged into a fierce battle on the runway and around the hangars. Many are hastily recalled Reservists. Their weapons are the 1930s Bren gun, the abysmal 1940s Sten gun, and the .303 bolt action rifle (essentially the same as the Lee-Enfield their grandfathers had in 1914). The Soviets have equipped the Egyptians with the best assault rifle in the world, the Kalashnikov AK47, and have trained them how to use it. By 1300, the Paras have lost four dead, thirty-six wounded and are almost out of ammunition. Somehow they hang on during the hours of darkness.

At first light on 6 November, 40 and 42 Commandos RM are ready to assault the beaches near Port Said. They come ashore in LVTs - Landing Vehicles Tracked - from the 1625 ton tank landing ships HMS PUNCHER and HMS LOFOTEN. One hour later they are joined by 45 Commando RM flown in by Fleet Air Arm Whirlwind and Sycamore helicopters from the modified carriers THESEUS and OCEAN. This is the first time helicopters have ever delivered troops directly into battle. Neither type was designed for the task but, by operating a high-speed shuttle, they disembark 450 marines and seven tons of stores in one hour. Some are hit by small arms fire, but none are lost.

There is a link-up with the Paras, streets are cleared, snipers tracked down, the position generally consolidated. Port Said is wrecked, many civilians are dead, the oil tanks will burn for days. Centurions of the 6th Royal Tank Regiment with 2 Para head off at speed down the Canal road towards El Quantara. They advance twenty-five miles against light opposition before being ordered to halt and dig in. It's all over. The US President Eisenhower has pulled the plug on the pound Sterling. Its value against the US dollar is falling faster than the Treasury's gold reserves can prop it up. The London Stock Exchange goes into free-fall. The Commonwealth governments are furious with Eden. In breach of all previous custom, he has not invited their opinions before taking his country to war, and now their own Sterling reserves are fast dropping in value. After Suez, the US dollar will replace the pound Sterling as the world's primary unit of exchange.

The ceasefire came into effect at midnight GMT (0200 local time). Ten hours later the first big gale hit the coast and all ship-to-shore movement ceased. Not until 22 December, six miserable weeks later, were the last of our unhappy beleaguered troops able to re-embark. Admiral Barjot had been proved right. The forty-eight hours land war, to echo the Iron Duke, was "the closest run thing". And the war at sea? The Royal Navy worked effectively and amicably with a French navy it had attacked with clinical violence only fifteen years earlier at Mers el Kebir. That tragic affair cost the lives of 1297 French sailors. It left a legacy of anger and resentment which has never entirely gone away.

On the British side, there were those who remembered Vichy France's bombing raids on Gibraltar, the cruel treatment of our airmen whenever taken prisoner during operations over Algeria, and the violent episode on 8 November 1942 at the port city of Algiers. As an element in the planned Anglo-American invasion of

*Anthony Eden's "collateral damage" worries were well-founded. Scores of townsfolk were killed, structural damage was comparable with that inflicted upon the city of Alexandria by the ships of Admiral Sir Beauchamp Seymour's fleet in 1882 (vide Part Four).*

*With all the melodrama of a Shakespearean tragedy, a clearly exhausted Anthony Eden sweeps into Buckingham Palace on the 9 January 1957 to tender his resignation as Prime Minister. Eden had campaigned at home on a popular platform of "Peace comes first, always" and yet privately he told Field Marshal Montgomery that the Suez campaign was an opportunity to "knock Nasser off his perch".*

*With its illogical "**Near East**" bar, the fourteenth issue of **The Naval General Service Medal** recorded the Royal Navy's last major operation before it was supplanted in 1962 by the all services **Campaign Service Medal**. Vice Admiral Durnford-Slater's Anglo-French fleet included 112 British ships of all types, hence the number of medals awarded (17,800) was exceptionally high.*

North Africa (Operation *Torch*), two 1800 ton destroyers, HMS BROKE and HMS MALCOLM, were ordered to enter the docks with troops embarked. After being landed on the quayside, the task of our soldiers was to occupy the port facilities and prevent their demolition. The planning staff believed with excessive optimism that their arrival would not be opposed by the French. They were wrong. The shore batteries blasted both of the destroyers at close range, the MALCOLM (Commander Archibald Russell, RN) in particular being hard hit. Ten of her men were killed, many others wounded, and she was forced to withdraw. Under fire, the BROKE (Commander Henry Fancourt, RN) disembarked her troops but was then hit again as she made her escape. Two days later she foundered under tow.

The bitter memory of all those events did not inhibit the professional relationship in 1956. For the Royal Navy, Suez was an outstanding success. At very short notice, it conducted to perfection its first significant amphibious operation since 6 June 1944. It engaged and sank with gunfire the DOMIAT (admittedly doomed from the outset). In the first-ever attack on a surface vessel by swept-wing jet aircraft, it shot one of them down (admittedly it was a "friendly"). The work of the Fleet Air Arm, both fixed-wing and rotary, was exemplary. Denied by political restraint from replicating the heavy 1882 bombardment of Alexandria (*vide* Part Four), our big-gun ships shouldered aside the US Sixth Fleet without open conflict and generally "maintained the presence". Anthony Eden's political career was ruined, but his nation's servicemen could return home with the feeling of a job well done. Ironically, those having the requisite skills were sent back to Port Said to salvage and remove the vessels scuttled by the Egyptians as blockships. Six months later the Canal reopened to traffic. Apart from the interruption of the fourth Arab-Israeli conflict (the 1973 Yom Kippur War), it has operated perfectly well ever since under Egyptian management.

Finally we come to 1982 and **The South Atlantic Medal.** Here the author must declare a personal interest and switch to the first person singular. In 1984 I was commissioned by the Royal Navy to write a book about that campaign. The main aim was to describe the role of the Fleet Air Arm, particularly during the critical opening phase of the war. The Admiral who was pressing the buttons gave me c*arte blanche* to move forward in my own way. As an historian, I have always been interested more in "how did we get into this thing in the first place?" and "what were the results achieved?" rather than the stirring clash of steel separating the two. For me, this was a particularly stimulating experience because my previous books had been "old history". The Falklands were "new history". I could talk directly with the diplomats, politicians, scientists and servicemen who had shaped it and could walk the littered ground where battles had been fought. In 1986, I completed *Operation Paraquat, The Battle for South Georgia, 1982*, published by Picton (Chippenham). Based upon two hundred personal interviews, the story-line had grown far beyond the Fleet Air Arm framework and thereby, coincidentally, had answered the question "how *did* we get into this thing in the first place?"

Anyone wishing to know more may read the book for themselves, if they so wish. Constraints of page space also prevent me from properly describing **The South Atlantic Medal** and, anyway, it is not necessary to do so. On the strength of *Paraquat,* I was asked by Spinks to contribute to their new (1988) edition of *British Battles and Medals.* Pages 266-268 provide all the details any researcher or collector might ever require.

Part Nine of these articles will be the last in the series. The title is "The Awards That Never Were". It will look at some of the battles and campaigns to which the Royal Navy has at times been committed by successive British governments, often with the loss of servicemen's lives, but which never received official recognition in the form of a medal. Due to its length, it will be presented in two parts with the narrative covering the decades 1820 to 1945, then 1945 to 2013.

# Part Nine (A) - The Awards That Never Were (1820 to 1945)

SO FAR we have been looking at the stories behind just a few of the campaign medals presented to members of the Royal Navy. The earliest was **The Naval Reward** (1588), the last to be mentioned were the retrospective issues of **The Naval General Service Medal** with bar **Canal Zone** (in 2003) and **The Arctic Star** (in 2012). The number of awards omitted has greatly exceeded the number featured. However, the limited scope of the survey has encouraged the author to concentrate upon medals which have received little exposure in the past or which are recorded in the standard reference works with questionable accuracy. Further, it has obliged him to write about awards of which he himself had little if any previous knowledge. The **Canada General Service Medal** (1866-1870) was a case in point (*vide* Part Four of this series of articles). In other words, he has frequently found himself sailing into unfamiliar waters. And this, surely, is the joy of collecting medals. Each has a story to tell but, to understand that story, we need to think, to read, and to ask questions. If these articles have stimulated in the reader an urge to research deeper - from other sources - they will have served a useful purpose.

Most British medal awards are logical and clearly justified. They represent specific events which self-evidently qualified for official recognition with the issue of a silver or bronze disc suspended from a length of coloured ribbon and bearing the effigy of a Monarch. But we may wonder why the authorities have at times allowed other episodes of naval significance to pass unrewarded. An obvious example was the work of the British West Africa and British East Africa Squadrons in their fight against black slavery between 1820 and the middle decades of Queen Victoria's reign (*vide* Part Three). Equally puzzling is the absence of a medal for the events known collectively as the Battle of Shimonoseki. First, we must examine the circumstances.

Initial European contact with Japan came in 1543 with the arrival of Portuguese Jesuit priests and Dutch merchant traders. Japan was a very structured feudal society, 2000 years old, consisting of various Princely clans each having allegiance to an Emperor deemed to be immortal and administered by an executive cabinet headed by a Shogun. In 1640 they banned Christianity, forbade overseas trade, and evicted all foreigners. Over the next two centuries, the Japanese isolated themselves from the outside world. Limited trade with Holland recommenced in the early 1800s and then the Americans began to show interest in establishing a dialogue with this "closed country". American naval missions attempted to do so in 1846 and 1849, but it was Commodore Matthew Perry, USN, who in 1854, with the

*Commodore Matthew Perry, USN.*

subtle hint of force, obtained a treaty to open certain ports to the West. Apart from three small gun-brigs presented to them earlier by America, the Japanese did not at that time possess a navy and had no knowledge of modern naval warfare, hence Perry's heavily armed steam-powered warships made a great impression. There were provincial Princes who, having seen those ships, wanted to acquire Western technology, but there were others who feared any Western intrusion into their culture. And therein lay the seeds of conflict.

Between the big home islands of Kyushu and Honshu there is a narrow seaway known as the Straits of Shimonoseki. It lay within the domain of Lord Mori Takachika, and he was one of those willing to defy the terms of the 1854 treaty. Like others, he was encouraged in 1863 by Emperor Konei who, breaking with centuries of tradition, challenged his own Shogunate with an edict ordering a complete expulsion of "the barbarians", the Europeans. The fat was now in the fire, Japan teetering on the brink of civil war.

The flames were fanned when Mori Takachika ordered his batteries to fire at foreign merchant vessels passing through the Straits. One, the PEMBROKE, was American. In retaliation, the USS WYOMING steamed into the Straits, sank two small vessels and fired on the shore batteries before withdrawing with fourteen of her men killed. That was on 16 July 1863. Three weeks earlier, the French naval despatch steamer KIENCHANG had come under fire from the shore and was fortunate to escape with only one sailor wounded. Despite warnings from the KIENCHANG's captain, the Dutch 16-gun sloop MEDUSA tried her luck in the Straits on 11 July and paid the price with nine seamen dead. All of this culminated on 20 July when two French warships under *Capitaine* Benjamin Jaures bombarded the coast and put ashore a brigade of 250 sailors and marines who set fire to buildings and destroyed a battery.

Jaures was thanked by the Shogunate for having punished the rebel Mori Takachika, but the French diplomat who ordered the attack was recalled because Paris was still hoping for a peaceful solution. And there the matter rested for more than a year while, surrounded by increasing violence, the European envoys struggled to agree a response. Crisis point came on 7 August 1864 when the British Vice Admiral Augustus Kuper, flying his flag in the 2400 ton frigate HMS EURYALUS, steamed into the southern port of Kagoshima with a squadron of nine Royal Navy ships. He was there to collect the reparations due for the murder by Samurai swordsmen eighteen months earlier of an Englishman, Charles Richardson. While the negotiations dragged on, Kuper's ships unexpectedly came under fire from the shore. A single cannon ball simultaneously removed the heads of EURYALUS's captain and first lieutenant. Eleven other men were killed, many more wounded. Kuper responded by burning several vessels in the harbour, then steamed north to Yokohama to await orders. He found the Allied envoys finally ready for action. They gave him command of a fleet of seventeen ships (including his own squadron) and he departed on 17 August for Shimonoseki.

It was a time when France was engaged in her disastrous war in Mexico and so could contribute only three ships to the expedition. The Dutch had four warships available, the Americans none at all. Matthew Perry and his squadron had long returned to America where President Abraham Lincoln and his people were immersed in their own cataclysmic civil war. However, to show support and in the absence of the WYOMING, the Americans did contribute to Kuper's fleet a chartered merchant steamer as a token flag-carrier. Despite these international commitments, the expedition was essentially a Royal Navy affair.

Admiral Kuper brought the Allied fleet into the Straits on 5 September and opened a heavy bombardment of the town of Shimonoseki and its defences. Fierce return fire badly damaged two of his ships and caused casualties, but on the second morning he sent in his landing parties (reportedly 2000 soldiers, seamen and marines). After ferocious hand-to-hand combat, the stockades and batteries were stormed and all resistance ceased. Subsequent mopping up was left to the forces of the Shogunate but, by the end of the second day, seventy-one of Kuper's men were dead or wounded and three awards of **The Victoria Cross** had been earned. The recipients, all Royal Navy, were 17-year old Midshipman Duncan Boyes, RN, Captain of the After Guard Thomas Pride, and the first American national to be so honoured, Able Seaman William Seeley.

Clearly, the British government approved of what had been done in its name at Kagoshima and Shimonoseki. Augustus Kuper himself was rewarded with a knighthood (KCB) and later promoted to full Admiral, but Queen Victoria was not invited to authorise a campaign medal for the Royal Navy and Royal Marines personnel who had served under him. This, surely, was very odd. She had approved only recently the issue of the all-ranks **China War Medal** (1856-1863), a campaign which likewise had been an international exercise in "gunboat diplomacy". Four

*Felice Beato, born in Venice, was one of a handful of early photographers who specialised in recording the aftermath of 19$^{th}$ century military conflicts. Somehow he attached himself to Vice Admiral August Kuper's assault force at Shimonoseki. While fires burn on the foreshore, British sailors and marines pose for his camera at the newly captured Choshu battery.*

years later she approved a medal for our almost bloodless invasion of Abyssinia (*vide* Part Four) but, for whatever reason, her Prime Minister, Viscount Palmerston, made no similar recommendation for Japan. With hindsight, such a medal would today remind us of the astonishing release of pent-up human energy which after 1864 swept that nation forward from feudalism to capitalism in less than half a century.

Captain K J Douglas-Morris, RN, was another writer who looked at what he called "no medal actions". It is a topic discussed in his scholarly *Naval Medals 1793-1856* (sadly, Japan did not come within that stated time-frame). As an example, he described the navy's work in Latin America in 1845-1846. Just like Lord Mori Takachika twenty years later, the dictator of Argentina, General Juan Manuel Rosas, chose to challenge foreign interference by blocking a major commercial waterway. In his case, it was the Parana river. From far inland it joins the River Plate which in turn feeds into the South Atlantic. He ordered the construction of a bank-to-bank boom, a formidable obstacle half a mile in length and consisting of twenty-four hulks lashed together with chains, stem to stern. On 20 November 1845, to reopen the Parana to traffic, men from six British warships successfully stormed the shore batteries and destroyed the boom. Thirty-six were killed or wounded. Commanding the operation - recorded as the Battle of Punto Obligado - was

*Depicted here by the noted marine artist Oswald Walters Brierly, the transitional sail and steam HMS Gorgon displaced 1100 tons and carried six large calibre guns. After serving at the 1840 bombardment of St Jean d'Acre (vide Part Two), in 1843 she joined the Royal Navy's deterrent flotilla patrolling the Atlantic coast of Latin America. The primary task was protection of Britain's trade with the emerging economies of that region. The 1845 Battle of Punto Obligado was a rare live-firing intervention in the hinterland.*

Captain Charles Hotham in HMS GORGON. He was honoured with a knighthood (KCB), but there were no medals for his sailors (even though as late as 1870 the elderly survivors were petitioning the Admiralty for such an award).

That affair had been preceded thirty-nine years earlier by a much more significant series of events. By late 1805, despite the triumph off Cape Trafalgar, the British found themselves still facing their enemies in almost every quarter of the globe. That meant confrontation at sea where we were at our strongest. With British interests under threat in India and the East Indies, it was important to establish permanent security for the sea route around the Cape of Good Hope. To this end, a naval expedition led by Commodore Sir Home Riggs Popham was sent from England to seize the Dutch settlement in Table Bay. With him were British Army regiments commanded by Lieutenant General Sir David Baird. The task force arrived on 4 January 1806 and, after a brief struggle, the Dutch capitulated. Baird became Governor General, his new garrison protected by Commodore Popham's squadron.

Popham looked around for further ways of employing his ships. Without waiting to consult London, he and the recently arrived General William Beresford settled upon Buenos Aires as a legitimate target. They persuaded Baird to lend them 1400 troops from the Cape Town garrison and they set off southwards for the River Plate in late April 1806. It seems not to have occurred to them that they should first investigate the political implications of their purely military action. They apparently did not know that the population of the Spanish-America Viceroyalty of the Rio de la Plata was looking for moral and material support in its ambition to break away from the control of Napoleon's puppets in Madrid.

*Despite the 1806 fiasco at Buenos Aires and his subsequent Court Martial, Commodore Home Riggs Popham was honoured by the City of London for "his endeavours to open new markets". As Rear Admiral, he went on to serve with great success in support of Welllington's Peninsular campaign. Before that, in 1803, he had invented an improved system of naval signal flags most famously used two years later by Horatio Nelson on the eve of the Battle of Trafalgar: "England expects every man will do his duty".*

When Beresford landed near Buenos Aires in early June, he and his troops should have been welcomed as allies and liberators. Instead, they treated the local people as enemies. After a short sharp fight, in which the British lost one man killed and twelve wounded, the town was occupied. The Treasury was immediately looted. Beresford was richer by £30,000, Popham by £6000, each private soldier by £18.50. They did not retain their new wealth for long.

A makeshift army of Buenos Aires and Montevideo militias led by General Santiago de Liniers surrounded the town. He held the British in his trap for forty-six days. On 12 August 1806, Beresford was forced to surrender after a final forty-eight hours of fighting. He and his men were marched away to be jailed in small towns in the interior. After six months in captivity, Beresford somehow managed to escape and found a ship to take him back to Cape Town.

The British government was furious when news of all this reached London. Commodore Popham was recalled to London to be censured by Court Martial, but national honour demanded the sending of another task force to obtain the release of the still captive General Beresford and his soldiers. Commanded by General Baird, the expedition arrived in October off Maldonado (in present-day Uruguay). The landings were contested by the local Spaniards but they were quickly put to flight. Again, the political initiative was lost when the town was subjected to three hours of drunken pillage.

Encouraged by that success, the British government sent a third force. On 3 February 1807, under the command of General Sir Samuel Auchmuty, it captured Montevideo at a cost of 100 British dead (800 Spaniards were killed). Five months later, on 5 July, Buenos Aires was again attacked, this time with a force commanded by General John Whitelocke. The assault was poorly planned, the British were beaten and (again) forced to surrender. Subsequent negotiations led to the total withdrawal of all British troops in the vicinities of Buenos Aires, Montevideo and Maldonado. And so ended Great Britain's last attempt at conquest on the mainland of South America.

The fact that ill-trained local militias had been able to defeat a professional army from Europe lit the fuse of rebellion. There were less than 600,000 people living in the area of the Rio de la Plata, and many of these were Amerindians and plantation slaves, but the powerful land owners were tired of paying taxes to the government in Madrid. They seized the opportunity provided by Europe's preoccupation with its own troubles to strike out for independence. Open revolt commenced in 1810 and within six years the long-standing Spanish link had been broken.

There followed a complete role reversal for the Royal Navy in southern waters. The populations of the newly emergent Latin American nations were being boosted by immigration from Europe and, as their economies expanded, British companies became major trading partners. The original Rio de la Plata settlers had hoped to find silver (*argentum*) just as others had discovered it in Peru, but there was none to be found. Even so, that was the name their successors gave to their new country when it became fully independent in 1820. As events were to show, their future lay not with silver but with farming and the export of grain, hides and salted beef. In return, the Argentines needed British machine tools and agricultural machinery and, later that century, a railway system.

To protect their shared commercial interests from foreign interference, the Admiralty ordered the creation in 1826 of a permanent South America Station. Its first commander was Rear Admiral Robert Otway and his initial task was to protect the people of Brazil. They had recently broken away from Lisbon, but the King of Portugal had ambitions to re-establish his country's former ownership of that vast territory. When Otway's squadron arrived in Brazilian waters it was such an intimidating deterrent that the new nation was able to retain its independence without open conflict. Other former Spanish colonies such as Chile and Peru likewise at times enjoyed the coastal security provided by the Royal Navy while they got on with their endless succession of internal wars and revolutions.

The South America Station expanded in 1837 and became the Pacific Station. Its ships conducted regular patrols along both the eastern and western coastlines of the Americas and of Western Canada. Based first at Valparaiso and then, after 1846, at Esquimalt (Vancouver Island), the Pacific Squadron maintained the maritime peace in those vast regions for nearly eight decades. That said, the description "peace" must be taken with a pinch of salt. The American Civil War (1861-1865) witnessed major conflicts at sea between "ironclads" such as the USS MONITOR and the CSS VIRGINIA, innovative designs which pointed the way forward in warship design.

The US Navy saw further action - if "action" is the correct word - on 15 February 1898 when the 6700 ton auxiliary cruiser USS MAINE exploded in Havana harbour. Three quarters of her 374 officers and men were killed. The cause of the disaster was never established with any certainty, but it was an event which aroused the fury of the American public and led to war with Spain and the invasion of Cuba. The Royal Navy was given no role in either of those episodes even though the Civil War badly damaged Lancashire's cotton industry and the war in Cuba interfered with British trade. There were limits to what could be done.

When Admiral Sir "Jackie" Fisher became First Sea Lord in 1904, one of his problems was deciding how best to utilise his assets in the face of Germany's ever-expanding naval power. Dozens of Royal Navy ships had been committed to the recent campaigns in South Africa and China and were returning to their home ports (or had already done so).

Many of the older ships were due for scrapping, and this meant that their personnel could be transferred to the new DREADNOUGHT Class and the various other new types under construction. He needed every experienced officer and rating he could lay hands on to boost the strength of the Grand Fleet. They were more urgently required at home than they were on the other side of the world. Accordingly, the Pacific Station was wound down in March 1905 and, as a permanent Royal Navy establishment, never replaced. Instead, the extensive dockyards and barracks at Esquimalt were handed over to the newly-formed Canadian Naval Service (renamed Royal Canadian Navy in 1911) and it has been the home of Canada's Pacific Fleet ever since.

Here we may pause for a moment. Looking back, we see that no medals other than those named to PHOEBE and CHERUB were ever issued in respect of the navy's services in the Western Atlantic and Eastern Pacific littorals after Napoleon

*America's Civil War generated a huge leap forward in warship design. In some ways even more radical than that of HMS Warrior (today preserved at the Portsmouth Historic Dockyard) the concept of the steam-powered "ironclad" opened new possibilities for naval architects worldwide. In total, sixty were built during that war but best remembered is the 1000 ton USS Monitor seen here showing her battle scars. A major engagement was the inconclusive clash with the Confederate navy's Virginia off Hampton Roads on 9 March 1862. Having made her mark on history, the Monitor sank under tow off Cape Hatteras less than a year after her launch.*

had departed for St Helena and after we made our peace with the Americans. However, in his book, Douglas-Morris makes the point that a man can be discovered to have taken part in one or more "no medal actions" by considering first his known awards - British and foreign - and then by researching the voyages of the ships in which he can be shown to have served. This applies, of course, not only to the Americas. His pages devoted to the Royal Navy's and Royal Marines' forgotten role in the Wars of Spanish Succession (the 1835-1839 "Carlist Wars") are particularly instructive in that context.

Additionally, he quotes the case of Charles Norman, an officer who received the **NGSM** with bar **Syria** for his 1840 services in HMS EDINBURGH. The Admiralty had rewarded him then with accelerated promotion from Lieutenant to Commander, but he received nothing for the Battle of Punto Obligado even though he was possibly at greater hazard there - in HMS COMUS - than he had been off the coast of Syria five years earlier. As a footnote, Captain Hotham's 1100 ton steam frigate GORGON also featured in the Syria story (*vide* Part Two), a fact which demonstrates the adaptability of those early side-wheelers.

In Part Five, we looked at some of the campaign medals resulting from the navy's role in various actions fought between 1890 and 1914. Prominent amongst those accounts was the story of the Second Anglo-Boer War of 1899-1902 and the two awards which commemorate it, **The Queen's South Africa Medal** and **The King's South Africa Medal.** Less well remembered is the conflict which preceded it, two decades earlier, the First Anglo-Boer War (the First War for Freedom). The troubled relationship between the British and the hardy descendents of the original 17$^{th}$ century Dutch settlers has already been described, so we shall focus now upon the events of 1880-1881.

Although the British government had formally recognised the independence of the Boer Republics of Transvaal and the Orange Free State in 1852 and again in 1854, we were still harassing them in the wake of the Zulu War of 1879. The entire region was in an unsettled state, the British continuing to impose (or attempting to impose) their vision of the future. In essence, they wanted to forge within the Empire a confederation of all the British colonists, the Boer settlers and the tribal leaders who between them controlled most of southern and south eastern Africa.

The policy of expansion was in the hands of Sir Bartle Frere, representing the British government. His military commander was Major General Sir George Colley, an officer well regarded for his past campaigning record. Ignoring the 1850s agreements, Frere had ordered the creation of seven small widely scattered British Army garrisons, numbering in total 2000 men, within the borders of the Transvaal. Matters came to a head on 20 December 1880 at Bronkhorst Spruit. A long column of military wagons, thinly escorted by the 94$^{th}$ Regiment of Foot, was passing through Boer territory when it was stopped and ordered to turn back. Lieutenant Colonel Philip Anstruther declined to give way and the encounter erupted into a one-sided fire-fight. Within minutes, 120 of his men, including all his officers, were dead or wounded. The mortally injured Anstruther ordered the survivors to surrender. There were two Boer casualties.

Despite this setback, General Colley was so concerned for the fate of the seven isolated garrisons that he formed a Natal Field Force with the intention of entering the Transvaal to rescue them. He was warned that the Boers could, if necessary, mobilise up to 16,000 men and that 2000 of them were waiting along his intended line of march. With little more than 1200 troops available, he called upon the navy to contribute a Naval Brigade. Unfortunately for him, there were at the time only two ships in nearby waters, the 1760 ton sloop HMS DIDO and the 4150 ton corvette HMS BOADICEA.

At the order of Commodore Frederick Richards, BOADICEA sent ashore seventy petty officers and seamen. Fifty more came from the DIDO. Additional to their rifles, the sailors brought with them two Gatling guns, two 9-pounder field guns and three rocket tubes. In charge of this small Brigade was Commander Francis Romilly, RN. His officers were Lieutenants Henry Ogle and Cornwallis Trower with Sub Lieutenants Augustus Scott and Henry Grant Monckton. They could not know it, but neither Romilly nor Trower had long to live.

Despite the distances to be covered and the potential scale of the opposition, Colley was gambling on a successful outcome. His optimism was ill-founded. The next clash came on 28 January 1881 at Laing's Nek. Colley tried to remove a strong force of Boers entrenched on high ground. The tactics were those of the Crimea - red-coated troops ordered into a bayonet charge up sloping open ground. By now the soldiers had been joined by sailors who brought into action their rocket tubes. After several hours of battle - in which nearly all Colley's regimental officers were sniped or killed in hand-to-hand combat - the British were forced to retreat. Their casualties - dead, wounded, captured - amounted to 150 (one third of those engaged).

For their part, the Boers suffered forty-one casualties, some most probably inflicted by the navy's rocket missiles. Two **Victoria Crosses** were awarded for this

When Commodore Richards sent men to aid General Colley in 1881, he had gained already a fine fighting record in the Second China War and the Zulu War. After service in the 1885 Burma campaign he became First Naval Lord. In that role, he master-minded a huge new construction programme which led to the resignation of Prime Minister William Gladstone. Retiring in 1899 as Admiral of the Fleet Sir Frederick Richards, his career epitomised a degree of political influence his $21^{st}$ Century successors could not imagine.

action which, it may be noted, was the last time a British infantry regiment - in this instance the 58th (Rutlandshire) Regiment of Foot - carried its Colours into action. Four young officers in succession were given that honour. All four were shot down.

A month later, on 8 February at the N'gogo River crossing, a wagon convoy commanded in person by General Colley was ambushed by 300 Boers. They killed or wounded 139 officers and men, half the strength of the escort, at no loss to themselves. Colley himself survived this disaster but seems to have been undaunted by it. He knew that Sir Bartle Frere and the Boer leader, Paul Kruger, were negotiating a peaceful settlement. Determined to salvage his reputation before the fighting stopped, he launched without Frere's authority yet another advance, this time up the undefended heights of the massive steep-sided Majuba Hill.

On 26/27 February he led an overnight march with 290 soldiers and sixty-eight sailors to occupy the cliffs overlooking the main Boer encampment. Reaching the summit, he found it to be out of rifle-shot range but nevertheless he ordered his men to stay where they were and awaited the Boer reaction. It came at daybreak, Boer scouts stealthily climbing 500 feet up through wooded ravines to identify the British positions and report them to their commander, Piet Joubert. By midday he was ready to strike with full force. Sub Lieutenant A L Scott, RN, subsequently reported: "The Boers had gained the top of the hill and were coming across in great numbers to cut off the men retreating. The enemy poured a tremendous fire down the sides of the mountain so that we were obliged to scatter and make the best of our way out of range". General Colley was killed almost immediately by one of the first shots fired.

What started as a general retreat quickly became a rout, every man for himself, some in their panic falling from the cliffs. Untrained in individual marksmanship, our men could do little to return fire. The soldiers' red coats and sailors' blue jackets made them easy targets. At a cost to themselves of just one dead and five wounded, the Boers shattered the British force. Lieutenant Trower died where he stood, shot through the lungs. Commander Romilly was shot through the gut and died four days later after being carried down by his men to the makeshift field hospital administered by Surgeon Edward Mahon, RN. Of the sixty-eight Naval Brigade personnel committed to this fiasco, exactly half were killed or seriously wounded.

When Commodore Richards came to write his despatch to the Admiralty, he quoted eyewitness reports that the Boers had treated with compassion the several dozen wounded left behind. They collected the British dead and buried them, soldiers and sailors alike, in two mass graves on the mountain top. They also agreed to the removal of Colley's body and that of young Trower for individual burial beside Surgeon Mahon's tented hospital.

The Boers had no facilities for holding large numbers of prisoners, so they were all unconditionally set free. One such was an officer of the Gordon Highlanders whose name was fated to become notorious thirty-four years later. Lieutenant Ian Hamilton was wounded at Majuba but soon recovered to resume his military career. By 1915 he was General Sir Ian Hamilton, in charge of Allied land operations on the Gallipoli peninsula. What happened there under his command has been touched upon in Part Six.

After just ten weeks of intermittent fighting, Majuba was the end of it. In March

*Evoking "Custer's Last Stand" at the Little Big Horn - a battle fought five years earlier - this Illustrated London News engraving attempts to preserve the final moments of Major General Sir George Colley on the high plateau of Majuba Hill. In the event, he was killed by a single shot through the forehead just as he emerged from his tent and therefore had no control over the battle. Critics claimed the stress of the earlier defeats had impaired his judgement, hence he avoided telling Sir Bartle Frere his orders could not be met with such limited resources.*

*Bearing little resemblance to eyewitness accounts, the scene on Majuba Hill is depicted by an artist faithful to the tradition of portraying Queen Victoria's soldiers at their most heroic. Although it is monochrome, his dramatic painting illustrates the Naval Brigade men (dark jackets) fighting alongside Colley's soldiers (pale jackets). Those wearing the kilt represent the 141 men of the $92^{nd}$ (Gordon Highlanders) Regiment of Foot who took part.*

it was all settled - the Transvaal would continue to be a self-governing Republic, the British would be responsible only for its external affairs. Strangely, when the Second Anglo-Boer War was in full flow twenty years later, a popular rallying cry was "Remember Majuba!". For their part, the authorities decided that Majuba was instead best forgotten, hence the Queen was never invited to approve the issue of a campaign medal.

In retrospect, we may question why General Colley acted as he did. An experienced officer, there is no doubting his personal bravery and he was one of the minority of his contemporaries who had attended the Staff College. He should not be dismissed simply as a fool. Whatever fault may be laid at his door it was that of failing to recognise his enemy's skills in fieldcraft and marksmanship. His successors, the generals who in 1899 commanded the British army during the opening phase of the Second Anglo-Boer War, made exactly the same mistake. However, like most senior officers and administrators then serving in South Africa, he had with him his wife. In Army circles - smart tea-time chatter amongst the other wives - Lady Colley was known as "Tiger". Yes, it was suggested that it was she who prodded her husband into making such flawed decisions, particularly at Majuba.

We now move forward to the conflicts of the $20^{th}$ century. Totally dependent upon first coal and then fuel oil, the Royal Navy could not have operated for long without the Merchant Navy. Operating far from any naval shore base, our warships were replenished by the Royal Fleet Auxiliary (established in 1905) but, before that could happen, all the raw materials of war needed to be brought to British shores

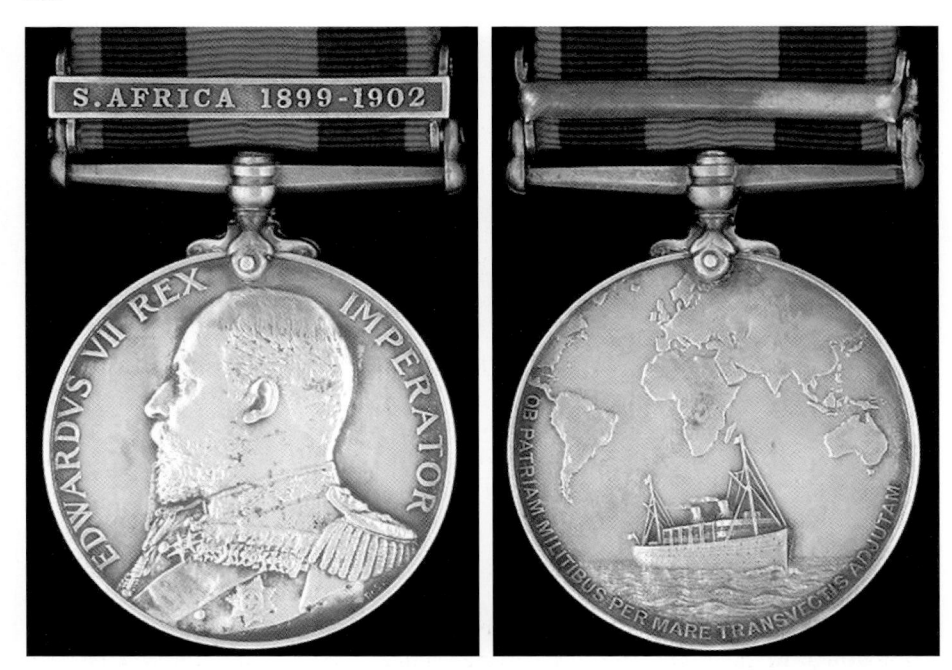

*(Above) This poignant example of **The Transport Medal** was awarded to Captain Edward John Smith, RD, RNR. He completed two trooping voyages to South Africa as Master of the White Star Line liner RMS Majestic. Following other important commands, he took the prestigious new RMS Titanic to sea in April 1912 only to die when she sank in the North Atlantic. (Below) If he had lived, and if still serving in the Great War, Captain Smith would have received **The Mercantile Marine Medal**.*

from the Americas and from every corner of the Empire. By the same token, soldiers and their weaponry could not be moved from one theatre of war to another except by civilian-manned troopships and requisitioned liners. Recognition first came in 1903 with the officers-only **Transport Medal.** Struck in silver, it was given to the Master and his eight most senior officers in each of the ships which had carried troops to South Africa (our second war with the Boers) and to China (the Boxer rebellion). The medal was fitted with bars: **S Africa 1899-1902** and/or **China 1900.** The officers of 174 vessels were granted this award, hence the total issued was 1566 (making it, numerically, as rare as **The Victoria Cross).**

In 1919, a completely new award was announced, **The Mercantile Marine Medal.** Struck in bronze, it was intended for issue (irrespective of rank or rate) to all civilian seafarers who had completed at least one wartime voyage through a designated "danger zone" in a ship of the British Mercantile Marine. In 1928, to honour its wartime services, the Mercantile Marine was given a new name by King George V when he appointed HRH The Prince of Wales as "Master of the Merchant Navy and the Fishing Fleet".

Between 1914 and 1918, 3305 British-registered ships were sunk. Nearly 15,000 of the men and women serving in them lost their lives. The Board of Trade was responsible for despatching the medals and, given the traditionally casual nature of employment in the merchant service (other than that of officers), the Board's task could not have been easy. Men of more than one nationality or ethnic origin might be signed-on by a First Mate from the "pool" at Southampton, then paid off in Liverpool before dispersing to join other ships (possibly in other ports). Their movements were recorded in the Registry of Shipping and Seamen but, by the early 1920s when the medal was ready for distribution, many were dead or had settled ashore or gone home to their country of origin. A total of 133,135 medals were issued, impressed on the rim with the man's forename and surname, but not his rate or the name of a ship. Researching his career can be difficult if he had a combination of names shared with several other recipients, but determined digging in the archives can often reveal a dramatic story.

There was no such official recognition at the end of the Second World War. Like their opposite numbers in the Royal Navy, merchant seamen qualified for one or more of the anonymous campaign Stars (*vide* Part Seven). However, the authorities chose not to follow the precedent of **The Mercantile Marine Medal.** The decision was probably based upon considerations of cost and "administrative convenience", but it left a legacy of resentment amongst the survivors (particularly those who had served in the North Russia convoys). Between 1939 and 1945, 3860 cargo and passenger ships were sunk or seriously damaged by enemy action. Thirty-two thousand British mariners lost their lives. More than 8000 are buried in Commonwealth War Graves Commission cemeteries scattered around the world, 24,000 more have "no other grave than the sea". Whenever a merchant ship was sunk by bomb or torpedo, the owners immediately stopped the pay of her crew (excepting the contract officers). Days or weeks spent in a lifeboat or hospital (for the lucky ones) did not count. So, "no money, not even a medal".

We turn now to the 1920s. China was in a state of chaos - powerful warlords,

Communist-inspired factions and a National Revolutionary Army (NRA) all fighting each other for territory. Since 1854, several European nations had enjoyed trading privileges based upon (at various times) thirty-six different Treaty Ports. Foremost amongst the bankers and traders were the Americans and the British. To protect those commercial interests, their governments routinely deployed warships to patrol China's coast and major rivers. One such Treaty Port was Nanjing (Nanking), sited on the banks of the mighty Yangtse.

Violence came to Nanjing in late March 1928 when the city was attacked by the NRA and by murderous gangs of bandits. With hundreds of Europeans trapped in the city, it was imperative to mount without delay a rescue operation. Nanjing is not far inland, and the river is at that point navigable to ocean-going vessels. Vice Admiral Sir Reginald Tyrwhitt was C-in-C China Station, and he despatched fourteen Royal Navy ships with orders to employ whatever fire-power might prove necessary to effect an evacuation. They were the heavy cruiser VINDICTIVE, the light cruisers CARADOC, CARLISLE and EMERALD, and the destroyers PETERSFIELD, VERITY, VETERAN, WILD SWAN, WISHART, WITHERINGTON and WOLSEY. Also engaged were APHIS, CRICKET and GNAT - three of the "Insect" Class gunboats featured previously in this series of articles.

The US Navy contributed five destroyers - JOHN D FORD, NOA, PILLSBURY, SIMPSON and the WILLIAM B PRESTON. They were joined by gunboats of the Japanese Navy (four), and of the Italian and French navies (one each). In combination, these vessels carried more than enough heavy weaponry to do the job, but Tyrwhitt and the American commander knew that the operation needed to be completed quickly before a prolonged land battle could develop.

After initial exchanges on 21 March, serious action commenced three days later when American and British ships opened fire with their main armament against identified NRA positions. By midnight the city was burning, some of its fine waterfront buildings reduced to rubble. Under cover of this bombardment, naval landing parties located and embarked most of the terrified foreign nationals (only forty, plus one British seaman, were dead or missing). The evacuees were taken out to two merchant vessels, the SS KUNGWO and SS WEN-CHOW. They were escorted down-river by American and British warships which, as had happened during the hours of the evacuation, were under persistent gunfire from the both banks of the river. For "the Nanjing Incident" and for other actions between 1926 and 1932, American sailors and marines received **The Yangtse Service Medal.** Vice Admiral Tyrwhitt's men received nothing.

Likewise, the Royal Navy's involvement in "the Panay Incident" of 12 December 1938 was allowed to pass unrewarded. By that year, large tracts of China were being overrun by the Japanese. Again, the city of Nanjing fell victim to violence but, compared with that of ten years earlier, it was inflicted on a nightmare scale beyond any imagining. It continued for six frenzied weeks, ending only when the invaders' appetite for blood and torture was fully sated. In what became known as "the Rape of Nanjing", 250,000 disarmed Chinese soldiers and unarmed civilians were murdered with the bullet, the bayonet and the sword. At least 20,000 women and children were raped and mutilated (some sources estimate 100,000). In Part Five (1890-1914), we looked at the appalling story of the outrages committed by European troops in Pekin (the 1900 Boxer Rebellion) under the brutal command of General Alfred Graf von Waldersee. Those atrocities were nothing compared with the medieval barbarity of the so-called soldiers of Imperial Japan.

Most of the European traders and missionaries had fled the city, but key members of the US Embassy were still at work. The USS PANAY was sent to rescue them. She was a 480 ton riverboat armed with two 3" guns and eight .30 calibre machine guns. After several years of Yangtse service, her fifty-nine officers and men were accustomed to riverbank sniping. Under the captaincy of Lieutenant Commander James M Lewis, USN, they coolly extracted the remaining foreign nationals before heading upriver, away from the fighting.

The "Insect" Class gunboats HMS BEE and HMS LADYBIRD were in the vicinity, heading to support their American comrades. Both came under fire, LADYBIRD suffering six hits from Japanese artillery shells (with unknown casualties). However, she and BEE were lucky compared with the isolated PANAY. Attacked from the air by Japanese aircraft, hit by bombs and machine-gun fire, she sank on the afternoon of 12 March. Three of her crew were killed. Forty-three more, plus five civilian passengers, were wounded. Reparations were paid, but the incident marked the beginning of the deterioration in US/Japanese relations which

*In 1938, at the city of Nanjing, gloating Japanese officers took hundreds of photographs of the atrocities committed by their troops. Most are too repulsive for reproduction in a publication like this. Shown here, Chinese civilians are about to be buried alive in a pit they had been forced to dig.*

*The Yangtse Service Medal*, *as issued for actions in China between 1926-1932. The medal, created in 1930, was awarded for service within the Yangtse river valley and for service ashore at Shanghai in direct support of landings relating to the Nanjing Incident.*

culminated on 7 December 1941 at Pearl Harbour.

**The Yangtse Service Medal** was replaced in August 1940 by the retrospective **China Service Medal**. It was issued to all US Navy and USMC personnel who served in that country in later years. The dangers of patrolling the Yangtse - often caught in the cross-fire of other peoples' wars - were indeed dramatically underlined by the sinking of the USS PANAY, but HMS BEE and HMS LADYBIRD were not the only White Ensign ships to come under fire during the 1920s and 1930s. Even so, after 1900, there were no more British medals for services in China until, in 1949, HMS AMETHYST attempted to carry supplies to the besieged British community in, once again, Nanjing. She was due to replace HMS CONSORT as guard ship. The story of that heroic episode is well known, it need not be re-told here. It is sufficient to note that the Admiralty did finally acknowledge that operating in China through often hostile territory - on occasion as much as 1000 navigable miles deep into the Asian landmass - could be unusually perilous. The tenth issue of **The Naval General Service Medal** was fitted with the bar **HMS Amethyst - Yangtse 1949.**

In Part Six, attention was drawn to the anomaly of that same medal having been granted with the bar **Palestine 1936-39** but the denial of a matching award for the blockade of Spain during those same years. For the navy, Palestine was bloodless. Spain was not. It was the period of the Spanish Civil War. At this distance in time it is difficult to grasp the scale and violence of that tragic conflict. Half a million people died, 450,000 fled. In a full-scale rehearsal for the global war about to erupt, Adolf Hitler and Benito Mussolini committed their naval and air forces to ensure that General Francisco Franco would be the winner.

The Royal Navy was given the dangerous task of patrolling the Spanish coastlines, north and south. The job was twofold - identifying blockade runners and protecting any innocent merchant shipping passing through those waters. Italy had the largest fleet of submarines of any nation in the world - eighty-three compared with the Royal Navy's thirty-eight. Of these, at any one time, twenty or more were operating covertly in the Western Mediterranean while Hitler's U-boats lurked off Spain's northern ports.

Before it was all over, 105 merchantmen of twelve different nationalities had been attacked by torpedo, by surface gunfire, by bombing, or by aerial strafing. Twenty-nine were British-flagged and, of these, three were sunk. The first, the 7000 ton oil tanker SS WOODFORD, went down following a torpedo attack on 1 September 1937 off Benicarlo (Cape San Sebastiano). The Second Engineer was the one man lost from her all-Greek crew. Two months later, on 30 October, the elderly 2350 ton cargo steamer JEAN WEEMS (Captain Everett) was bombed and sunk while on passage from Marseilles to Barcelona with a cargo of wheat. There were twenty-six survivors.

Then, on 21 January 1938, the 887 ton SS ENDYMION (Master and part-owner Captain Adolphus Verano) was on passage from Newport (South Wales) to Cartagena with a cargo of coke when, off Cape Tinoso, she was torpedoed by the Italian submarine TORRICELLI (it was operating under Nationalist colours as the GENERAL SANJURJO). Of the fifteen members of the ENDYMION's crew, only four survived. One who died was Laura Verano, the Gibraltar-born daughter of the ship's Master. Probably the ship's cook, she had been signed on as Ordinary Seaman.

In the language of the time, all these ships were damaged or destroyed by "insurgent forces". This meant, in the main, German or Italian aircraft or submarines from which all original identifying marks had been removed. Royal Navy ships could not know until the last moment whether or not they were about to be attacked. Their "non-intervention" neutrality status was no guarantee of immunity. During an air raid at Valencia on 23 February 1937, Captain T B Drew,

*While there was no medal for Royal Navy men who served during the Spanish Civil War, Hitler's Nazi government was not so shy. Announced in April 1939,* **The Spanish Cross** *(Der Spanienkreuz) was given to the 26,117 German servicemen who had "volunteered". Struck in either bronze, silver or gold, it had six levels of seniority. The highest was the "Gold with Diamonds" version of which twenty-eight were presented. Three of those recipients - Adolf Galland, Werner Molders and Walter Oesau - were Luftwaffe fighter pilots. Lessons learned in Spain made them formidable opponents in the 1940 Battle of Britain.*

RN, and four of his men in the battleship HMS ROYAL OAK were injured by an errant anti-aircraft shell fired from a shore battery. At other locations and at different times, ROYAL OAK and the destroyers BLANCHE, FEARLESS, GALLANT and GIPSY were each attacked from the air. None were seriously damaged.

On 7 September, the destroyer HMS HAVOCK was patrolling off Alicante when her lookouts saw the wake of two torpedoes passing close by. While her sister-ship HASTY came racing to her support, HAVOCK responded with a salvo of seven depth-charges. They brought to the surface a large spread of oil, but then her ASDIC unit broke down and the submarine escaped. It was the 620 ton Italian IRIDE. In command was Prince Junio Valerio Borghese and he was lucky to survive. The charges exploded so close to his boat that not only was a fuel tank ruptured but two of his men were reportedly hurled against machinery and fatally injured.

In 1940 the remarkable *Capitano di Fregata* Prince Borghese invented the *maiali* ("pigs") - the two-man "human torpedoes" soon to be copied by the British. It was he who commanded the submarine SCIRE when, in December 1941, it carried three *maiali* from La Spezia to Alexandria for the daring attack which sank at their moorings the battleships HMS VALIANT and HMS QUEEN ELIZABETH.

Meantime, off Southern Spain on the afternoon of 13 May 1937, the recently commissioned 1350 ton destroyer HMS HUNTER was patrolling the Gulf of Almeria. Unknown to her Captain, two German E-boats (flying Nationalist colours) had some weeks earlier laid mines in the approaches to the port. When HUNTER struck one of these mines she was crippled and came close to sinking before being towed into Almeria harbour by her sister-ship HYPERION. The explosion killed eight of the ship's company and injured twenty-four others.

More would have died without the actions of Lieutenant Patrick Noel

*Long before the British began to form units such as the Special Boat Section, the Italian submariner Prince Junio Valerio Borghese was pioneering his own concept of "special forces". Only by the chances of war was he spared when, off Alicante, HMS Havock failed to kill him in 1937. His greatest success in WWII was the sinking at their moorings of HMShips Valiant and Queen Elizabeth, a blow which radically reduced for many months the strength of our Mediterranean Fleet. An ardent Fascist, he fought on against the Allies after Italy changed sides in 1943. Post-war, for political reasons, he was imprisoned for four years by his own government.*

Humphreys, RN. The ship was listing heavily. Hearing the shouts of men trapped in the dark and stench of a shattered Mess Deck, he took charge and jumped down into chest-deep sea water and fuel oil. With four others helping him, he dragged up several bodies and ten barely alive seamen and stokers. To remain there amongst the torn steelwork, struggling to free burned and fuel-blinded casualties, required immense courage. It was recognised by an announcement in *The London Gazette* (12 November 1937) of his award of **The Empire Gallantry Medal (Military Division),** more formally titled **The Medal of the Order of the British Empire for Gallantry**. On the initiative of HM the King, the **EGM** was superseded in September 1940 by **The George Cross,** a new award equating to **The Victoria Cross** but for acts of valour "not in the face of the enemy". Holders of the **EGM** were permitted to exchange it for **The George Cross,** and Pat Humphreys was one who did so.

Additionally named in *The London Gazette* were the four men who volunteered to work alongside him in that terrifying incident. Petty Officer James Smail likewise received the **EGM (Military Division)** while Able Seamen James Collings, Ernest Thomas and Herbert Abrahams each were awarded **The British Empire Medal.** After extensive repairs and refit, HMS HUNTER returned to service and joined the Home Fleet. During the ferocious close-quarter First Battle of Narvik (10 April 1940), again badly damaged, she was in collision with her sister-ship HOTSPUR, then rolled over and sank. Eight months later HMS HYPERION was lost in the Mediterranean. Pat Humphreys himself did not survive very much longer. He had transferred in 1938 to the Fleet Air Arm, qualified as an Observer/Navigator in Swordfish biplanes, then went to the Mediterranean in HMS EAGLE.

While on loan to HMS ILLUSTRIOUS he had taken part in the Taranto attack (*vide* Part Seven). His pilot that night was Lieutenant (A) J W G Wellham, RN. As part of the second wave of attacking Swordfish, they made a wide low-level circuit through the fierce *flak* rising from the inner docks before heading towards the battleships moored in the outer harbour. Skirting the balloon barrage - their aircraft badly damaged by machine-gun fire and a 40 mm shell - they flew towards the massive bulk of the 38,000 ton VITTORIO VENETO. In 1940 this powerful modern ship had been fortunate to survive the Battle of Cape Matapan. She was attacked three times on that occasion by Fleet Air Arm aircraft which inflicted serious damage with their torpedoes. Returned to active service after five months in dockyard hands she was one of the prime targets at Taranto but, again, her luck held. Even though Wellham pressed his attack to 500 yards before releasing his torpedo, he failed to obtain a hit. He and Pat Humphreys were themselves fortunate, managing to guide their battered Swordfish back to the distant ILLUSTRIOUS.

Pat Humphreys was posted subsequently to HMS DAEDALUS (the Royal Naval Air Station at Lee-on-Solent) and from there to the RAF's No 96 Squadron based at West Malling, Kent. Equipped with the De Havilland Mark XII Mosquito night fighter, the squadron operated anti-intruder patrols. On the night of 26 November 1943, he and his pilot, Lieutenant (A) G M Walker, RN, were killed when shortly after take-off their aircraft lost height and crashed into a tree two miles west of the airfield.

*First commissioned in early 1940, the identical 38,000 ton 30 knot Littorio and Vittorio Veneto outclassed all British battleships then stationed in the Mediterranean. If equipped with radar, they would have been even more dangerous. Prime targets at Taranto, they survived the raid although the Littorio needed five months to repair.*

The next and final edition of this series - "The Awards That Never Were", Part Nine (B) - will consider the decades between 1945 and the present day. The two most contentious events were the three "Cod Wars" with Iceland (1958 to 1976) and the dispute with Southern Rhodesia (1966 to 1975). They will beg an important question. Assuming that in our complex modern world we do still need a navy, what is a fit and proper role for it in the defence of our national interests?

## Part Nine (B) - The Awards That Never Were (1945 to 2013)

LOOKING BACK, and as remarked in Part Nine (A), we can see that there have been numerous occasions when men of the Royal Navy have been committed to battle, even honoured with awards for their bravery, but which were never recognised with the issue of a campaign medal. Certainly there is a case for arguing that the navy's long-running 19$^{th}$ century anti-slavery campaigns, its services in the 1830s Carlist Wars, in the 1840s in Latin America, in the 1860s Japan conflict, in South Africa 1881, and then during the 1930s Spanish Civil War, should each have earned a medal. However, and by contrast, there is reason to be thankful that two very much later Royal Navy campaigns were permitted to pass unrewarded. One such was the Beira Patrol and this, in condensed form, is the story behind it.

Having shed responsibility for India in 1947, the British set about abandoning Africa. In rapid succession, each Colony and Protectorate gained independence with a floodlit midnight ceremony attended by a member of the Royal family. The exception was Southern Rhodesia. It was governed by a white European minority of 250,000 led by Ian Smith, a farmer whose battered face was testimony to his wartime service as a Spitfire pilot. He was just one of thousands of Rhodesians, black and white, who loyally volunteered to fight for Britain in the two world wars. Told by our Prime Minister Harold Wilson that he must accept the principle of "majority rule", Ian Smith declined. The two met and talked, but there could be no meeting of minds. Rhodesia's economy was *per capita* the strongest and most productive in all Africa. The predominant tribes, four million Mashona and Matabele, were at peace and, argued Smith, they were not ready for Wilson's concept of democracy. Ian Smith might well have questioned how they could be expected to make that transition in a few months while the British, beginning with the Magna Carta of 1215, had inflicted upon themselves seven centuries of civil conflict before finally embracing universal suffrage with the Representation of the People Act of 1928.

Tired of Wilson's threats and bullying, Ian Smith's otherwise intensely pro-British Cabinet reluctantly issued, on 11 November 1965, its "Unilateral Declaration of Independence" (UDI). Wilson responded by recruiting the whole world against him. In New York, his diplomats somehow persuaded the United Nations Security Council to agree a series of increasingly harsh sanctions which made Rhodesia an outcast from the international community. Exactly how that small country's breakaway from the British Crown might jeopardise the security of the world was not explained.

At home, public opinion was divided on the Rhodesia issue. Thousands of RAF aircrew had trained in that beautiful country during the war, hundreds returned later to settle. Many British families had friends and relatives in Rhodesia, just as they did in Canada, Australia or New Zealand. On the other hand, there were those who argued that white supremacy in *any* African country was morally wrong. The same view prevailed in the UN General Assembly. Some members proposed that, if sanctions did not work, Great Britain must mount a military invasion. They were supported by the Archbishop of Canterbury, Michael Ramsay, who announced: "If

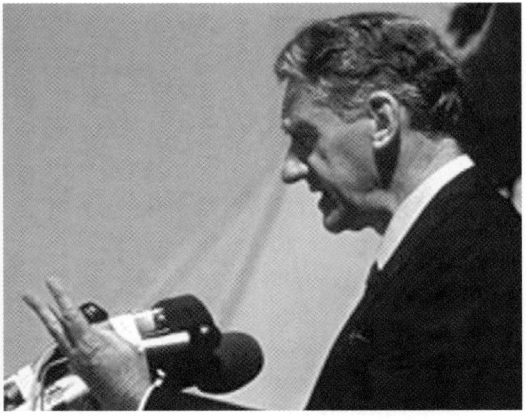

Images: BBC Archives/Wikipedia

*Although Harold Wilson seems amused by Ian Smith's raised two fingers, these photographs are not directly connected. The Rhodesian leader was simply making the second of three points at a political rally. He died in Cape Town in 2007, age eighty-eight. His bitter opponent resigned the British premiership in April 1976 and shortly afterwards was diagnosed as having Alzheimer's Disease. By coincidence, the navy's long-running Beira Patrol had ended ten months earlier and the third "Cod War" ended two months later.*

British soldiers are sent to fight in Rhodesia, I am certain that God will be on their side". But, as the years rolled by, British public interest in the affairs of Africa was overtaken by the fascination of watching the nightly TV coverage of America's democracy-loving activities in Viet Nam. Then, after Edward Heath replaced Harold Wilson in 10 Downing Street in 1970, people were more concerned with the endless strikes, the power cuts and the "three day working week".

At the heart of Wilson's strategy was an oil embargo. Rhodesia imported part of its oil requirements by road tanker from South Africa, part by rail tanker from Laurenco Marques (now Maputo), and part *via* 185 miles of inland pipeline from Beira. Six hundred miles apart, the latter are ports sited on the coast of what was then Portuguese East Africa (now Mozambique). The South African government's policy of *apartheid* made it sympathetic to the Smith regime. Portugal was helpful because she had fears for the future of her own Colonies. Rejecting authoritative advice to the contrary, Wilson convinced himself that the only way to stop the flow of oil would be a blockade in one of the world's busiest sea lanes, the Mozambique Channel.

The eminent naval historian C S Forester wrote: "The mightiest weapon of sea power, the blockade, can cause a nation an enormous amount of immediate inconvenience". The key word here is "immediate". The very threat of armed interception at sea has at times swiftly discouraged every merchant shipping company from even attempting to continue its normal trading activities. The Royal Navy's blockades of Germany in 1914-1918 and 1939-1945 were major contributors to that nation's downfall by starving its people of food and its industries of raw materials.

In the Mozambique Channel context, the navy had insufficient ships to meet every possible scenario, so Wilson opted to focus just on Beira with (initially) two frigates and a Fleet carrier. Lorenco Marques would be left undisturbed. The operation commenced in March 1966 and did not expire until June 1975. During those nine years, at great financial cost, seventy-six Royal Navy ships were rotated through, some of them several times over. The first to arrive were the carrier HMS ARK ROYAL and the frigates LOWESTOFT and RHYL, with ARK ROYAL's excellent Fairey Gannets providing early warning radar surveillance. Whenever they reported a suspect inbound tanker it was over-flown by the Ark's Scimitar and Sea Vixen strike aircraft in the hope of intimidating its captain. After three weeks ARK ROYAL was relieved by the carrier HMS EAGLE, but then she also was deemed too valuable for such mundane work. Her departure after six weeks on station deprived the patrolling frigates of air-borne long range radar cover.

Flight Lieutenant (later Air Commodore) Graham Pitchfork was one of two RAF exchange officers serving with the Buccaneers of 800 NAS in HMS EAGLE. He recalls: "I was the navigator (observer) on my first 'ship plot' sortie on 16 March 1966 and so began a long and tedious series of operations, some up to 500 miles from the carrier. They were not without risk. We flew at maximum range with very small fuel reserves. The swell in the Mozambique Channel made some landings challenging and, with no diversion airfield for aircraft to head for in the event of an emergency or a foul deck, the pressure was always on. During the Beira patrol, a Buccaneer and one of ARK ROYAL's 890 NAS Sea Vixens were lost. Sadly, the observer of the latter did not survive despite the gallant efforts of his pilot to save him".

Graham is referring here to the accident on 10 May 1966 when Lieutenant (A) Allan Tarver, RN, piloting Sea Vixen XJ520, experienced a double engine failure at 12,000 feet. His Observer/Navigator was Lieutenant (A) John Stutchbury, RN. With their aircraft descending rapidly towards the sea, John followed Tarver's instruction by trying to eject. The Observer's seat in a Sea Vixen was offset from that of the pilot and had its own access hatch, but now it failed to open fully. This inhibited the ejection seat cartridge from firing, so John tried to physically force his way out. Tarver twice inverted the Sea Vixen in the hope he would fall free, but he was trapped halfway out of the hatch and possibly losing consciousness. There was no movement when Allan Tarver several times reached back and pushed at John's feet. By now the aircraft was rolling into its final dive. When Allan activated his own ejector seat in the last seconds before the crash it was too late for the parachute to deploy. High speed impact with water is normally fatal. Almost miraculously, he survived and was plucked from the sea by one of the Ark's rescue helicopters. The *London Gazette* of 26 August 1966 carried the announcement of the award to Lieutenant Allan Leigh Tarver of **The George Medal.**

So far the French government had stayed out of this essentially British quarrel, but it was then persuaded to grant Royal Air Force landing rights in Madagascar. Detachments of Avro Shackleton (MR2) maritime reconnaissance aircraft were allowed to commence operations from the airport at Majunga. At various times and in succession, Nos 37, 38, 42, 204 and 210 Squadrons each contributed three aircraft. Flying twelve hour (daylight only) patrols, they maintained an increasingly patchy cover until Madagascar gained independence from France (as Malagasy) in 1971. Ordered out by the new government, operating by then just two aircraft, the Shackleton crews were happy to be relieved of that wearisome five-year deployment and revert to their primary role of tracking Soviet submarines and surface vessels.

Despite operating at such a great distance from conventional RAF bases, and despite chronic problems with the Shackleton's temperamental Griffon engines, the ground crews kept their charges at the highest level of serviceability. If one of them had been forced by technical failure to "ditch" in that vast stretch of ocean, the absence of an air-sea rescue organisation would have given its crew little chance of survival. Between 1941 and 1946, from Iceland to the Arabian Gulf, the Air Sea Rescue Directorate had operated a fleet of high-speed launches plus dozens of detachments from twenty different Squadrons of assorted aircraft, all specially equipped to recover injured and hypothermic airmen from the sea. There were no such assets at Majunga.

When on 9 April 1966 the UN Security Council had adopted Resolution 221, it called upon the British government "to prevent, by force if necessary, the arrival at Beira of vessels reasonably believed to be carrying oil destined for Southern Rhodesia". Of the fifteen members of the Council, five abstained from voting while ten voted in favour. They included China (which even then had long-term ambitions for Africa and its natural resources) and the United States of America (they seem to have forgotten their own successful breakaway from the Crown in 1776). All of this, for the navy, raised the ever-recurring question - what exactly were "the rules of engagement"? What were the implications of "by force if necessary"? Little more than two years after the start of the Beira Patrol, the rules had escalated to the point at which, if all else failed, a Royal Navy captain was authorised to fire high explosive shells from his main 4.5 inch armament into the machinery spaces and bridge superstructure of any suspect vessel which refused to stop or change course. High explosive in a tanker's engine room would inevitably cause a fire which, in turn, would most probably spread with predictable consequences to the volatile cargo.

It was a sign of Wilson's increasing petulance that his government should even contemplate such a thing, but seemingly it felt obliged to raise the stakes to that appalling level in the light of two earlier episodes. On 3 April 1966, one of EAGLE's Sea Vixens of 899 NAS sighted a suspect tanker 500 miles south of Beira. At first light on the following morning, two Buccaneers of 800 NAS were launched to intercept and photograph it. She was the Panamanian-owned Greek-flagged JOANNA V, laden with 18,000 tons of oil. As she approached her destination she was ordered by HMS PLYMOUTH to heave-to, but her captain refused to comply. Watched by the world's Press, the JOANNA V sailed into Beira with PLYMOUTH trailing tamely in her wake. The British government then leaned hard on the Portuguese who for a long time refused to accept her cargo of oil.

A few days later, on 10 April, the frigate HMS BERWICK intercepted the oil tanker MANUELLA. This ship, a sister of the JOANNA V, had been reported heading for Beira from the south. A Buccaneer circled overhead while she was boarded by a party of sixteen seamen armed with Sterling sub-machine guns. They were headed by Lieutenant D B Mansergh, RN, and Lieutenant J H Graham, RN.

The Greek captain was persuaded by Mansergh that he must change course and divert to the South African port of Durban. And that was the end of that episode.

Thereafter, following the withdrawal of HMS EAGLE in May, the navy had only one other significant encounter with suspect tankers. On 19 December 1967, HMS MINERVA intercepted the French tanker ARTOIS, also heading for Beira. Even though MINERVA fired live warning shots, the ARTOIS held to her course and safely discharged her cargo.

Images: courtesy of Air Commodore Graham Pitchfork, RAF (retd)

*During the failed attempt to intimidate her captain, one of a pair of HMS Eagle's Blackburn Buccaneers sweeps at first light over the oil tanker Joanna V. To increase the range of the Buccaneers, all wing stores and pylons have been removed. Some aircraft were fitted with bomb-bay photographic packs containing six cameras. This image (above) was taken on 4 April 1966 by Lieutenant Commander David Howard and Flight Lieutenant Graham Pitchfork. Six days later, 500 miles off Beira, Graham and Sub Lieutenant David Brittain capture the scene as HMS Berwick lowers her sea boat preparatory to boarding the Manuella.*

Those new "rules of engagement", ordered by the MoD (Navy) on 21 March 1968, had extremely grave implications. Did the diplomats who voted for Resolution 221 truly understand the ecological impact of great quantities of oil spilling into the Mozambique Channel and, much more importantly, the associated deaths of non-belligerent seafarers? Thankfully that never happened but, if a tanker *had* been destroyed, would the politicians have really stood by the Royal Navy captain who sank her? After he had so successfully carried out his orders, would the Queen have been asked to present him with some sort of decoration?

In the event, the ARTOIS episode was the last. Over the next seven years, our ships had nothing to do but wait for Downing Street to change their orders. Warned that the Royal Navy was now instructed to use direct live fire, the international shipping community abandoned Beira as a destination for its tankers. And anyway it no longer mattered because, by then, Rhodesia was receiving (with careful rationing) all the oil it required *via* Lorenco Marques and from South Africa. The Beira-Umtali pipeline, no longer needed, was taken out of service. Reduced to a single frigate on station (HMS SALISBURY was the last), the Beira Patrol ended on 25 June 1975. The matelot's perspective was neatly summarised by Geoffrey Dykes (he served in the frigate HMS ROTHESAY): "During those nine long years - equating to 78,840 hours of sea time - the navy had just twelve hours of real action, the incident with MINERVA and the ARTOIS. What a waste of time! It was bloody boring but, what the hell, as long as they paid me".

Geoffrey Dykes' analysis of the Beira Patrol reflects to perfection the

*The 2500-strong ship's company of HMS Eagle remained out of sight of land for seventy-one days and fitness training became a necessary daily routine. Aircraft of the ship's Air Group are represented here by a Sea Vixen FAW2 of 899 NAS, four Wessex helicopters and a Fairey Gannet.*

consequences whenever a politician - any politician - exploits Her Majesty's armed forces as an extension of his own personal bigotry. Harold Wilson's vendetta against Ian Smith was totally unrelated to Great Britain's national interests, and Parliament failed our servicemen and our tax payers by not bringing an end to the farce very much sooner.

When after fourteen years of struggle Ian Smith eventually acknowledged defeat, it had been inflicted not by lack of oil but by the sanctions which banned Rhodesia's exports of tobacco and grain (throwing great numbers of black Africans out of work) and the economic drain of a brutal war with Marxist guerillas encroaching from Mozambique (the Chinese and North Koreans moved in when the Portuguese moved out).

The government of Prime Minister Margaret Thatcher played the key role in sponsoring the creation on 18 April 1980 of the new nation, Zimbabwe, under the Presidency of Robert Mugabe. Ceasefire negotiations held in London in 1979 had brought a temporary return to Crown administration and the dispatch of a British and Commonwealth contingent to supervise the disarmament and election arrangements. Soldiers, police officers and civilians who took part and who served at least fourteen days received the Sovereign's cupro-nickel **Rhodesia Medal (1980)** and **The Zimbabwe Independence Medal.**

Summing up his time with the Beira Patrol, Air Commodore Pitchfork writes: "Our efforts, and those of the other Royal Navy and Royal Air Force units involved, were not thought worthy of either **The Rhodesia Medal** or a clasp but, as Allan Tarver's award demonstrates, they were not without risk. As an outsider - one of the two RAF officers in EAGLE - I was able to witness at first hand the Royal Navy's centuries-old capability to carry out a tedious but internationally important operation, quietly, effectively, with the minimum of fuss".

Beginning with **The Naval General Service Medal** bar **Nile (1798),** more than forty different official and semi-official medals - some bearing a multitude of bars - were issued in recognition of campaigns fought on and around the continent of Africa. **The Africa General Service Medal** bar **Kenya** commemorated the so-called Mau-Mau Emergency (1952-1956). It is believed that certain specialist Royal Navy and Royal East African Navy personnel were amongst the 33,000 recipients. With the end of Empire it seemed at the time almost certain to be the last in that long succession of such awards. But then came the Rhodesia dispute. It is just possible that there were Royal Navy staff officers or observers who qualified in 1980 for one of the 2500 Sovereign's **Rhodesia Medals** but, as they were unnamed, only the original rolls could provide an answer. Ironically, twenty-eight years later, in 2008, the government of Prime Minister Gordon Brown tried (but failed) to invoke United Nations sanctions against the still firmly entrenched Robert Mugabe. So much for Wilson's concept of democracy.

The **Naval General Service Medal** (second series), introduced in 1915, was replaced in 1962 by the all-services **Campaign Service Medal.** In theory, and following precedent, it could have been issued with a bar **Beira Patrol,** or something similar. Between 1966 and 1975, thousands of our men - Royal Navy, Royal Fleet Auxiliary and Royal Air Force - sweated out their tours of duty on and over the

Mozambique Channel. Trained and equipped to hunt Soviet submarines in the North Atlantic, they were stuck with a job which gave them no opportunity even for maintaining those skills. A medal might have been a token reward for the years of boredom, but would they really have wanted to wear it anyway?

The same question comes to mind when we look at another "no medal action" of that same period. It was a campaign which took the Royal Navy back, once again, to Arctic waters all-too-familiar from the war of 1939-1945. During those tumultuous years the aircraft carrier GLORIOUS, the potent fast cruiser EDINBURGH and "the mighty HOOD" were lost. Hitler's magnificent capital ships SCHARNHORST and BISMARCK were hunted to destruction. At a terrible cost in ships and lives, in the teeth of incessant U-boat and aerial attack, the vital Allied supply convoys were shepherded through to North Russia. But then, beginning in 1958, in these same waters, the Royal Navy faced a new enemy - a handful of small lightly-armed patrol vessels of the Icelandic Coast Guard Service (the ICGS). The contrast could not have been greater (or, depending upon your point of view, more unworthy).

Iceland, the size of England and Wales, is covered almost entirely by rock, ice and tundra. Administered by its own parliament since 930 AD, ruled since the late 1300s by Denmark, it became a self-governing dominion of the Danish kingdom in 1918. Historically, the human population rose and fell in the wake of successive natural disasters and emigrations to the USA before stabilising in the 1930s. The rest of the world had little interest in the lives of the Icelanders and their neighbours until the outbreak of the Second World War. But then, in the Spring of 1940, there were two events which helped to shape the future Battle of the Atlantic.

On 9 April 1940, the day of Germany's invasion of Denmark and Norway, HMS SUFFOLK disembarked 250 Royal Marines at Torshavn, capital of the Faroe Isles, (dependencies of Denmark). Later the marines were replaced by Scottish troops. The British Army maintained an effective garrison force on the Faroes right through to 1945.

On 10 May, the very same day that Germany smashed into Holland, Belgium and France, the navy delivered 750 Royal Marines to Reykjavik, capital of Iceland. The flotilla consisted of the cruisers BERWICK and GLASGOW escorted by the destroyers FEARLESS and FORTUNE. Like the earlier Faroes operation, Reykjavik was uncontested. Soon after, and even before the United States officially entered the war, 4000 American soldiers replaced the British marines. The US Army continued to maintain a strong garrison on the island for the remainder of the war, hence there was never any risk that it might be seized by the Germans.

Concentrated mainly in Reykjavik, the post-war population of Iceland was 300,000 and rising. Before their disastrous venture into international banking between 2001 and 2007, their healthy economy was based exclusively upon just two natural resources - hydro-electric and geothermal power, and huge stocks of fish. More than 400 species thrive in the offshore waters where the Gulf Stream collides with the Arctic Ocean. Three in particular are commercially important - cod, haddock and herring. Prior to the 1930s (when deep freezing was introduced), Iceland's only exports were salted dried fish and cod-liver oil.

Such abundant marine wealth had attracted the attention of foreign fishermen since the 18$^{th}$ century but, with so many grounds available in other parts of the North Atlantic, there was enough for everyone. That changed when sail was replaced by steam and then by diesel. Fishing vessels became ever bigger, able to spend longer at sea, and to employ increasingly heavy gear. Their skippers were no longer catching the cod by hooked long-line as in centuries past. Their heavy trawls were ripping them out of the ocean on an industrial scale. The Icelanders could see what was happening on the Grand Banks, the once immensely prolific waters off Newfoundland. The first factory ship arrived on the Grand Banks in 1951. In just fifteen years, eight million *tons* of cod were landed, far more than had been caught in the previous 400 years. The remaining stocks collapsed entirely in 1992. Marine biologists now believe the Grand Banks cod is unlikely ever to return.

In the 1920s and 1930s, hundreds of steam trawlers were operating from our East Coast ports such as Aberdeen, Grimsby and Hull in pursuit of the North Sea herring. Landings peaked in the 1950s, then declined steeply before the final collapse of 1979. Obliterated by commercial greed and reckless disregard for conservation, the silvery herring has gone the way of the Grand Banks cod. High cliffs in the Norwegian fiords once clamorous with thousands of nesting sea birds are now silent. The big Polish and Russian factory ships no longer bother to visit, it is not profitable to do so. Even the humble mackerel is under threat.

The concept of "territorial waters" goes back a long way, back to the days when the heaviest cannon in a coastal battery could fire no more than three miles. Beginning in the 17$^{th}$ century, several countries laid formal claim to sovereignty over their coastal waters, but that concept evolved in modern times with their declaration of "economic exclusion zones". Iceland laid her own claim to four miles when, in 1944, she declared independence from German-occupied Denmark and became a Republic.

The Charters of the United Nations and of the North Atlantic Treaty Organisation each provide for peaceful negotiated resolutions to international disputes. Iceland had joined NATO in 1949, hence the quarrel which came to be known as "the Cod Wars" was uniquely a conflict between two fellow-Members. A succession of international conferences and Court hearings failed to reach any meaningful long-term agreement when Iceland extended her claim to twelve miles, then to fifty, ultimately to two hundred.

The five other trawling nations having a stake in Iceland's fish stocks - the Faroes, Norway, Belgium, Denmark and West Germany - accepted the extensions, but the British government contested the issue every step of the way. We finally threw in the towel in 1976 under pressure from the Americans. The government of Iceland was hinting that it might withdraw from NATO. If that happened the US air base at Keflavik could be closed and the West's ability to monitor the passage of Soviet submarines through the Denmark Strait significantly reduced. In 1977 the British government belatedly fell into line with the Icelanders by imposing a 200 miles economic exclusion zone on our own home waters.

Before all that came to pass, the Royal Navy was involved in three separate conflicts with the ships of the ICGS. The first "Cod War", 1958 to 1961, was triggered by Iceland's unilateral claim to twelve miles of sovereignty (instead of the previous four). The second, September 1972 to October 1973, followed her extended claim to fifty miles. The third and final "Cod War", and the most violent, lasted from November 1975 to June 1976. Each was marked by incidents which easily could have resulted in a heavy loss of life (one ICGS sailor was in fact killed). The catalogue of deliberate rammings, warp (net) cuttings and live gunfire, spanning in total a period of eighteen years, is too long to be listed here. However, the whole protracted saga has been recorded in exemplary detail in a book by Captain Andrew Welch, RN (retd), an officer who served in HMS CHARYBDIS in the second "Cod War".

Amongst so many, just one episode will serve to illustrate the extent to which the Royal Navy was sucked into the British government's obsession with fishing quotas. On the evening of 6 May 1976, the 2150 ton frigate FALMOUTH (Commander Gerald Plumer, RN) encountered the Icelandic patrol vessel TYR (Captain Kjaernested Guomundur, ICGS). A trawler, the CARLISLE, was fishing inside disputed waters and TYR was seen to be trying to drag her warp cutters across CARLISLE's wake. The British frigate was racing to intervene at twenty-six knots when she and the TYR, moving at twenty knots, collided. To quote Captain Plumer: "The effect of the collision was awful, the TYR heeled over seventy degrees to starboard as she rapidly pivoted around my stem until the two ships were lying stem to stern, our port sides grinding past at three to four knots". Both ships were badly damaged.

Few vessels could normally be expected to recover from a roll of seventy degrees but, undaunted, Captain Guomundur regained control and finished the job of cutting CARLISLE's warps. He then headed off in pursuit of another British trawler and there was a second heavy collision with FALMOUTH. Nobody was killed by either impact but, if the TYR had capsized and her men drowned, what would have been the repercussions under international law? In the accepted sense of the word, the dispute was not, and never could be, a formally declared "war". It was not even (as defined in United Nations terminology) "a state of armed conflict", so who would have been answerable?

In the mid-1970s as many as 110 British trawlers were operating off Iceland at any one time. Policing them were eight ICGS patrol vessels. The largest, AEGIR and TYR, displaced 1150 tons. The smallest, at 200 tons, was the ALBERT. During the eight months of that third "war", the Royal Navy deployed in succession twenty-two different frigates supported by seven ships of the Royal Fleet Auxiliary, four of the Royal Maritime Auxiliary, and six chartered ocean-going tugs. The Royal Air Force also was involved. Making the long haul north from Scotland, its Nimrods and Shackletons provided radar coverage whenever conditions permitted. A much larger commitment than the Beira Patrol, the Iceland campaign likewise diverted valuable specialist warships away from their primary training and operational tasks without achieving its objective. Further, the "David and Goliath" scenario did nothing to enhance our navy's reputation around the world.

The 19th century German soldier-philosopher Karl von Clausewitz wrote: "All wars are an extension of diplomacy by other means". In 1982, when diplomacy

*A dangerous game in dangerous waters. Above, the Leander class frigate HMS Bacchante veers sharply across the bow of the ICGS vessel Tyr. Below, in another encounter, the captain of the Baldur uses the same tactic of intimidation by racing across the bow of HMS Mermaid. This sort of jousting led to frequent collisions with significant damage to the competing ships.*

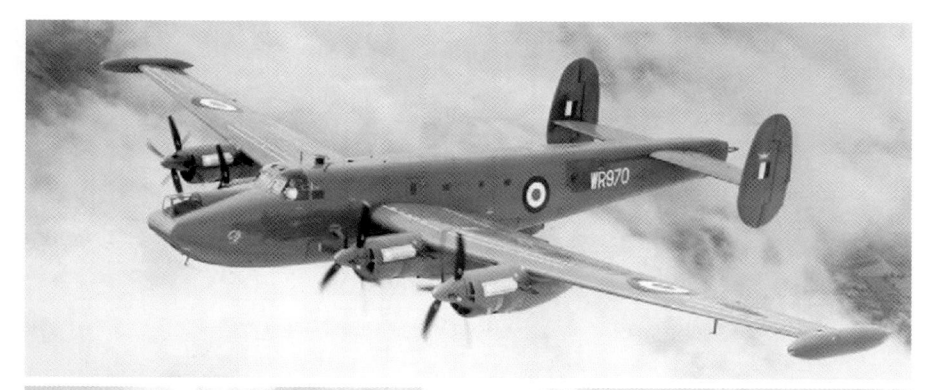

*Between 1952 and 1991, the RAF's Avro Shackleton operated in all aspects of anti-submarine warfare and maritime surveillance in many parts of the world. Based on Roy Chadwick's Lancaster and Lincoln bombers, it had a ten-man crew and a flight endurance of fourteen hours. Beginning in 1969, it was replaced progressively by Hawker Siddeley's turbofan Nimrod (itself a derivative from a much earlier aircraft, the Comet jet civil airliner). In 1993 the MoD ordered an updated MRA4 version but in March 2010, vastly over budget, seven years late and not a single craft completed, the contract was cancelled. Once again, we turned to the American aviation industry and purchased seven of the well-proven Boeing Sentry e-3 aircraft (a derivative of the 1958 Boeing 707 airliner). Operating at 30,000 feet, it has an exclusively radar surveillance and communications role. Unlike the Shackleton and Nimrod, it has no integral strike capability*

failed (almost inevitably so), Margaret Thatcher accepted the need for armed force against Argentina. Few Britons would dispute either the legitimacy or the morality of her decision to fight for the Falkland Islands. But the Beira Patrol? British territory, British lives, were they in jeopardy, in need of protection from an aggressor nation? That wearisome campaign had its origins in nothing more than head-butting between two politicians, Ian Smith and Harold Wilson. And the dispute with Iceland? At home, there was justified fear of job losses in our major fishing ports, but what *national* interests were threatened by the Icelandic people's stubborn determination to conserve their one and only (finite and diminishing) exportable natural resource? With Labour MPs holding comfortable majorities in all the British distant-water fishing ports and with Harold Wilson back in 10 Downing Street, the (third) "Cod War" was inspired exclusively by domestic party politics, not international diplomacy. It was, in this writer's opinion, an abuse of executive power.

The First Sea Lord and Chief of the Naval Staff at the time of the third "Cod War" was Admiral of the Fleet Sir Edward Ashmore. How did he feel about the policy he was being instructed to pursue? His destroyers and frigates - costing many millions of pounds, packed with high-technology equipment operated by expensively trained specialists - were being used as primitive battering rams. It made no sense but, as a serving officer, he was bound to obey his government's orders. Either that or be sacked.

Sir Edward had personal experience of operating in the extremes of Arctic weather. In 1942, as First Lieutenant in the "Hunt" Class destroyer HMS MIDDLETON, he took part in convoy escort operations carrying war materials to Archangel. In March 2013, having submitted his claim, he received his **Arctic Star.** Not through the post but, as befitted someone of his rank, in person from a nominated serving officer, Commander Alec Parry, RN. At ninety-three, Sir Edward is not the oldest recipient of **The Arctic Star** but he is surely the most senior.

When Harold Wilson unexpectedly resigned in March 1976 he was replaced by James Callaghan who, interestingly, appointed Anthony Crosland as his Foreign Secretary. And which constituency did Mr Crosland represent in the House of Commons? It was Grimsby. That was perhaps coincidental, but we may wonder why Wilson and Callaghan each persisted with a strategy so clearly ineffectual when there was available to them a much simpler alternative. Blockade.

 The oil blockade of Rhodesia failed because there were too many points of leakage. For its own oil needs, Iceland likewise is entirely dependent upon importations. But, unlike Rhodesia, it is an island and has only one port capable of discharging tankers. We had more than enough ships to seal off Reykjavik and thereby to perhaps bully the Icelanders into agreeing the terms we wanted for our trawler owners and their bank managers.

Alternatively, we could have warned the Icelanders that we were preparing to lay mines off Reykjavik and around the fiords where ICGS ships sheltered at times of foul weather. We still had two mine-layer destroyers in commission during those years - first, HMS ORWELL (scrapped in 1965), then HMS ABDIEL (scrapped in 1988). British submarines also had the capability to lay mines of various types, and stocks were routinely held by the Ministry of Defence until 1992. Even if the British government never seriously considered adopting that tactic, the bluff might at least have delayed the inevitable. What the implications would have been under international maritime law are uncertain.

Neither the Beira Patrol nor the "Cod Wars" earned a medal, but even if such awards had been authorised, they would surely never have commanded the level of respect otherwise given to British campaign medals in general. Our men followed their orders with their customary dedication, it was the nature of the work given to them by their political masters which did not sit comfortably with the traditions of the Senior Service.

The 2011 war against Libya was in a totally different category. It was based upon a broad international (essentially European) consensus. Consisting of two principal regions, Cyrenaica (eastern) and Tripolitania (western), Libya had been colonised progressively from 1911 onwards by Italy. For centuries a province of the Ottoman Empire, they were ceded to Italy after the Italo-Turkish War of 1911-1912. That conflict had posed at the time a dilemma for Prime Minister Henry Asquith and his Cabinet. Great Britain was on friendly terms with Turkey and equally with Italy. The warships and troop transports transiting south from mainland Italy to the Gulf of Sirte were passing though seas where the Royal Navy had long claimed to be top dog. In theory, Admiral Sir Edmund Poe, C-in-C Mediterranean Fleet, could have been ordered to intervene, but Libya's oil deposits were not discovered until 1959. With no vital British interests at stake, Italy was left free to continue with her ultimately failed attempt to create her own empire on the African continent.

Libya was liberated from Italian control by Montgomery's 8th Army British, Indian, Australian, New Zealand and Free French divisions after their hard-fought Western Desert campaign of 1940-1942. In 1951, with Anglo-American support, the distinguished Senussi leader, Idris, became monarch of a united Kingdom of Libya. In 1969, after nearly eighteen years of relatively stable administration, he was overthrown in a military *coup* led by Colonel Muammar Gaddafi. By 2011, tribal quarrels and Gaddafi's erratic rule were provoking a civil war. Given his regime's known violation of human rights, its past exports of weaponry to foreign terrorist groups but especially his control of Libya's immense reserves of oil, a series of United Nations Security Council Resolutions culminated with the authorisation of "no fly" zones and a coastal blockade. At this point the Royal Navy became involved.

Led by the French President Nicolas Sarkozy, nine nations formed a Coalition which then evolved, on 24 March 2011, into a NATO operation to which eleven more nations contributed additional ships, aircraft and humanitarian aid. They included warships from Romania and Albania. In the event, and although hundreds of civilians were killed by "collateral damage", the seven months operation was essentially a bombardment from the air of Gaddafi's military infrastructure. Either in the attack or logistical roles, 26,500 sorties were flown by eleven different national air forces. At the forefront in the strike role were the French, the Danish and the Norwegian.

At sea, the Royal Navy contributed the destroyers LIVERPOOL and YORK,

211

the frigates WESTMINSTER and CUMBERLAND, the mine hunter BROCKLESBY and the amphibious warfare ship OCEAN. Shore targets were hit by Tomahawk missiles launched from the nuclear attack submarine TRIUMPH (the TURBULENT was also there), but the Libyan Navy itself offered little threat. Eight of its frigates and corvettes were effectively destroyed in their ports by air strikes on the night of 20 May. Two more were seized by rebel forces in Benghazi. Six Soviet-built "Foxtrot" Class submarines acquired in 1982 had long ceased to be operational.

No British fixed-wing aircraft carriers took part because the last of them, HMS ARK ROYAL, had been de-commissioned just thirteen days before the new NATO Operation *Unified Protector* was authorised. Worse, the Fleet Air Arm's highly effective Sea Harrier FA2 had been scrapped in 2006. It was replaced temporarily by the RAF's GR7 and GR8 variants, but in 2010 they also were taken out of service. In sharp contrast - which some readers may think an alarming contrast - the Italian Navy's AV8B version of the Sea Harrier made numerous sorties against Libyan ground targets while operating from the 14,000 ton carrier GIUSEPPE GARIBALDI. They were joined by AV8Bs operating from America's 41,000 ton amphibious assault ship KEARSARGE.

For its part, the French Navy was able to deploy the 42,000 ton nuclear-powered carrier CHARLES DE GAULLE. Her forty embarked aircraft included the excellent Super Etendard - successor to the type which sank HMS SHEFFIELD

*Demonstrating that air power can be projected worldwide at relatively modest cost, this is the Italian Navy's 30 knot Giuseppe Garibaldi. Built by Fincantierri at Monfalcone (Trieste), commissioned in 1985, displacing 14,000 tons (war load), her aircraft took part in operations over Kosovo and Afghanistan before she joined the NATO campaign against Gaddafi's Libya in 2011. Her armament - air, surface and sub-surface - exceeds that of any single ship currently in service with the Royal Navy. In 2009 she was joined by the even more potent multi-role 30,000 ton carrier Cavour.*

*A French semi-stealth delta-winged Dassault Rafale "M" being prepared on the flight deck of the Charles de Gaulle for its next mission over Libya. The type first entered naval service in 2002. Demonstrating even more the worrying extent to which the Fleet Air Arm has fallen behind, the Rafale has a combat radius with full war load of more than 1000 miles at twice the speed of sound. Understandably, Press statements released by the MoD in 2011 made no reference to the French and Italian carriers.*

*Although British service personnel who took part in the 2011 war with Libya did not receive a Sovereign's medal, they did qualify for the NATO award as shown here.*

and the MV ATLANTIC CONVEYOR off the Falklands in 1982. Like the Italian and American Harriers, its task in 2011 was bombing and strafing Gaddafi's military assets. One third of all the *Unified Protector* ground attack missions were flown from the CHARLES DE GAULLE.

In the overall context, Britain's contribution both in the air and at sea was no more than modest. We simply did not have enough of the right ships and the right aircraft. When Admiral Sir Mark Stanhope, the First Sea Lord and Chief of the Naval Staff, made it known that the navy could not continue to meet its commitments off Libya for more than ninety days without restricting its training and operational tasks elsewhere, he raised the hackles of David Cameron. The Prime Minister is reported to have said: "I'll do the talking, you do the fighting". Stanhope and the other two Chiefs of Staff were summarily sacked from their membership of the Defence Board. It then became an all-civilian monthly forum representing a range of defence equipment contractors. Whether or not this was the best way of preserving the nation's security is a matter of opinion but even Winston Churchill, at the height of his wartime powers, might have hesitated from wielding the axe in that way.

The armed forces have since been reinstated with two seats at the high table. At the time of writing (April 2014) they are occupied by General Sir Nicholas Houghton, Chief of the General Staff, and Air Chief Marshal Sir Stuart Peart, Vice Chief of the General Staff. The Royal Navy has no direct representation. Documents emanating from Whitehall no long refer to the Royal Navy, it has become "the naval services". Former Sea Lords would weep.

Muammar Gaddafi was caught and butchered by his own people on 20 October and that, effectively, was the end of it. The original purpose of the campaign - "regime change" - had been achieved with a new transitional government given international recognition. It may seem unlikely that the Royal Navy will be involved in a similar operation in the immediate future but, even so, is "regime change" for its own sake a fit and proper role for our armed forces?

The answer is debatable, but it begs the associated question - what is the Royal Navy *for*? To secure the self-evident vital interests of our nation and of our NATO partners or, as was the case with Suez (1956, Anthony Eden's hatred of Colonel Nasser), Southern Rhodesia (1965-1975, Harold Wilson's vendetta against Ian Smith), Iceland (1958-1976, Wilson's obsession with fish) and Iraq (2003, Tony Blair's fabricated weapons of mass destruction "evidence" against Saddam Hussein), is it to satisfy the aspirations of individual politicians? As we have seen, an extremely fine line may (or may not) distinguish one from the other. Each of those four conflicts were modern versions of the 19$^{th}$ century concept of "gunboat diplomacy". They rendered even more apposite an alternative interpretation of the von Clausewitz maxim: "All wars are an extension of *politics* by other means". In the final analysis, "orders is orders", but any officer hoping to one day command the Fleet may find food for thought in all of this.

The main problem for that officer is the near impossibility of anticipating the future directives issued by politicians who, no matter how well intentioned, may lack any deep understanding of naval power and its application. In the wars of 1914-1918 and 1939-1945, the world consisted of "the good guys" wearing white hats and "the bad guys" wearing black hats. It was all so simple. Everyone knew where they stood. Since then, the dynamics of inter-nation power-plays have become increasingly ambiguous, to say the least.

Domestic politics *per se*, it must be recorded, have not been the only driving force behind Britain's post-WWII use of "gunboat diplomacy". In 1961, for example, Iraq's *Quassem* regime was threatening to occupy its small neighbour, Kuwait. It had been under British protection since 1899 and its potential oil wealth was at that time being actively explored. Prime Minister Harold Macmillan ordered an immediate all-arms response. Royal Navy ships hurried to the Arabian Gulf from Aden, Mombasa and Singapore, Royal Marine Commandos from Malta, British Army regiments from Cyprus and Kenya. The RAF still possessed at that time the Short company's Belfast heavy-lift aircraft needed to speedily deliver from widely-scattered bases their vehicles and bulky equipment. The carriers VICTORIOUS, CENTAUR and BULWARK each had central roles in the operation. In the face of such a powerful show of force the crisis soon evaporated - British troops handing over to units of the Arab League. However, the 1961 Operation *Vantage* did emphasize the continuing importance of retaining "fire fighting" and deterrent resources ready to deal with the unexpected even in the greatly changed world of what was at that time the post-Empire era.

Currently (2013) there are 5.5 million British nationals living or working overseas. Some are located in countries which politically are not entirely stable. In a crisis, as has happened in the past, they might require protection or evacuation at short notice. The British Commonwealth comprises fifty-four independent sovereign states with a combined worldwide population of 2.2 billion people. Canada, Australia and New Zealand are amongst those having modern navies of their own, but many of the widely-scattered smaller nations would almost certainly turn to Britain in times of trouble.

That has not always been the case. The most obvious exception is Grenada, the Caribbean island first occupied by the British in 1627 and which became a Crown Colony in 1877. Granted independence within the British Commonwealth on 7 February 1974, its new administration was based upon the Westminster model of freely elected representatives. The Prime Minister was Eric Gairy while representing the Crown was Governor General Sir Leo Victor de Gale,

Heading the opposition was Maurice Bishop, likewise Grenadian-born. A London-trained barrister, he was a graduate of the London School of Economics. In 1979 he overthrew the Gairy administration and made himself Prime Minister of a People's Revolutionary Government. It was a one-party government in the Soviet style, and Bishop used it to introduce a wide range of initiatives connected with advances in social housing, education, gender equality, healthcare, racial discrimination, and so forth. His model was the egalitarian regime of Castro's Cuba and it worked. However, on 14 October 1983 and after four years in power, he and his senior colleagues were arrested and murdered by hard-line Communist political opponents who had their own agenda. Rioting broke out, so the island's 1500-strong People's Revolutionary Army (PRA) stepped in and formed a military council to run the country. The constitution was suspended and martial law declared. And it was this latest *coup* which triggered the most amazing rupture in the Anglo-American relationship since the War of 1812-1815.

The Queen's representative on the island was Grenadian-born Governor General Sir Paul Scoon (he had succeeded Sir Leo Victor de Gale in the previous year). Scoon was a graduate of three British universities and a former Deputy Director of the Commonwealth Foundation in London. Even though Britain's armed forces had demonstrated their ability to conduct long-range operations only eighteen months earlier - when they ejected the Argentines from the Falkland Islands - Sir Paul presumably decided it would take too long for them to mount a relief force and despatch it across the Atlantic. Swift and decisive action was imperative. The fact that the British government was now busy decommissioning or selling off some of the Royal Navy's key ships - and still debating the cost of replacing the ships sunk in the Falklands war - may also have been on his mind. Whatever the case, he asked the Americans to intervene.

In President Ronald Reagan - sensitive like his predecessors in the White House to the Soviet influence in Cuba - he found a receptive ear. A British-led consortium was completing on the island an airport with a runway designed to accommodate the next generation of big wide-bodied commercial jet aircraft. Tourism was central to the island's future economy. However, Reagan and his advisors had to assume that the new Point Salines International Airport might soon become a Soviet base for spreading Communism in Latin America and other islands of the Caribbean. Their belief was reinforced by the comings and goings of Russian-built long range transport aircraft delivering military hardware (it included armoured combat vehicles and multi-barrelled anti-aircraft guns together with enough small-arms to equip at least 10,000 revolutionary fighters).

About 700 of the men working at the airport were Cuban construction workers, most of them Cuban Army engineers. Bizarrely, they had twenty-four North Koreans of unknown status working with them. The evidence was enough to sound the alarm in Washington. There were 740 US citizens (including 595 medical students) on the island, and their safety was an added concern. President Reagan authorised an immediate military response. Already two weeks in the planning, the Pentagon gave it the code name Operation *Urgent Fury*. Melodramatic that title may have been, but it did reflect the impressive speed with which it was mounted. Less than a week after the latest coup, American troops were on the ground and fighting hard.

Launched in part from the island of Barbados and in part from bases in the United States, an air-borne invasion commenced at early dawn on 25 October 1983. Supporting it were dozens of helicopter gun-ships and ground attack fighter-bombers. The naval task force of twenty ships was centred upon the 80,000 ton carrier USS INDEPENDENCE. In total, the Pentagon committed 7300 combat personnel to the operation, of whom nineteen were killed and 116 wounded (an unknown number by accident or "friendly fire"). According to whatever source one chooses to consult, 9000 of the **Armed Forces Expeditionary Medal** were issued with a further 5000 medals "for merit or gallantry". Personnel employed in the supply chain and in the Pentagon qualified for these awards, hence the high numbers.

In four days it was all over. The Cuban and Grenadian PRA soldiers fought as well as they could, but they were swamped by American firepower. Along with twenty-four civilian dead, more than 200 of them were killed or wounded. The post-mortem then commenced. The invasion was overwhelmingly condemned by the UN General Assembly as being "a flagrant violation of international law". A similar Security Council resolution was blocked by the US veto. On Capitol Hill, opinion was divided but veered towards "the ends justified the means". President Reagan, when questioned, said the negative UN votes "had not spoiled his breakfast".

That may have been so, but the invasion itself certainly caused severe indigestion in Downing Street and Buckingham Palace. Washington had given no warning that

*The twenty American warships committed to Operation Urgent Fury were led by the massive conventionally-powered USS Independence. The crew (including 2089 air wing personnel) amounted to 5360 all ranks and they operated ninety strike and surveillance aircraft. The British government abandoned the Royal Navy's own sea-borne fixed-wing capability when, in March 2011, HMS Ark Royal was de-commissioned for the last time. However, currently under construction (2013) are two 70,000 ton Queen Elizabeth carriers powered by diesel electric and gas turbine engines. Each are intended to operate, at a currently estimated purchase price of $100 million each, forty Lockheed Martin F-35B supersonic strike aircraft. All being well, the Queen Elizabeth will enter full operational service before 2018.*

it was about to attack a country of which our Queen was (and still is) nominally the Head of State. Indeed, the Operation *Urgent Fury* commanders seem to have been unaware that this was the case. But, even if they had been so aware, it was no business of theirs what the diplomatic fallout might be. Their Chief had ordered them to go in with all six-guns blazing, and that is precisely what they did.

The boldly aggressive military commander was Major General Norman Schwarskopf, the officer who seven years later commanded the Coalition forces in the Iraq war. Having endured as a junior officer the 1960s muddle and command indecisions of Viet Nam, he was determined to hit fast and hit hard. Perhaps with hindsight it was over-kill, but it worked. Regardless of world opinion, the Americans had made it abundantly clear that never again would there be a repetition of the extraordinarily dangerous 1962 Cuban missile crisis.

The American nationals on the island were evacuated without loss or injury and Sir Paul Scoon likewise was set free. He was being held captive in his official residence by the PRA until a detachment of US Navy SEALS made a daring raid to rescue him. It is reported that he and his aides remained entirely calm and composed while, for several hours, a severe fire fight raged all around the building. If nothing else, Her Majesty's Governor General had maintained in adversity the British "stiff upper lip" tradition.

Just as they failed in 1982 to anticipate trouble in the South Atlantic, Britain's Intelligence services failed to identify the sudden huge build-up of American naval forces in the Caribbean. On the evidence available, the British High Commissioner's office on Barbados neglected to inform the Foreign & Commonwealth Office of the sudden arrival on that island of the US Special Forces units. Or, if it did, the information was ignored. British journalists based in Washington - normally well tuned to any tremors in the White House and the Pentagon - seemingly went deaf. GCHQ wasn't listening. The radar sets on any British warship in the Caribbean - if there was one - failed to spot the intense air and surface activity. Until the last moment, *Urgent Fury* was a top secret operation and the Americans were admirably

*A US Navy Sikorsky Sea Stallion hovers over a Soviet-made ZU-23 anti-aircraft weapon prior to removing it for disposal. At least four assault force helicopters were either shot down or disabled before the fighting ceased. Pilots reported that ground fire during the first hours of the assault had been unexpectedly intense, a fact which emphasises the good fortune of the Fleet Air Arm aircrew who conducted the first ever such helicopter assault at Port Said (the Suez affair) in 1956.*

*A US soldier stands guard beside wrecked Soviet-made armoured personnel carriers, two of several found post-battle on Grenada. The Cuban regime, presumably with the full knowledge and approval of Moscow, was rapidly converting this small tropical island into an armed camp. The escalating delivery of such heavy combat equipment was far in excess of anything needed for normal internal security duties. If Washington had waited much longer, the invasion might have been contested even more violently and with much greater civilian and service casualties.*

efficient in keeping the secret. Whitehall was gloriously ignorant of what was about to happen.

The first inkling trickled through to Downing Street early on the morning of 25 October. At 1230, Prime Minister Margaret Thatcher instructed the Cabinet Office to despatch a message on her behalf to the American President, hinting that Parliament might not agree to the installation of his cruise missiles in the UK if his country "intervened in the internal affairs of a small independent nation, however unattractive its regime".

As a threat, this communication carried no conviction whatsoever. Drafted almost certainly by a senior civil servant - not the normally blunt-speaking "Maggie" herself - it was implying that the House of Commons was the final arbiter on the strategic deployment of the NATO nuclear shield. It was excessively optimistic to believe that Washington would give more than a moment's consideration to such a feeble argument. It was totally irrelevant to the situation as viewed from the White House. President Reagan and his advisors were less concerned that American missiles might or might not be welcomed in the UK at a date yet to be determined, they were far more worried that within days Soviet nuclear-armed ballistic missiles might begin to arrive on Grenada. Once established on site, getting them removed could entail a major confrontation not only with Havana but also with Moscow. It would be a replay of the 1962 crisis when President John Kennedy and Premier Nikita Krushchev had gone eyeball-to-eyeball and the world had held its breath.

Twenty minutes later, receiving no reply, Mrs Thatcher called him in person on the telephone. It is not known exactly what was said, but he is quoted as assuring her: "An invasion is not contemplated". He explained later that he had been intimidated by the emphatic tone of her voice. As he well knew, the invasion had commenced nearly nine hours earlier and the skies over Grenada were full of his fighter-bombers and Cobra attack helicopters. With the operation barely started, his Chiefs of Staff would anyway have wanted keep the details from the outside world for as long as possible and so avoid foreign interference.

It is said that, when news of the assault reached the Queen, she was deeply angry. At every level - military, political, diplomatic, Intelligence - the British had been exposed and humiliated. For their part, the great majority of the 110,000 Grenadian people welcomed the Americans as liberators. Democratic government was restored and, each year, 25 October is celebrated as Thanksgiving Day.

There is an interesting footnote to this episode which may possibly explain why Great Britain was excluded from it. As stated above, Grenada gained its independence on 7 February 1974. Following the pattern of the previous decade whenever a British Colony or Protectorate was making that historic transition, it might have been expected that a member of the Royal family would attend the floodlit midnight handover ceremony. Grenada was different. It had been planned that HRH Prince Richard, Duke of Gloucester, would travel to the island with his wife as representatives of his cousin, the Queen. Instead, because the island was currently experiencing civil unrest, strikes and power cuts, his intended visit was cancelled. She was represented instead by then Governor General, Sir Leo Victor de Gale.

*The fighting has stopped. On a street in the small capital city of St George's, a trooper of the 82nd Airborne Division (the "All Americans") chats with admiring young Grenadians. Assuming it ever came to their attention, this photograph should have angered three members in particular of the British establishment. Apart from Her Majesty the Queen and her Prime Minister Margaret Thatcher, they were Francis Pym (Foreign & Commonwealth Secretary), Sir Patrick Wright (Chairman of the Joint Intelligence Committee), and Admiral of the Fleet Sir John Fieldhouse (First Sea Lord and Chief of the Naval Staff). Their subordinates let them down badly. They had entirely failed to warn them that a member State of the British Commonwealth was about to be invaded.*

The British government was represented by Mr Peter Blaker, MP, a well-travelled but relatively unknown junior Minister in the expiring Edward Heath administration. By contrast, President Nixon sent the high profile diplomat and statesman Cyrus Vance - "the confidant of Presidents" - to represent the United States of America. The Grenadian people were left to draw their own conclusions.

The Grenada affair happened thirty years ago. Whenever the teaching staff at the Joint Services Command & Staff College (Shrivenham) is looking for a fresh topic with which to challenge its students, the tutors might care to offer the 1983 Grenada scenario. If Sir Paul Scoon had appealed for help to London and not Washington, how might we have responded? Would the British have handled the problem any differently? Would we have had the political will to act militarily? More importantly, if that or something similar arose today (2014), would we have the ships and the aircraft needed? Would the MoD (Navy) still possess the capability to mount at very short notice an effective task force and the logistical resources ashore in the UK to sustain it at sea? If the answer is "yes", well and good. If "no", then to repeat myself, what is the Navy *for*?

Admiral Sir Mark Stanhope was appointed First Sea Lord and Chief of the Naval Staff in July 2009. He proved to be an outspoken advocate of the need for

Great Britain to maintain a strong and balanced defence posture despite severe budgetary constraints. In a keynote speech to the Royal United Services Institute, on 5 July 2012, he defined the role of the Royal Navy. In essence, he was arguing the case for a "global navy", able *inter alia* to police the sea lanes frequented by Britain's mercantile trade. In many ways it was the same case propounded by former First Sea Lords such as "Jackie" Fisher (1904-1910 and 1914-1915), Ernie Chatfield (1933-1938), Caspar John (1963-1966), Edward Ashmore (1977-1979) and Henry Leach (1979-1982), all of them, like Admiral Stanhope, vigorous defenders of the Senior Service in the rough and tumble of the Whitehall arena.

The earliest of those officers were looking at a scenario which began to change with the end of Empire, the post-war introduction of "flags of convenience", and the offshore tax advantages enjoyed by many of Britain's mercantile competitors at sea. In 2008, the year before Mark Stanhope's elevation to the top post, events moved forward suddenly and radically. Following a ruling by the International Maritime Organisation, the British government entered into a convention titled the Red Ensign Group (the REG). This London-based organisation keeps a record of all vessels registered in the United Kingdom of Great Britain and Northern Ireland plus those of all the Crown Dependencies and Overseas Territories (twelve of which are named in the schedule). The Ministry of Defence confirms that, according to current British defence strategy, the REG Agreement does indeed apply to "those Territories and Dependencies having no means of offensive capability and relying directly upon Her Majesty's Government on matters other than self-defence". The wording is fluffy but the intention is clear enough.

Although their ships fly their appropriately "defaced" versions of the Red Ensign, and although their owners may not pay UK taxes, they are deemed to be "British". Attacked or threatened, we would no doubt go to their aid anyway, but there is now a legal obligation. Strangely, the Agreement makes no stated provision for merchant ships associated with major Commonwealth nations such as Canada, Australia and New Zealand. However, there is a proviso which implies that, in a wartime situation, they too would be legally entitled to the shared protection of the Royal Navy.

As of January 2014, there are 3959 ocean-going vessels (displacing in total 50.1 million tons) registered under REG jurisdiction. This makes it the sixth largest combined merchant fleet in the world. Adding then the ships of the other Commonwealth members, the Royal Navy's nineteen destroyers and frigates are committed to assisting in the protection of 5000 or more merchant vessels. However, that figure is insignificant compared with the overall global scale of maritime trade. According to the authoritative *World Fleet Monitor* - and discounting warships, deep sea trawlers and the like - there are currently 87,483 ocean-going vessels circulating around the globe. Even the US Navy, with nearly 300 ships in commission, would find it impossible to provide anything other than token protection for such a vast armada.

Adding to the daunting statistics is the important fact that much of the world's commercial shipping is insured with Lloyds of London. Regardless of the national flag flying at their stern, those merchantmen and their cargoes represent a significant investment by the City of London and thereby the British economy. It follows that ships not covered by REG but registered in tax havens such as Panama, Liberia, the Bahamas and the Marshall Islands might also need protection in times of a "hot war" at sea.

Singapore became an independent member of the British Commonwealth in 1966. Its commercial port is the busiest of all such ports anywhere in the world. On average, 700 ships arrive or depart every twenty-four hours, delivering or collecting 60,000 containers. At any one point in time, there are 1000 ships in the docks or anchorage. The scale of all this sea-borne activity, in which British exporters and financial institutions have such a massive stake, is staggering. The Republic of Singapore has no need for an extended-range "blue water" navy, but it has invested heavily in protecting the vital maritime trade upon which, lacking any natural resources of its own, it is entirely dependent. With six modern frigates, six corvettes, thirteen fast patrol craft, four amphibious warfare ships and four submarines, Singapore's navy is arguably at the present time relatively more "fit for purpose" than is the Royal Navy of the United Kingdom. And, for top cover, it has the support of its nation's 143 modern combat aircraft.

Of all the world's maritime trading countries, Singapore, Japan and the United Kingdom are uniquely vulnerable to conflict on the high seas. Island nations, lacking natural resources, their economies can be wrecked or held to ransom at any time. By contrast, the continental nations have their own domestic food production and material resources, with integral road, rail and canal infrastructures. They could keep going for very much longer.

In the overall strategic context, the problem for the Royal Navy is that it no longer possesses the overseas shore-side repair and logistical bases which were available to Admiral Stanhope's predecessors. British membership of NATO entails open access to Italian and Greek naval yards but, for the rest, the picture has changed. Stretching half-way around the world from the sovereign base at Gibraltar to HMAS COONAWARRA - the northern Australian naval base at Darwin - there is not a single naval dockyard where in future decades our ships can be absolutely certain of a friendly welcome and logistical support in times of strife. In their absence, an extension of our full-time naval capability around the world and along the ocean highways can be effective only in the form of independent self-supporting task forces comparable with the permanent US Navy fleets operating in the Indian Ocean, the Pacific and the Mediterranean. The British Labour government took the first step along that road in 2007 by ordering the construction of the 70,000 ton aircraft carrier QUEEN ELIZABETH (to be followed by a sister ship, PRINCE OF WALES).

These new super-carriers will be conventionally powered, not nuclear powered, and therefore will require the attendance of a fleet train incorporating unarmed oil replenishment ships of the Royal Fleet Auxiliary. The supply chain will be very long indeed if one or both of these carriers are committed to a conflict in, shall we say, the seas around South East Asia. That hypothesis will be explored later in this article.

As currently planned, the carriers themselves will be armed with machine-guns and the Phalanx point defence system. Clearly, therefore, any task force centred upon one of these huge vulnerable carriers will need to include a significant number of frigates and destroyers to guard her whenever she is deployed in a potentially hostile environment. The number of such ships so committed will represent at least half of those currently available. Unless additional frigates and destroyers are ordered soon, the creation of one or possibly two carrier-centred task forces will weaken the navy's ability to deal simultaneously with other tasks elsewhere. The phrase "all your eggs in one basket" comes to mind.

Relevant to that argument is the number of ships judged necessary by the US Navy when it was preparing for Operation *Urgent Fury* in 1983. Even though at Grenada there was no surface or sub-surface threat, no air threat, no sea-skimming missile threat, no enemy coastal batteries to be overcome, Vice Admiral Joseph Metcalf III was given a fleet of twenty warships of various types to permit him to carry out his mission. The US Department of Defence is no more profligate with its budget than is Britain's Ministry of Defence. If it assessed that twenty was the right number, then twenty was what it was. Grenada was a tiny microscopic invasion compared with Normandy or Okinawa but, as a demonstration of global strategic maritime muscle-flexing, *Urgent Fury* was a classic. In that context alone it was money well spent.

The current mission statement of the US Navy is unequivocal. It makes no mention of "protecting the national interest" - the Royal Navy's own stated but ill-defined primary duty - but is phrased in terms which allow for no misunderstanding. Quote: "The mission of the Navy is to maintain, train and equip combat-ready naval forces capable of winning wars, deterring aggression and maintaining freedom of the seas". The words "capable of winning wars" are particularly significant. They go right to the heart of any debate regarding the cost of building and sustaining a fleet which is "fit to fight".

In pursuit of its mission, the US Navy operates 3700 aircraft and 290 ships (including ten "big deck" carriers). A truly global navy, its tonnage is greater than the navies of the next thirteen largest national fleets combined. As a "fleet in being", it exercises immense influence upon the conduct of international diplomacy. The American General George S Patton (1885-1945) was a soldier, not a sailor, but his succinct remark "superior firepower is an invaluable tool when entering negotiations" said everything that needed to be said in that context.

In the 1983 Grenada affair, Vice Admiral Metcalf's force was a "fleet in action". However, the stated importance of "a fleet in being" dates back to First Lord of the Admiralty Lord Torrington (1690). A classic demonstration of its value was the Commodore Matthew Perry expedition to Japan in 1854-1855 (*vide* page 175). Without a life lost, the visible latent power of his flotilla would in time bring that country into the 20$^{th}$ Century. Returning to America, he published at his own expense a three-volume narrative of his journey. Widely read, it shaped his nation's perceptions of the Western Pacific region and opened the door for future trade. The projection of maritime power does not necessarily lead to clouds of gunsmoke and long casualty lists. Today that power is encapsulated in the most specialised of all types of warship, the aircraft carrier.

Carriers are the most complex machines of war ever invented. It is the close integration of seamanship and airmanship which imposes such a huge workload on the ship's company. Exceptional skills are required at both levels. The unnecessary sinking of HMS COURAGEOUS and HMS GLORIOUS early in the Second World War revealed the problems of preparing such complex ships - but especially their commanding officers - for active service. The lessons highlighted in 1939 and 1940 were not fully absorbed until 1945 when Admiral Fraser's British Pacific Fleet began to operate in company with the US Navy under the intense pressure of attack by the *kamikaze* (*vide* Part Seven).

At the time of writing, we are looking at a hiatus of at least (say) six or seven years between the scrapping in 2011 of HMS ARK ROYAL and the expected arrival in full operational service of HMS QUEEN ELIZABETH (hopefully complete with her full fixed-wing air component). There must be some concern that the knowledge and experience gained in the past may by then have withered on the vine, old lessons needing to be re-learned from scratch. The weaponry changes, the fundamentals remain the same.

The same applies to the Fleet Air Arm, only more so. It has not operated its own fixed-wing combat aircraft since 2006 (when the sub-sonic Sea Harrier force was sold off to the US Marine Corps for spare-part breaking). As announced, the FAA's 809 NAS will begin to operate sometime around 2016 a vastly more complicated strike aircraft, the Lockheed Martin F-35B. That means another hiatus - in this context of at least ten years - in the continuity of British naval aviation. The game of "catch-up" will be an immense challenge not only for the aircrew and maintainers but also for the officers responsible for their training and tactical deployment. Again, old lessons to be remembered, new lessons to be learned.

The prototype F-35 was rolled out at Fort Worth, Texas, in 2006. Subsequently, at prodigious cost, its three variants have been plagued by seven years of design, construction, propulsion and avionic deficiencies. Our Defence Board's considered choice, the short-range F-35B version, is shaped to the requirements of the US Marine Corps. Like the Sea Harrier, it is a V/STOVL aircraft. This means that it can take off either vertically or after a short level run. The Defence Board's initial choice had been the long range F-35A, but that version requires expensive steam-powered launch catapults, arrester wire gear and an angled flight deck as incorporated in the construction of conventional Fleet carriers. To reduce the build-cost of the QUEEN ELIZABETH, the original specification was changed. It now includes a "ski jump" but not the launchers and arresters. The bean-counters have over-ruled the naval architects.

This author leaves it to the aviation experts to assess whether or not the F-35B will be ready in 2016 or 2017 (or whenever) to meet the operational needs of the Fleet Air Arm at sea and whether, at Mach 1.6, it will match the speed and agility of its competitors in combat. What is certain is that the QUEEN ELIZABETHs will be restricted to handle (apart from helicopters) only V/STOVL aircraft. Committed to a joint UN or NATO exercise or operation, they will be unable to accommodate (say) a French or American pilot needing to land-on in a hurry. One may also ask why, if a V/STOVL type aircraft is just what the Royal Navy needs, it was necessary to build such whacking big 70,000 ton carriers in the first place. Carriers of

*The Lockheed Martin F-35B is, in essence, a go-faster stealth version of Hawker Siddeley's 1960s sub-sonic Sea Harrier. It can operate from flight decks very much smaller than the eight acres of the Queen Elizabeth Class carriers. This F-35B is making trial flights from the 41,000 ton LHD (landing helicopter dock) amphibious warfare ship USS Wasp. She is not fitted with a ski-jump. Even so, in September 2013 Squadron Leader Jim Schofield, RAF, was able to make conventional short take-off test launches from the Wasp while carrying a weapons load.*

considerably less displacement - and costing significantly less - can do the same job. The Italian Navy is purchasing the F-35B for future deployment in its carrier, the CAVOUR. At 30,000 tons, she is less than half the size of the QUEEN ELIZABETHs.

The decisions have been made, the die is cast. However and with hindsight, instead of opting for the super-carrier solution in protecting our national interests, it might perhaps have been wiser to follow the housewife's rule that you always need three of everything - "one on, one off, one in the wash". For the navy, the rule translates as "one on station, one working up, one in for refit". Rather than commit 140,000 tons of steel to building just two ships (assuming the PRINCE OF WALES will indeed one day come into full service), the same tonnage would have produced three 42,000 ton carriers like the French navy's excellent nuclear-powered CHARLES DE GAULLE. She already has twelve years of operational experience under her belt. And, as a bonus, there would have been enough tonnage left over to build another amphibious warfare ship to join the lonely HMS OCEAN.

Yes, such ideas can probably be dismissed as simplistic, and hopefully the members of the Defence Board took all that into account when they made their historically crucial decision in 2007. Time and the emergence of the next major international crisis will tell whether or not the decision was a good one.

Its members may not have realised it at the time, but the Board's decision was as revolutionary as the Admiralty's 19th century switch from sail to steam and its reluctant early 20th century acceptance of John Philip Holland's pioneering submersible. The task force-oriented Royal Navy of the future - intended, we are told, to serve our needs for the next fifty years - will be in many ways very different to that which has gone before.

In the context of international affairs, fifty years is a very long time. We need only to look at what happened between 1914 and 1945 to understand that this is so. When the next crisis comes, it will quite possibly be in the Far East, but there are plenty of other potential flash-points in distant waters.

China began to study aircraft carrier designs in 1987 and has since been advancing rapidly towards the creation of a multi-role "blue water" fleet. Her navy already operates the ex-Soviet re-fitted 67,500 ton carrier LIAONING and intends to have four additional domestically-built similarly large carriers in commission by 2018. For the past two years, the LIAONING has been exercising as a training ship, her sailors and air-crew coming to terms with the complexities of carrier operations. Their future stealth strike aircraft will be the Shenyang J31, an aircraft which according to unsubstantiated reports will be capable of Mach 2.4 with a ceiling of 65,000 feet. Allegedly, its technology is based in part upon classified files stolen from Lockheed Martin sub-contractors.

If Beijing achieves its stated objectives, it seems that by the time HMS QUEEN ELIZABETH has completed her own working-up trials, Chinese naval aviation capability will have overtaken that of the Royal Navy by a significant margin. An added concern is the Chinese submarine fleet. At the present time (2013) it includes four (possibly five) nuclear-powered 11,000 ton boats fitted with long range ballistic missiles able to reach cities in several countries with which Great Britain has close ties. To counter-balance such strategic threats the most effective weapons in Britain's armoury are the four excellent VANGUARD Class submarines.

The new British super-carriers and their strike aircraft are designed - like our submarines - for all-out war. Or, at the very least, as "a fleet in being", offering the threat of great retaliatory violence to anyone tempted to throw down the gauntlet. To escort them and shield them from attack, the Royal Navy has in its inventory, at the last count, nineteen technologically sophisticated destroyers (8500 tons) and frigates (5000 tons) in various states of operational readiness. In years gone by they would have been classified as cruisers and light cruisers. Their quality and combat capabilities are outstanding but these are "blue water" ships, arguably too big for confined inshore operations in which the navy might conceivably become involved (the "island rich environment" of South East Asia, for example).

Then, if Admiral Stanhope's proposition that the navy should protect commercial sea lanes is valid and accepted, we do not possess the smaller (and far less expensive) warships suited to the general shepherding of merchant ships, the defence of commercial ports, and low-intensity operations.

Currently the Royal Navy has in service the four "River" Class offshore patrol vessels. Employed in fishery protection duties around the UK and the Falkland Islands, they are the same size, at 1700 tons, as a typically much faster hard-hitting Fleet destroyer of WWII and the 1950s and 1960s. Designed for a maximum speed of 20 knots, the "River" Class are armed with nothing more aggressive than a single 20 mm cannon and a brace of machine-guns. No doubt excellent in the role for which they are intended, they would struggle if attacked to defend either themselves or any merchantman placed in their charge.

The Second World War demonstrated that you cannot have too many of what were then classified as sloops (1300 tons), corvettes (950 tons) and "armed trawlers" (average displacement 600 tons, vide Part Seven, HMS MULL). Apart from their numerical value in showing the White Ensign over wider stretches of ocean, "keeping an eye on the opposition", escorting merchant vessels and rescue work, their 21$^{st}$ Century equivalents would offer every promising young officer the prospect of obtaining a captaincy. The experience so gained is essential if he is to be moved on to higher appointments within the service. How many of our junior officers can hope to one day stand on their own bridge? It is the only way they can develop "hands on" personal initiative and practical ship management skills.

Computer software can never replace hard-headed seamanship. On 7 July 2002, the bridge officers in HMS NOTTINGHAM failed to recognise surface turbulence as a sign of shallow water. When they drove their Type 42 destroyer onto the Wolfe Rock (Lord Howe Island, Queensland) they ripped a ninety foot gash in her hull. She was saved only by the ship's company's courageous damage control response drills. Greater familiarity with conventional Admiralty printed charts, combined with eye-ball experience in "reading the waves", would have prevented the disaster.

Eight years later, on 22 October 2010, the 7000 ton nuclear-powered submarine HMS ASTUTE hit the headlines by trying to hit the Hebridean island of Skye. By the grace of that Providence which watches over befuddled sailors, the officers on watch brought their charge to rest, by simple good luck, on a flat ridge of soft sand

and shale, not the ragged rocks which otherwise might have torn into her hull and even tipped her onto her beam-ends. For eleven hours she was stranded, helpless. While she had been progressing steadily in darkness towards the shore, nobody noticed that the depth of water under her keel was shoaling rapidly and menacingly from forty-five metres to one metre. Given the ASTUTE's close proximity to land - less than 500 metres - the officers of an earlier age would have had a man stationed at the bow, heaving a lead line. The Royal Navy had long ago abandoned such primitive kit, replacing it with the electronic echo sounder. Normally it works perfectly well but, on that morning, in the ASTUTE, it was switched off. And that was only one of the basic errors identified by the Court of Inquiry.

When young men or women join the Royal Navy they are not simply starting a professional career, they are joining a brotherhood of the sea, a trade, a guild, a body of sailors, mariners, coastguardsmen, trawlermen, yachtsmen, all married equally to the sea and each of them alert to its ever changing moods. In Nelson's day the navy trained its future officers by recruiting boys who had yet to attain puberty. Their school was the sea, their teachers were the waves and the wind. The admirals who distinguished themselves in the war of 1939-1945 had joined the service at the age of thirteen. The navy was their mother and their father, the ocean their life-long home.

With relatively low impact on the Defence Budget, today's budding young officer can start to acquire that same awareness by being given command of a small craft comparable with the Motor Torpedo Boats (MTBs), Motor Gun Boats (MGBs) and Harbour Defence Motor Launches (HDMLs) built in their hundreds in 1939-1945 and operated in every theatre of war.

Their post-war successors were the heavily-armed 90 ton BRAVE Class fast attack craft (FACs). Only two were ever commissioned, restricted to trial and experimental work. Capable of 52 knots, HMS BRAVE BORDERER and HMS BRAVE SWORDSMAN would have been ideal for coastal raiding and anti-piracy operations in confined waters. Built by Vospers, the type was popular with foreign buyers but the Royal Navy abandoned it in 1970. They were followed by three more Vosper craft of a new type - the 102 ton 40 knot SCIMITAR, CUTLASS and SABRE - but the Class was never enlarged. By contrast, many other navies have continued to develop the missile-armed FAC concept and to deploy them in large numbers. Numerically in the lead are Iran (a lurking menace to warships guarding tanker traffic in the Straits of Hormuz) and North Korea (with 300 reportedly in service).

Major units such as aircraft carriers will find themselves in serious trouble if attacked by a multiple "swarm" of FACs. And not only at sea. In December 1971, half of Pakistan's warships and 90% of its naval fuel-oil storage facilities were destroyed by a squadron of Indian Navy FACs. The 245 ton missile-armed VIDYUTs made two daring attacks on the naval base at Karachi and got away without loss.

In October 2000 the missile destroyer USS COLE was alongside in Aden docks, taking on fuel, when two men in a solitary suicide speed-boat killed or wounded fifty-nine of COLE's crew and came close to sinking her. What could a "swarm" of even such primitive craft like that one achieve against a major naval base?

The golden age of the battleship ended, finally, in 1945. Will the carrier-centred task force likewise lose its relevance in the face of rapidly changing warship design, missile capability and electronic magnetic warfare? Readers seeking possible answers may wish to research deeper. There is a raft of disturbing evidence to suggest that "bigger" may no longer be in itself "better". It is possible that future

*Fast attack craft (FACs) are operated by many of the world's navies. Shown above is a typical conventional example. Operated by the Chilean Navy, it is based upon a German design. Displacing 265 tons, capable of 36 knots, it carries four Exocet and four Harpoon anti-ship missiles. With a crew of twenty, man for man, ton for ton, it possesses immense hitting power, but vastly more potent designs are evolving all the time. In a "Star Wars at sea" scenario, and if professional forecasts are to be believed, there will be 80 knot FACs armed with every kind of missile and 200 knot torpedoes. Shown below are four Australian designed catamaran Houbei Class of the Chinese PLA Navy. Sixty or more have entered service since 2006. At the time of writing, Britain's Royal Navy has nothing remotely comparable on the stocks.*

battles at sea may be fought by large numbers of smaller craft (some of them displacing up to 3000 tons with an operational range of 3000 miles and capable of 80 knots) rather than by small numbers of much bigger ships. If this proves to be the case, and if the Royal Navy accepts that proposition, many more of its junior officers must be prepared for captaincy far sooner in their careers than is currently feasible with so few ships in commission.

In the 1980s and 1990s, the ARCHER Class came into service with the University Royal Naval Unit. Its fourteen widely dispersed 49 ton boats are manned by small regular crews whose job it is to teach seamanship and navigation to future deck officers. They provide those young men and women with a groundwork understanding of the sea, and that is good. However, they cannot teach captaincy. In time of peace or time of war, only the challenge and privilege of command will reveal a naval officer's true quality.

Image: BAE Systems

*After seven years of debate, the MoD (Navy) has opted for the big (6000 ton) 28 knot Type 26 to replace the frigates currently in service. According to recent Press releases, the first keel will be laid in late 2015, the complete ship to be commissioned in 2020. There will be an initial order for eight, with seven more to follow. If, as announced, one is launched each year, they will be up to strength by 2030. These forecasts should be set against the facts described in the preceding pages.*

But now we must return to the topic of campaign awards. What are the prospects for the issue of any more "medals to the navy"? The Falklands War of 1982 was the one occasion in the past thirty-one years when the Fleet has been committed to a major "live-fire" operation on the high seas and, rightly, it earned a war medal. While we must maintain the hope that the navy will never again be ordered into another similar conflict it is always prudent and necessary to "speak softly and carry a big stick". President Theodore Roosevelt first uttered that phrase in 1901. More than three centuries earlier, the Elizabethan statesman William Cecil had said "seek peace but prepare for war". For the Royal Navy, their combined wisdom is even more relevant today than ever it was in the past. The dilemma, though, is deciding "what kind of war? what kind of ship?".

For the time-being, deployments of a very different order are still being conducted and are likely to recur. For example, "aid to the civil power". There have been numerous occasions when one of our ships has been sent speeding to assist the people of some unfortunate island or coastal town stricken by a hurricane or other natural disaster. Such work has never been recognised by the award of a British medal, but it can be stressful, even dangerous. The potential hazards were emphasised on 2 April 2005 when a Royal Australian Navy Sea King helicopter crashed on a mercy mission over Indonesia following the *tsunami* flooding of that month. Nine servicemen died, their next-of-kin receiving the Australian government's **Humanitarian Overseas Service Medal**.

When in 1908 much of eastern Sicily was devastated by an earthquake - triggering a massive Royal Navy response - the Italian government was quick to show its gratitude to our sailors with its **Messina Earthquake Medal**. We have never followed the Italian or Australian lead. It is not suggested that a new medal should be struck every time our sailors are engaged in such humanitarian work, but a **Civil Aid Medal** with appropriate place-name or date bars for truly major disasters would be an appropriate acknowledgement of their achievements.

**The Naval General Service Medal** (second series) was issued with a bar commemorating our anti-piracy patrols between 1909 and 1915 in the Persian Gulf. Only a few years earlier, fourteen Royal Navy ships were engaged in identical work around the Horn of Africa. Their men received **The Africa General Service Medal** with bar **Somaliland 1902-04**. Today, a new generation is fulfilling the same task off that same coast but it is largely unreported. It would be consistent with precedent to issue **The Campaign Service Medal** with bar **Somalia**. Nobody wishes to see "putty medals" being handed out simply for the sake of personal adornment, but today's Somalia anti-piracy and Caribbean anti-drug smuggling operations do arguably merit such recognition.

Numerically, the Royal Navy is now a shrivelled shadow of what it was in those decades. This does not mean that its work is any less important in protecting the national interest. And, by "national interest", we should encompass its role in fighting the international drug trade, combating the Indian Ocean pirates, and providing humanitarian aid wherever and whenever it may be needed. By extension, the navy's role in Sierra Leone (2000) and Libya (2011) demonstrated its value in supporting UN and NATO operations.

So where does our navy go from here? The future Admiral may wish to consider the words of the Royal Navy prayer: "… that we may be a safeguard unto our most gracious Sovereign Lady, Queen Elizabeth, and her Dominions, and a security for such as pass on the seas upon their lawful occasions". The reader is invited to decide whether or not those sentiments provide some sort of an answer. In our complex modern world, what *is* the navy for?

## Farewell to the Crimson and White...

At any Remembrance Sunday parade of the past fifty-odd years you will have seen a diminishing number of ex-servicemen wearing the distinctive crimson and white ribbon of **The Naval General Service Medal**. Evoking the colours of the White Ensign, it stands out from all the others. Introduced in 1915, unique to the Senior Service and to the Corps of Royal Marines, it was superseded in 1962 by the purple and green of the all-services **Campaign Service Medal**. Seventeen bars were authorised:

**Persian Gulf 1908-1914** (7127 awarded)
A long-running Royal Navy campaign to suppress piracy in the Gulf and in the Arabian Sea.

**Iraq 1919-20** (116)
Operations on the Tigris supporting Britain's sponsorship of a Hashemite kingdom in the wake of the Turkish army's removal from that region (known during the war as Mesopotamia).

**NW Persia 1920** (4)
Medals given to the four recipients (*vide* Part Six) were initially fitted with the bar **NW Persia 1919-20**. They were asked later to return it for replacement with the bar **NW Persia 1920**. It is not known whether they troubled so to do.

**Palestine 1936-39** (13,600)
Coastal operations intended to restrict Jewish immigration from Germany. The exodus was prompted by Nazi persecution of their families and communities in that country.

**SE Asia 1945-46** (2000)
Post-war naval support, following the defeat of Japan, for British and Indian Army forces fighting to re-establish order in French Indo-China and the Dutch East Indies.

**Minesweeping 1945-51** (4750)
Clearance of the thousands of mines laid by both sides during the war. A huge operation, extending from the North Sea to the coast of mainland China.

**Palestine 1945-48** (7900)
The blockade of immigrant ships transporting Holocaust survivors. Previously they had been held captive in forced labour and concentration camps spread throughout every part of Europe.

**Malaya** (7800)
The Communist-inspired "emergency" of 1948-1960. Royal Marine Commandos had a prominent role in this essentially jungle-centred campaign.

**Yangtse 1949** (1450)
The well-known HMS AMETHYST incident in which HMShips BLACK SWAN, CONSORT and LONDON were also engaged.

**Bomb and Mine Clearance 1945-53** (145)

**Bomb and Mine Clearance 1945-56** (number unknown, but rare)

**Bomb and Mine Clearance Mediterranean** (60)
The rules of entitlement for these three bars are explained in Spink's *British Battles & Medals* (1988).

**Cyprus** (4300)
The "enosis" campaign (1955-1958) when Greek-Cypriot nationalists were seeking political union with Greece. Royal Navy ships blockaded the coast, Royal Marine Commandos operated in the Troodos mountains.

**Near East** (17,800)
The short-lived 1956 Middle East campaign triggered by Colonel Nasser's nationalisation of the Suez Canal. The circumstances are described in Part Eight.

**Arabian Peninsula** (1200)
When the Sultanate of Oman was threatened by rebel forces (1957-1960), British warships and aircraft supported military operations ashore. The majority of the **NGS** medals issued with this bar went to Royal Marine Commandos.

**Brunei** (900)
The speedy suppression of a rebellion against the Sultan in December 1962. In an interesting throwback to the qualifying rules for much earlier campaign medals, Royal Navy and Royal Marine personnel received the **NGS** medal (or bar) only if they had been detached from their parent ship for service ashore or with inland river craft.

**Canal Zone** (number unknown)
This bar was sanctioned in 2003 as tardy recognition of service in Egypt between October 1951 and October 1954. The historical background to this award is described in Part Eight.

"Jolly Jack", "bootneck Royal", "intrepid aviator", today their medals are the most visible record of who they were and what they achieved. Just as the original **Naval War Medal** of 1848 served its purpose, came and then went, **The Naval General Service Medal** of 1915-1962 is unlikely to be granted a rebirth.

## For Valour ...

Much of this book has been devoted to a miscellany of battles or campaigns each of which prompted the issue of a distinctive medal to be worn on the breast of every man who had served. It was tempting to venture into the parallel sphere of medals recording acts of individual gallantry, or awarded for long service or meritorious service. It would have been pointless to have even attempted such a thing. The impressive *British Gallantry Awards,* by P E Abbott and J M A Tamplin, was first published in 1970. A work of high scholarship, it describes the origins and regulations relating to all such decorations.

The complex evolution of the **Naval Long Service & Good Conduct Medal**, and the **Naval Meritorious Service Medal** (for which sailors and marines are equally eligible), were many years ago researched and recorded with academic precision by a retired naval officer, Captain K J Douglas-Morris, DL.

To those closest to him he was "Kenneth", to his friends and fellow-researchers he was "Douggie", to the medal collecting fraternity at large he was "the Captain".

In his lifetime he produced two books which today are essential sources of reference. The first, published in 1982, was *The Naval General Service Medal Roll, 1793-1840*. It was not the first such publication, others had trod the same path in former years but, having passed many hundreds of hours in what was then the Public Record Office, Kew, "Douggie" created a Roll of recipients so accurate that it is unlikely ever to be bettered.

His second book, *Naval Medals, 1793-1840*, was published in 1987. The entries related mainly to officers and ratings whose medals and other awards formed part of his own vast collection, but they provided in the wider context an explanation of the administrative procedures leading to their issue. Collectors having an interest in the **LS&GC** "anchor type reverse" and the "wide suspension/narrow suspension" variants, as examples, may learn much from "Douggie's" profound knowledge.

One of the many treasures in his collection was the **Victoria Cross/Conspicuous Gallantry Medal** group won by a Cornishman, Ordinary Seaman John Trewavas (the Sea of Azoff, 1855, *vide* pages 50-51). In total there have been 117 **Victoria Cross** awards to men of the Royal Navy, plus a further ten to Royal Marines. The Trewavas VC recognised one of the earliest acts of valour, by any seaman, in the decades of Queen Victoria's long reign. The following five examples demonstrate how his successors gained fame and glory not only in surface vessels but also on land, under the sea and above it.

### Surgeon William Job Maillard, Royal Navy

His VC was yet another of those awarded following what "Douggie" Morris categorised as "no medal actions". The setting was the island of Crete, the year was 1898. The mainly Christian population was once again in open revolt against its

Muslim Ottoman rulers. Instability on such a strategically important island was contrary to the interests of the principal European powers so they agreed to impose a peaceful settlement by installing a combined military occupation force.

On 6 September, when Royal Navy craft were putting troops ashore at Candia, they came under heavy rifle fire. It inflicted casualties on two parties of seamen from HMS HAZARD. Surgeon Maillard was already ashore when he was asked to assist. Leaving his place of safety, he crossed the beach and attempted to lift a dying seaman from one of the boats. Even though it was hopeless, he persisted in trying to save him. With the boat drifting away from the beach, Maillard had to abandon the attempt. By the time he regained cover, "his clothes were riddled with bullets". By a near-miracle he was uninjured.

**Captain Lewis Straford Tollemache Halliday, Royal Marines Light Infantry**

On 24 June 1900, 30 year-old Captain Halliday was commanding a party of RMLI men defending the British Legation at Pekin when a group of Boxers broke into some of the outbuildings and set them on fire (*vide* pages 85-87). To drive them out, a hole was knocked in the Legation wall and Halliday then led six of his men through it to tackle the Chinese in a hand-to-hand fight. Three of them he killed with his own hand, but severe injuries (including a punctured lung, a damaged arm and loss of blood) forced him to withdraw, telling his men "carry on, don't mind me". He walked back into the Legation unaided.

After returning to duty eighteen months later, he went on to become a General, VC, KCB. His medals are held by The Royal Marines Museum, Southsea.

**Squadron Commander Richard Bell-Davies, Royal Naval Air Service**

In January 1915, he and another RNAS pilot, in the face of fierce ground fire, bombed the U-boat base at Zeebrugge at very low level. He continued the attack even though he was losing blood from a wound in a thigh. For this and similar operations over the Belgian coast he was admitted to the **Distinguished Service Order**.

He was then sent to the Middle East where, commanding No 3 Squadron RNAS, he took part in the Salonika campaign. On 19 November 1915, flying in company with Flight Sub Lieutenant Gilbert Formby Smylie, he made a low level bombing attack on the Ferrijik railway junction (near the Turkish-Bulgarian border). Ground fire was intense. Smylie was forced to make a crash-landing in a nearby marsh when his aircraft was hit and disabled. Climbing out unhurt, he set fire to it. One of his bombs had not fallen free, so he hoped the fire would ignite it and completely destroy the aircraft before Turkish troops could arrive.

At this point, seeing that Richard Bell-Davies was circling and coming down to his rescue, and might be killed when the bomb exploded, he ran back and set if off with a shot from his revolver. Ignoring the flames, the flying debris and rifle fire from approaching enemy troops, Bell-Davies swooped down, gathered up his friend, stuffed him into the cramped front compartment of his single-seat Nieuport 10, and flew back to his base with neither man injured. Bell-Davies received the **Victoria Cross**, Smyllie the **Distinguished Service Cross**.

Retiring in 1941 as Vice Admiral, VC, CB, DSO, AFC, Bell-Davies joined the Royal Naval Reserve in the rank of Commander. Employed first as a convoy Commodore and then as commissioning captain in the new escort carrier HMS DASHER, he finally left the service in 1944 having completed forty-three years in uniform. Such men were seemingly indestructible. His medals are held by the Fleet Air Arm Museum, Yeovilton (Somerset).

**Ordinary Seaman John Henry Carless, Royal Navy**

On 17 November 1917, at the Battle of the Heligoland Bight, 21 year-old John Carless was one of the team serving a 6" gun in the light cruiser HMS CALEDON. An enemy shell wounded or killed most of the men in the turret. His VC citation tells the rest of the story: "Although mortally wounded in the abdomen, he still went on serving the gun at which he was acting as rammer, lifting a projectile and helping to clear away the other casualties. He collapsed once, but got up, tried again, and cheered on the new gun's crew. He then fell and died. He not only set a very inspiring example, but he also, whilst mortally wounded, continued to do effective work against the King's enemies".

In 1920, by public subscription, a bronze bust of John Carless was unveiled in his home town of Walsall. His medals are thought to be held by Walsall Town Council.

**Sub Lieutenant Basil Charles Godfrey Place, Royal Navy**

He was commanding the midget submarine X7 when, on 22 September 1943, he took part in the latest attempt to destroy the "the beast", the battleship TIRPITZ, at her anchorage in Kaafiord, Northern Norway. Operating with him that day was his friend Lieutenant Donald Cameron, RNR, commanding X6. He also, subsequently, was awarded the **Victoria Cross**.

The battleship was tucked deep within the fiord, fifty miles from the sea. The two young officers penetrated the elaborate German defences - mines, patrol craft, hydrophone listening stations - without being detected. The last obstacle - anti-torpedo nets surrounding the target ship - failed to stop them when they evaded that also.

They were then attacked with depth charges and gunfire. Escape became impossible and they were obliged to scuttle and surrender. Meantime they had released under the battleship's hull their two-ton side cargoes of Amatol. When the charges exploded the concussion was such that some of her engine mountings and a main gun battery mounting were unseated. Even though RAF reconnaissance photographs taken the following day suggested that the attack had failed, TIRPITZ was in fact ruined and non-operational until such time as she might reach a dockyard in Germany. It was her enforced move down the coast of Norway which brought her within range of Bomber Command (*vide* page 144).

In 1950, Godfrey Place took the unusual step of transferring from the Submarine Branch to the Fleet Air Arm. Qualifying as a pilot, he joined HMS GLORY and flew Sea Fury ground attack missions over Korea with 801 NAS (*vide* pages 158-163). His medals and decorations are held by the Imperial War Museum, London.

**The VCs that never were ....**

The Victoria Cross was founded by Royal Warrant on 29 January 1856. Article 12 states that it can never be given "without conclusive proof of the performance of the act of bravery for which the claim is made". Indisputable supporting eye-witness statements are required, and that is right and proper. However, there have been occasions in the past when someone is known to have gone far beyond the normal calls of duty, has possibly lost his life "in the presence of the enemy", but whose actions could not be fully authenticated at the time.

When Commander C E Glasfurd, RN, took his HMS ACASTA into action, operating in company with another small (1350 ton) destroyer, HMS ARDENT (Lieutenant Commander J F Barker, RN), he must have known that he and his men were facing certain death. The date was 8 June 1940, the place was the Norwegian Sea, their opponents were two of Germany's most powerful capital ships, SCHARNHORST and GNEISENAU.

The full story of the tragic loss of the two British destroyers, and of the aircraft carrier they were defending, HMS GLORIOUS, must be studied elsewhere. All three ships were lost with virtually 100% fatalities. When it was all over, the captain of GNEISENAU "ordered her battle flag to be lowered to half mast and his crew were brought to attention to honour the ACASTA's brave fight". She had fought that fight for two hours, scoring a torpedo strike and hits with her 4.7" guns before disappearing in a welter of shell bursts. There was one survivor, Leading Seaman Cyril Carter.

The ARDENT capsized, still traveling at speed, after repeated German strikes but not before launching her torpedoes and scoring at least one 4.7" hit. The First Lieutenant of the SCHARNHORST later reported: "She fought with outstanding resolution ... extremely skillfully ... in a situation that was hopeless for her". Two men were picked up five days later by a German seaplane. AB Roger Hooke had somehow lived through the intense cold, the other man did not.

Given the absence of eyewitness accounts other than those of the German bridge officers there could be no award of the Victoria Cross to either of the two gallant destroyer captains. And that was a source of lasting personal sadness to Captain "Nick" Barker, son of ARDENT's captain. By 1982, "Nick" had himself gained command of a ship, the famous "red plum", HMS ENDURANCE, in which he had a key role in the build-up to the Falklands war.

# Addendum

The ten "Medals to the Navy" articles first published in *The Review* (and subsequently expanded in this book) were followed in 2013 by an unrelated article devoted to the operation code-named *Jubilee*. With the exception of a Canadian readership, what happened on the French coast at Dieppe on the morning of Wednesday, 19 August 1942, is a story curiously unfamiliar in many quarters. And yet it was by far the largest amphibious operation ever undertaken by the Royal Navy up to that time.

Since 2013 the story-line has been even further developed, and I believe it merits a permanent place in the historiography of the Second World War. Why? Because it analyses crucial aspects of the Dieppe Raid never mentioned in previous publications. Over-riding any other consideration, however, is my wish to commemorate and salute in print all those fine men whose lives were so carelessly thrown away. Soldiers, sailors, Royal Marines, US Rangers, they were ordered into a trap from which there was from the outset little, if any, prospect of escape.

They and their air force comrades left grieving families throughout the British Commonwealth, the majority of them in Canada. Most of the Canadian soldiers who died had already contributed several years of voluntary part-time service to their local militia regiment when, in the autumn of 1939, they departed their peace-time jobs and their home-towns to mobilise for full-time service overseas.

Having crossed the Atlantic, they were held in England for nearly three years before being committed to their first battle, the Dieppe Raid. Some were in their early twenties, but typically their ages were twenty-five to thirty-five. One of the oldest to be killed was Private James Duncan Campbell of the South Saskatchewan Regiment. When his parents, wife and children waved him off to war from their small prairie township of Arcola, he was already forty-three. Even older was Private Eugene Adalbert Neale of the Essex Scottish Regiment, an American-born grey-beard of fifty when he died on Dieppe beach. One of the youngest soldiers to be killed was eighteen year-old Private Robert Boulanger of Les Fusiliers Mont-Royal. He must have been well under age for military service when he enlisted.

The carefully tended graves and headstones of these three men are to be seen in the war cemetery at Hautot-sur-Mer, a bare two miles from the beaches where they were cut down. Today, seven decades later, the local staff of the Commonwealth War Graves Commission continue to give them in death the regard which those who were responsible for planning the Raid entirely failed to give them in life.

In time of war, a nation's fighting men are its most precious resource. They must be trained and equipped to the highest standard and placed under the command of officers who are not only competent in their chosen professions but who also understand the concept of "duty of care". Readers of the following pages may well conclude that James Campbell, Eugene Neale and Robert Boulanger, along with hundreds of others like them, were denied the leadership and respect which might otherwise have allowed them to live, to fight another day and, at the end of it all, to come safely home.

## Fabian Ware

Over the centuries, by storm, by mischance, by prestilence, by enemy action, untold numbers of British sailors have lost their lives beyond our shores. Some died on land and so gained the dignity of a burial, the great majority have no other grave than the sea.

Before 1914 there was no procedure for perpetuating their names in a way accessible to the public. Any influential family, having lost a naval son, could commission a memorial in their Parish church. A coastal community which had witnessed the foundering of a ship on their nearby shore might voluntarily erect a plaque, recording the event. For the rest, White Ensign or Red Ensign, too many ships and their lost crews were remembered only by the grieving families.

It was a civilian named Fabian Ware, a Red Cross volunteer working on the Western Front, who began informally to record the graves of men killed in the early Great War battles. It was an enormous task. In May 1915 his work and that of his colleagues was given official recognition by the War Office as the Graves Registration Unit. Two years later, responding to Ware's dynamic personal leadership and to public demand, the government sponsored the creation by Royal Charter of the Imperial War Graves Commission ("Imperial" later amended to "Commonwealth", here abbreviated as CWGC).

Fabian Ware laid down two rules which have ever since held inviolate. First, that CWGC headstones and memorials should make no distinction between rank. The design and material is the same for the most senior and the most junior. Secondly, men who died on land must remain buried where they fell or be re-interred at the nearest "concentration" cemetery. Regardless of wealth or social status, no family can lay claim to their man's body for repatriation.

Those of the thousands who were never found are commemorated on memorials throughout the Commonwealth. Untraced ranks and ratings of the Royal Navy and Royal Marines are listed on the CWGC Naval Memorials sited at the three principal manning ports: Plymouth, Chatham and Portsmouth. Royal Naval Air Service personnel from WWI are named on a memorial at Lowestoft, those of the Fleet Air Arm from WWII at Lee-on-Solent. Men of the Mercantile Marine and its successor Merchant Navy who have no known grave are recorded on the CWGC memorial beside the Thames at Tower Hill.

Not all of the men who lost their lives in the Dieppe Raid - particularly the naval personnel - were ever found. The soldiers whose bodies were immediately afterwards buried in mass graves by the Germans were re-interred in 1947-1948 by the CWGC at nearby Hautot-sur-Mer. Captured men needing medical treatment had been taken to military hospitals inland. The headstones of those who then died of their wounds are to be seen in the CWGC St Sever Extension cemetery in the great city of Rouen.

On the evening of 18 June 1815, 15,000 of Wellington's soldiers lay dead or dying on the battlefield of Waterloo, their bodies stripped by foraging peasantry, their abandoned remains left to rot. Exactly one hundred years later, Fabian Ware's drive and initiative ensured that then and for ever since, the war dead of Great Britain and the Commonwealth have always been given the respect which is their due.

## Dieppe 1942 - Who was to Blame?
## A Personal View

In 1948, age sixteen, returning from Switzerland with a school holiday group, I made my first visit to the small historic French port of Dieppe. The cross-Channel ferry was behind schedule so I wandered off from the railway station, the *Gare Maritime*, to walk along the sea-front. I knew little of the battle fought six years earlier, only that Canadian tanks had been put ashore on this beach with orders to fight their way over the high sea-wall, then across the wide esplanade and into the town. What lingered in my mind after that brief experience was the character of the beach. It was very steep, with tidal strands of pebbles, gravel, and coarse sand. It was the pebbles which impressed the most. The size of a large potato, unstable, they slipped and slid from under my shoes. If these strands were so difficult to traverse on foot, how could a heavy tank have climbed them without shedding a track or becoming stranded? Boys of my wartime generation of course thought we understood such things. Also, growing up on the quayside of the Devon fishing port of Brixham where I had my own boat, I knew a bit about beaches and the sea.

Years later I began to read published accounts - British, Canadian, German, French - of the 1942 Operation *Jubilee* Dieppe Raid. Whatever the source, they described an event of otherwise unimaginable horror. In 2008, with the tentative thought that I might write a book of my own, I travelled to Dieppe to spend three days walking the ground where those doomed Canadian soldiers had fought their brief battle (or where they would have fought if the odds against them had not been so impossibly high). At the end of my visit, and having viewed the cemeteries, I came away with a feeling of profound anger. In every possible context, Operation *Jubilee* was wrong. Immeasurably wrong.

Later I decided that the market for Dieppe Raid publications was already well sated and so abandoned the idea of a book. However, I had accumulated in the interim the fat research file upon which the following account is based. I shall not attempt to describe the military events of 19 August 1942 in any detail - other writers have dealt with that aspect of the story. Instead, and following the principle that nothing happens unless somebody has caused it to happen, I shall focus upon the leading architects of the disaster. They were the men who, by reason of their incompetence, inexperience or unreasoning enthusiasm, engineered an event comparable with the worst disasters of the First World War. The difference was that, on the Western Front, wounded and shell-shocked men could crawl back to their trenches. At Dieppe, there was no such option.

Only four hours after landing, scores of desperate men were fleeing the carnage ashore and swimming out to sea. Between them and sanctuary lay seventy miles of cold English Channel. Some, wounded and semi-naked, were seen and rescued, others were swept away on the ebbing tidal flow and never found. It is an outrage that they should have been forced into that situation.

Primary responsibility lay with Vice Admiral Lord Louis Mountbatten, head of the sprawling Directorate of Combined Operations. Man of action, handsome, charming, vain, he was the epitome of a dashing captain of destroyers. At times

*Before his promotion to Combined Operations, Captain Lord Mountbatten commanded HMS Kelly. She was a K-Class Fleet destroyer displacing 2700 tons (war load) built on the Tyne in 1938 by Hawthorn Leslie. Commanded throughout her short existence by Lord Mountbatten she was capable, like her captain, of great dash and high speed. Here, on an early trial run, her twin propellers (backed by 40,000 shaft horse power) are raising her bow and driving down her stern. Not the luckiest of ships, she saw active service for less than two weeks during the first fourteen months after commissioning. Storm damage, a mine, a ramming and a torpedo each in succession put her back in dockyard hands. On 23 May 1941, she and her sister-ships Kashmir and Kipling were operating south of Crete without air cover when they were attacked by a flock of twenty-four Ju87 Stuka dive-bombers. Kelly and Kashmir were both sunk, half of Mountbatten's ship's company being lost. He himself nearly drowned, trapped under his own bridge when the Kelly rolled over. With the other survivors, he was picked up by Kipling and taken to safety at Alexandria.*

reckless, a disregard for his own personal safety but also the safety of people for whom he was responsible would lead to his assassination in 1979 by Irish republicans during his annual summer holiday on the coast of County Sligo. In 1939 his wife Edwina had inherited Classiebawn Castle, an imposing mid-19th century Baronial-style property near the fishing and tourist village of Mullaghmore. Mountbatten retained the Castle after Edwina died prematurely in 1960 and it was here that he came every August with close family members to relax and enjoy time in their company.

The local people were always glad to see them, making them welcome in their own unobtrusive way, but Mullaghmore was only sixteen miles from the border with Northern Ireland. Members of the Irish Republican Army often took refuge in the surrounding area, a fact well known to the security services.

In every previous year the *Garda Siochána* (the Irish Police) had provided a strong close protection team (in some years as many as twenty-eight officers working around-the-clock shifts). In the days preceding the family's arrival, they made regular security checks on Mountbatten's twenty-nine foot motor boat, *Shadow V,* moored in Mullaghmore harbour. There were no such arrangements in August 1979. He assumed that, as a non-politician and now in his 80th year, he was no longer at risk and he therefore told them they were not needed.

It was a fatal decision which he allowed other people to make for him. Unlike some other members of the royal family he had never had a personal bodyguard but he did from time to time invite advice from authorities who, in theory, were better able than he to assess the risk of a terrorist attack. That year, before leaving for Ireland, he consulted William Whitelaw, Home Secretary, and Robert Marks, Commissioner of the Metropolitan Police. Marks in turn consulted his opposite number in the *Garda* and it was the consensus opinion that the risk was probably minimal. Evidently, for them, that was good enough. Their advice was, of course, influenced by political considerations. Commissioner Marks, although privately telling Mountbatten that he personally advised against the visit, quoted his *Garda* colleague as saying "we can't show the white flag to the IRA". Understandably, the Irish could not admit to perhaps having lost control of events in their own country. Protection was scaled down to just four plain-clothes officers watching the Castle at night, two discreet escorts during the day. They were no more than a token gesture.

How could Whitelaw, Marks and Dublin not understand that, as a high profile embodiment of the British establishment, a cousin of Her Majesty the Queen, Mountbatten was an obvious target? In terms of his personal safety, they had left him stark naked. Barely five months earlier, the wartime hero Airey Neave, MP, had been murdered by bomb blast within the heavily-policed House of Commons underground car park. If the republican bombers could do that, they could certainly kill Mountbatten - together with members of his family - in sleepy County Sligo. A more cautious man might have either cancelled the trip or simply requested the same level of protection provided in former years. It would certainly have been given. He was a strong-minded man with many admirable qualities, but "caution" was not one of them. The final decision was his and his alone

On the sunny Bank Holiday Monday morning of 27 August, he and six others departed Mullaghmore harbour in *Shadow V* and headed out towards a nearby lobster fishing ground. They were his daughter Patricia, her husband John Brabourne, their twin 14 year-old sons Timothy and Nicholas, the 83 year-old Dowager Lady Brabourne and 15 year-old Paul Maxwell, a well-regarded local fisher lad.

Five hundred yards out from the shore, the boat exploded. Activated by remote control radio signal, a five pounds charge of dynamite hidden under the floor-boards blew it to pieces. Mountbatten, Nicholas and Paul died instantly, Lady Brabourne later that night. The three survivors were left with terrible injuries.

Why did he take such a pointless gamble with all their lives? His plan for the Dieppe Raid - involving as it did the lives of 6000 soldiers and marines, plus 4000 airmen and sailors - was even more dismissive of potential danger. But, given his bold character and the importance of the event, given that he was the senior officer in overall command, it is surprising - indeed, almost unbelievable - that he chose not to accompany the Dieppe expedition in person and thereby provide on-the-spot leadership to the bewildered officers in the offshore command ships HMS CALPE and HMS FERNIE. His preferred role was that of a distant observer, attempting to follow their infrequent and confusing wireless (radio) reports as best he could back in England.

Images: Allan Warren and The Belfast Telegraph

*The life of "Dickie" Mountbatten (1900-1979) was by any standard exceptional. He retired from his last active post, Chief of the Defence Staff, in 1965. For two decades and more, he had been at the centre of the United Kingdom's national and international affairs. His rewards were an Earldom, a Knighthood of the Order of the Garter, and the Grand Cross of four other illustrious Orders of chivalry. Long fascinated by such marks of distinction, by heraldry, by royal genealogy and ceremonial ritual, he began in 1971 to compile the details of his own eventual State funeral. The planning was meticulous. What he could not anticipate was the fate that awaited him, his body wrapped in a blanket on an Irish beach.*

I have tried but failed to recall any other occasion in British history when 10,000 men were committed to battle by a leader who, on the day, stayed passively at home. There were 237 vessels flying the White Ensign that day. At the very least, and if only out of professional curiosity, surely he should have been motivated to observe the conduct of his subordinate officers while they were crossing the Channel, clearing the minefields and approaching the French coast?

He had invited a group of journalists to accompany him when on the previous morning and afternoon he toured the embarkation ports. Cap tilted at jaunty angle, he posed for their cameras with smiling Canadian and British servicemen who, unaware of what awaited them, might within hours be dead or condemned to three years in a prisoner of war camp. I found no evidence that he came back to greet the lucky ones upon their return.

In its preparatory stages there were many cooks stirring the Dieppe witch's brew. Too many. A few, as will be shown later, had previous experience of inter-service cooperation. Most had none at all. One of Mountbatten's basic failures was to ensure that each of the three services would indeed work together in a "combined" operation. For the RAF, Operation *Jubilee* was viewed as an opportunity to provoke the *Luftwaffe* into a major aerial encounter and to inflict heavy losses upon it. For the Canadian Army, it would be a land battle. For the Royal Navy, the job would be to convey the troops to the French coast, let them fight their battle, then bring them home again. How those three strands might best be woven together was a conundrum discussed but never resolved.

Mountbatten's major failure, however, was that of not insisting upon a full in-depth analysis of the risks involved. For that he depended upon his Senior Intelligence Officer, the Marques de Casa Maury. It was this man's assessment that "Dieppe is not strongly defended". To find an explanation for Mountbatten's trust in him - to understand why he so readily accepted his opinion - we need to look at the friendship between them. Unexplored by any other author, it may explain the cause of the disaster. In my opinion, it was the primary cause, hence the nature of that friendship needs to be examined and, in particular, the character and personal background of Casa Maury.

Known as Pedro to his family and later as Peter or "Bobby" to his lovers and high-society friends, he was born in 1896 of Spanish parents in Baracoa, Cuba. His father was a wealthy businessman who aspired to higher social standing. In 1897 he applied to the Vatican for the granting of a Papal title. As justification he listed his "good work for the Church", a "promise to show his gratitude with deeds", and much more besides. In consideration of two substantial cash payments, the submission was approved by His Holiness Pope Leo XIII. And so, Don Pedro Jose Mones y Maury became the Marques de Casa Maury. The title was hereditary in the male line, hence it passed to Peter when his father died. London journalists would later refer to Peter as "a Spanish nobleman", an attribution he made no attempt to deny. That was understandable because, combined with his sophisticated charm and dark good looks, it made him even more attractive to women.

Following the 1896 popular uprising in Cuba and with an American invasion of that island imminent, the newly-appointed Marques moved his family and his fortune to Madrid and, soon after, to the fashionable Avenue Kleber, Paris. His son Pedro (Peter) received his early education from French tutors and subsequently (1907-1913) from the Jesuit priests at Beaumont College, Old Windsor. Next, having an aptitude for things mechanical, he studied engineering at the University of London and specialised in engine design at the Royal College of Science. In 1917, age twenty-three, he was granted a temporary commission in the Royal Flying Corps as a Lieutenant (Acting Captain) employed in the development of aero engines. During this time he formed a passion for fast cars. Leaving the RAF in February 1919 he devoted himself to motor racing. Recruited by Enrico Bugatti as a works driver, he competed in the 1920s at Le Mans, in a great many TT races and in the French, Italian and Spanish *Grands Prix*.

In 1927 he was appointed to the Board of Bentley Motors, makers of luxury cars and the iconic green racing machines. He was made Managing Director jointly with W O Bentley. The company was succeeding on the race tracks but struggling financially. The majority share-holder was Woolf Barnato, heir to a diamond fortune and himself a racing driver. Although they knew each other well, Barnato was under the mistaken impression that Peter was a financial expert, able to bring order to the company's affairs. He instead devoted his efforts to improving its marketing image and designing bodywork for new models. He did both jobs exceedingly well before he and W O Bentley were both removed from the Board in 1930. The company went bust soon afterwards and was taken over by Rolls Royce. Peter's first marriage ended in divorce that same year. He had married Paula Gellibrand, a famed social beauty and favourite model of the society photographer Cecil Beaton.

After losing money in the Wall Street crash, Peter restored his finances by creating in 1934 the ultra-modern Curzon Cinemas in Mayfair and Shaftesbury Avenue, Soho. They attracted audiences from "the smart set", upper levels of society of which he was a popular member. In those pre-television years, a visit to the cinema was a "dressing up" event similar to a visit to a West End theatre. Theirs was a privileged group which enjoyed a remarkable sexual freedom unknown to the lesser classes. A merry-go-round of promiscuity and divorces, it was exclusive to the aristocracy and to those who, like Peter, possessed the wealth and stamina to match their pace.

He first encountered the Mountbattens in Valetta, Malta, sometime around 1928. "Dickie" Mountbatten was serving with the Mediterranean Fleet. He and his wife, Edwina, had established a temporary home on the island. Like them, Peter had a luxury yacht and there were the usual parties and entertainments. Subsequently he became close to them both and often visited the family home (first Adsdean, later Broadlands). Their daughter, Lady Patricia, told me she was too young at the time to remember much about him other than his slightly foreign accent. Doubtless it added to his allure.

From a letter quoted verbatim by Philip Ziegler - Mountbatten's authorised biographer - it is evident that "Dickie" accepted Peter as yet another of his wife's many lovers. Ziegler makes the point that Mountbatten was strangely tolerant, treating those men as long-term friends. Theirs was what is known as an "open marriage". When Peter applied for British nationality, Mountbatten was one of his four distinguished sponsors. I believe it was solely as a consequence of their close personal friendship that Mountbatten invited the novice Peter - rather than any other available officer - to be his Senior Intelligence Officer at Combined Operations Headquarters (COHQ). Given all that had passed between them and Edwina over the years, did he think it impolite (or even domestically undiplomatic) to thereafter replace him with someone more capable? Or was he simply oblivious to the dangers?

In 1938, age forty-two, with war looming, Peter had applied for a commission with the Royal Air Force Volunteer Reserve. It was granted on 4 April 1939. His fluency in three languages made him an obvious candidate for training in Intelligence work. Having completed the basic induction course and holding the rank of Acting Probationary Pilot Officer (Admin & Special Duties) he was posted, by odd coincidence, to RAF Mountbatten, Plymouth. It was the home of 15 Group RAF Coastal Command and of the all-Australian 10 Squadron operating Short Sunderland flying boats. In common with the rest of Plymouth and Devonport, it was badly battered during the blitz.

Peter departed 15 Group on 16 December 1941 and returned to London to join the inner circle of "the Mountbatten Court" at COHQ. At the same time, to give him enhanced status, Mountbatten arranged with the Chief of the Air Staff, Sir Charles Portal, for Peter's instant promotion to Acting Wing Commander. He must have been delighted with the additional rings on his jacket cuff and to be reunited with people of his own kind. Bomb-wrecked Plymouth and the cheerful Aussies could never compete with the delights of Mayfair, Park Lane and the West End. Peter was one of numerous pre-war personal friends of the Mountbattens who, regardless of their varied competence, were plucked from lesser roles in the war effort to share the glamour of "Combined Ops".

For reasons I cannot establish, Peter was Mentioned in Despatches (*London Gazette*, 1.1.1942). This may have related to his work as a 15 Group Intelligence Officer or he may have distinguished himself during the Plymouth blitz. It might even have been for an act of bravery during the bombing, I do not know. Certainly he had shown bravery when, in 1937, he married the 44 year-old divorcee Mrs Freda Dudley Ward. She was formerly the long-time confidante and mistress, before he met Mrs Simpson, of Edward, Prince of Wales. A familiar figure on the London social scene and country house party circuit, she had not long ended an affair with her latest lover, a cousin of the Earl of Pembroke. That marriage (Peter's second) ended in divorce in 1954 after he was cited as one of four correspondents following a scandalous affair with the very much younger Laura, Countess of Dudley. He was then age fifty-eight. Peter may have performed badly at COHQ but in other respects he cannot be faulted.

Reading about these people and their peacetime self-indulgent lives, I wonder whether those of their men serving in uniform truly understood their wartime moral responsibilities. Mountbatten boasted to his friend Sir Robert Scott: "Edwina and I spent all our married lives getting into other people's beds". Philip Ziegler names several ladies with whom "Dickie" had intimate relationships before the war and he

Images: Reproduced courtesy of the Bugatti Trust/ National Portrait Gallery

*"Bobby" Mones Maury, as he was then known, drove his first race for Enrico Bugatti on 16 October 1921. The event was the Spanish Grand Prix. Driving a Type 13, he completed the thirty lap race in second place. In this photograph, kindly provided by The Bugatti Trust, he is behind the wheel with his usual mechanic, Zirn. The 1923 studio portrait, by Bassano, affirms the handsome persona which made him so acceptable to the British aristocracy. In December 1941, totally lacking in military or naval experience, he will be recruited to assemble the information needed for that most complex category of warfare, amphibious assault.*

took a life-time pleasure in the company of intelligent beautiful women, but there is no evidence that his private life might have interfered with his professional duties in the months leading up to the Dieppe Raid. On the other hand, there is the inevitable suspicion that some of his courtiers at COHQ may have been too pre-occupied with their off-duty activities to have much regard for the ordinary sailors and soldiers who would be committed to it.

What is beyond dispute is that Mountbatten's own thoughts in the early months of 1942 were quite certainly *not* devoted 100% to preparations for Operation *Jubilee*. He was a cinema *aficionado*, an enthusiasm dating back to his junior officer days and to the 1922 honeymoon spent partly in Hollywood where he and Edwina were lavishly entertained by the great and the good of the American film industry. Friendships were formed then which continued for many years and which he mobilised later to sponsor the creation of the non-profit Royal Naval Film Corporation. An excellent initiative, officially launched in April 1938, the Corporation supplied popular films for the entertainment of sailors serving at sea or at isolated shore establishments. Only someone with Mountbatten's unique network of personal contacts - civilian and naval, British and American - could have pulled it off.

One of those connections was a friend of many years' standing, the playwright and actor Noel Coward. Mountbatten had persuaded the Admiralty to allow him in 1937 and 1938 to visit various ships in the Home Fleet and the Mediterranean Fleet so that he could discover what categories of film would be most appreciated by the sailors. The answer was "anything that made them laugh". They were amused (or possibly bemused) by the flamboyant overtly homosexual Noel, but he did the job. Questions were asked in the House of Commons, but the grumbles subsided when it was told that he was paying all the travel costs from his own pocket.

Logically, Mountbatten was instantly responsive when three years later, in the autumn of 1941, Coward asked for his advice. He had obtained the backing of the Ministry of Information to produce a morale-boosting film, *"In Which We Serve"*. It was the story of a fictional destroyer, HMS TORRIN, and her fictional commanding officer, Captain Kinross. The plot was essentially the real-life story of HMS KELLY, the ship in which Mountbatten had so nearly died when a few months earlier she was bombed and sunk off the coast of Crete. Noel Coward would play the role of Captain Kinross.

Aware that Coward's heroic screen portrayal of him might provoke personal resentment amongst his fellow officers and at the Admiralty, Mountbatten tried hard to distance himself from the public image it would present. Amongst the dozens of archived Press and publicity photographs dating from that period, I did not find a single one which showed the two men together. Even so, he characteristically devoted his great energy and enthusiasm to every aspect of Coward's production - including the writing of the script, the auditioning of leading actors and even the selection of the two hundred bit players, the "extras". He was determined that the Royal Navy would appear on the screen as it really was, not as a civilian script writer or director might otherwise imagine it to be. In this he was entirely successful. When the film was released onto the cinema circuit in

*Preparing himself for the role of Captain Kinross in the film "In Which We Serve", Noel Coward studied Admiral Lord Mountbatten's mannerisms and style of command in every detail. The result was a triumph, the actor successfully shedding every vestige of the stage character so familiar to his pre-war theatre-going public.*

September 1942 - one month after the Dieppe Raid - it was received to wide public and critical acclaim and was nominated for an Academy award. Directed by the brilliant young David Lean, of almost documentary quality, *"In Which We Serve"* still appears from time to time on our television screens and it has lost none of its 1942 authenticity.

Attempting to soak up the nuances of naval language and ship-board life, Noel Coward spent much of the autumn and winter months once again visiting Royal Navy ships and shore establishments and consulting with "Dickie" (who at the time was establishing himself in his new job at COHQ). In 1937 and 1938, Coward had been talking to the lower decks about their peacetime taste in films. This time he was listening to all ranks and ratings under the very different circumstances of war.

He had never himself served in uniform but, under "Dickie's" tutelage, he learned quickly and well. The ultra-sophisticated pre-war "silk dressing gown and gold cigarette holder" stage *persona* was replaced by that of a naval officer shaped in the Mountbatten mould. Filming commenced at Denham Studios, near London, in February 1942. That was four weeks before the high risk St Nazaire Raid and just when *Jubilee* was entering the crucial formative stages of planning. We shall never know how much time was dedicated by Mountbatten to his conferences with Noel Coward and the production team, how many journeys he might have made to the Denham Studios. Ziegler states that they were "frequent". Nor can we know to what extent this film in which he took such a passionate interest might have encroached upon his mental focus as head of Combined Operations.

Whatever the answer, *"In Which We Serve"* was undeniably a diversion of effort from his primary duty - master-minding the Dieppe Raid plan. Furthermore, his involvement with Coward's film must have been well known to his COHQ staff. How did they respond? Did Mountbatten's enthusiasm for that project in any way diminish their personal commitment to their own allotted duties? Maximum dedication by all concerned was essential if *Jubilee* was to succeed, and that could be enforced only by tight management and strong leadership. Judged by the events of 19 August, not everyone employed at COHQ was ever persuaded of the gravity of their responsibilities.

The Casa Maury family became involved in the film when Mountbatten persuaded David Lean to add Pamela Dudley Ward to the cast. A professional actress, she was one of Peter's two step-daughters. We may wonder whether he and his wife will have frequented Denham Studios to share in the "show-biz" glamour. If so, it would have been yet another distraction from primary duties.

After Pamela's own marriage ended in divorce, she married the film director Sir Carol Reed. He had been one of Peter's four sponsors when Mountbatten was arranging for the Cuban to become a British citizen. Always central to the Mountbatten story are the deep-rooted bonds of friendships and personal loyalties.

Another indication of Mountbatten's lack of "grip" over his staff was the inadequacy at Dieppe of the wireless (radio) arrangements. Depending upon the source consulted, the RAF's ship-to-air communications worked well enough at first but then failed during the withdrawal. The navy's ship-to-shore communications, on the other hand, broke down almost as soon as the assault commenced. Given the chaos on the beaches that was understandable at the tactical level, but no meaningful reports from Hughes-Hallett (the expedition's naval force commander, of whom more later) or Roberts (the land force commander, also of whom more later) ever reached Mountbatten back in England.

Although he carefully avoided during his pre-war career the trap of being permanently categorised an "expert" - something which could have inhibited his long-term promotion prospects - Mountbatten was technically better informed on the subject of signals than any other officer in the Navy List. In 1924 he attended the Long Signals Course at HMS MERCURY, a shore base in HM Barracks, Portsmouth. Established in 1904 following the arrival in service of Marconi's new equipment, it taught all aspects of wireless telegraphy and encryption to officers and ratings alike. As usual, Mountbatten worked ferociously hard, passed the course, then joined the Mediterranean Fleet as Assistant Fleet Signals Officer.

Two years later he was back at MERCURY, this time as an instructor. On his own initiative he completely re-wrote the "Admiralty Handbook of Wireless Telegraphy" and devised an innovative method of illustrating the diverse circuits. This *tour de force* was followed by several more years in the Mediterranean, this time as the Fleet Signals Officer. According to Ziegler, he was constantly checking the work of each ship's telegraphists, getting to know them individually, guiding and encouraging, dramatically improving their efficiency. His reputation as the top man spread throughout the navy.

Summing up, there was no other serving officer better qualified to ensure that the *Jubilee* communication systems should be perfect in every way. They were not, and this suggests that he had entrusted the task to one of his COHQ subordinates and then left him to get on with it. Whoever he was, that officer self-evidently lacked the skills required to devise an agreed inter-service "joined-up" signals net. Once again, Mountbatten had picked the wrong man.

The Operation *Jubilee* air commander was Air Vice Marshal Trafford Leigh-Mallory, head of Fighter Command's 11 Group. On the morning of the raid, awaiting news, he remained at the Group's headquarters, RAF Uxbridge (on the outskirts of London). Mountbatten, having delivered rousing speeches to the departing troops at Portsmouth, Shoreham, Great Yarmouth and Newhaven, had motored up to join him on the previous evening. The Army Commandos landed at 0400, the first Canadians at 0445. Thereafter, given the breakdown in communications, Mountbatten had no control over what was happening on the other side of the Channel and, if so minded, to issue fresh orders. He could not possibly comprehend how the plan to which he had given his personal approval was so swiftly collapsing into bloody ruin.

All of this brings us back to Wing Commander Peter de Casa Maury. Beginning

*Air Vice Marshal Trafford Leigh-Mallory shared Mountbatten's reckless streak. Beginning in 1941, as the ambitious head of 11 Group Fighter Command, he ordered an intensive campaign of low-level "sweeps" over France. Hundreds of aircrew were lost, mainly to ground fire, without furthering the progress of the war. As justification, "lessons were learned". In 1943 he joined SHAEF as Eisenhower's Air C-in-C. Then, following the Normandy breakout, he was appointed to SEAC as Mountbatten's Air C-in-C. Weather predictions for the first leg of the outbound flight to Ceylon on 14 November 1944 were bad. According to the Court of Enquiry, he "persuaded" the pilot to take off anyway. When the Avro York crashed in the French Alps, everyone on board was killed (including Leigh-Mallory's wife).*

*Sir Robert Laycock became a professional soldier in 1927 when he was commissioned into the Royal Horse Guards. In WWII he saw action with the Army Commandos in Crete and North Africa before his appointment as Chief of Combined Operations in 1943. In the context of the Dieppe story, his main contributions were to unhorse Wing Commander Peter de Casa Maury and to subsequently impose upon "Combined Ops" the professionalism which previously it had so woefully lacked. Later appointed Governor General of Malta during the difficult Dom Mintoff period, he suffered poor health and died prematurely, age sixty, in 1969.*

with the 1920s, he emerges as a man who had devoted much of his life to fast cars and fast ladies before being invited to gather and assess the information needed for a pioneering major amphibious operation. He was in many ways a fascinating individual, but Mountbatten's loyalty to this particular old chum would be laughable if the consequences at Dieppe had not been so tragic.

No heads rolled in the wake of the raid. Mountbatten kept his job and for the next six months he retained his Senior Intelligence Officer. Peter's removal from COHQ required the intervention of someone who, as it happened, had no direct involvement with either the planning or the execution of *Jubilee*. He was Brigadier Sir Robert Laycock, head of the Army Commandos, the Special Service Brigades. In September, returning to London after a series of daring actions in the Middle East, he soon heard the stories then circulating and spoke with the two Army Commando leaders who had taken part, Lieutenant Colonels John Durnford-Slater and the Lord Lovat. All the evidence pointed to disgracefully bad Intelligence as having been the root cause of the failure.

Mountbatten was showing no sign of wanting to sack Peter, but Laycock was in a unique position. In 1935 he had married Angela Dudley Ward, daughter of the Mrs Freda Dudley Ward mentioned previously and who two years later married Peter de Casa Maury. By that union, Peter became Robert's step son-in-law. It is impossible to imagine that the two men did not know each other very well indeed. Without involving Mountbatten, Laycock went directly for the jugular.

On 9 December 1942 he wrote a personal letter - "Bob" to "Bobby" - in which he condemned the accuracy of Peter's *Jubilee* Intelligence and suggesting that he should hand over to an officer better trained in such work. Peter replied immediately with a long explanation of his pre-raid research, but he must have been shaken by Laycock's letter. He consulted his friend "Dickie" who offered to arrange for him an alternative Wing Commander's job "if you would like it". Those five words reveal everything we need to know about the ethos of Combined Operations as it was at that time.

Peter decided instead that he should move on. In a letter dated 22 February 1943 he wrote again to Laycock: "The Senior Intelligence Officer in this headquarters must have the full confidence of all. I felt that after your letter of 9 December last, this was not the case and immediately (*sic*) handed in my resignation to the CCO (Mountbatten). I did not think it fair on him - or me - that under such circumstances I should bear the responsibility of future operations".

Having tried but failed to persuade Mountbatten to arrange a further promotion - to Group Captain - Peter was permitted to resign his RAFVR commission while retaining the honourary substantive rank of Wing Commander (retired). For any officer to voluntarily walk away from his duties in the middle of a war is highly unusual. My record is incomplete, but I believe it was the result of further exchanges between Mountbatten and Sir Charles Portal. Whatever the explanation, looking for new employment, Peter had been talking with pre-war motor racing friends. Several were serving with the all-civilian Air Transport Auxiliary (ATA) created by a leading City figure, Gerard d'Erlanger. Between 1939 and 1945, he recruited a wide range of outstanding men and women to serve as ferry pilots supporting the RAF. One such was Diana, daughter of Woolf Barnato, another was the record-breaking driver John Cobb, hence Peter was re-joining friends from his time with Bentley Motors. He had not flown with the RAF but, helped by his engineering background and despite his age (47), he passed the flying and physical tests and that, I assume, was what he did for the remainder of the war.

His wife, Freda, was unhappy that he was no longer part of "Dickie's" inner court. That was a natural reaction as a loyal wife but it diminished her own perceived social status. She may also have been disappointed that Peter's name did not appear in the long list of *Jubilee* honours and awards published in early October. In response, Mountbatten sent her a sympathetic letter explaining the difficulties of interpreting aerial photographs and other aspects of Jubilee which were attracting criticism. Apart from his abandonment in 1936 of his cousin the Duke of Windsor - after the Abdication - Mountbatten was always endearingly loyal to his friends.

In December 1943, a new Anglo-American organisation (SHAEF) was established to plan the intended liberation of France. It absorbed the British-led planning cell (COSSAC) created nine months earlier by Lieutenant General Sir Frederick Morgan. It also subsumed the role of COHQ. Appointed to command SHAEF was the American General Dwight D Eisenhower, an officer with modest family roots in Kansas. A good judge of men and an experienced organiser, he had directed the Anglo-American forces in North Africa (Operation *Torch*) and then Sicily (Operation *Husky*). His officers were appointed and promoted on merit. Personal wealth, social status and old friendships counted for nothing. Officers who failed to meet Eisenhower's demanding standards were swiftly returned whence they came.

Mountbatten's own career was approaching a cross-roads. Although claiming to have learned so much at Dieppe about amphibious operations, he was given no role in planning the 1944 Normandy assault. He was in fact removed entirely from the European theatre of war. He had been hoping for a sea-going appointment but, in August 1943, he was promoted to full Admiral and made C-in-C of a new South East Asia Command (SEAC). He established another stylish "Court", this time in the pleasant hill town of Kandy, Ceylon's ancient capital, where he amassed a remarkably large headquarters staff of several thousand service men and women.

The fighting in that region was on land, so the choice of a sailor rather than a soldier to supreme command of the "forgotten" British, Indian, African, American and Chinese forces serving in Burma might seem strange. Objections were raised in high places but Churchill had made up his mind and, as events were to show, it was a good choice. Both before and after the Japanese surrender in August 1945, the role of "Supremo" enabled Mountbatten's previously unrealised talents as an inter-Allies facilitator to emerge and blossom. Undaunted by the complexities of dealing with very senior British and American officers - all significantly older than himself, each highly protective of his own command and his own personal reputation - he developed the sort of measured judgement so conspicuously absent from *Jubilee*. Back in London, control of Combined Operations passed to the tough professional soldier "Bob" Laycock. There were no more Dieppes.

Meantime, 1942 was for the Allies the most perilous year of the war. The RAF's bombing of Germany was a campaign in its infancy. Convoys in the Atlantic and tankers in the Caribbean were being savaged by increasing numbers of U-boats. Rommel's *Afrika Korps* was threatening to capture the Suez Canal. Powerful German armies were at the doors of Moscow and Leningrad. Stalin was pressing Churchill for an immediate full-scale invasion of France, hopefully forcing Hitler to transfer many of his divisions from Russia and the Ukraine. But with American industry and recruitment still gearing up for global war, Churchill knew there was no prospect of a cross-Channel invasion before 1943 or even 1944. In essence, his thinking was: "Something must be done. Dieppe is something, so let's do it".

As enthusiasm for the operation gathered pace, more and more people were drawn into the *Jubilee* orbit. One such was Canadian-born Rear Admiral Harold Baillie-Grohman. Exceptionally, this officer had attended both the Military Staff College and the Naval Staff College. They taught the disciplines of careful planning and efficient administration. That training paid off when he was given the task of rescuing the British and Commonwealth troops who had been committed to Churchill's ill-conceived 1941 adventure in Greece. Posted to COHQ as the Naval Force Commander, he found himself working alongside Commodore Lord Louis Mountbatten, an officer qualified in signals but not in staff work.

It was an anomaly of the command structure that Baillie-Grohman carried the higher rank. In October 1941, when Mountbatten replaced Admiral of the Fleet Sir Roger Keyes at COHQ, he had been made "Combined Operations advisor" to the IGS, the Imperial General Staff committee. That meant everything and nothing, depending upon interpretation. He rightly decided it meant he was *de facto* the man in charge and he acted accordingly. However, the three Force Commanders - sea, land and air - were each senior to him, each thinking in terms of his own service. It was a poor arrangement so, in March, the clock ticking, Churchill ordered

Mountbatten's promotion to Acting Vice Admiral (the youngest ever). His role was confirmed with the title "Chief of Combined Operations" and he was given a seat on the IGS committee. The First Sea Lord, Admiral Sir Dudley Pound, wrote a deferential letter to Churchill, questioning the wisdom of thrusting such an inexperienced young officer into the heart of the nation's war effort, but he did not press the point. It might have been better if he had done so.

Meantime, Baillie-Grohman adjusted well to the strange COHQ command arrangements. He had been Mountbatten's senior officer in the pre-war Mediterranean Fleet and was twelve years older. Unfortunately, he seems not to have advertised widely his stated opinion that Peter de Casa Maury was "utterly useless". If that was his belief then, by virtue of his greater experience, it was his duty to confront Mountbatten and tell him candidly that he was backing the wrong horse.

The issue never reached that stage because, after being engaged in the early phase of planning, Baillie-Grohman fell ill and was obliged to hand over as Naval Force Commander to Captain John Hughes-Hallett, RN. This officer, of nearly the same age as Mountbatten, was a torpedo specialist. He chaired the Raid Planning Committees for the St Nazaire raid in March and the Dieppe assault in August. He did not go along with his predecessor's estimation of Peter as being "utterly useless". To the contrary, Philip Ziegler quotes him as saying that Peter "did his work with astonishing despatch, displaying considerable skill, artistry and imagination". Set against the scale of the disaster, why such flowery words of praise? Was Hughes-Hallett overawed by the charismatic Mountbatten - anxious to please him by endorsing his choice of Senior Intelligence Officer - or did he genuinely not understand why the raid had gone so badly wrong?

*Rear Admiral Harold Baillie-Grohman was the first of Lord Mountbatten's two successive Naval Force Commanders. He was particularly experienced, having served with the Grand Fleet and the Dover Patrol in WWI, then as captain of HMS Ramillies in a major action against the Italian Fleet in 1940. Forced by ill-health to depart COHQ in early 1942, he recovered sufficiently to be Flag Officer in Charge at Harwich (1944) and at the captured north German naval bases at war's end. He died in 1978, age ninety.*

*In August 1942, Captain John Hughes-Hallett, RN, commanded the largest armada of warships and amphibious vessels committed to action up to that time. Additional to eight small destroyers, fifteen minesweepers and thirty-nine Fairmile "C"-class Motor Gun Boats, it included 175 transports and landing craft of various types. Within the constraints of an inherently flawed plan, his men did all and more than might ever have been expected of them. He himself was admitted to the Distinguished Service Order. Subsequently he held a succession of senior posts before retiring in 1954 as a Vice Admiral. He then became a Conservative MP serving under his old Dieppe boss, Sir Winston Churchill. He died in 1972, age seventy-one.*

On the fateful day, Captain Hughes-Hallett crossed the Channel in HMS CALPE. She was the main command and control ship, one of the eight small (1340 ton) "Hunt" Class destroyers deployed at Dieppe. Looking down from her open bridge he saw for himself a consequence of his committee's handiwork. By mid-morning her decks were so crowded with evacuated casualties - more than two hundred of them - she was for a while unable to traverse or fire her guns. The *Jubilee* force did not include a fully-equipped medically-staffed hospital ship.

After the raid, Hughes-Hallett was amongst the first to propose that, if even a very small harbour like Dieppe could not be seized by storm, the Allies would need to take their own port with them when eventually they returned to France for a full-scale invasion. The seed had been sown in his mind when he saw some initial designs prepared in 1940 by Guy Maunsell, a highly regarded civil engineer. The Welsh engineer Hugh Iorys Hughes submitted similar designs.

Winston Churchill was a quarter of a century ahead of them all. In 1917, having been restored to the Cabinet as Minister for Munitions, he submitted what was at the time a revolutionary concept. He was proposing the construction of huge concrete *caissons* which could be towed across the North Sea to create an artificial harbour on the enemy coast. Ignored at the time, his paper lay dormant, gathering dust. But then, when Hughes-Hallett submitted his own recommendations, he found that Churchill had remembered his 1917 proposal and had returned to the same basic theme. The Churchill Archives (Cambridge) contain his original memorandum, dated 26 May 1942 (addressee not recorded), in which he urged the construction of "Piers for use on beaches" designed to rise and fall with the tides. It was the genesis of the Mulberry harbours. That was three months *before* the Dieppe raid. The coincidence of dates demolishes the argument that Mulberry was somehow a "lesson learned" from Operation *Jubilee*.

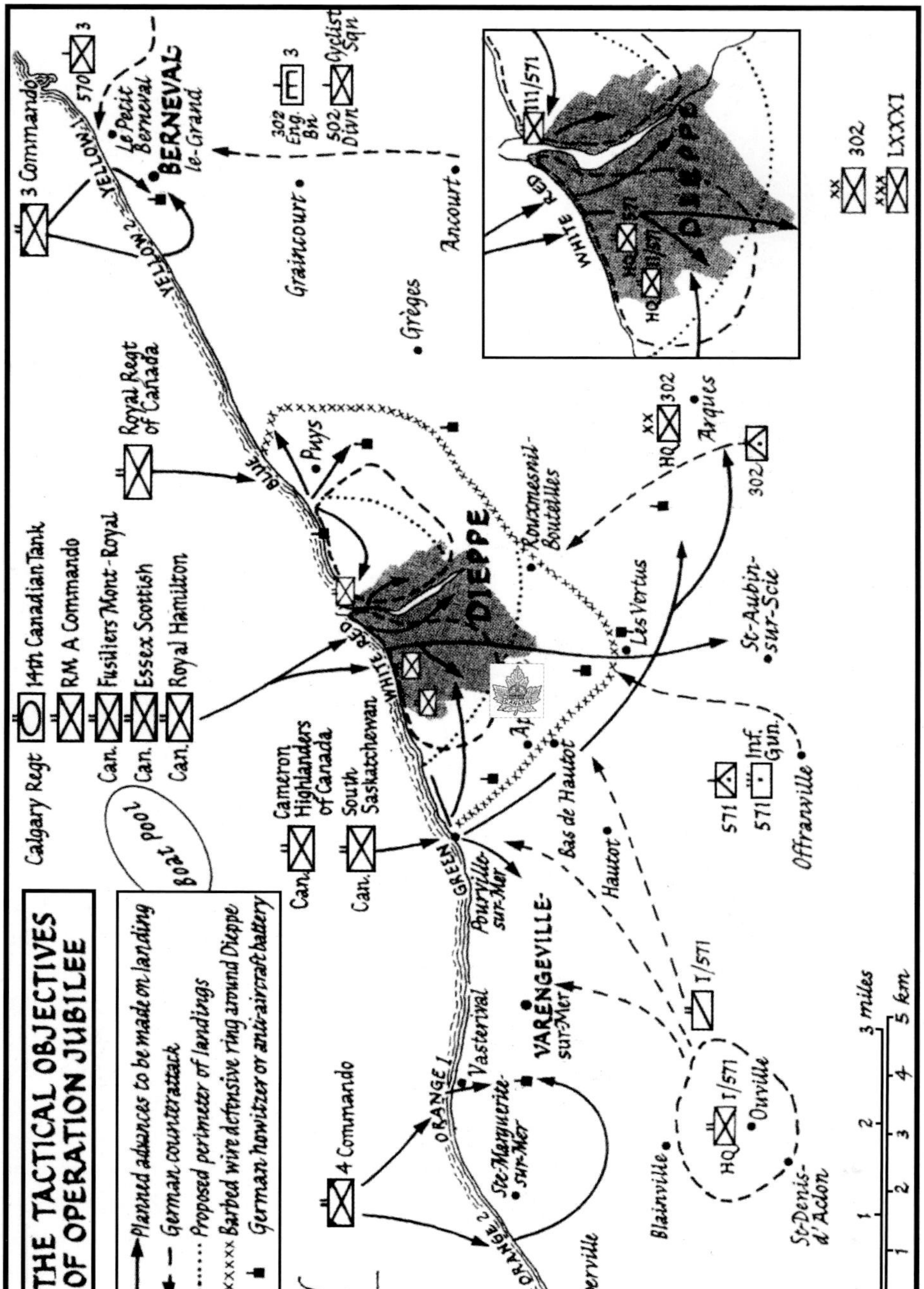

THE TACTICAL OBJECTIVES OF OPERATION JUBILEE
Planned advances to be made on landing
German counterattack
Proposed perimeter of landings
Barbed wire defensive ring around Dieppe
German howitzer or anti-aircraft battery
boat pool
Calgary Regt
14th Canadian Tank
R.M. A Commando
Can. Fusiliers Mont-Royal
Can. Essex Scottish
Can. Royal Hamilton
Royal Regt of Canada
3 Commando
Can. Cameron Highlanders of Canada
Can. South Saskatchewan
4 Commando
YELLOW 1
YELLOW 2
BLUE
RED
WHITE
GREEN
ORANGE 1
ORANGE 2
DIEPPE
Puys
Le Petit Berneval
BERNEVAL le-Grand
Graincourt
Ancourt
Grèges
Arques
Rouxmesnil-Bouteilles
Les Vertus
St-Aubin-sur-Scie
Bas de Hautot
Hautot
Offranville
Pourville-sur-Mer
VARENGEVILLE-sur-Mer
Vasterival
Ste-Marguerite-sur-Mer
Quiberville
Blainville
Ouville
St-Denis-d'Aclon
570
302 Eng. Bn
502 Divn
Cyclist Sqn
HQ 302
302
571
571 Inf. Gun.
I/571
HQ I/571
III/571
HQ
XX 302
XXX LXXXI
0 1 2 3 miles
0 1 2 3 4 5 km

# THE ASSAULT ON DIEPPE

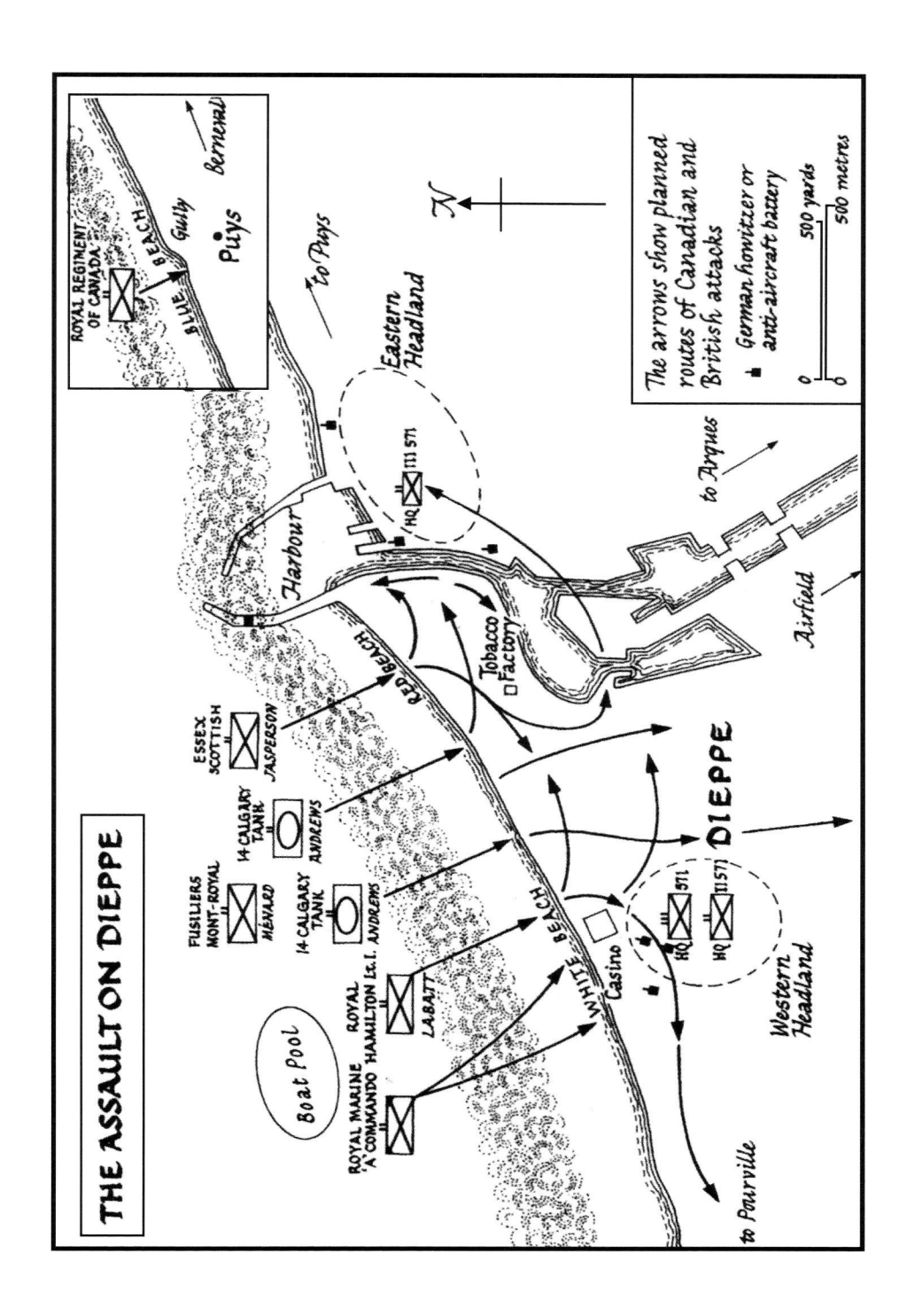

It was evident that the artificial harbours could handle only part of the tonnage which would be needed ashore. Pre-war studies had recommended the construction of flat-bottomed craft capable of discharging men, vehicles and stores directly onto open beaches. Not nearly enough was being done to develop such vessels until Mountbatten, age 41, replaced the elderly Sir Roger Keyes. To his great credit, he quickly recognised the need and did something about it. At his urging, substantial orders were placed with American yards and, soon after, a dedicated training programme was set in motion. By 1944, an innovative family of Royal Navy and US Navy landing craft (the largest displacing 3000 tons) had been tried and tested in the North Africa, Sicily and Italy invasions. They were integral to the success of the Operation *Neptune* landings in Normandy.

Off Dieppe, standing beside Hughes-Hallett on CALPE's bridge, was a man for whom I have the greatest sympathy. He was Major General J H "Ham" Roberts, MC. Wounded towards the end of his four years service on the Western Front with the Royal Canadian Horse Artillery (RCHA), he recovered and joined the skeletal Permanent Force which, denied adequate government funding, endeavoured throughout the 1920s and 1930s to train Canada's all-volunteer part-time militia regiments. Many had (still have) strong associations with Scotland and France, countries from which their forebears migrated long ago. For French-Canadian soldiers, Dieppe has a particular resonance. It was from this port that the first pioneers had sailed, in 1608, to establish a colony at Quebec and thereby founded modern French-Canada.

In the 1914-1918 war, 620,000 Canadians volunteered for overseas service. They won their spurs, at enormous sacrifice, at Festubert, Ypres, St Eloi, on Vimy Ridge and on the Somme. Sixty thousand were killed, 293,500 wounded (a casualty rate of nearly 50%). Their sons rallied again to Britain's cause in 1939, the first arriving in England in December. "Ham" Roberts was at that time commanding 1$^{st}$ Field Regiment, RCHA. When the German *blitzkreig* tore through the British and French armies in northern France in May and June 1940, he was ordered to join them as part of a desperate attempt to stem the flood. After landing, he had advanced halfway across Brittany when he was ordered to halt and return to Brest for evacuation. It was here that his troubles began. The Atlantic ports and their approach roads were jammed with thousands of frightened refugees and disorganised British and French troops. Under frequent aerial attack, they were hoping to find a ship to take them to England. At St Nazaire, the liner LANCASTRIA had just finished loading when she was struck by three bombs. An estimated 6500 soldiers went down with her.

"Ham" Roberts got his regiment away intact with all its guns and most of its vehicles. He was the only Allied commander to do so. It was a masterly display of determination and strong leadership. In April 1941 he was given command of the 2$^{nd}$ Canadian Division, its sub-units spread across the southern Counties. Increasingly restless, his soldiers were engaged in endless exercises and rehearsals for unknown future battles on land. Then, in May and June 1942, their training was directed specifically at the Dieppe scenario and they were as well prepared for it as any troops ever could be under the circumstances. Not that it mattered - *Jubilee* was

*Major General J H "Ham" Roberts, the Military Force Commander at Dieppe, seen here in typically robust mood. His medal ribbons tell us this photograph was taken before the raid. Afterwards, he endured the criticisms with quiet dignity, not seeking to lay the blame on others. Retiring in 1945 after thirty-five years of Regular service with the Canadian Army, he joined the Commonwealth War Graves Commission before settling in the Channel Islands. He died in 1962, age seventy-two.*

so badly planned that most of those who landed would have been lost anyway.

By nine o'clock on the morning of the raid, standing beside Hughes-Hallett on the bridge of HMS CALPE, Roberts was concluding very reluctantly that the main assault was failing. Even so, heroic rescue attempts by the Royal Navy were not abandoned until 1215. He was criticised afterwards for having committed part of his floating reserve when the battle was already lost. It is important to understand the pressures under which he was working. For many months, the Canadian government and Press had been asking with increasing insistence what the British intended to do with their troops. Told that he would be the *Jubilee* Military Force Commander, he was obliged to accept the plan as it was, not as he might have wished it to be. A rugged straight-talking soldier with origins in the farmlands of Manitoba, he must initially have found it difficult to adjust to the *ambience* of COHQ where so many people seemed to know each other socially. Mountbatten was from a different planet and, assuming that General Roberts obtained a personal briefing from Peter de Casa Maury, what on earth did he make of that exotic individual?

Far more unsettling was the fate of The Winnipeg Grenadiers and The Royal Rifles of Canada. By 1941 it was clear that Hong Kong might soon be invaded. The Colony's defences were sufficient for no more than a token resistance. Asked if they would send troops to boost those defences, the Chinese Nationalists replied they were too busy fighting the Japanese Army on the mainland and could not (or would not) spare any troops for Hong Kong. Churchill then asked the Ottawa government if it could assist. The response was immediate, the Grenadiers and the Rifles being sent halfway around the world from their temporary war stations in Jamaica and Newfoundland. Under-trained and ill-equipped, they disembarked just three weeks before the Japanese attacked. They fought bravely but had no chance of influencing the inevitable outcome. All those fine men who, given time, could have matured into first-class soldiers, were callously thrown away in a futile political gesture.

Eighteen months later, was "Ham" Roberts privately wondering whether the men of his 2$^{nd}$ Division were about to be sacrificed in the same way? Dominion troops were rarely committed to a British campaign without the prior consent of their respective governments. His immediate boss in England was Lieutenant General "Harry" Crerar, DSO, commanding 1$^{st}$ Canadian Corps. In theory, Crerar could have reported to Ottawa that *Jubilee* would kill a lot of Roberts' men to no good purpose. That was never an option. Neither he nor Roberts possessed the knowledge of amphibious warfare needed to make a judgement. Mountbatten, Hughes-Hallett and all the others seemed to know what they were doing and Churchill was the driving force. The Canadian government wanted to have its soldiers fighting the Germans and helping to win the war. After training them for a year or more, Roberts himself needed to test his regiments in battle. He was not to know that Dieppe was the wrong battle.

Aboard the CALPE, "Ham" had peered through the dense banks of artificial smoke shrouding the shoreline. The scene was one of violent turmoil, the ship's decks a carpet of distressed wounded soldiers, wireless communications almost useless, dozens of small landing craft bobbing around amongst the shell-bursts and looking for new orders. In such dire circumstances he did the best he could and no man can do more. Although the citation for his subsequent award of the DSO acknowledged his "ability, courage and resolution" at Dieppe, he was later relegated to command his country's training units stationed in the United Kingdom.

Bernard Montgomery was the only British Army general to be involved, albeit briefly. Before he was ordered to Cairo to take over the 8$^{th}$ Army, he was C-in-C Eastern Command (UK). Having attended an initial joint-services briefing for what was at that stage titled Operation *Rutter*, he condemned the plan as "amateur". It had sixteen different objectives and five separate landing sites. Montgomery knew something of which he spoke. In 1937, as a Brigadier, he had planned and conducted a large-scale amphibious training exercise which earned high praise from his superiors and led to his promotion as Major General. He argued that, instead of dispersing the assaulting troops along ten miles of coast, the town itself should be the one and only target. I believe he would have held a very different view if he had not been told: "Dieppe is only lightly defended". Like the others, he unwisely accepted this at face value. And why not? The Intelligence assessments had been rubber-stamped by Mountbatten. As an outsider at COHQ, Montgomery was in no position to challenge them.

In 1940, following the collapse of the Belgian and French armies, he had brought his 3$^{rd}$ Division BEF back to England more or less intact. But, having personally endured the Operation *Dynamo* evacuation from Dunkirk, he should have understood at least one of the risks implicit in *Rutter/Jubilee*. Getting ashore is one thing, getting off again is something very different.

Montgomery may have sneered at Mountbatten's preparations for the Dieppe raid but if he thought the *Rutter/Jubilee* plan was "amateur" it was brilliant by

Image: Reproduced courtesy of the Imperial War Museum

*The location and date are unknown, but Mountbatten's shoulder epaulettes and Montgomery's black beret with its Royal Tank Regiment badge (adopted while commanding the 8th Army) might suggest 1943. Somehow they contrived to meet for the sort of photo-opportunity they both encouraged. Here they are examining what appears to be a school atlas.*

comparison with that drawn up for Operation *Agreement*. When he arrived in Cairo on 12 August to assume command of the 8th Army, he found waiting on his desk the details of an intended highly complex combined services night-time assault on Rommel's principal supply base, the port of Tobruk. Just like *Rutter*, the intention was to occupy the port for fifteen hours while demolition parties blew everything to pieces and generally caused alarm and despondency to the enemy. In another echo of the Dieppe plan, it assumed that the German and Italian garrison troops would let them go about their business more or less unchallenged and they would then sail triumphantly back to Alexandria.

The plan involved Long Range Desert Group (LRDG) and SAS attacks from inland with simultaneous amphibious landings by 11th Battalion, Royal Marines, and infantrymen of The Royal Northumberland Fusiliers and The Argyll & Sutherland Highlanders. No conventional landing craft were available so, in the style of Gallipoli in 1915, most of the assaulting troops would be delivered to the shore in barges towed by motor-boat tugs. There was no full-scale rehearsal and none of the fighting units were Commando-trained (11th Battalion RM was a port defence unit). Weather forecasts then turned out to be totally wrong. Tow ropes parted in the heavy seas, nearly all the barges foundered or were smashed on the rocky shore. Great numbers of men were crushed or drowned.

Commanding the Mediterranean Fleet was Vice Admiral Sir Henry Harwood, knighted and promoted for his skilled handling of the 1939 Battle of the River Plate (the destruction of Germany's battle-cruiser GRAF SPEE). He had no previous experience of combined operations but he agreed to make available for the operation three of his most valuable ships. They were the 6" gun cruiser HMS COVENTRY and two modern "Tribal" Class destroyers, HMS ZULU and HMS SIKH. In addition, he contributed two "Hunt" Class destroyers - HMS CROOME and HMS HURSLEY - and eighteen MTBs. Caught in a blaze of port-side searchlights, blasted at point-blank range by 88mm shore artillery, or dive-bombed next day on their way home, COVENTRY, ZULU and SIKH were sunk along with one third of the MTBs.

Understandably, having so recently taken command of the 8$^{th}$ Army, Montgomery's main priority was re-organising it in preparation for his future El Alamein battle, but even a superficial examination of his GHQ Staff's plan for Tobruk should have sounded the alarm bells. It was intended to take place during the night of 13/14 September. That was four weeks after *Jubilee*. Given his 1937

*On the evening of 15 September 1942 the last surviving Operation Agreement vessels were limping back to harbour at Alexandria, laden with dead, wounded and men pulled from the sea. Without adequate air cover, they were dive-bombed throughout the daylight hours after escaping from Tobruk. Seen here on the morning of 19 September, their C-in-C, Vice Admiral Sir Henry Harwood, makes a formal visit of inspection to HMS Canopus, the navy's Alexandria shore base. What has he been doing for the past four days? Has he demanded from Montgomery and from his own Staff a full explanation of exactly what went wrong, so that lessons might be learned? Or has he, like Mountbatten after Dieppe, moved on?*

experience as an organiser of amphibious exercises, given his earlier exposure to the *Rutter* planning process, it is strange that he did not look harder at the Operation *Agreement* plan. Tobruk would be the first major 8$^{th}$ Army operation since his arrival in Egypt, his first claim (if it succeeded) to be the aggressive fighting commander for whom Churchill was so desperately hoping. In the event, he allowed *Agreement* to go ahead without revision or critical analysis. It was doomed by inadequate Intelligence, poor inter-service coordination, lax security and faulty Royal Navy navigation.

Churchill had passed through Cairo on 4 August - sacking the victor of the First Battle of Alamein, Auchinleck - before travelling on to Moscow for his historic first meeting with Stalin. He had named Lieutenant General "Strafer" Gott as Auchinleck's successor, but that officer was killed on 7 August in a 'plane crash. Churchill's second choice, the unknown Montgomery, was then named as successor to Gott. He landed in Egypt from the UK *via* Gibraltar on 12 August. By then Churchill was in Moscow so the two men did not meet at that time. Their first one-to-one talks commenced on 19 August (the very day, coincidentally, of the Dieppe raid). While returning from Moscow on his way back to London, Churchill spent four days in consultation with the newly-arrived Montgomery, but apparently there was no discussion between them regarding the impending attack at Tobruk. If there had been such a conversation, surely Churchill would have talked about Dieppe? Despite the official claims of success and the misleading signals from Mountbatten, he should by then have worked out broadly the truth of what had happened. The appalling Canadian losses alone were enough to tell him that something was very wrong, but absolutely nothing was being learned. The Tobruk raid went ahead anyway.

Despite their best efforts in the face of the port's powerful defences, nearly all the assaulting troops who managed to get ashore were killed or taken prisoner. That was a tough way to earn **The Africa Star**. In total, 746 men were lost. A handful managed to evade capture and walk the 500 miles back across the desert to reach, weeks later, the 8$^{th}$ Army's forward patrols. Not all of them survived the trek. Vice Admiral Harwood should have been a very angry man. To no good purpose, Operation *Agreement* had squandered three of his most important warships together with the lives of 280 of his seamen and 292 Royal Marines. German and Italian casualties were sixty-six dead and wounded, but Tobruk's port facilities remained intact.

Apologists for Mountbatten and his staff have argued that little was known in 1942 about landings on a hostile shore. Dieppe was the beginning of a learning process, necessary in order to gain experience. This is demonstrable nonsense. In terms of the fundamentals, there was not a single lesson to be learned that had not been learned long before. The Royal Navy and Royal Marines had been conducting operations of that type since the 18$^{th}$ century. Horatio Nelson himself lost his right arm in just such an action in July 1797. It was an attempt to storm, in small boats, the fortified port of Santa Cruz, Tenerife. The weaponry had changed but that was all. The retrospective **Naval War Medal**, authorised in 1848, carried fifty-five different bars for "boat service" actions, but they were authorised only if the officer in command was rewarded with accelerated promotion. There were many other such engagements which did not earn a medal. The Admiralty always took coastal actions very seriously. In 1756, Vice Admiral John Byng attempted without success to seize the island of Minorca. Found guilty by Court Martial of "failing to do his utmost", he was shot on his own quarter-deck by a Royal Marines firing squad.

Turning to modern times, had the planners not heard of Gallipoli, the opposed landings at Cape Helles and ANZAC Cove? Winston Churchill most assuredly knew that story because the disastrous Gallipoli campaign had been his idea. In 1915, our troops had faced Turkish machine-guns and barbed wire. They were backed by the fire-power of a combined Anglo-French battle fleet. Seventeen years later, at Dieppe, their successors were confronted by reinforced concrete and large calibre coastal batteries with virtually no naval gunfire support whatever.

In 1918, the Zeebrugge and Ostend raids had each more or less done what was expected of them, but those objectives were very limited compared with the complexities of the *Jubilee* plan. Although costly in lives, the St Nazaire raid in March 1942 had been brilliantly successful but it had only one purpose - the destruction of a dry dock.

The fruits of those past experiences were absent from the *Jubilee* plan. And that is strange because all five senior officers involved had witnessed in person the hazards of rescuing soldiers from a close-pursuing enemy. Foremost amongst them were Hughes-Hallett and Mountbatten himself. In HMS DEVONSHIRE and HMS KELLY, each was engaged in May 1940 in the evacuation of British and French soldiers trapped in Norway. Baillie-Grohman had witnessed the shambles on the Peloponnese, Montgomery the evacuation at Dunkirk, Roberts the chaos on the Atlantic coast.

What nobody identified was the absence from the Dieppe plan of a contingency "what if" clause. To repeat myself, getting ashore is one thing, getting off again is something very different. There was no prior agreement as to what action should be taken in the event that the initial assault force might become stalled on the beaches and in need of immediate evacuation. It was cheerfully assumed that all would proceed according to plan without troublesome interference from the Germans. In truth, they were never a significant part of the equation. It has long been a cardinal rule of warfare: "know thine enemy". That rule was ignored.

The first full rehearsal for Dieppe took place on 13 June at Bridport, Dorset. Mountbatten did not attend. Churchill had sent him to Washington to convince President Roosevelt that it was not possible to mount an invasion of the continent before 1943 at the earliest. In the event, the Bridport exercise fell apart in disorder. A repeat performance was held ten days later. Although lacking the mock realism of a contested landing, the naval element was better organised. The decision was made to proceed with the raid as soon as considerations of tide, moonrise and sunrise might permit. The weather then turned sour and 19 August became the next opportune date. This left a hiatus of four or five weeks during which further rehearsals might have been conducted but, bafflingly, nothing was done.

Meantime, Mountbatten began to wobble. There was dismay when he let it be known that he was uncertain about the wisdom of proceeding with the plan in its

Image: Reproduced courtesy of the National Archives of Canada

*Taken at one of the two Bridport pre-raid training exercises, this photograph emphasises the unreality of the preparations for the Dieppe assault. On the landing craft, the guns are unmanned. The sailors (without anti-flash gear) have stripped to the waist in the warm sunshine while their officers gossip on the beach. A prime target for any machine-gunner, the gaggle of Canadian soldiers exhibits no tactical awareness. If any lessons were learned, it was the need to train under live-firing conditions, the "battle inoculation" exercises as created in early 1944 by the Americans at Slapton Sands, South Devon.*

current form. His foremost worry, understandably, was the absence of heavy naval gunfire support. A few months earlier, in late December 1941, a small force of Army Commandos had raided the German-occupied Norwegian islands of Vaagso and Maaloy (Operation *Archery*). They were supported by four destroyers (CHIDDINGFOLD, OFFA, ONSLOW, ORIBI) and the 10,500 ton 6" gun cruiser HMS KENYA. Resistance had been much stronger than expected. It was overcome mainly by naval gunfire, and Mountbatten wanted more of the same for *Jubilee*. However, following the navy's horrendous losses to aerial attack in the Far East and Mediterranean, his request for the temporary loan of a battleship or at least a couple of heavy cruisers had been turned down flat by Admiral of the Fleet Sir Dudley Pound: "Battleships in daylight off the French coast? You must be mad, Dickie!".

Battleships were one thing, cruisers were another. Pound had been willing in 1941 to release from the Home Fleet a significant proportion of his available 6" gun cruisers and big 4.7" gun destroyers in support of the army's raids in Arctic and Norwegian waters, none of which enjoyed the benefit of adequate (or any) air cover. So what was different about Dieppe, a target for which abundant air cover was available and which was very much closer to home?

If the vastly experienced First Sea Lord thought it too dangerous for the most powerful warships in the Royal Navy to enter the English Channel, why did anyone believe the small "Hunt" Class destroyers would fare any better? Displacing 1400 tons, they were excellent in their design role as convoy escorts and U-boat hunters but were totally unsuited for contested shore bombardments. The high explosive shells from their 4" guns lacked the power to demolish reinforced concrete.

The thinking was illogical but, however reluctantly, Mountbatten accepted Pound's ruling and at that point *Jubilee* became an even greater gamble. Pound and Churchill had collaborated successfully at the Admiralty during the first year of the war and he was now in a position to tell the Prime Minister that, having seen the *Jubilee* plan, he judged it to be unsound. For whatever reason, he did not do so.

As the deadline approached there was a flurry of exchanges between Mountbatten and Churchill and Sir Alan Brooke, Chief of the IGS. It is enough to state that those exchanges resulted in a decision which beggars belief. The plan was based upon the element of surprise. To maintain secrecy, the raid would go ahead without any member of the IGS other than Brooke himself knowing about it. Surely it was not seriously believed that an IGS officer might pick up his 'phone and "spill the beans" to Berlin? It is far more probable that Churchill was worried that IGS support for the scheme might be withdrawn. In the event, no executive order was ever drafted, hence nobody was required to sign it.

One result of this security clampdown was that several highly-placed individuals were able, rightly or wrongly, to deny afterwards any prior knowledge of the raid and therefore any culpability for what went wrong. The "secrecy" idea is rendered even more illogical by the decision to involve the Americans. That in itself was a good idea. It would be a friendly gesture to our new Allies and perhaps they would be interested to see how the British conducted an amphibious operation. However, it did mean they were privy to information denied to some of our own top commanders. This in no way enhanced Mountbatten's subsequent popularity or even credibility.

Entering into the spirit of the occasion, the Americans offered to send twenty-four B17 Flying Fortress bombers to hammer the *Luftwaffe* fighter base at Abbeville, thirty miles north of Dieppe. It was only their second independent mission over occupied France (they had bombed targets at Rouen two days earlier). Their Abbeville raid was successful, but it had little if any impact on the aerial battle. It had no influence whatever on the Canadian landings because it was timed for 1035. By then, Roberts knew for certain that the land battle was lost and, in scenes of terrible death and destruction, the Royal Navy was trying to save his men.

Much more useful would have been a pre-dawn precision bombing attack on the town and its defences. This did not happen because American bomber pilots were trained to operate only in daylight and anyway, as happened at St Nazaire, it could have alerted the defenders that something unusual was imminent. Also, despite some wavering, Churchill was anxious to keep civilian casualties to a minimum. What he did not know, and what Peter de Casa Maury should have discovered, was that Dieppe had been emptied of most of its citizens. Their homes were needed to accommodate the great numbers of German garrison troops. Sea-front hotels and luxury villas had been requisitioned and converted into strong-points. Some had been demolished to improve fields of fire.

One of the early arrivals in England from the United States was Brigadier General Lucian Truscott. This excellent officer admired the British concept of special Commando units. He raised and trained the 1$^{st}$ Ranger Battalion, US Army, and by June 1942 it was ready for action. Truscott was watching from the bridge of HMS FERNIE when forty-nine hand-picked Rangers, dispersed in small sections, went ashore alongside the Canadians and the Army Commandos. They were there "to gain experience". Most of his men were either killed or captured. How fortunate he was that Mountbatten did not invite him to contribute much greater numbers of his eager young Rangers. The propaganda value of those few who did cross the Channel emerged in an American newspaper headline: "Yankees Land in France First Time Since 1917".

Eleven days after the raid, Captain Hughes-Hallett submitted a despatch to Admiral Sir William James, C-in-C Portsmouth, describing the events of the day as he himself had witnessed them. His report was suppressed until August 1947, two years after the war. General "Pug" Ismay, in his very detailed memoirs published in 1960, failed to mention Dieppe even once. This despite the fact that he was Churchill's right-hand man throughout the war, channelling information and instructions to and from Downing Street and the IGS. Given that *Jubilee* was the first major assault on Hitler's "Fortress Europe", surely he could have granted it a line or two in his book? Arthur Bryant's 1957 biography of General Brooke, based upon that officer's war diaries, gave Dieppe no more than passing comment.

In 1999 the respected British military historian John Laffin produced a book titled *Raiders*. Prefacing the short chapter devoted to Dieppe, he described it as "a raid carried out by 5000 Commandos". Award-winning historian Antony Beevor, in his *The Second World War*, published in 2012, dismisses the Dieppe Raid in just two (factually incorrect) paragraphs. For the British, Operation *Jubilee* was, and

*A softly-spoken Texan, General Lucian K Truscott, Jnr, was one of the least known but most effective military leaders of WWII. He was asked to contribute only a token element of his new US Army Rangers to the Dieppe Raid but later he commanded much larger formations in Italy and France. Having risen to high office after the war, he died in 1965 (age 70) and was buried in the Arlington National Cemetery, Washington DC.*

Image: Reproduced courtesy of the National Archives of Canada

*Of the forty-nine US Rangers who took part in Operation Jubilee, three were killed, most were captured. Lieutenant Edward Loustalot was the first American soldier to be killed in Europe in the Second World War. In this photograph of Dieppe beach, second furthest from the camera and wearing the distinctive US Army pattern gaiters, is the body of another Ranger (said to be that of Lieutenant Joseph Randall).*

seemingly still is, an episode best forgotten. Not so in Canada. For that nation it was, and still is, a deeply felt source of pride and of sorrow. And of not a little anger.

In London, the rush of events in the autumn of 1942 - Alamein and Stalingrad - swiftly overtook Dieppe as a topic for debate. There was no independent investigation, no systematic attempt to find out what had gone wrong. That was in marked contrast with what happened in the wake of the Gallipoli *debacle* in 1915. In August, as soon as the accusations began to fly thick and fast, Prime Minister Asquith had ordered the setting up of a Royal Court of Enquiry with authority to interview witnesses under oath. It was a Court with teeth. Two hundred individuals - including Winston Churchill - were required to appear and submit themselves to cross-examination.

When the findings were published, in late 1917, they blasted the reputations of almost everyone involved. One of the few exceptions was the tough no-nonsense General Sir Charles Monro. Having replaced the "feather-brained" General Hamilton - Prime Minister Asquith's description of him - it was Monro who had so skillfully organised the bloodless evacuations. But, as Churchill said after Dunkirk, "wars are not won by evacuations". The judgement of the Court was summarised with this elegant understatement: "the risks that had been taken when planning and executing the operation had always been greater than the chances of success". Exactly the same epitaph applied to Operation *Jubilee*.

To conduct a similar Court of Enquiry in 1942 was unthinkable. Any washing in public of British dirty linen could only damage the Allied cause. People both at home and abroad were already struggling to absorb a rapid succession of depressing headlines, there was no point in adding yet another. But, in the absence of such forensic analysis, how exactly and in practice were (as claimed) "new lessons" learned at Dieppe? The amphibious warfare techniques which made the 1944 Normandy landings so successful would, I believe, have evolved anyway and without the cruel human wastage of Operation *Jubilee*.

In the context of "blame analysis" there is a great disparity between peacetime and wartime procedures. In the former, if a Quartermaster cannot account for all the blankets supposedly held in his Stores, a Court of Enquiry is convened. If a pilot damages his aircraft in an allegedly clumsy landing, the circumstances are officially investigated. If a Royal Navy ship hits the rocks, her Captain is granted a Court Martial which will hear his explanations and then either exonerate him or find him guilty of negligence. The rules change as soon as the guns begin to speak. Traditionally, senior officers who blunder are quietly put out to pasture or promoted sideways. In the Great War, the crass incompetence on the Western Front of Generals such as John French and Douglas Haig - commanders who orchestrated a succession of battlefield catastrophes - was rewarded by elevation to the Peerage. Haig received a tax-free bonus of £100,000 voted by Parliament "by a grateful nation".

Gallipoli was different. General Hamilton was replaced and given no further employment, Winston Churchill was sacked from government. It seemed his political career might never recover. But then, two decades later, and setting aside his early blunders in wartime strategy, he emerged as the inspired and inspiring saviour of Western freedom and democracy at a time when much of the world had already lost those privileges. To quote President John Kennedy: "He mobilised the English language and sent it into battle". That was good and fine but, in the specific context of *Jubilee*, Churchill was alone amongst the key players to have personal knowledge of Dieppe and its environs. He enjoyed frequent pre-war holidays at the nearby sporting estate owned by his friend the Duke of Westminster. Located a few miles inland, it maintained a pack of hounds. Attired in hunting pink, Winston had ridden far and wide over that large estate in pursuit of fox and wild boar. From the saddle, with his "soldier's eye for country", he had gained a clear understanding of the local topography.

It is surprising, therefore, that he at first supported Montgomery's idea of dropping one or more parachute battalions to attack Dieppe from the rear while the Canadians came ashore on the beaches. In that broken landscape, dropping at first light, their losses to landing accidents would have severely degraded their fighting ability well before engaging the enemy.

As far as the town itself was concerned (and as related by his policeman bodyguard, Inspector Walter Thompson), Winston usually crossed the Channel via the Dover to Calais ferry before travelling down the coast to Dieppe by rail. This brought him to the dock-side *Gare Maritime*. So, from the train and then during the chauffeured road journey inland to the Duke's property, he had ample opportunities to see how Dieppe is confined within vertical cliffs on either side and rising ground to the rear. Dominating the town and its seaward approaches is a massive cliff-top 15th century castle and former barracks, the *Chateau de Dieppe*. Perhaps, by 1942, the memory of all that had faded?

Whether it had or not, the fact remains that, for the British in general, Dieppe was not the dark side of the moon. At the turn of the century, one quarter of the population was English, mainly wealthy retirees attracted by the climate and comfortable life style. Known as *La Colonie*, they had their own "social season". It was for decades visited by upper-class English tourists. It was so fashionable that, in 1894, the celebrated author Oscar Wilde chose it for his ill-fated honeymoon. In 1899, Churchill's future mother-in-law, Lady Blanche Ogilvy, lived there with her daughter Clementine. Of all the northern French seaside resorts, Dieppe was the most familiar and most photographed.

When in 1951 he came to publish his own version of events, Churchill recorded a pre-raid Downing Street meeting (undated) between himself, Mountbatten, Brooke and Hughes-Hallett (curiously, neither Leigh-Mallory nor Roberts were invited). To quote from his account: "From available Intelligence it appeared that Dieppe was held only by German low-category troops amounting to one battalion, with supporting units making no more than 1400 men in all". Even though it was of crucial importance, nobody questioned the accuracy of this information. Why did Mountbatten not bring Peter de Casa Maury with him to this meeting so that he could explain himself? Ten minutes of interrogation would have revealed the poverty of his research.

For example, how hard had he looked at the aerial photographs? At the hundreds of pre-war picture postcards? At the Dieppe street map? The town had been rebuilt following a heavy Anglo-Dutch naval bombardment in 1694. The Calgary Regiment's 38-ton Churchill tank had a track width of eleven feet and a length of twenty-five feet. It was the largest and heaviest of any of the tanks at that time operating in any of the Allied armies. When I walked through the narrow jumbled 18th century streets which crowd to the rear of the long line of seafront hotels and villas, I concluded that - with or without the help of friendly German traffic police - the majority were impassable to Churchill tanks. But, if opposed by a well-organised defence, any which did somehow succeed in by-passing the concrete obstacles and entering the maze could easily have been trapped between the debris of buildings brought down by German demolition teams. Tanks are notoriously vulnerable when caught up in street fighting.

When told by Churchill that he was to replace Sir Roger Keyes at COHQ, Mountbatten had written to his wife: "For the first time in my life, I am apprehensive about my new job - what do I know of soldiering?". Peter de Casa Maury possessed even less understanding, indeed none at all. However, he did have access to several specialist resources if he chose to consult them (or if so ordered). The Joint Intelligence Committee, established in 1936, reported regularly to the Prime Minister's Cabinet Office. It was a short walk from the COHQ offices in Richmond Terrace. The Special Operations Executive, created in July 1940, was located a cab-ride away, in Baker Street. The French Resistance movement was a proven source of reliable information. Officers of the army's Intelligence Corps, established in July

1940 at Maresfield, East Sussex, were skilled in probing all aspects of German military activity. RAF Medmenham, based in a large country house near the small Buckinghamshire village of that name, had been the home of the Central Interpretation Unit since April 1941. It analysed the thousands of RAF photo-reconnaissance images covering every part of Western Europe and the Mediterranean. Churchill's daughter, Sarah, was working there as a leading interpreter. Bletchley Park had broken the German Army's Enigma codes in December 1941 and must have identified the military units lining the French coast. Each of those agencies had much to offer to someone in Peter's position. How then could he have failed to assess correctly the strength of Dieppe's defences?

I did for several years wonder whether or not *Jubilee* was from its inception deliberately intended to fail - Mountbatten having been instructed by Churchill to ensure that it would fail. Politically and strategically, such an order would have made good sense.

Before 22 June 1941, when Hitler launched his Operation *Barbarossa* invasion of the Soviet Union, Joseph Stalin had collaborated with him by sharing in the conquest of Poland and then by aiding the Nazi war economy with vast tonnages of oil and grain. By 1942, with the German Army on the rampage in Mother Russia, Stalin had changed his tune entirely. He was accusing the British of "cowardice" for not mounting a cross-Channel "second front" to take the pressure off his struggling Red Army.

*The Free Belgian, French and Polish navies were represented at Dieppe. Seen here returning to Portsmouth is the 1400 ton "Hunt" Class ORP Slazak. First ordered as HMS Bedale, the Poles had commissioned her barely four months earlier. In the thick of the fight, attacked repeatedly from the air, she shot down four German aircraft and rescued eighty-five Canadian soldiers. Her Captain, Lieutenant Commander Tyminiski, was awarded the (British) Distinguished Service Cross.*

Before 7 December 1941, despite their crucially important Lend Lease support, the United States had officially stayed out of the fight until suddenly thrust into it at Pearl Harbour. Now the American economy was fast emerging from the 1930s Great Depression, the recovery fuelled in part by British contracts for guns, vehicles and aircraft. America's long-standing resolve to never again be sucked into a European war had been replaced by a fever of enthusiasm for an immediate "second front" invasion of Western Europe. Churchill was being criticised by many of America's top people for Britain's "half-hearted" role in this new war which they themselves had barely begun to enter. Their combatative "let's go" spirit was admirable and welcome, but it ignored the realities. The Allies possessed only a fraction of the fleets of landing craft needed for such a venture and the new untrained American regiments were still on the wrong side of the Atlantic.

Germany's U-boats were devastating the Allies' trans-ocean convoys, threatening to cut Britain's lifelines. Merchant vessels were being sunk faster than the shipyards could replace them. The most productive western regions of Russia and the Ukraine had fallen, three million Soviet troops had been taken prisoner. Hitler was hurling 300 of his best divisions - four million men - into the enormous eastern front campaign. If Stalin and his generals were to crack, those divisions would be free to attack in the west. The Arctic convoys were helping to keep the Soviets in the war, but the tide was still flowing strongly in Hitler's favour.

If Churchill was to convince Stalin and the American leadership that to attempt a full-scale invasion of France in 1942 could end only in bloody failure, he needed solid evidence to support his case. Dieppe provided that evidence. Not only did it strengthen his hand with our new Allies, it silenced his critics at home. Stirred by left-wing MPs and newspaper editors, street demonstrators in London had been demanding a "second front now". As the truth leaked out, they fell silent.

I found nothing in the written record to suggest that Churchill might have expressed relief when *Jubilee* ended as it did, but he would certainly have found himself in difficulty with Moscow and Washington if it had been a success.

So, were all those dead Canadian soldiers and British sailors the victims of a conspiracy or of a cock-up? Rightly or wrongly, I believe Operation *Jubilee* was just one more of Churchill's many other impractical schemes to strike back at Germany at a time when the Allies were in trouble on every front, and that the man he placed in charge had absolutely no idea how to conduct such an operation. It was a cock-up.

The stated original purpose of *Rutter/Jubilee* was to test our ability to seize and temporarily occupy a French port. However, as the weeks went by, in a classic instance of "mission creep", the plan expanded into a multi-task operation with supplementary objectives added to it. It gained surreal "add ons" dreamed up by Peter de Casa Maury but also by numerous others. They did, yes, make good sense, but only if uncontested by a German defending force. One such was a proposal by Peter Murphy, a trusted confidant dating back to Mountbatten's undergraduate days at Cambridge University and now embedded at the heart of COHQ. He recommended that the assaulting troops should be accompanied by selected bi-lingual "political officers". They would mingle with the local population and explain the significance of the raid for the future liberation of their nation.

Then, the Air Ministry knew there was a Freya radar station near Pourville - the southern flank landing site at which The South Saskatchewan Regiment and The Queen's Own Cameron Highlanders of Canada would go ashore. Peter therefore briefed RAF Flight Sergeant Jack Nissenthall to break in and bring away its technical equipment. Despite his youth, Jack had exceptional knowledge of radar. Escorted by eleven bodyguards who had orders to kill him rather than let him fall into German hands, he was also given a suicide pill. As a Jew, his prospects if captured were in any case limited. The small-scale raid at Bruneval in February had yielded excellent results, so why not try it again at Pourville? Jack Nissenthall later recorded his impressions of Peter de Casa Maury (who was not only Jesuit-educated but also a pre-war acquaintance of Oswald Mosley, leader of the British Union of Fascists). He found him condescending, arrogant, and anti-semitic. Jack did in fact reach the Freya station where, under close-quarter fire, he at least managed to cut the telephone cables before escaping with the last two survivors from his bodyguard.

Another "add on" related to the known presence in Dieppe's inner harbour of several barges. They were the rusting remnants of the 1700 self-propelled Rhine river vessels assembled in French and Belgian ports two years earlier when Hitler ordered them to be adapted as landing craft for Operation *Sealion* (the aborted invasion of southern Britain). What a lark it would be if some Royal Marines could sail them back in triumph to England! They had no practical value but the newspapers would love it, a great publicity *coup* for "Combined Ops". Naturally, the Germans would have maintained them in seaworthy condition, fuel tanks topped up, batteries fully charged, ready to be cast off. That task was given to a platoon from "A" Commando (later re-titled 40 Commando RM).

Oh, and while you are there, would you please break into the dock-side *Kreigsmarine* office and pinch all the secret stuff? Hoping for a repeat of the successful Lofoten raid of March 1941, the Bletchley Park people were asking for the latest version of Enigma and the naval code books. In response, Admiral John Godfrey, Director of Naval Intelligence, ordered Ian Fleming (future creator of 007 James Bond but at the time a Lieutenant Commander, RNVR) to brief thirty Royal Marines from his 30 Assault Unit for that purpose. One of them, reportedly, was a professional "peter man", someone who knew how to blow open a safe without the prior consent of the owner.

Command of this part of the operation was given to Commander Robert Ryder, RN. In his 580 ton shallow-draft HMS LOCUST, he would follow the channel inside the long curving outer mole, then proceed through the narrow harbour entrance to disembark his passengers directly onto the inner quay. Casa Maury may or may not have identified the artillery gun emplacement sited on the mole but evidently not the machine-guns concealed within tunnels excavated into the left-hand cliff-face.

Robert Ryder had previous experience of schemes like this. In March, winning his Victoria Cross in the process, he led the flotilla of MGBs which accompanied HMS CAMPBELTOWN at St Nazaire. Now, at Dieppe, he was again under point-

*Commander Robert Ryder, VC, RN, hero of the St Nazaire Raid. He took the courageous personal decision at Dieppe to abort the intended penetration into its confined inner port area. Both he and his ship survived to witness the return of peace, he as a Captain, the Locust as a RNR drill ship.*

blank fire from a fully alert garrison and the ship took a heavy hit. Including port demolition teams, there were nearly 200 Royal Marines packed tight on his open deck. They were suffering dreadful wounds, many of them fatal, it was pointless to persist with this mad plan. Having reported to Captain Hughes-Hallett, he was sent to support the Canadians on Dieppe beach.

The *Jubilee* final score statistics are distressingly familiar. The Canadians lost 3369 dead, wounded and captured. The Royal Navy lost 550 officers and men, thirty-three landing craft and the destroyer HMS BERKELEY. Royal Marine casualties were more than one hundred dead, the Army Commandos lost 172 dead and captured. In the aerial battle, the RAF lost 106 aircraft (with 153 aircrew), the *Luftwaffe* had forty-eight of its own 'planes shot down. German casualties, dead and wounded, were 593 all services. But figures alone cannot convey the truth of that day. Most published accounts focus on Dieppe itself - the heroic efforts by the Calgary Regiment's tanks to reach the esplanade, the fight for the Casino, and so forth. The southern flank attack at Pourville by The South Saskatchewan Regiment and The Queen's Own Cameron Highlanders of Canada is clearly described. Not only their chaotic initial landing but also the advance inland, the withdrawal from a close-pursuing enemy, then the subsequent shambles when, under the weight of men frantically trying to save themselves, over-loaded landing craft were stranded under fire on the falling tide. They were shot to pieces. That was bad enough, but even Pourville did not compare with the massacre at Puys. Let me take you there.

We drive over high ground two miles north from Dieppe. Then, descending a steep narrow road, we pass through a huddle of cottages and summer holiday villas. They are confined within a defile, one of the few breaks in the long line of chalk cliffs stretching north towards Le Treport and Boulogne. We arrive at a car park, an enclosed level area measuring twenty yards by seventy adjoining the sea-wall. The "feel" of this place is intensely claustrophobic.

Going back to 1942, Puys has been selected by COHQ as a Canadian landing site. It has also been selected by the Germans, and they agree - Puys beach is indeed a potential landing site. It is, in fact, a perfect close-range killing ground. Having come ashore, your battalion's orders are to advance up the valley, turn right over the high ground, then march down into Dieppe town for re-embarkation. Along the way, with your 556 buddies of The Royal Regiment of Canada and with 111 men of The Black Watch (Royal Highland Regiment) of Canada, you will capture a four-gun coastal battery, destroy an anti-aircraft gun battery, and overrun an army barracks. The time allowed is seven hours. Your CO, Lieutenant Colonel Douglas Catto, has been threatened with the sack for questioning the practicality of all this.

It is 0550, shoreline features are fast gaining definition in the dim light of dawn. You are one of Colonel Catto's 556 Royal Regiment soldiers, thirty of you

*The "little ships" of British Coastal Forces were given the task of protecting the Jubilee amphibious craft in transit to and from the French coast. Their weaponry was too light to have much impact on the German shore defences but, with Hughes-Hallet's armada under prolonged Luftwaffe attack during the voyage home, their firepower helped to reduce any further losses.*

crouching within the hull of a Landing Craft Assault (LCA). Raising your head you can see, beyond the boat's bow gate, a narrow pebble beach. At most 250 yards long, it is backed by a high sea-wall. The wall is topped with coils of barbed wire. At each end there is an access ramp, also thick with wire. To the right is a low sheer cliff. On the left, a steep hillside on which there are some houses and two concrete bunkers. Apart from the throb of the boat's engine and the sound of gunfire coming from Dieppe, all is quiet.

Guided here by a solitary MGB which initially had lost its way, your flotilla of LCAs is an hour late. Undisturbed by the Royal Navy or by the RAF, the sixty-man defending force watches your approach. Waiting behind their mortars and machine-guns, the Germans have had many months in which to range their weapons and pre-set the sights. They hold their fire until the first boats are about to touch down. The killing then begins.

You scramble forward to the foot of the sea-wall, desperately seeking shelter from the storm of bullets and mortar explosions. You cannot see your enemy, you cannot use your rifle. Your friends are falling all around you, some silently, others screaming in pain. Helpless, terrified, you can only wait to die or surrender. This, your first battle, is over before it could even begin. Originating in 1862 when Toronto families first began to contribute their sons for service to the British Empire, your proud all-volunteer regiment has in moments been annihilated.

The machine-gunners and mortar crews of The Black Watch of Canada have been landed at the narrow foot of the right-hand cliff. Cowering under its overhang, German soldiers lobbing hand grenades down amongst them, they cannot bring their weapons into action. Four are killed outright, the rest can only surrender.

From the two regiments, just sixty-five officers and men escape back to England in those of the very few landing craft still intact and still having a crew to handle them. Manning one of those craft is 20 year-old Leading Seaman Coxswain Michael Boultbee, today a retired clergyman living in Dawlish, Devon. Almost certainly the last surviving eye-witness, he still wonders: "How did I live through that? How did any of us live through it?".

Michael's flotilla of LCAs had been carried across the Channel in the early hours aboard the converted Belgian pre-war Ostend-Dover ferry HMS PRINSES ASTRID. "As we drew near the coast, the order came to 'man the landing craft'. Boat crews were first aboard, followed by the troops that each was to carry. All the while the boats remained secured to the davits. A choppy sea below looked singularly uninviting. After lowering, and as instructed, the two columns of our flotilla followed the dim blue light showing at the stern of a Coastal Forces MGB. However, two small 'hiccups' arose. First, we 'found' the wrong vessel and, struggling in the dark to find the right one, found ourselves tangled with a small German convoy of some form. Several minutes later than intended, we found the right vessel to follow. We were on our way".

According to other sources, the MGB leading these landing craft veered off track, heading south towards Dieppe. In the darkness of the final two miles of the approach, it was a mistake easily made. More time was lost. Realising his error, the officer commanding the MGB changed course, guiding his flock northwards

*Two thousand Landing Craft Assault (LCA) were operated worldwide during the war. Early models, with a crew of three to five, were powered by Ford or Chrysler 65hp petrol engines producing a cruising speed of 8 knots. Displacing 9 tons, they carried a load of 35 fully-armed troops. Dieppe was their savage baptism of fire.*

parallel with the line of cliffs. Michael remembers being illuminated by searchlights, presumably mounted on the cliff-tops.

"There was more than a hint of dawn as we approached Puys beach. Expectations in high places, we gathered, were that the defence would be light because crack German troops who had been there were away at the (Russian) front. German high command can't have been listening. As we approached the beach - it gives me the creeps even now to remember it - there was an eerie silence. Why didn't the guns fire? Someone had once said that the profile of an LCA was so low that they could easily be missed by viewers from the shore. We wanted to believe it".

Michael continues: "We were perhaps fifty yards offshore when all hell let loose. How could anyone survive the onslaught? Remembering to lay out our kedge anchor to ensure that, if we survived we could pull off the beach, we touched down. As Cox'n I signalled to my seaman to lower the bow gate for our soldiers to run ashore. Our small world was ablaze with fire and noise. Understandably there was some reluctance among the Canadian troops to leave the boat. Into the tension of the moment came the calm 'frightfully posh' voice of Lieutenant Bill Welch, RNVR, our flotilla's Divisional Officer: 'I say, Boultbee, the natives are bloody hostile!'. Just loud enough for all to hear. It was enough. The moment's tension eased. The troops poured out of the boat. Those were the last steps many of them would take before they died".

Most of the LCAs were shattered, their crews killed or wounded. A handful hauled off and found shelter in the smokescreen drifting up from Dieppe. There was no sign of the PRINSES ASTRID or the MTB. "We hung around offshore for a couple of hours, maybe more, wondering what to do next. By then we were on our own. We had started off from the Isle of Wight, but when finally we agreed to go home our first sight of land was Newhaven. The sea was like a millpond, it was a peaceful trip, almost enjoyable. What a contrast to what we had just seen at Puys! I have never ceased to be amazed that our three-man crew came back in one piece".

278

Images: Reproduced courtesy of the National Archives of Canada

*Photographed on the afternoon of 19 August 1942, this is Puys. Already, a great many of the Canadian and Royal Navy dead and wounded have floated away on the falling tide. The dead who remain will be transported to mass graves inland. Of the 556 Royal Regiment of Canada men who sailed from England, 227 have been killed within minutes of struggling ashore on this tiny beach. Slaughtered by mortar bombs and by machine-guns concealed within the two skillfully-sited bunkers (as indicated above), their families will be told "their sacrifice was not in vain".*

The young officer commanding the German machine-gun and mortar teams later wrote his own account. In his post-action report, he recalled standing on the sea-wall and "looking down on a scene of horror".

In 2008, when I made my own journey to Puys beach, I crouched tight against that sea-wall, trying to imagine the nightmare scene on the morning of 19 August 1942. If I leaned back out of direct line-of-sight of the two German machine-gun bunkers, I might live. If I moved one pace away from the wall, I was dead. It was as simple and as brutal as that. In microcosm, it is the story of Mountbatten's so-called "reconnaissance in force". After the war he claimed that lessons learned at Dieppe had saved thousands of lives two years later in the Normandy invasion: "The Battle of D-Day was won on the beaches of Dieppe. It was one of the most vital operations of the Second World War. It gave the Allies the vital secret of victory".

Only the most convoluted train of thought could arrive at that self-serving conclusion. He never explained what that "vital secret" might have been and, if the operation really was so "vital", why did he himself take no active part in its execution?

From Cairo, immediately after the raid, Churchill reported back to his Cabinet colleagues in London: "My general impression of *Jubilee* is that the results fully justified the heavy cost. The large-scale air battle alone justified the raid". How could he have formed that impression unless someone in COHQ had sent him a grossly misleading signal? It could not have been sent without the authority of Mountbatten. Presumably it did not inform him *inter alia* that the RAF had lost twice as many aircraft as the *Luftwaffe*. Or, if it did, he chose to ignore it. It was the first attempt at denial of the truth.

With the last weary survivors returning to their south coast camps, COHQ was busy distributing a Press statement. Repeated that evening by the BBC news service, it told the world: "The raid has been completed as planned". German radio gave it a more realistic assessment: "The raid served only political purposes but defied all military reason".

On 8 September, Prime Minister Churchill rose to his feet in the House of Commons to present a broad summary of the current war situation. When reading the following extract from his speech in which he referred to Dieppe, we must keep in mind the great peril in which the Allies then stood on each of the main fighting fronts. A few weeks earlier, on 2 July, a small coterie of disgruntled MPs had tried to bring him down with a Vote of Censure. It had been overwhelmingly rejected by the House, but the fact that such a thing could happen had not been understood in Washington and Moscow. Their systems of government did not allow for similar back-stabbing attacks on a national leader, especially in time of war. If he was to maintain Allied solidarity, Churchill could not risk a second Vote of Censure so quickly in the wake of the first.

Obliged to put the best possible face on the nation's difficulties, and after describing recent events in the Mediterranean, this is what he said: "The second important operation was the attack upon Dieppe. It is a mistake to speak or write of this as a 'Commando raid'. Commando troops distinguished themselves remarkably in it. The military credit for this most gallant affair goes to the Canadian troops who formed five-sixths of the assaulting force, and to the Royal Navy, which carried most of them back. The raid must be considered a reconnaissance in force. It was a hard, savage clash such as are likely to become increasingly numerous as the war deepens. We had to get all the information necessary before launching operations on a much larger scale. This raid, apart from its reconnaissance value, brought about an extremely satisfactory air battle which Fighter Command wish they could repeat every week. It inflicted upon the enemy in killed and wounded as many as we suffered ourselves. I, personally, regarded the Dieppe assault, to which I gave my sanction, as indispensable to full-scale operations".

Readers who have followed the Operation *Jubilee* story thus far will recognise the gaping holes in Churchill's account. The same picture was painted eleven months later by the very capable Mr A V Alexander, MP, First Lord of the Admiralty throughout most of the war. Addressing the House of Commons on 3 July 1943, he referred to *Jubilee* as "the great naval operation splendidly planned and carried out". For the sake of public and international confidence nobody could afford to confess that it had been anything less than a triumph.

Churchill's monumental six volume history of the Second World War was compiled by a team of writers working under his direction and editorship. When referring to *Jubilee*, his 1951 volume titled *The Hinge of Fate* devoted only two pages to it and they were written for him by Mountbatten. Unsurprisingly, given their authorship, they supported the "lessons were learned" argument. Churchill was

Images: Reproduced courtesy of the National Archives of Canada

*The White Ensign still flutters over Dieppe beach, but there is no movement amongst the hundreds of Canadian dead. None were conscripts, all had volunteered to join the Allied cause. Inspired by pride in their historic regiments and in their close family ties, they found themselves in a trap from which there was no escape. Despite the later claims by Mountbatten and his supporters, there could be no valid excuse.*

bound to give his name to that version because it was he who consistently promoted Mountbatten's stellar career. Even so, the eulogy - "Honour to the brave who fell. Their sacrifice was not in vain" - is disturbingly reminiscent of the unsavoury excuses put forward after the brainless slaughter of 1914-1918.

As far as *Jubilee* was concerned, Mountbatten shared the same mentality as Haig and his fellow generals who likewise, on the Western Front, sent men to die in suicidal frontal attacks which they themselves chose not to witness. Before he succumbed to a heart attack in 1928, Douglas Haig had been promoted to Field Marshal, showered with honours and awards and granted an earldom. Before his assassination five decades later, "Dickie" Mountbatten had become the most highly decorated Admiral of the Fleet, also elevated to an earldom and, like Haig, honoured by the nation with the exceptionally rare distinction of a full State funeral. When the distinguished mourners gathered in Westminster Abbey in 1928 and 1979 to pay their final respects, were they joined by the ghosts of Passchendaele and Puys? As reminders of the past, they would not have been made welcome.

*"Once more into the breach dear friends, once more. I see you stand like greyhounds in the slips straining upon the start. The games afoot!". The analogy between William Shakespeare's King Henry V inspirational speech to his troops before the walls of Harfleur in 1415 and Lord Mountbatten's speech to his own men as they embarked in 1942 is impossible to resist. The analogy ends with what then happened in France. The battle at Agincourt was for Henry and his bowmen a great victory, the battle at Dieppe was for Mountbatten and his Canadians a bloody defeat.*

Preparations for *Jubilee* had gathered their own momentum as the weeks went by. Could the death-toll have been avoided or at least greatly reduced? There were four opportunities to achieve one or the other. First, an independent evaluation of Casa Maury's opinion - "not strongly defended" - would have demonstrated that he was talking through his hat. Secondly, if the Royal Navy would not risk one or more capital ships, the RAF and USAAF could have been ordered to continuously smother the defences throughout every stage of the operation. Thirdly, and because the assault depended upon surprise, there should have been a contingency plan if surprise was lost. When part of the naval force got into a severe fire-fight in the early hours with German armed trawlers, it could have been assumed that the defenders ashore had been aroused and the raid abandoned accordingly. Although unsure of what was happening out at sea, at least one local commander did declare a partial alarm (in the event, this made little if any difference to the outcome). Fourthly, and in the same vein, when it became obvious within the first few minutes that the landing sites - contrary to Intelligence briefings - were covered by all manner of weaponry, Hughes-Hallett and Roberts should have been empowered to stop the whole thing in its tracks. Mountbatten's plan did not give them that option. If he had been with them on HMS CALPE's bridge - seeing for himself what was happening - he could have intervened and changed their orders. Instead, and despite his "man of action" reputation and love of personal publicity, he had given himself the day off.

The thinking of the COHQ planning staff is hard to fathom. "Time and tide wait for no man" and in every amphibious operation they are determinant factors in equal measure. In the Dieppe context, a protracted operation would give the Germans time in which to bring reinforcements rushing to the coast from inland. On the other hand, a short in-and-out attack might give the Canadians too little time in which to reach their goals and then withdraw in good order. The original *Rutter* plan envisaged an operation lasting fifteen hours. High tide at Dieppe was 0403. Re-embarkation would be conducted on the afternoon incoming tide and completed at its peak (1900). But then, in early July, it was learned that a *Panzer* division had arrived in Amiens, barely forty miles from Dieppe. It seemed to be a routine "rest and refit" movement, but it radically altered the balance of threat.

In response, the time-scale for the new *Jubilee* plan was reduced by half. Re-embarkation would finish sometime after dead low tide, or in any event not much later than 1300. That, at least, appears to have been the intention. Presumably it did not worry the planners that - given the English Channel's strong tidal currents - the sea level at Dieppe would by then have fallen twenty-six feet. The beaches would have become very much broader, more exposed to enemy fire and, on the ebb flow, with an increased likelihood of evacuation craft becoming stranded. The South Saskatchewans and Queen's Own Cameron Highlanders of Canada discovered all this to their cost while they were attempting to escape from Pourville.

In my much younger years I served as an army intelligence officer. Looking at the topography and calculating the distances to be covered, I concluded that, even as blank-firing training exercises, neither *Rutter* nor *Jubilee* could be completed within the time-frames allotted to them. The truncated *Jubilee* time-table especially was much too compressed.

Departing England, free of any time constraints and not under fire, the expedition had needed four different ports of embarkation. The intended return journey, working against the clock, would be made mainly from Dieppe's one small harbour and its adjoining unstable beach. Whether it was an eight hours operation or a fifteen hours operation, I believe it would have been a logistical impossibility for 5000 or more troops (assuming none of them to be stretcher cases) to have reached all their designated objectives and then re-embarked (complete with their total allocation of fifty-eight tanks plus their armoured cars, Jeeps and Bren-gun carriers) even if on that day there had been not a single German soldier anywhere within twenty miles. Unhappily, the Germans *were* there and they turned it into a battle. Someone described Dieppe as "the charge of the Light Brigade in boats". That just about covers it.

So, who *was* to blame? It is a time-honoured Royal Navy custom that, when decisions are to be made, "there is only one captain on the bridge". Mountbatten was that captain and Churchill put him there. To better understand the horror they cooked up, and if you have not already done so, read one or two "Dieppe Raid" books. What you will not find is more than passing (if any) reference to the Marques de Casa Maury. And yet, in my opinion, it was Mountbatten's flawed appointment of this man as his Senior Intelligence Officer which, from the outset, infected and blighted the entire operation. Young men died who, if properly commanded, should have lived. If you doubt the truth of that statement, do as I did and go there. I believe you will marvel at the courage and regimental spirit of *Jubilee*'s trusting victims. I believe also that you will come away, as I did, angered that their trust had been so grossly betrayed.

It is a quirk of history that reputations can be damaged or enhanced on the strength of a single episode. In the 1920s, Winston Churchill was taunted by his critics as "the butcher of Gallipoli". The Dieppe Raid never attracted the same condemnation even though he had been its prime mover. Today he is recalled, rightly, as the greatest Englishman of the 20$^{th}$ century. Lord Louis Mountbatten, for his part, is remembered as the Viceroy who, charged in 1947 with the task of negotiating the independence of India, did so with enormous patience in the face of irresolvable political obstacles. By then the "over-promoted destroyer captain" - as he was sometimes labelled - had matured into a statesman. But, even to his many admirers, Dieppe remains an enduring stain on his fifty years of service to the Royal Navy and to the nation.

*Hautot-sur-Mer, the silent legacy*

# SOUVENEZ-VOUS
# REMEMBER

Some selected sources and acknowledgements:

*Archivio Segreto Vaticano* (Vatican City), The W O Bentley Memorial Foundation, The Bugatti Trust, Act Productions Ltd (Curzon Cinemas history), *Mountbatten, The Official Biography*, Philip Ziegler (1985), The Mountbatten Archive (University of Southampton), The Churchill Archives Centre (Cambridge), *Churchill's Bodyguard*, Tom Hickman (biography of Inspector Walter Thompson), *The London Gazette* (12.8.1947 Supplement), *The War at Sea* (Roskill, Vol II), MoD Naval Historical Branch, the *Bundesarchiv*, RAF Innsworth (Personnel Records), *The Turn of the Tide*, Arthur Bryant (biography of FM Viscount Alanbrooke), *The Memoirs of General the Lord Ismay* (1960), *Churchill, The Power of Words*, Martin Gilbert (2012), *Behind Closed Doors ... Story of the Duchess of Windsor*, Hugo Vickers (2011), *In Command of History*, David Reynolds (2004), *Hansard's Parliamentary Debates*, and especial thanks to Peter G L John, Wing Commander Jim Routledge, RAF (retd), Kim Lindsay, Susan Davie, Heather Barr, Lady Patricia, the Countess Mountbatten of Burma, Captain Mark Reid (Canadian War Museum), and Dr Bernardo Rodriquez Caparrini (Cadiz).

# INDEXES

## Battles and Campaigns

Abyssinia, **61-65**
Agreement (Operation), **261-263**
Alexandria, **73-76**
Algiers, **29, 39-40, 100**
America (1812-1815), **33-39**
Anglo-Boer War (1st), **80, 183-187**
Anglo-Boer War (2nd), **79-85**
Anklet (Operation), **155**
Antwerp, **97**
Archery (Operation), **155, 261**
Arctic, **153-156**
Armada, Spanish, **3, 6** *et seq*
Ashantee, **47**
Atlantic, **127-131**
Azoff, **50, 51**
Bali Strait, **140, 141**
Baltic (1854-1855), **51-55**
Baltic (1918-1920), **121**
Basque Roads, **39**
Barfleur, **18-19**
Beachy Head, **17**
Bear Island, **154**
Beira Patrol, **198-204**
Belmont, **82**
Bloemfontein, **83**
Bomarsund, **53-54**
Britain, **13, 125**
Bruneval, **273**
Buenos Aires, **179-180**
Cadiz, **6, 13**
Camperdown, **39**
Cape St Vincent, **27, 31**
Chemulpo Bay, **92**
China (1900), **85-88**
China (1928), **189**
China (1938), **189**
Claymore (Operation), **154**
Copenhagen, **39**
Coronel, **91, 98**
Crete, **241**
Crimea, **49-51**
Dardanelles, **108-112, 136**
Dieppe, **239** *et seq*
Dogger Bank, **91, 98**
Dungeness, **16, 17**
Dvina River, **117**

Dynamo (Operation), **260**
Egypt, **74-76**
Eshowe, **72**
Falklands (first), **91, 98**
Falklands (second), **13, 174, 229**
Fenian Raid, **65-67**
Fishguard, **25**
Gallipoli, **98, 108-112, 136, 261, 264, 283**
Gamlarkleby, **53**
Gauntlet (Operation), **154**
Gibraltar, **20-21**
Gingindlovu, **72**
Glorious First of June, **25-28, 102**
Graspan, **82, 83**
Grenada, **214-219, 222**
Havre, Le, **18-19**
Heligoland Bight, **91, 98**
Helsinki, **55**
Hogue, La, **19, 21**
Hong Kong, **259-260**
Husky (Operation), **252**
Iceland (Cod Wars), **204-210**
Inyezane, **72**
Isandlwana, **70, 71**
Java Sea, **140**
Jenkin's Ear, **12**
Jubilee (Operation), **239** *et seq*
Jutland, **91, 94, 98**
Kertch, **50**
Kimberley, **81, 82**
Kola, **56, 57**
Korea, **158-163**
Kronstadt, **120**
Kuantan, **132-134, 136-139**
Kut-al-Amara, **116-117**
Kuwait (1961), **213-214**
Ladysmith, **81**
Leghorn, **16**
Leyte Gulf, **146**
Libya (2011), **210-213**
Lingayen Gulf, **146-147**
Lofoten, **154, 155**
Lowestoft, **17**
Mafeking, **81**
Magersfontein, **84**

Majuba Hill, **72**, **185-187**
Malacca Straits, **142-143**
Maldonado, **180**
Malloy/Vaagso, **155**
Malta, **126**, **150-151**
Matapan, **150**
Mau-Mau, **204**
Mesopotamia, **117-119**
Modder River, **83**
Montevideo, **180**
Muskateer (Operation), **166-174**
Namsos, **153**, **154**
Nanjing, **190-192**
Narvik, **153**, **154**
Natal Rebellion, **72-73**
Navarino, **29**, **39**, **40**
Neptune (Operation), **258**
New Orleans, **33-34**
Nile, **39**
North Cape, **155**
North Russia, **119**
Okinawa, **147**, **149**
Ostend, **112**, **264**
Palestine (1936-39), **123**
Palestine (1945-48), **157**
Paraquat (Operation), **174**
Pedestal (Operation), **126-127**, **150-151**
Pekin, **85-87**
Persia, **120**
Petropavlovsk, **55-56**, **57**
Punto Obligado, **178-179**, **182**
Rhodesia, **197-204**
Ridgeway, **66**
River Plate, **256**
Rutter (Operation), **260**, **268**, **282**

Saintes, The, **22**, **30**
St Jean d'Acre, **40-42**
St Nazaire, **264**, **266**, **273-274**
St Tropez, **20**
Scheldt Estuary, **127**
Scheveningen (Texel), **16**, **17**
Seventh Frontier (Transkei), **69**
Shimonoseki, **176-178**
Siberia (1854-55), **55-57**
Siberia (1918-1921), **121-123**
Singapore, **139-140**
South Atlantic, **174**
South Russia, **120-121**
Spanish Civil War, **123**, **192-195**
Spitzbergen, **154**, **155**
Suez (Operation Muskateer), **163-174**
Sunda Strait, **140**
Sveaborg, **54-55**
Syria, **39**, **41-42**, **51**
Taganrog, **51**
Taranto, **134-135**, **195-196**
Tel-el-Kebir, **76**
Tobruk, **231-263**
Torch (Operation), **252**
Trafalgar, **13**, **28**, **39**
Tsushima, **79**
United States (1812-1815), **33-39**
Urgent Fury (Operation), **215-219**
Vaagso/Malloy, **155**, **259**
Valparaiso, **38-39**
Vantage (Operation), **214**
Vigo Bay, **19-20**
Walcheren, **127**
Zeebrugge, **112**, **264**
Zululand, **69-72**

## Campaign Medals

1914-1915 Star, 1914-1918, **97**, **117**,
Abyssinia, 1867-1868, **61**, **65**
Africa General Service, 1902-1956, **48**, **203**, **230**
Africa Star, 1940-1943, **149**, **150**, **263**
Air Crew Europe Star, 1939-1944, **125**, **155**
Allied Victory, 1914-1918, **97**, **98**, **117**, **121**
Arctic Medal, 1818-1855, **56**

Arctic Star, 1939-1945, **153**, **155**, **175**, **209**
Armed Forces Expeditionary (USA), **215**
Army of India, 1799-1826, **29**, **57**
Ashantee, 1873-1874, **47**, **49**
Ashanti, 1900, **48**
Atlantic Star, 1939-1945, **127**, **131**, **153**
Baltic, 1854-1855, **55**

British War Medal, 1914-1918, **97, 98, 117, 121**
Burma Star, 1941-1945, **131, 143, 149**
Callis, 1742, **20**
Campaign Service, 1962, **173, 203, 230**
Canada General Service, 1866-1870, **65, 66, 67, 175**
Central Africa, **48, 49**
China Service (USA), 1935-1957, **192**
China War, 1840-1842, **29, 42, 43, 57, 85, 159**
China War, 1856-1863, **59, 85, 177**
China War, 1900, **84, 85, 86**
Commonwealth Naval, 1658, **16, 18**
Crimea, 1854-1855, **50, 55, 57**
Dangers Averted, 1589, **10, 11**
Dominion of the Seas, 1665, **17**
Earl St Vincent's, c.1801, **31**
East & Central Africa, 1879-1899, **48**
East & West Africa, 1891-1898, **48, 49**
Egypt, 1882-1889, **73, 76**
Endymion Crook, c.1815, **35-36**
France & Germany Star, 1944-1945, **127, 155**
General Elliott's, 1782, **20**
General Picton's, 1782, **20**
General Service, 1918-1962, **91**
Hogue, La, 1692, **19**
Humanitarian Overseas Service (Aus), **230**
India General Service, 1854-1895, **57**
Indian Mutiny, 1857-1858, **57**
Italy Star, 1943-1945, **149, 150**
King's South Africa, 1901-1902, **84, 183**

Korea (Queen's), **158, 159, 161**
Korea (UN), **161, 163**
Libya (NATO), **212**
Mercantile Marine, 1914-1918, **98, 189**
Messina Earthquake, 1908, **230**
Midshipman's Badge, c.1815, **35-36**
Natal Rebellion, 1906, **72, 73**
Naval General Service, 1793-1840, **23** *et seq*
Naval General Service, 1915-1962, **91** *et seq*
Naval Gold Medals, 1794-1815, **28, 37**
Naval Good Shooting, 1905, **89, 90**
Naval Reward, 1588, **10, 11, 175**
New Zealand, 1845-1866, **59**
Pacific Star, 1941-1945, **146, 149**
Polar, 1904, **91**
Punjab, 1848-1849, **159**
Queen's South Africa, 1899-1902, **84, 183**
Red Hot Shot, 1782, **20, 21**
Rhodesia, 1980, **203**
St Jean d'Acre, 1842, **42, 43**
South Africa, 1834-1853, **59**
South Africa, 1877-1879, **69, 70**
South Atlantic, 1982, **174**
Spanish Cross (Germany), 1938, **193**
Transport, 1899-1902, **188, 189**
Triumph, 1652, **17**
Vigo Bay, 1702, **20**
Yangtse Service (USA), 1926-1937, **190, 192**
Zimbabwe Independence, 1980, **203**

### British Ships of War (with relevant dates)

Abdiel, 1980s, **209**
Acasta, 1940, **153, 236**
Acavus, 1943, **130**
Achilles, 1759, **21**
Active, 1877, **69, 70**
Active, 1944, **152**
Agincourt, 1914, **99**
Ailsa Craig, 1943, **152**
Ajax, 1914, **93**
Ajax, 1947, **157**

Albatross, 1944, **162**
Alberta (HMY), **102**
Albion, 1816, **39**
Albion, 1956, **169**
Alert, 1813, **37-38**
Alexandra, 1882, **74**
Algerine, 1900, **87**
Amethyst, 1949, **158, 192**
Anson, 1945, **145**
Antelope, 1941, **154**

Anthony, 1941, **154**
Aphis, 1928, **119, 150, 190**
Archer, 1943, **131**
Archer, c.1990, **229**
Ardent, 1940, **153, 236**
Arethusa, 1941, **155**
Ark Royal, 1588, **8**
Ark Royal, 1941, **135**
Ark Royal, 1966, **199, 211, 216, 223**
Ark Royal, 2011, **211**
Astute, 2010, **226-227**
Audacious, 1914, **93, 94**
Audacity, 1941, **130**
Aurora, 1866, **67**
Aurora, 1940, **154**
Bacchante, 1915, **110**
Bacchante, 1970s, **207**
Bedale, 1944, **151, 271**
Bee, 1928, **190, 191**
Belfast, 1950, **158**
Belfast, **295**
Ben-my-Cree, 1915, **136**
Berkeley, 1942, **270**
Berwick, 1940, **204**
Berwick, 1966, **200, 201**
Birmingham, 1914, **93**
Bittern, 1854, **56**
Black Swan, 1951, **158**
Blanche, 1937, **194**
Blonde, 1914, **92**
Boadicea, 1879, **70, 72, 184**
Boadicea, 1914, **92**
Brave Borderer, c.1960, **227**
Brave Swordsman, c.1960, **227**
Britannia, 1692, **18**
Brocklesby, 2011, **211**
Broke, 1942, **173**
Bulwark, 1956, **169, 214**
Caledon, 1917, **235**
Calpe, 1942, **237, 260, 282**
Campbeltown, 1942, **273**
Camperdown, 1893, **79**
Canopus, 1942, **262**
Captain, 1797, **27**
Captain, 1870, **77**
Caradoc, 1928, **190**
Carlisle, 1919, **122, 190**
Centaur, 1961, **214**
Centurion, 1900, **86**

Centurion, 1914, **93**
Ceylon, 1956, **168**
Charybdis, 1973, **206**
Chelmer, 1915, **111**
Cherub, 1814, **38, 181**
Chesapeake, 1813, **35**
Chiddingfold, 1941, **265**
Cicala, 1919, **119**
Clio, 1920, **120**
Cockchafer, 1919, **119**
Colossus, 1916, **126**
Comus, 1845, **183**
Conqueror, 1805, **28**
Conqueror, 1982, **13**
Consort, 1949, **192**
Coonawarra (RAN), **221**
Cornwall, 1942, **141**
Cossack, 1940, **145**
Courageous, 1939, **131, 223**
Coventry, 1942, **262**
Crane, 1956, **169**,
Croome, 1942, **262**
Cricket, 1919, **119, 150, 190**
Cumberland, 2011, **211**
Cutlass, c.1970, **227**
Cyclops, 1840, **41**
Daedalus, 1943, **195**
Dasher, 1942, **235**
Defence, 1794, **26, 52**
Deloraine (RAN), 1942, **141**
Devonshire, 1942, **264**
Dido, 1881, **184**
Doris, 1899, **81, 82**
Dorsetshire, 1941, **132, 141**
Dragonfly, 1915, **118**
Dreadnought, 1692, **18**
Dreadnought, 1906, **78, 89, 181**
Dublin, 1914, **95**
Dublin Castle, 1919, **120**
Duke of Wellington, 1871, **77**
Duke of York, 1945, **145, 155**
Duncan, 1866, **66, 67**
Duncan, 1944, **131**
E15, 1915, **112**
Eagle, 1692, **18**
Eagle, 1940, **195**
Eagle, 1956, **169, 170**
Eagle, 1966, **199, 200, 201, 202, 203**
Eclipse, 1900, **101**

Eclipse, 1941, **154**
Edinburgh, 1840, **183, 204**
Edinburgh, 1942, **204**
Edinburgh Castle, 1919, **120**
Electra, 1941, **132, 141**
Elfin (HMY), **102**
Elizabeth Bonaventure, 1588, **9**
Emerald, 1928, **190**
Encounter, 1942, **141**
Endurance, 1982, **236**
Endymion, 1815, **28, 36, 37**
Erin, 1914, **99**
Eskimo, 1940, **153**
Espiegle, 1920, **120**
Essex, 1814, **38**
Euphrates, 1879, **70**
Euryalus, 1863, **176**
Exeter, 1942, **140, 141**
Express, 1941, **132, 133**
Falmouth, 1976, **206**
Fearless, 1937, **194**
Fearless, 1940, **204**
Fernie, 1942, **237, 267**
Firefly, 1915, **118**
Formidable, 1945, **145, 147, 149**
Forester, 1879, **70**
Fortune, 1940, **204**
Furious, 1917, **116**
Gadila, 1943, **130**
Gallant, 1937, **194**
Ganges, 1917, **115**
Ganymede, 1817, **54**
Gipsy, 1937, **194**
Glasgow, 1940, **204**
Glorious, 1940, **153, 204, 223, 236**
Glory IV, 1919, **119**
Glory, 1951, **160, 236**
Glowworm, 1919, **119**
Gnat, 1941, **150, 190**
Goliath, 1915, **111**
Gorgon, 1840, **41, 45, 178, 179, 183**
Greenfly, 1915, **118**
Guerriere, 1812, **36**
Hardy, 1940, **153**
Hasty, 1937, **194**
Havock, 1937, **194**
Hazard, 1898, **234**
Hermes, 1942, **141**
Hesperus, 1944, **131**

Himalaya, 1879, **70**
Hood, 1941, **89, 135, 204**
Hornet, 1854, **56**
Hotspur, 1940, **153, 193**
Howe, 1945, **145**
Hunter, 1937, **153, 194, 195**
Hursley, 1942, **262**
Hydra, 1840, **41**
Hyperion, 1937, **194, 195**
Icarus, 1941, **154**
Illustrious, 1940, **127, 134, 195**
Impregnable, 1816, **39**
Impregnable, 1914, **100**
Indefagitable, 1914, **92, 94**
Indefagitable, 1945, **145**
Indomitable, 1942, **126, 132, 145, 162**
Inflexible, 1882, **76**
Inflexible, 1915, **109**
Invincible, 1882, **76**,
Iron Duke, 1914, **99**
Irresistible, 1915, **109, 110**
Jackdaw, 1943, **131**
Jamaica, 1956, **168**
Java, 1812, **36**
Jervis Bay, 1940, **128**
Jupiter, 1942, **141**
Kashmir, 1941, **240**
Kelly, 1940, **240, 247, 264**
Kent, 1919, **122**
Kenya, 1941, **265**
King George V, 1914, **93, 99**
King George V, 1945, **145**
Kipling, 1941, **240**
Kruger, 1919, **120**
Ladybird, 1941, **150, 191, 192**
Legion, 1941, **154**
Leopard, 1854, **53**
Lion, 1692, **18**
Lion, 1914, **92**
Liverpool, 1914, **94**
Liverpool, 2011, **210**
Locust, 1942, **273-274**
Lofoten, 1956, **171**
London, 1881, **48-49**
London, 1949, **232**
Lowestoft, 1966, **199**
M28, 1918, **106**
Majestic, 1915, **111**
Malcolm, 1942, **173**

Mantis, 1919, **119**
Mary Rose, 1510, **15**
Matchless, 1943, **155**
Mercury, 1904, **249**
Mermaid, 1970s, **207**
Middleton, 1942, **209**
Minden, 1816, **39**
Minerva, 1966, **201, 202**
Miranda, 1854, **56, 57**
Monarch, 1854, **52**
Monarch, 1899, **81**
Moth, 1919, **119**
Mull, 1944, **152-153, 226**
Naiad, 1900, **84**
Neptune, 1914, **93**
Newfoundland, 1956, **168-169**
New Zealand, 1914, **92**
Nigeria, 1940, **154**
Nile, 1854, **52**
Niobe, 1900, **84**
Nith, 1956, **168**
Norfolk, 1941, **154**
Nottingham, 1914, **93, 94**
Nottingham, 2002, **226**
Nymphe, **23, 25, 39**
Ocean, 1915, **109**
Ocean, 1950s, **160, 171**
Ocean, 2011, **211, 225**
Odin, 1854, **53**
Offa, 1941, **265**
Oiseau, 1793, **25**
Onslow, 1941, **265**
Oribi, 1941, **265**
Orontes, 1879, **70**
Orwell, 1960s, **209**
Osborne (HMY), **100, 101, 102**
Pathfinder, 1914, **111**
Perth (RAN), 1942, **140, 141**
Petersfield, 1928, **190**
Phoebe, 1814, **38, 181**
Phoenix, 1840, **41**
Plymouth, 1966, **200**
Porpoise, 1945, **143**
Powerful, 1840, **41**
Powerful, 1899, **81**
President, 1854, **56**
Prince of Wales, 1941, **132-139**
Prince of Wales, 2020, **221, 225**
Princess Royal, 1914, **92**

Prinses Astrid, 1942, **276, 277**
Puncher, 1956, **171**
Punjabi, 1940, **154**
Pylades, 1866, **66, 67**
Queen Charlotte, 1816, **39, 40**
Queen Elizabeth, 1941, **194**
Queen Elizabeth, 2014, **216, 223, 225**
Queen Mary, 1914, **92, 94**
Raglan, 1918, **106**
Ramillies, 1940, **254**
Repulse, 1941, **132, 138-139**
Rhyl, 1966, **199**
Rothesay, 1975, **202**
Royal George, 1797, **29**
Royal Oak, 1937, **194**
Sabre, c.1970s, **227**
Salisbury, 1975, **202**
Sandwich, 1797, **30**
San Fiorenzo, 1797, **25**
Scarab, 1943, **150**
Scimitar, c.1970s, **227**
Scorpion, 1943, **155**
Serapis, 1779, **19**
Shah, 1879, **70**
Shakespeare, 1945, **143**
Shannon, 1813, **34, 35**
Sheffield, 1982, **211**
Sikh, 1942, **262**
Snapper, 1939, **129**
Southampton, 1914, **93**
Sparrowhawk, 1940, **125**
Starling, 1944, **131**
Statesman, 1944, **143**
Stonehenge, 1944, **143**
Stork, 1944, **131**
Stratagem, 1943, **143**
Stromboli, 1840, **41**
Suffolk, 1919, **122**
Suffolk, 1941, **154, 204**
Sybille, 1854, **56**
Sybille, 1901, **84-85**
Swan, 1588, **7**
Talbot, 1904, **92**
Tally-ho, 1944, **143**
Tamar, 1879, **70**
Tartar, 1940, **154, 156**
Temeraire, 1882, **76**
Tenedos, 1879, **70**
Tenedos, 1941, **132, 141**

Terpsichore, 1900, **84**
Terrapin, 1945, **143**
Terrible, 1900, **84**
Theseus, 1950's, **160, 171**
Tonnant, 1815, **33**
Torbay, 1702, **19**
Trenchant, 1945, **143**
Triad, 1920, **120**
Triumph, 1652, **16, 17**
Triumph, 1915, **111**
Triumph, 1951, **160**
Triumph, 2011, **211**
Truant, 1943, **142**
Trusty, 1943, **142**
Turbulent, 2011, **211**
Tyne, 1956, **166**
Unicorn, 1951, **160**
Valiant, 1941, **194**
Vampire (RAN), 1941, **132, 141**
Vanguard, 2013, **226**
Venus, 1900, **101**
Verity, 1928, **190**
Vesuvius, 1840, **41**
Veteran, 1928, **190**

Victoria, 1893, **79**
Victoria & Albert II (HMY), **102**
Victoria & Albert III (HMY), **101, 102**
Victorious, 1945, **145**
Victorious, 1961, **214**
Victory, 1692, **18**
Victory, 1797, **28, 30-32, 43**
Ville de Paris, 1797, **30-32**
Vindictive, 1928, **190**
Vulture, 1854, **53**
Walker, 1944, **131**
Warrior, 1860, **78**
Weasle, 1804, **43**
Westminster, 2011, **211**
Whiting, 1900, **87**
Widgeon, 1901, **84**
Wild Swan, 1928, **190**
Windsor Castle, 1919, **120**
Wishart, 1928, **190**
Witherington, 1928, **190**
Wolsey, 1928, **190**
W T Robb, 1866, **67**
York, 2011, **210**
Zulu, 1942, **262**

## Personnel

Abrahams, AB Herbert, **195**
Agar, Lieut Augustus, **121**
Andrewes, Adm Sir William, **162**
Anstruther, Lt Col Philip, **183**
Armstrong, Mid T C, **83**
Ashmore, Adm Sir Edward, **209, 220**
Atcherley, Capt James, **28**
Auchmuty, Gen Sir Samuel, **180**
Auchinleck, Gen Sir Claude, **263**
Aynsley, Sig W H, **71**
Bader, Sqn Ldr Douglas, **126**
Baillie-Grohman, Adm H, **253-254**
Baird, Gen Sir David, **179, 180**
Ball, Capt Albert, **113**
Barker, Lieut Cdr J F, **236**
Barker, Capt N J, **236**
Bateman, Lieut (A) C R, **133**
Battenberg, Adm Prince Louis, **91, 107**
Bayley, Sub-Lieut (A) G W L A, **134**
Beatty, Adm Sir David, **92**
Bell-Davies, Sqn Cdr R, **234**

Bennington, Lieut Cdr Leslie, **143**
Beresford, Gen William, **179, 180**
Black, Adm Sir George, **56**
Blake, Sir Robert, **16, 17**
Booker, Maj Charles, **113-114, 117**
Boultbee, L/S Michael, **276-277**
Boyes, Mid Duncan, **177**
Bridgeman, Adm Sir Francis, **91, 103, 105, 107, 134**
Bridport, Adm Lord, **30, 31**
Brittain, Sub Lieut David, **201**
Brodie, Lieut Cdr Theodore, **112**
Broke, Capt Philip, **35-36**
Brooke, Gen Sir Alan, **266, 267**
Brownrigg, Capt Charles, **48-49**
Bruce, Cdre H W, **56**
Buckley, Lieut C W, **57, 58**
Buckner, Adm Charles, **30**
Bulkeley, Lieut R G P, **143**
Burgoyne, Capt Hugh, **77**
Byng, Adm John, **264**
Callis, Capt Smith, **20**

Cameron, Lieut Donald, **235**
Carden, Adm Sir Sackville, **100, 107-108**
Carless, OS John, **235**
Carter, L/S Cyril, **236**
Cartwright, Cdr F J, **133**
Casa Maury, W/Cdr Peter, **243** *et seq*
Catto, Lt Col Douglas, **275**
Chappell, W/Cdr Roy, **137**
Chatfield, Adm Lord, **164, 220**
Chelmsford, Gen Lord, **69-71, 100**
Childers, Mid Leonard, **77**
Cochrane, Adm Sir Alexander, **33**
Codrington, Adm Edward, **40-41**
Coker, Mid Lewis, **72**
Coles, Capt Cowper, **77**
Colley, Gen Sir George, **183-187**
Collings, AB James, **195**
Collingwood, Capt Cuthbert, **27**
Collishaw, Lt Col R, **113, 117**
Congreve, Col William, **51**
Cook, Capt James, **127**
Cooke, Capt James, **25**
Cooper, Boatswain Henry, **57, 58**
Cork, Lt Cdr (A) Richard, **126, 127, 151**
Cowan, Adm Sir Walter, **121**
Crerar, Gen H D G "Harry", **260**
Cunningham, Adm A B "ABC", **134, 135, 150**
Curzon-Howe, Adm Sir A, **102**
Dacres, Capt James, **36**
Dallas, Maj Stanley, **113, 117**
Dampier, Capt C F, **94**
Dickason, PO H, **120**
Douglas-Morris, Capt K, **39, 55, 178, 183, 233**
Dowding, AM Hugh, **125**
Drake, Sir Francis, **6, 7, 8, 14, 45**
Drew, Capt T B, **193**
Dreyer, Capt Frederick, **89**
Drysdale, Lieut Col Douglas, **161**
Duff, Adm Sir Alexander, **122**
Duncan, Lieut D C, **143**
Dundas, Adm Sir Richard, **54-55**
Dunning, Cdr Edwin, **116**
Dunsterville, Gen Lionel, **120**
Durnford-Slater, Lieut Col John, **251**

Durnford-Slater, Adm R, **166, 173**
Dykes, L/S Geoffrey, **202**
Edmonds, Flt Cdr Charles, **136**
Eliott, Gen Sir Augustus, **20**
Exmouth, Adm Lord, **39, 100**
Fall, Flt Cdr Joseph, **113, 117**
Fancourt, Cdr Henry, **173**
Fegan, Capt Fogarty, **128**
Fieldhouse, Adm Sir John, **219**
Finch, Flt Lieut J, **151**
Fisher, Adm Sir John "Jackie", **89-91, 98, 100, 101, 103, 107, 108, 111, 134, 181, 220**
Fisher, Adm Sir William, **164**
Fitzherbert-Brockholes, Lieut R, **119, 122**
Fleming, Lieut Cdr Ian, **273**
Ford, Rev William Lewis, **122**
Fowles, 2nd Lt G H, **114**
Franklin, Capt Sir John, **56**
Fraser, Adm Sir Bruce, **145, 146-147, 148, 155, 223**
French, Gen Sir John, **269**
Frobisher, Sir Martin, **7**
Gambier, Capt James, **26**
Gamble, Adm Sir Douglas, **99**
Gaselee, Gen Sir Edward, **87, 88**
Gaze, Master John, **39**
Glasfurd, Cdr C E, **236**
Glyn, Col Richard, **70**
Godfrey, Adm John, **273**
Gordon, Lieut Bernard, **152-153**
Gott, Gen W E H "Strafer", **263**
Graham, Lieut J H, **200**
Gray, Lieut (A) Robert, **149**
Grenville, Sir Richard, **7**
Gretton, Cdr Peter, **131**
Haig, AB C B, **120**
Haig, FM Douglas, **269, 281**
Halliday, Capt L S T, **234**
Hamilton, Gen Sir Ian, **110, 185, 268, 269**
Harwood, Adm Sir Henry, **262**
Hawkins, Sir John, **6, 45, 47**
Hezlet, Lieut Cdr A R, **143**
Hillyar, Capt James, **38-39**
Holland, Lieut Hubert, **85**
Hope, Capt Henry, **28, 37**

Horrocks, Sub Lieut (A) H, **131**
Hotham, Capt Charles, **179, 182, 183**
Houghton, Gen Sir Nicholas, **213**
Howard, Charles, **6-9, 11**
Howard, Lieut Cdr David, **201**
Howe, Adm Lord, **26-28, 102**
Huddart, Mid Cymbeline, **82, 83**
Hughes-Hallett, Capt J, **249, 254-255, 258, 267, 270, 282**
Humphreys, Lieut P N, **194-195**
Hutchinson, Mid R B C, **83**
Ismay, Gen H L "Pug", **267**
James, Adm Sir W, **267**
Jervis, Adm Sir John, **30-32**
John, Adm Sir Caspar, **220**
Jones, AB William, **85**
Keightley, Gen Sir Charles, **166, 167, 169**
Kennedy, Lieut Ludovic, **156**
Keyes, Adm Sir Roger, **253, 270**
King, Lieut W D A, **129**
Kitchener, Gen Lord, **98**
Koughnet, Mid E B van, **67**
Kuper, Adm Augustus, **176, 177**
Lambert, Capt Henry, **36**
Laugharne, Capt T L P, **37**
Laycock, Brig Sir Robert, **251, 252, 253**
Layton, Adm Sir Geoffrey, **142**
Leach, Adm Sir Henry, **220**
Leach, Capt J C, **132, 133**
Leigh-Mallory, AVM Trafford, **250, 270**
Limpus, Adm Arthur, **99-100, 107**
Little, Capt Robert, **113, 117**
Loader, AB Roy, **169**
Lockyer, Capt Nicholas, **33**
Lovat, Lieut Col the Lord, **251**
Lowe, Warrant Gunner E E, **83**
Lumsden, Gen Sir Herbert, **146, 147**
Lyons, Capt Edmund, **56-57, 58**
Lyons, Adm Lord, **58**
McCudden, Capt James, **113**
Macintyre, Cdr Donald, **131**
Mahon, Surgeon Edward, **185**
Maillard, Surgeon Job, **233**
Mannock, Maj Edward, **113**
Mansergh, Lieut D B, **200**

Martin, Capt Byam, **51**
Martin, AB Dan, **70**
Methuen, Gen Lord, **82, 83**
Miller, Capt C B, **95**
Miller, Capt Ralph, **27**
Milne, Adm Sir Alexander, **100**
Milne, Adm Sir Berkeley, **70-71, 100-107, 134**
Moffat, Lieut Cdr (A) John, **135**
Monckton, Sub Lieut H G, **184**
Monro, Gen Sir Charles, **268**
Montgomery, Gen Sir Bernard, **210, 260, 261, 262**
Morgan, Gen Sir Frederick, **252**
Morton, Sub Lieut Bryan, **147**
Mountbatten, Adm Lord Louis, **166, 239** *et seq*
Murphy, Col Peter, **272**
Napier, Adm Sir Charles, **41-42, 51-54**
Napier, Gen Sir Robert, **61-65**
Neale, Capt Sir Harry, **25**
Nelson, Adm Horatio, **13, 16, 27, 28, 43, 263**
Nissenthall, Flt/Sgt J, **273**
Nixon, Gen Sir John, **118**
Norman, Cdr Charles, **183**
Norris, Cdre D T, **120-121**
Ogle, Lieut Henry, **184**
Osmond, Lieut Edward, **134**
Otway, Adm Robert, **181**
Packenham, Gen Edward, **34**
Paine, Adm Godrey, **115, 117**
Parry, Cdr Alec, **209**
Pearson, Col Charles, **70**
Peart, AVM Sir Stuart, **213**
Peel, Capt Sir William, **57**
Pellew, Capt Edward, **23, 39**
Percival, Gen Arthur, **139, 140**
Pertwee, Lieut H G, **120**
Phillips, Adm Sir T S V "Tom", **132-136**
Picton, Gen Sir Thomas, **20**
Pitchfork, Air Cdre Graham, **199, 201, 203**
Place, Sub Lieut B C G, **235**
Plumer, Cdr Gerald, **206**
Plumridge, Adm Sir James, **52-53**

Poe, Adm Sir Edmund, **102-103, 104, 210**
Popham, Adm Sir Home, **179, 180**
Portal, AM Sir Charles, **245, 252**
Pound, Adm Sir Dudley, **125, 126, 127, 133, 265-266**
Power, Adm Sir Arthur, **145**
Price, Adm David, **55-56**
Pride, PO Thomas, **177**
Prothero, Capt Reginald, **81, 82**
Prowse, Capt C J, **94**
Ralegh (Raleigh), Sir Walter, **8, 15**
Rawlings, Adm Sir Bruce, **146**
Rawlinson, L/S John, **152-153**
Reed, Pte William, **122**
Richards, Cdre Frederick, **184, 185**
Robeck, Adm John de, **109, 110, 111, 112**
Roberts, Gen J H "Ham", **249, 258, 259, 260, 282**
Rodney, Adm Lord, **21-22**
Romilly, Cdr Francis, **184, 185**
Rooke, Adm Sir George, **19**
Russell, Cdr Archibald, **173**
Ryder, Cdr Robert, **273-274**
Samson, Cdr C R, **97**
Saunders, Adm Sir Charles, **102**
Scarlett, Lieut (A) Norman, **135**
Schofield, Sqn Ldr Jim, **224**
Scott, Sub Lieut A L, **184, 185**
Scott, Capt Percy, **89**
Scott, Capt Robert Falcon, **91**
Seeley, AB William, **177**
Seymour, Adm Sir Beauchamp, **74, 172**
Seymour, Adm Sir Edward, **86, 87**
Sharman, Ord Seaman James, **43, 44**
Shelford, Capt Thomas, **111**
Slaughter, Lieut (A) H J, **134**
Smail, PO James, **195**
Smith, Capt Callis, **20**
Smith, Capt Edward John, **188**
Smylie, Flt Sub Lieut G F, **234**
Somerville, Adm Sir James, **145**

Sowerby, Capt C F, **94**
Stanhope, Adm Sir Mark, **212, 219, 221, 226**
Stopford, Adm Sir Robert, **41, 42**
Stutchbury, Lieut John, **199**
Sueter, Cdre Murray, **115, 117**
Swanston, Lieut David, **143**
Syfret, Adm Edward, **150, 151**
Tait, W/Cdr J B "Willy", **144**
Talbot, Capt H F G, **111**
Tarver, Lieut Allan, **199, 203**
Tennant, Capt W G, **132, 133, 137, 139**
Thomas, AB Ernest, **195**
Thompson, Insp Walter, **269**
Townsend, Gen Charles, **118**
Trewavas, OS John, **233**
Troubridge, Adm Sir Ernest, **101**
Trower, Lieut Cornwallis, **184, 185**
Tucker, Cdr Thomas T, **38-39**
Tudor, Adm Sir Frederick, **122**
Turner, Lieut Cdr H B, **143**
Tyrwhitt, Adm Sir Reginald, **190**
Vaughan-Lee, Adm C L, **115, 117**
Verschoyle-Campbell, Lieut D, **143**
Vian, Adm Sir Philip, **145, 146**
Vigors, Sqn Ldr Tim, **137**
Walker, Capt F J "Johnnie", **131**
Walker, Lieut (A) G M, **195**
Warrender, Adm Sir George, **93-95**
Welch, Capt Andrew, **206**
Welch, Lieut "Bill", **277**
Wellham, Lieut (A) J W G, **195**
Wellington, Gen Duke of, **14, 42**
Whitelocke, Gen John, **180**
Williams, Capt Hugh, **85**
Williams, Adm Hugh Pigot, **99**
Williamson, Lieut Cdr (A) K, **135**
Wilson, Adm Sir Arthur, **91**
Woodward, Adm Sir J "Sandy", **13**
Wolseley, Col Sir Garnet, **47, 69**
Wreford-Brown, Cdr Christopher, **13**
Wrottesley, Lt Cameron, **54**

## About the Author

Roger Perkins was born in 1932 in Dartford, Kent, but long ago he moved to the beautiful southern slopes of Dartmoor National Park. He and his wife Evelyn Patricia raised six splendid children who, in turn, have produced numerous grandchildren and great grandchildren.

A qualified agronomist and animal nutritionalist, based first in London and then in Lisbon and Milan, he was for twenty years associated with international companies engaged in the poultry and dairy industries. Returning from Italy in 1969, he changed course and entered the financial services industry. None of which had any connection whatever either with medals or with the Royal Navy.

An early passion for such matters originated with stories told by his father, Harry. While a 16 year-old Boy 1st Class, he witnessed the Battle of Jutland as messenger on the flag bridge of HMS BENBOW (later he served in "L" Class submarines). Another stimulus was the WWII career of Roger's future father-in-law, Arthur Thatcher. He commanded an American-built mine sweeper operating in the North Sea.

As a teenager, Roger himself gained an early taste for the sea as occasional spare hand on Brixham trawlers and then, in his early twenties, with the Merchant Navy as a traveling stockman aboard Union Castle and Donaldson Line freighters. He delivered thoroughbred horses and farm breeding animals to new owners in South Africa and Canada. The swelling deep blue of the South Atlantic and the grey stormy waters of the North Atlantic made a lasting impression.

Much later, having settled back in Devon with a young growing family, Roger needed an additional interest other than running his business and weekend duties as a Special Constable with the Devon & Cornwall Constabulary. A chance encounter with Max Powling, one of the "old and bold" of the medal collecting fraternity, opened up an entirely new world. He became Roger's mentor. Life-long enthusiasms for military history, for research and for writing then all came together as one.

Over the past forty years they have generated an irregular succession of books devoted to varied aspects of British history. Most relevant to today's world was *Operation Paraquat, The Battle for South Georgia, 1982*. Commissioned by the Fleet Air Arm Museum (Yeovilton) and sponsored by the Ministry of Defence (Navy), it coincidentally identified the less obvious root causes of the Falklands War. Two very much earlier naval episodes had led to the co-authored publication of *Gunfire in Barbary - The Battle of Algiers, 1816* and *Angels in Blue Jackets - The Navy at Messina, 1908*.

In the 1950s, as a National Service officer, he had served in Kenya and Uganda with 4th Battalion, The King's African Rifles. That experience gave him a lasting respect and liking for his *askari*. They were the fighting men whose forebears had "followed the drum" by joining the multitude of units recruited at various times throughout East and Central Africa.

Researching their histories made him aware of how little he knew about their contemporaries in other lands around the globe: Australians, Canadians, New Zealanders, South Africans, West Africans, Sikhs, Hindus, Gurkhas, they and many more like them. Not even in the time of Rome had the concept of empire brought together so many different creeds and races to serve in a common cause under a shared banner.

All of that prompted the decision to record their stories in a unified source of reference. The result was the weighty *Regiments - Regiments and Corps of the British Empire and Commonwealth, 1758-1993 - A Critical Bibliography of their Published Histories*.

*Regiments* was nominated in 1995 for the British Library Association's annual Besterman Medal (it was placed second out of several hundred diverse reference works published that year). In the same year it was judged "Best Specialist Reference Work" by what was at the time the University of Paisley's Literati Club. Further recognition came when The British Council selected *Regiments* as one of its exhibits at the prestigious Frankfurt Book Fair.

It has all been tremendous fun, with many friendships made, but *"Medals to the Navy"* will be the last to bear the Roger Perkins imprint. He gladly leaves it to the next generation of researcher to explore the astonishing four hundred years of British history in which the Royal Navy has so often taken the leading role.